THE PROFESSIONAL CHEF'S

BOOK OF BUFFETS

BY GEORGE K. WALDNER AND KLAUS MITTERHAUSER

Edited by Jule Wilkinson

Published by Van Nostrand Reinhold Company

BY GEORGE K. WALDNER AND KLAUS MITTERHAUSER

Edited by Jule Wilkinson

Published by Van Nostrand Reinhold Company

A CBI Book
(CBI is an imprint of Van Nostrand Reinhold Company Inc.)

ISBN 0-8436-0505-7

Printed in the United States of America

Van Nostrand Reinhold Company Inc.
115 Fifth Avenue
New York, New York 10003

Van Nostrand Reinhold Company Limited
Molly Millars Lane
Wokingham, Berkshire RG11 2PY, England

Van Nostrand Reinhold
480 La Trobe Street
Melbourne, Victoria 3000, Australia

Macmillan of Canada
Division of Canada Publishing Corporation
164 Commander Boulevard
Agincourt, Ontario M1S 3C7, Canada

16 15 14 13 12 11 10

THE MODERN BUFFET

One of the finest and most exciting expressions of the Chef's art is the modern buffet, and there is no doubt of its increasing importance in the culinary industry.

The shortage of qualified personnel, the increased difficulty and costliness of service at a high level continually escalate the economic disadvantages of formal food service. One of the soundest and most attractive answers is a glamorous, even spectacular buffet.

It eliminates many of the headaches of waiter availability and training, poor but costly service, cold food, friction and complaints. It permits an appetizing, exciting display with greater lead time for preparation. It permits tremendous variety without many of the risks of consumption guesswork. Economically, it permits greater value because even an "all-you-can-eat" policy with a moderate price can be profitable.

The buffet exemplifies and glorifies the visual art of the food "decorateur," but it is vital that the beautiful, exciting display should not result in disappointment when the food is tasted, for flavor is the final goal of all culinary effort. That is the reason that at the Culinary Institute students must fulfill exacting cooking requirements before being eligible for the Buffet Catering course.

The objective must not only be visual beauty, but art *in edible foods,* not the profusion of papier mache, styrofoam and other such materials often found at buffets and food displays. To achieve this objective calls for a high order of artistic skill, not only in food decoration but in sugar work and ice carving.

Finally, one of the great values of the buffet is the opportunity to expand on a wide variety of themes—patriotic, ethnic, seasonal—to a degree not possible in formal dinners.

Jacob Rosenthal
President Emeritus
Culinary Institute of America

ACKNOWLEDGMENTS

Jane Wallace, Editor-in-Chief, Institutions/VFM Magazine

Editor: Jule Wilkinson

Art Director: Antonios Pronoitis, Medalist Publications

Design by: Queenie Burns, Assistant Art Director, Medalist Publications

Photography Designed and Styled by: Carl O. Hofmann

Black and White Photography: Klaus Mitterhauser, George K. Waldner, John Hugelmeyer

Assisted by: Victor Hellberg, Tony Gramkowski

Antiques used in photography from
The Yankee Silversmith Restaurant, Meriden, Conn.

Buffet Tools: William Brand Cutlery Co., Inc., New York

Cheese Photos: The Kraft Kitchens, Chicago

Morris Bryant Inn Photo: Florida Citrus Commission

Hawaiian Food Preparation: Emerson Holmes, Culinary Institute of America

Ice Carvings: Joe Amendola, Culinary Institute of America

Pastry and Bread Preparation: George Willmott, Culinary Institute of America

TABLE OF CONTENTS

ABOUT THE AUTHORS

Interwoven in the pages of The Professional Chef's BOOK OF BUFFETS is the best of two culinary worlds: one, the era when practitioners of le haute cuisine ruled the kitchens; the other, the present, when a cost conscious approach to food service prevails.

George K. Waldner and Klaus Mitterhauser, authors of this book, were both grounded in classic methods of food preparation by recognized masters of the old traditions of fine food. However, continuing experience in modern food service made clear to them the necessity for new time-, ingredient-, and labor-saving methods.

These qualified buffet chefs refused to give up the high standards of food service drilled into them during their early training. Instead, they began to invent shortcuts, to adapt methods to new requirements, always keeping what was important of the original dish but accomplishing its preparation in ways that are workable today.

This is the secret of their success in bringing high style buffet preparation to today's tables. These are the methods they have selected for this comprehensive book on buffet preparation.

GEORGE K. WALDNER

Apprenticeship, Eden Hotel, Berlin, Germany; Executive Chef: Governor Clinton Hotel; Belmont Plaza; Salisbury Hotel; Overseas Press Club, New York City. Senior Chef Instructor, New York City Community College; Cornell University; Pratt Institute; Culinary Institute of America, New Haven, Conn. (ret. 1967). Past President International Chefs Assn.; charter member Les Amis Escoffier Societe. Author of "65 Quality Menus for Quantity Service"; Contributing Editor, Chef's Magazine. First awards for culinary excellence presented in the '20s; notable among them: Silver Medal of French Republic, 1930; Grand Prize, New York Hotel Exposition, 1950; Gold Medal Eugen Lacroix, Frankfurt, 1956; Gold Medal American Culinary Federation, 1956; Special DeBand Award, 1957; Gold Medal, Societe Culinaire Philanthropique, 1964; Gold Medal Verband du Koche Deutschland, 1965.

KLAUS MITTERHAUSER

Graduate: Culinary Arts School, Vienna, Austria. Apprenticeship: Lucerne, Switzerland. Garde Manger: Restaurants Bachi Wapen, La Ronde, and Riche, Stockholme, Sweden; S.S. Kungsholm. Chef: Canadian Embassy, Rio de Janeiro; Chateau de Paris, Minneapolis; Grandview Inn, Columbus, Ohio; Bellevue Stratford Hotel, Philadelphia; Buffet Catering Department, Culinary Institute of America, New Haven, Connecticut; J.F. Bell Research Center, General Mills, Minneapolis. Currently: Chairman and Executive Chef Instructor, Food Service Department, Hennepin Technical Vocational Center South, Eden Prairie, Minnesota. Among many prizes awarded: Antonin Careme Silver Medal, New York Coliseum, 1969; Reserve Grand Champion, Detroit Culinary Show, 1971; Gold Medal for Cold Buffet, Culinary Olympics, 1972; two Silver Medals for Cold Buffet, Culinary Olympics, 1976; Judges' Award, Salon of Culinary Arts, American Culinary Federation and National Restaurant Association, 1977.

CHAPTER I
Introduction

□ Service—buffet style—introduces a festive dimension to food whatever the occasion. Elaborate buffets can be scaled to match the most sophisticated gourmet tastes, yet service from a buffet table will give a special flair to quite simple breakfast, lunch and dinner menus.

The versatility of the buffet makes it adaptable to all types of food service occasions in every kind of setting. In this "Book of Buffets," preparation and service of buffet foods is described step by step.

Material is arranged so that anyone who has mastered the fundamentals of cooking can add to those skills the techniques needed to preparate and decorate the whole hams, turkeys, fish and other display pieces that are attention-getters on buffet tables. Decorating ideas have been grouped and varied in difficulty for various food categories.

With practice, you will develop the skills needed to create the many food items that make up the grand buffet. Detailed plans for setting up a grand buffet have been worked out in Chapter XIX.

Dramatizing an occasion by building a buffet around a colorful theme draws favorable comment from patrons. To help in creating a theme buffet, the decorating elements and foods needed to develop 21 themes are described and pictured in Chapter XVI.

However, mastery of all this material is not required before a simple buffet is attempted. Such a buffet can be produced by selecting a limited number of items and perfecting their preparation. As more techniques and recipes are mastered, buffets can be enlarged or varied to include the new dishes. Bear in mind that every platter on the buffet table does not have to be a time-consuming masterpiece.

Buffets can be planned around the "star system". Two or three decorated pieces, perhaps a whole fish, a capon and a canned ham, will give a simply planned buffet the necessary highlights.

Garnishes can heighten the effectiveness of the remaining dishes so that the total picture meets the basic buffet requirement of "showmanship in action".

For food service operations, buffets have such built-in advantages as:

- Simplified menu planning
- Maximum service with minimum help
- Food production in multiple units
- More productivity from cooks
- Food savings through imaginative use of leftovers
- Opportunities for dramatic food and culinary art display
- Reputation building for the entire food service operation
- Lower menu printing costs
- Increases in private party business
- Easier entertaining for special occasions in industrial plants, hospitals and schools

Whether simple or high style, every buffet should start with a master plan. The person in charge should:

1. Put the complete schedule for the buffet on paper.
2. Review the entire plan well ahead of time with all of the workers who will be assisting in preparation and service.
3. Post the plan where workers may refer to it so they can pace their progress to meet the time schedule.

The master planning sheet should list: decorations; foods to be served; source of recipes for all dishes; containers for finished displays—trays, bowls and platters most effective for each dish; directions for positioning food on the table.

Job assignments to cover each area of buffet preparation should also be clearly made so that workers understand what they are to do and when they are to do it.

Buffet service may be concentrated in a short period or stretched over a more extended period. The designated speed for service affects the way foods are arranged on the buffet table. A table diagram for each type of service is shown in this section. For other diagrams, see Chapter XIX.

For each category of service a separate dessert table is suggested. On tables set up where guests may eat, place water, glasses, forks, knives, spoons, butter and napkins.

The arrangement of food differs for the two types of tables, but the same basic categories are covered: appetizers, salads, breads, relishes and entrees. On the dessert table, selections are to be made from cakes, pastry, cheese and fruits.

The number of items offered in each category determines the cost and elaborateness of the buffet. However, with proper presentation, fewer dishes will also make an impressive display.

Decorative elements can also be used to create a more lavish impression. Ferns and leaves are simple yet quite effective buffet decorations. Ice carvings—traditional buffet highlights—can be used as decorative pieces or to hold flowers or food. Shrimp are often dispensed from an icy, carved fish container.

Decorated hams, poultry, colorful salad molds gain added attention when there is careful planning to develop maximum color contrasts with the foods that will surround them on the buffet table.

The buffet table should never give the impression of being static. Introduce the "action" element by using both high and low serving dishes as well as those of different shapes, styles and materials. Use dishes that have to be replenished during the serving period; the smaller sized chafing dish which is refilled mid-way through service keeps late comers from feeling they're getting less than the best.

Consider arranging the buffet table so that foods are presented on different levels. Building up part of the table with risers permits seated guests to "feast their eyes" even when there is a waiting line of customers.

14 POINT PROGRAM OF BUFFET PRESENTATION

1. Avoid the use of too heavy coating of chaudfroid on meat, poultry or fish items.

2. At all times, be sure aspic is crystal clear, well seasoned, flavorful and the right color.

3. Always plan decorations so patrons will know what the basic item is. It is preferable to have piece portioned or sliced for easy service.

4. Only use sockles where absolutely necessary to heighten display. Since they are not edible, they should be avoided as much as possible.

5. Be sure the platter, bowl or tray selected is the right size for the food item it is to hold. Never let food extend beyond; the salmon head and tail should both fit well inside the edges of the containers.

6. Never put any inedible display piece or material on a platter with food.

7. Do not put so many items on a platter, tray or dish that it looks crowded. This reduces the appeal of the food.

8. Do not overdecorate. Simply decorated pieces are the most effective and take less preparation time.

9. Don't color aspic red, blue or green. A few drops of yellow food coloring is effective in fish aspic and a few drops of tomato red food coloring for a game platter are permissible exceptions.

10. Don't spend too much time creating a display piece that cannot either be eaten or be used to display food that will be eaten.

11. Don't decorate or garnish a food piece with items which do not properly complement it, i.e., do not put cornets of salami with salmon.

12. Don't cover duck, beef rib roast, leg of lamb or other meat items with white chaudfroid sauce or seafood items with a brown or dark chaudfroid sauce.

13. Flowers made of raw potatoes, beets or turnips should not be placed on containers with salads. If you want to use them, place them among green leaves on the table.

14. When using pheasant plumage, be sure it does not get so close to the food that there is a possibility of the feathers getting into the food.

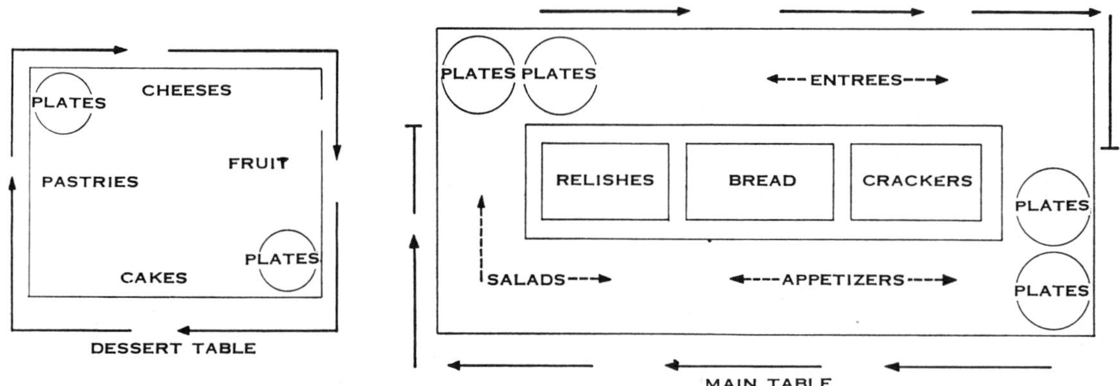

FOR BUFFET SERVICE COVERING A SERVING PERIOD OF SEVERAL HOURS.

1. MAIN TABLE
   A. TWO SEPARATE LINES
   (1) APPETIZERS AND SALADS
   (2) ENTRIES
   B.B RISER IN CENTER OF TABLE TO HOLD RELISHES, BREADS, CRACKERS. CAN BE REACHED FROM EITHER LINE.
2. DESSERT TABLE—ONE LINE
   GUESTS MAY WALK COMPLETELY AROUND TABLE AND CHOOSE FROM ALL DESSERTS. TWO STACKS OF PLATES AT OPPOSITE CORNERS FOR CONVENIENCE ONLY.

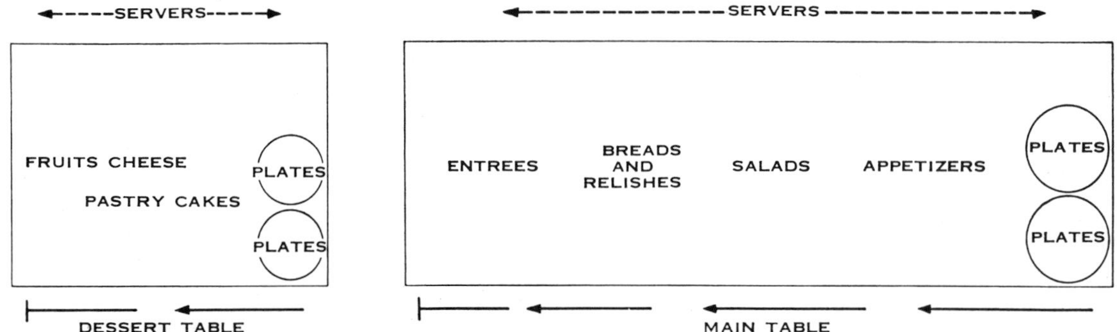

FOR BUFFET SERVICE COVERING A RELATIVELY SHORT SERVING PERIOD.

1. MAIN TABLE—ONE LINE WITH SEVERAL PEOPLE STANDING BEHIND TABLE TO SERVE THE GUESTS AS THEY PASS DOWN THE LINE.
2. DESSERT TABLE—ONE LINE WITH 1 OR 2 PEOPLE STANDING BEHIND TABLE TO SERVE THE GUESTS AS THEY PASS DOWN THE LINE.

HAND TOOLS AND UTENSILS REQUIRED FOR BUFFET WORK

NAME OF TOOL	USED FOR
Knives	
French knife (12 in.)	Chopping of small quantities; basic cutting and slicing procedures.
Paring knife (3 in.) stainless pref.	Most important for minute decorating work and fruit carvings.
Boning knife	For all butchering procedures on meat and fish.
Slicer (10-14 in.)	When the slicing machine cannot be used, this knife will accomplish the best possible job on bread and all boneless meat and poultry.
Scalloped knife	To cut fancy shapes from different vegetables, beets, carrots, etc.
Oyster and clam knife	
Steel and stone	
Special Tools	
Lobster or poultry shears	To open up lobsters to remove the meat; for special boning procedures on whole fish.
Parisian scoop (3 sizes)	To make melon balls; to scoop out fruits and vegetables.
Meat saw (22 in.)	To achieve smooth cuts through bones; butchering ham, crown roast of pork.
Spreader	To apply butter spreads and other fillings.
Offset large spatula (9 in. long, 3 in. wide, stainless)	To lift and transfer whole meat or fish pieces from decorating rack to a platter.
Tweezers	For minute decorating work on chaudfroid base.
Scalpel	To cut leeks and curving shapes out of vegetables for decorating purposes.
Cester	To cut grooves or different grooved designs into citrus fruits, cucumbers or melons.
Trussing needle (6 in.)	For galantines, stuffed suckling pig, salmon grosse pieces.
Egg slicer	To cut hard boiled eggs into uniform slices; a job that cannot be done with any other tool.
Larder	To insert strips of salt pork or bacon into lean meat items, such as saddle of venison, beef a la mode, rabbit.
Pastry bag and a set of tubes, waterproof preferably	A basic requirement for the preparation of canapes and for piping decorations on buffet pieces.
Scissors	Always handy, but especially to create large papillotes (paper frills) to embellish hams and poultry.
Butter Curler	An attractive tool that shapes butter into curls; widely used in Europe.
Carving tools	For sculpturing work on tallow; an inexpensive set of 12 different blades made in Japan is appropriate for this purpose.
Pastry brush	Perhaps one of the most important gadgets, used in many tasks from canape making to aspic work.
Small paint brushes	For aspic and chaudfroid painting.
Cutters	
A set of 10 round cutters	The most important and widely used type; required for croutons and decorating work of all kinds.
A set of 10 scalloped round cutters	Used primarily for aspic designs and vegetables.
Fancy aspic cutters miniature, medium, large	The most common set, widely used for making decorations to go on chaudfroid base.
Geometrical design cutters	A very expensive set made in Europe, but perhaps the most interesting and sophisticated set on the market. Based on the principles of geometry, unusual designs can be accomplished (see decorating ideas).
Numbers and Lettering	These are hand-made, are very expensive, but worth while and time saving.
Unique flower designs	An extravagant set, hand-made, but time saving in creating flower designs from chaudfroid base, vegetables.

American Buffet
Steamship Round
Roast Turkey

Whole Alaskan King Crab
Baked Beans
Tomato Salad
Cranberry Relish
Corn Relish

Wooden risers 12 to 18 in. in width and 8 to 12 in. in height are most often used. The length of the riser will depend on the length of the table.

A carver will contribute action to a buffet. Put him on-stage in spotless white wearing a tall chef's hat. Be sure his carving stance is erect.

Angle bowls and platters in ice beds or use inverted containers to provide pedestals that will make decorated hams, roasts, poultry or whole fish more dominant. Ice holders for bowls and dishes containing cold food are easy to make; hollow out half-blocks of ice with ice picks.

Garnish each platter, bowl or tray of food for maximum color effectiveness. Avoid over garnishing; clashing colors are more unappetizing than too little color. The goal in working out colors is a happy medium; if in doubt, tone colors down.

Space between dishes on the buffet table heightens the effectiveness of the individual items. Give each display piece its own chance to shine against the plain background of the table covering.

Skirts for the buffet table add to its impressiveness and should hang within ¼ in. of the floor. Table skirts are often pleated.

Spotlights can also be used to give extra focus to the more elaborate arrangements on the buffet table. Table lighting will be even more effective if the rest of the lighting in the room is subdued.

Other decorative effects that can be assets for the buffet table include letters spelling the name of the host organization cut from plastic foam (plastic foam when colored also makes attractive artificial fruit or flowers); candelabra holding candles in colors that accent the central theme; unusual vases, copper and silver-plated chafing dishes; striking antiques—lanterns, copper utensils, wrought iron work, figurines, wood carvings, driftwood, slender logs with colorful bark; instant mashed potatoes made into flowers via the pastry tube and blushed pink, blue and green as decorative additions to platters and trays.

Breakfast buffets for business groups or organizations before a day of meetings are an accepted practice. Though these are often informal, the host organization is almost certain to have an emblem or a piece of advertising that will add special interest, if displayed prominently on the buffet table.

Since breakfast groups usually gather slowly, a separate table of iced portioned fruit and juices—and when requested a selection of Bloody Mary's and Salty Dogs—can be set up for early arrivals. Coffee should always be ready for early guests, too.

Cereals, toast, rolls or coffee cake, eggs, sausages or other breakfast meats can be picked up from the buffet table. Hot foods can be served from chafing dishes.

The brunch buffet is more elaborate and most commonly served on Sundays and holidays. One typical brunch buffet menu:

Fresh Fruits
Broiled Canadian Bacon
Creamed Sweetbreads in Patty Shells
Brookfield Sausages
Tiny Golden Pancakes
Scrambled Eggs
Hashed Browned Potatoes
Assorted Sweet Rolls
Coffee Cakes Preserves
Coffee Tea Milk

Another brunch plan suggests serving fruits and juices at the table after which patrons go to the buffet table for: Roast Round of Beef, Baked Ham, Chicken, A Selection of Vegetables, Potatoes, Chicken Livers, Chicken Giblets, Beef Sausage, Bacon, Scrambled Eggs, Corned Beef Hash, Chef's Salad, An Assortment of Molded Salads, Danish Pastry, Cheese Cake, Cheese Coffee Cake.

There is a growing trend to buffet service in executive dining rooms at luncheon. Many of these dining rooms are being furnished with permanent buffet set-ups.

Usually tables are set in advance, then beverages are served by the same waitress. Two buffet set-ups, one hot and one cold, are presided over by other workers. A typical menu for the executive luncheon buffet:

On the Cold Buffet

Assorted Fruit Bowl Cold Ham Platter
Bowl of Carrot Sticks, Radishes, Celery and Green Onions
Lazy Susan Holding Spiced Peaches, Sweet Gherkin Pickles, Olives and Pickled Onions
Platter of Assorted Sandwiches
Platter of Cheese Slices—Cheddar and Swiss
Hard Cooked Eggs, Stuffed
Tossed Combination Salad Bowl
Bowl of Cottage Cheese
Cherry Gelatin with Cantaloup Balls
Bowl of Onion and Parsley Dip
Assorted Crackers
Cole Slaw Souffle

On the Hot Buffet

Hot Soup
Braised Sirloin Tips, Mushrooms
Buttered Noodles
Buttered Broccoli Spears

Buffet Desserts

Strawberry Shortcake, Whipped Cream
German Chocolate Cake Ice Cream

Dinner buffets are usually more elaborate, are often presided over by a carver. A dinner buffet might follow this pattern. In the center, at the back of the buffet table, position an illuminated ice piece, carved to hold small pieces of fresh fruit or small flower arrangements.

In front of the ice carving, center such decorated whole pieces as a turkey, chicken, ham, salmon or an arrangement of lobster or crab. At either end of the row of decorated pieces, place bowls or platters of salads—potato, macaroni, cucumber, cole slaw or vegetable. Dishes of celery, olives, radishes and containers of appropriate cold sauces can be interspersed where space permits.

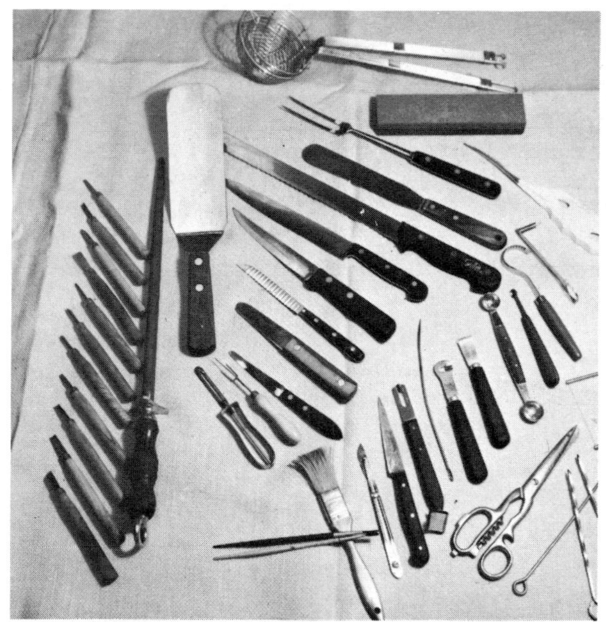

DECORATING TOOLS AND KNIVES

From lower right to left—FIRST ROW: Metal skewers, lobster or poultry shears, brushes, scalpel, paring knife, 3 cesteurs, trussing needle, parisian scoop-large, parisian scoop miniature size, butter curler, spiral cutter, shrimp deveiner; SECOND ROW, from left: peeler, sandwich fork, grapefruit knife, clam or oyster knife, scalloping knife, boning knife, medium french knife, bread knife or slicer, spatula or spreader, meat fork, sharpening stone, potato nest maker; THIRD ROW: carving tools for tallow work, sharpening steel, extra wide stainless steel spatula.

DECORATING CUTTERS AND SMALL TIMBALES

LOWER RIGHT: Empty cans for aspic timbales, pastry bag with 14 different tubes, bird of paradise cutter, row of enforced decorating cutters; LEFT: set of ten round cutters (plain), scalloped cutters (oval and round), set of fancy decorating cutters (in box); UPPER RIGHT: timbales (heart-shaped, oval, round), special cutters for floral designs.

Introduction

Breakfast buffet menu, Morris Bryant Inn, West Lafayette, Ind.: assorted dry cereals, bowl of citrus sections, grapefruit halves, fresh fruit, prunes; eggs, poached, scrambled; bacon, sausage, ham; home fried potatoes; hot rolls, danish, muffins, toast; hoosier apple butter, preserves; on alternate days, chicken hash (above); corned beef hash-poached eggs, creamed smoked fish, swedish style.

At the front of the table, position chafing dishes on matching trays. Popular items for chafing dish service:

- Chicken a la King on Toast
- Lobster or Seafood Newburgh with Rice
- Curried Shrimps with Chutney
- Chicken Creole with Rice
- Chicken Livers with Spaghetti
- Beef Stroganoff with Noodles
- Chicken Fricassee
- Chicken Pot Pie
- Beef Bourginonne
- Hungarian Beef Goulash

A separate dessert table is the usual rule for dinner buffets. Desserts do not need to be elaborate; fresh fruit and cheese is a popular dessert choice on buffets.

Whatever the type of buffet scheduled, there is assistance for planners and production people in the chapters that follow.

They provide detailed information on preparation and presentation of: canapes, knife and fork hors d' oeuvres, hard cooked fancy eggs, ham, poultry, fresh salmon and brook trout, king crab and lobsters, wild game birds, fruit carving and cheese display, aspic, aspic molds and fruit molds, chaud froid coating, mousse, farce, special salads, grosse pieces, pates and galantines, ice carvings. Step-by-step illustrations make procedures easy.

Other areas of importance to buffet production are also outlined. Buffet set-ups are diagrammed; themes are outlined; smorgasbord menus, simple and elaborate, are listed; decorating ideas for salmon, poultry and ham are described step-by-step.

The authors of the Book of Buffets had this aim: "If it goes on the buffet, we want to tell how to put it there." Their comprehensive coverage puts the essential information about buffets in easily-mastered, practical form.

NOTES

NOTES

Canapes, in American cuisine, are usually thought of as items to serve at large gatherings where people eat and drink while standing.

The terms "canapes" and "hors d'oeuvres" are often used to mean the same thing; but in this chapter canapes are defined as tidbits that can be picked up without utensils. They are served either on a baked base, on toothpicks or with toothpicks. Hors d'oeuvres, on the other hand are foods served on plates to be eaten with knife and fork as a first course at dinner or supper. Hors d'oeuvres will be covered in the next chapter.

Since both canapes and hors d'oeuvres are eaten first at a meal, they are also often referred to as appetizers. It is better to use the more specific words "canapes" and "hors d'oeuvres" since preparation of a knife and fork item for a canape table could have embarrassing consequences, if the sauce were to drip on a guest trying to consume it while standing in a crowd.

Canapes, in addition to being easy to eat, must also be colorful, piquant, spicy or salty. Saltiness is an especially desirable contrast when cocktails are being sold as it will definitely increase the guest's need for liquid.

Canapes may be either hot or cold. For a large group, they are usually displayed on a buffet table, with the cold canapes arranged on large platters and the hot canapes served from chafing dishes at the table or brought hot from the kitchen to be passed to the guests on trays.

Centerpieces for Canape Trays

Colorful centerpieces for trays of cold canapes designed for table display can be made from whole fruits or vegetables. Bite-size canapes can be embedded with picks all around the fruit or vegetable centerpiece. Sometimes a hollow is made in the top of the fruit or vegetable for a container of dip.

Among fruits and vegetables suggested for centerpiece displays: watermelon, pineapple, large or small pumpkin, honeydew and spanish melons and a large head of cabbage wrapped in foil.

Large carved turnips, roses made from tomatoes or cream cheese, figures made from lobster shells and whole cheeses such as edam or muenster add decorative color to canape table arrangements.

Any vegetable or fruit selected to hold pick-embedded canapes, with or without dip container, must be heavy enough to stay put while canapes are being removed from it.

Suitable bite-size canapes include medium shrimp with cocktail sauce or russian dressing for dip; ham or turkey cubes with dip of cream cheese, chives, chopped hard cooked eggs, prepared mustard; smoked oysters with dip of cream cheese, bacon crumbs, chopped watercress and grated onion; swiss cheese cubes with dip of cream cheese, crumbled blue cheese and chives; olives with same dip suggested for ham or turkey cubes; beef cubes with pickles and dip used with ham and turkey cubes; other smoked meats with dip suggested for smoked oysters.

Cold Canapes

The assembled items or *mise en place* for canape making include:

1. Whole unsliced pullman bread (rye and white) about 2 days old.
2. Butter spreads which have been held at room temperature long enough to have the creamy consistency that makes them easy to spread quickly.
3. Garnishes arranged on a sheet pan; capers, pimentos, and similar items are used to garnish.
4. Canned goods—opened and drained.
5. Silver platters or other metal platters covered with fancy paper doilies.
6. Centerpieces for trays—made ahead, if possible.
7. Bread cutters.

Canape Bases

Bread: Pullman white or rye, whole wheat, french bread, german pumpernickel or boston brown bread are most frequently used.

Alternates: All kinds of crackers; puff paste; pate au choux; melba toast.

Croutons: The most desirable canape base because it is crisp and can be stored satisfactorily. It can also be cut into many different shapes.

To Make Croutons:

1. Slice white pullman bread ½ in. thick, leaving crust on. This may be done in a slicing machine, but the loaf will have to be cut in half as it is too long for the machine. A 12-in. slicer can be used; but the slices will not be as uniform, and it will take longer.
2. Lay slices out on a table and cut into desired shapes with cutters.
3. Brush melted butter over sheet pan (margarine may be substituted for half the butter). Place bread cut-outs in rows on sheet pan; when pan is filled, brush more melted butter over the bread.
4. Bake in a 450° F. oven till crisp and brown on both sides. Regulate oven so both sides of crouton bake at the same time. This will make it unnecessary to turn the croutons, which is very time consuming. At this temperature croutons will be done in 5 to 8 minutes.
5. Baked croutons, when properly crisp, can be stored in a closed container up to two weeks or longer.

(Croutons are sometimes deep fried or crisped under the broiler. Neither of these methods is as satisfactory as baking. Regular toast is not as satisfactory for crouton bases either as it stales faster.)

Note: Egg white can be brushed over croutons before they are baked to provide a moisture-proof film which is especially desirable if the canapes are to be finished, decorated and then stored.

CANAPES:

COLD CANAPES AT LEFT FROM TOP TO BOTTOM—Genoa Salami, American Cheese Tartlettes, Carrot Caviar, Blue Cheese Balls on Pumpernickel, Shrimp Canape, Smoked Oyster and Liver Pate.

HOT CANAPE TRAYS AT RIGHT FROM TOP TO BOTTOM—Anchovy Rolls, Hot Swisse Canape, Crabmeat and Hollandaise, Petite Croque Monsieur, Canadian Canape, Anchovy Egg, Pizza Canape, Clam and Cheddar Cheese, Tuna and Cheddar Cheese. At far right, unbaked canapes.

Hot, Cold & Uncooked

Yields from one pullman loaf: Squares—160; rounds—100; diamonds—100 to 120; rectangles—100 to 120; half moons—120 to 130; long triangles—120 to 140. Special shapes like animals or stars will yield only about 60 to 70 croutons which makes these shapes too costly for many occasions.

Butter Spreads

The butter spreads charted on the facing page can be spread or piped on canape bases as a first layer, or they may be combined with other ingredients as a topping.

The main ingredient added to give butter a special flavor and color should always be chopped fine. Ingredients can be added to taste, but it is best to experiment with a small amount first. Butter will blend best if it is of creamy consistency; never use melted butter.

Basic whipped butter is prepared with softened butter or margarine whipped fluffy with a wire whip or electric beater. Basic seasoning is dry mustard, worcestershire sauce, or liquid hot pepper sauce. Use of whipped butter will help prevent moist fillings from soaking into canapes.

Other Canape Spreads

Cream Cheese Variations: To add flavor to cream cheese add any of the following, finely chopped: ham and other smoked meats; chives; pimientoes; olives, green ripe or stuffed; caviar. Cream cheese spreads do not have the same consistency as butter spreads and require more care in spreading.

Spreads Made from Meat, Fish or Hard-Boiled Eggs: Almost any type of roasted poultry, beef or veal, salmon or other kinds of cooked fish combined with mayonnaise and properly seasoned can be made into a spread. Meats or fish have to be pureed. These spreads are used mainly in pinwheel and layer canapes.

These canapes, framed by a silver tray and arranged to emphasize interplay of color and shape, were planned to delight the eye and the palate. These finger foods have maximum appeal for sip and savor groups. Variety is an essential and, happily, an easy ingredient of canape preparation. Materials for canape bases, spreads and garnishes are so numerous that the possible combinations are limited only by the energy and imagination of the person planning a canape assortment.

On smaller tray, crouton-based canapes: row 1 at top—half moon cheese tartlet; row 2—diamond-shaped with salmon rollatini; row 3—rounds with caviar; row 4—squares with liver spread. On larger tray, toast-based canapes: row 1 at top—bismarck herring and sardines; row 2—cheese tartlets; row 3—caviar and onion; row 4—blue cheese balls; row 5—liver butter spread anđl olives.

Simple yet eye-catching arrangement of gourmet ingredients. Toast triangles topped with smoked salmon and edged with cream cheese piping; stuffed eggs topped with mounds of black caviar.

Canapes on Crouton Bases for Cold Assortment

Since there is no limit to the variety possible in canapes, the following chart is offered only as a starting point. In working out a canape assortment, it is important to be sure that cheese, smoked meats and seafood are all included.

In the chart below the canapes are listed by main ingredient used.

Mass Production Set-Up for Canapes

This method is faster than the crouton-based method, but canapes will not be quite so crisp. It is most helpful when several hundred or thousand canapes must be produced. The basic preparation is the same as that described in the section on making croutons, but the preparation steps are different.

1. Split 2-day-old pullman loaves in half and trim crust in slicing machine or by hand with 12-in. slicer.
2. Slice trimmed blocks lengthwise into ¼-in. slices.
3. Arrange sliced bread in rows on a wooden work bench or other surface where cutting can be done.
4. Apply spread with pastry bag or spatula; butter spreads are recommended rather than mayonnaise

BUTTER SPREADS

	Color	Ingredients
Anchovy Butter	Brown	Pureed anchovy fillets or anchovy paste, chopped parsley, chives, lemon juice; 1 tsp. anchovy to 1 cup butter.
Horseradish Butter	White	Prepared horseradish; 3 tsp. per cup butter.
Caviar Butter	Black, White or Red	Black caviar and minced onions; whitefish caviar or Russian caviar with hot pepper sauce, worcestershire sauce, lemon juice, to taste.
Roquefort or Blue Cheese		Equal parts cheese and butter creamed in dicer-chopper; chives optional.
Shallot Butter		Minced shallots, parsley.
Pimiento Butter	Red	Pureed pimiento scraps, with lemon juice, hot pepper sauce, worcestershire sauce mixed with butter; chives or parsley optional.
Lobster Butter	Red	Lobster coral (red part of cooked lobster) and lobster trimmings; shrimp pieces mixed with butter, lemon juice, a pinch of paprika, hot pepper sauce, catsup.
Green Butter	Green	Boil following for 3 minutes: parsley, watercress, chervil, tarragon, fresh spinach, chives. Drain and puree in blender with capers and gherkins or with lemon juice. Mix with butter. Plain chopped parsley with juice can also be used to make green butter.
Mustard Butter	Yellow	Prepared yellow mustard.
Truffle Butter	Dark Brown	Finely chopped truffle peelings or pieces are mixed in blender with butter. Sherry or brandy is used for flavor.
Tuna Butter		Canned tuna and butter mixed.
Curry Butter	Yellow	Chopped onions and curry powder sauteed briefly and pureed in blender with mango chutney.
Smoked Salmon Butter		Smoked salmon trimmings put through meat grinder or strained through sieve.
Sardine Butter		Strain sardines through sieve, add lemon juice, hot pepper sauce, catsup. Use skinless sardines.
Caper Butter		Chop well-drained capers, add butter seasoned with tarragon vinegar and worcestershire sauce.
Smoked Oyster Butter		Chop oysters very fine, mix into butter, add lemon juice, worcestershire sauce, hot pepper sauce.

Note: When storing butter spreads in refrigerator, keep containers covered. Other seasonings may be added or substituted to change butter spread flavors; experiment first with a small quantity.

CANAPES ON CROUTON BASES

	Base	Spread and Topping	Garnish
Caviar I	Square Crouton	Red and black caviar mixed with minced onion and spread over buttered crouton	Arranged in checkerboard formation on tray
Caviar II	Round Crouton	Shallot butter, hardboiled egg slice, caviar on yolk	Piped cream cheese border
Caviar III	Round Crouton	Fancy piping on edge of crouton with caviar butter	Tiny onion rings, capers, radishes
Ham	Any shape	Mustard butter, chopped eggs mixed with parsley over ham	Small ham cubes on picks
Anchovy I	Round Crouton	Green butter, egg slice, anchovy ring with caper in center	Pimiento circle
Anchovy II	Any shape	Anchovy butter piping	Radish
Liver Pate	Diamonds	Canned liver puree mixed with butter and piped on with flat tube	Chopped smoked tongue, sweet gherkin
Smoked Oyster	Round Crouton	Pimiento butter, egg slice, slice of dill pickle	Smoked oyster on frill
Salami (Genoa)	Round Crouton	Horseradish butter, egg slice, pickle, small tomato slice	Salami cone, very thinly sliced
Blue Cheese	Any shape	Blue cheese butter piped on pumpernickel bread; also serve with pumpernickel fingers or sticks	Radish rose
Shrimp		Tomato butter, lettuce circle, egg slice, split shrimp on pick	Piped mayonnaise with black pepper, fresh dill
Smoked Salmon	Any shape	Salmon slices rolled with cream cheese placed on green butter	Fresh dill, capers

SET-UP FOR MASS PRODUCTION OF CANAPES

The set-up below is planned for mass production of canapes. Assembled in this mise en place are bowls of butter spreads, pastry tubes, opened canned items, other ingredients in individual dishes to be arranged on the lengthwise slices of pullman bread. (Dark rectangles are toasted bread.) Butter spreads keep moisture from toppings out of bread base. Cover bread with butter spread, add desired topping, as at right. If topping is to be an individual item—a sardine, shrimp or salami roll—space properly for cutting. Decorate and garnish before cutting. Chill items before cutting if possible. Cut into squares, long rectangles, triangles or diamond-shaped canapes, right below. Place on serving platters, cover with foil or transparent wrap until time for service. An efficient way to turn out canapes by the hundreds, or thousands for large parties.

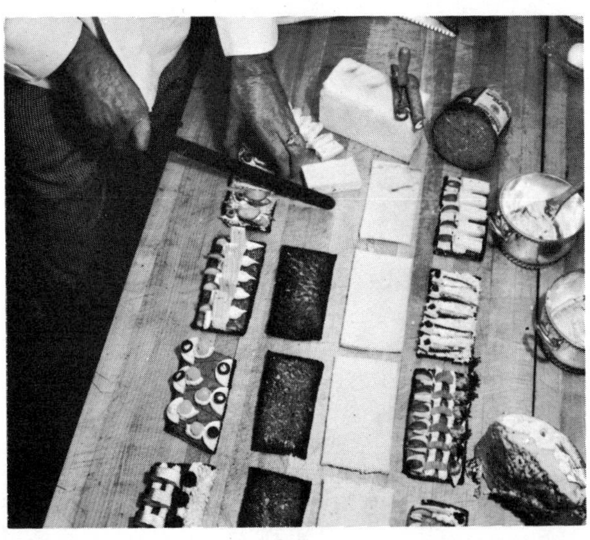

COLD CANAPE COMBINATIONS

	Base	Spread and Topping	Garnish
Ham	Pumpernickel rye rectangle	Mustard butter, asparagus tips rolled in ham	Chopped parsley
Anchovy	White triangle	Anchovy butter	Pimiento strips, olives
Cream Cheese	White or rye, any shape	Cream cheese pimiento, ham spread	Gherkins or pickles
Sardine	White rectangle	Parsley butter, briesling sardines, chopped eggs	Capers, parsley twigs
Salami	Rye diamonds	Green butter, salami rolls filled with egg spread	Pickles or olives
Cheese Checkerboard	Rye squares	Pimiento butter, white and yellow American cheese	Pimiento designs

OTHER COMBINATIONS

Fillets of anchovies on toast with pimientos
Red or black caviar on round crackers
Chicken liver pate on crackers
Coronets of imported salami on crackers with ham paste
Stuffed celery hearts with blue and cream cheese
Butterfly shrimps on tuna salad on melba toast
Sliced pate de foie gras in aspic on crackers
Egg paste on cracker topped with red caviar
Cream cheese on cracker topped with stuffed green olive
Puree of ham with sliced pickle on cracker
Stuffed devilled egg quarter topped with one-fourth ripe olive
Tuna salad with slice of hard cooked egg on rye circle
Ham roll filled with piquant egg paste and sliced pickle served on cracker
Smoked salmon rolled with cream cheese and chives
Small tidbits of herring on crackers with sliced pickle
Puree of smoked beef tongue on cracker with dill pickle
Herring fillet rolled with pickle and onion
Smoked eel on toast or crackers

MAKE AHEAD ASSORTMENT

Make-ahead assortment of canapes keeps well in the freezer. A light coating of aspic seals in freshness. From top to bottom, below, are rows of: Chicken liver pate with green olives. Pureed chicken salad covered with white chaud froid sauce, truffle square added. Smoked salmon rolled with cream cheese and chives, pimiento figure in center. Tuna fish salad spread topped with caviar. Cornets of salami stuffed with egg paste. Triangles of king crabmeat with chaud froid coating topped with slices of crab meat. Chicken liver pate made into a roll; sliced; slice placed on bread rectangle with a mushroom cap on top. Shrimp paste placed on bread, covered with chaud froid sauce. Skinless, boneless sardines cut in strips. Salmon spread, chaud froid coated, on bread triangles, decorated with ripe olive slices.

Assortment below starting at bottom row: 1. Round crackers with cheddar, cream cheese mixture topped with green stuffed olive slice. 2. Square crisp toast with anchovy filet and pimiento slice. 3. Liver pate on cracker with truffle slice, aspic coated. 4. Stuffed quarter deviled egg with pimiento decor. 5. Cracker, egg slice, cucumber, caviar. 6. Sliced king crabmeat on toasted bread square. 7. Sardine with pimiento on toast. 8. Goose liver puree piped on cracker, topped with small mushroom cap. 9. Decorated piece of fresh salmon on toast. 11. Square layer sandwich with tongue and cheese fillings. 12. Slice of smoked salmon pinwheel made with cream cheese and chive filling on cracker. Most of these canapes should be made close to time they are to go on the buffet table.

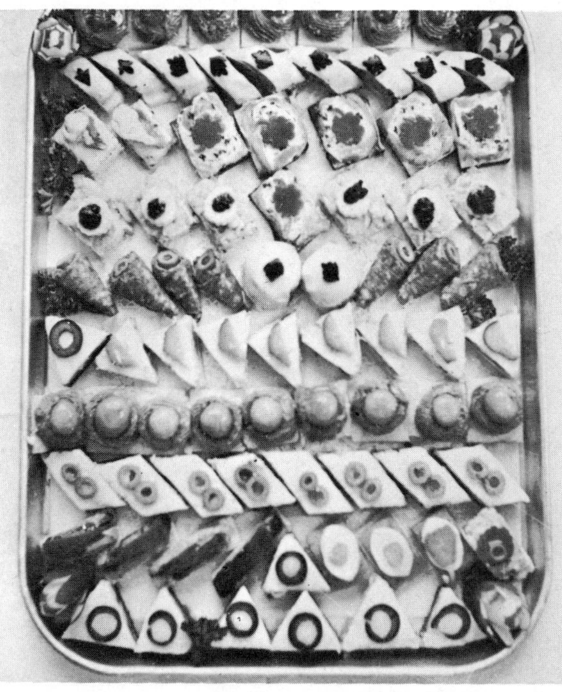

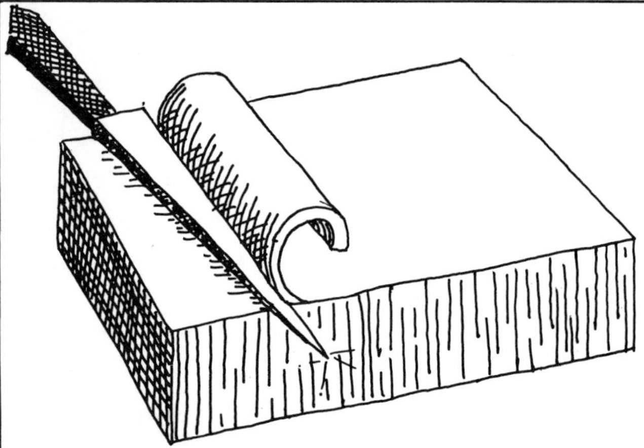

To Make Pinwheel Sandwiches

1. Slice pullman loaf of bread in half lengthwise. Trim crusts off. Cut lengthwise slices from each half making slices as thin as possible. Spread selected filling over entire slice. If cream cheese and jelly layers are to be used as filling for pinwheel, cover slice of bread first with cream cheese; soften it so it goes on smoothly. Next put on layer of jelly as evenly as possible, making layer fairly thick for maximum color contrast in the pinwheel.

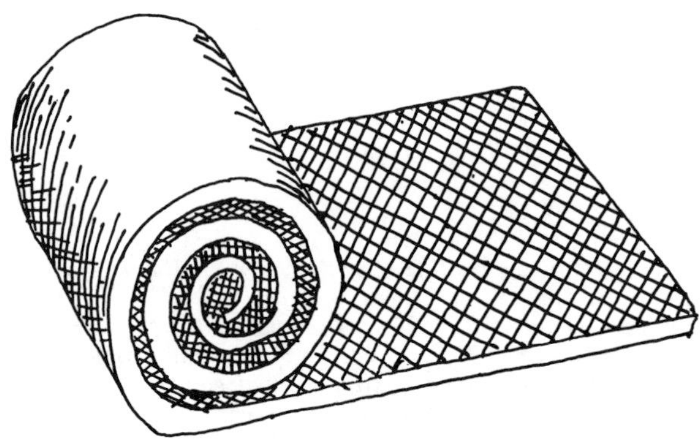

2. After slice of bread is spread with preferred fillings, roll slice the long way making roll tight. Wrap roll in wax paper and refrigerate.

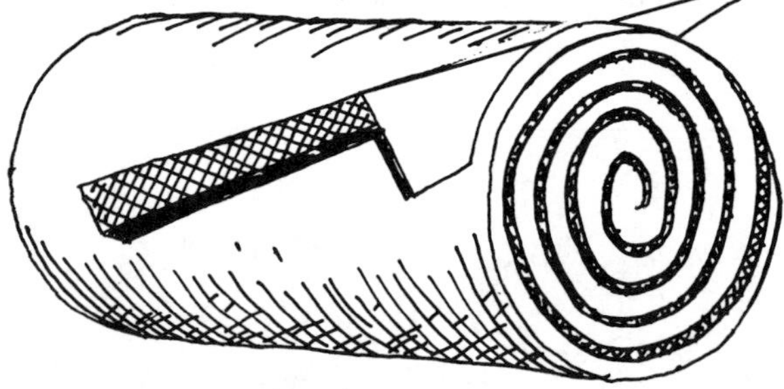

3. To cut pinwheels into slices for canape tray, first dip knife into hot water. Cut slices into desired width.

Pinwheel Sandwich Fillings

1. Mix two parts cheddar cheese with one part cream cheese, dash of worcestershire sauce and dash of liquid pepper sauce. Blend thoroughly. Pinwheels made with this filling can be refrigerated for two days before service.

2. Mix cream cheese with soft butter to spreading consistency.

3. To mixture of cream cheese and soft butter, add chopped nuts. Spread evenly on slice of bread, then top with chopped pimento or parsley bits.

4. Add chopped olives or chopped chives to mixture of cream cheese and soft butter.

5. First spread mixture of cream cheese and soft butter, then cover with thick layer of currant or mint jelly.

6. Spread cream cheese and soft butter mixture and arrange lox over it.

To Make Layer Sandwiches

This pattern for layer sandwiches specifies deviled egg paste for the spread and meat for fillings. Other spreads and fillings can also be used. Bread is sliced lengthwise as thin as possible. Use three or four slices of bread for each layer sandwich. Put egg paste (butter spreads may also be used) on both sides of slices of bread going into the middle of the layer. For 3-layer sandwich, put spread on top of bottom slice of bread; cover with filling; top filling with slice of bread that has been spread on both sides; cover second slice with more filling; add slice with spread on filling side to complete 3-layer loaf. (For 4-layer loaf, add one more slice in middle.) Wrap finished loaf in wax paper and refrigerate.

Layer Sandwich Fillings

1. To make deviled egg paste, rub egg yolks through a sieve, then mix with soft butter. Season mixture with worcestershire sauce, salt, pepper and english mustard and thin to spreading consistency with mayonnaise.

2. An alternate for deviled egg paste can be made using liver pate. Place pate in bowl and blend in soft butter until mixture reaches spreading consistency. Season mixture with salt and pepper and sherry.

3. To make ham paste, mix ground cooked ham with mustard, pepper and worcestershire; thin with mayonnaise to spreading consistency.

4. Chicken, tongue, tunafish, lobster and shrimp can also be used to make paste spreads for layer sandwiches.

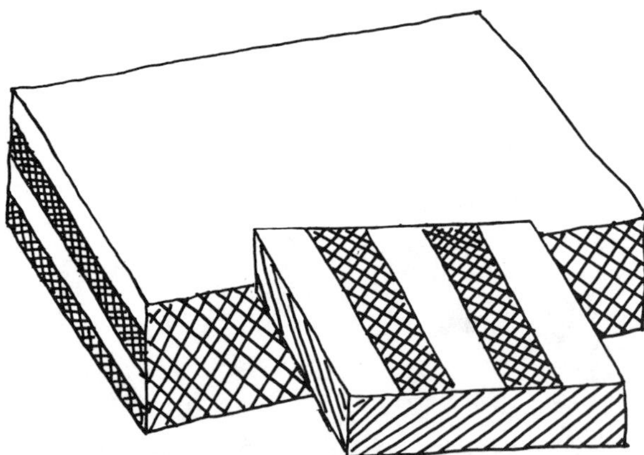

First step in slicing layer sandwiches: dip knife in hot water and slice loaf into layers of desired width.

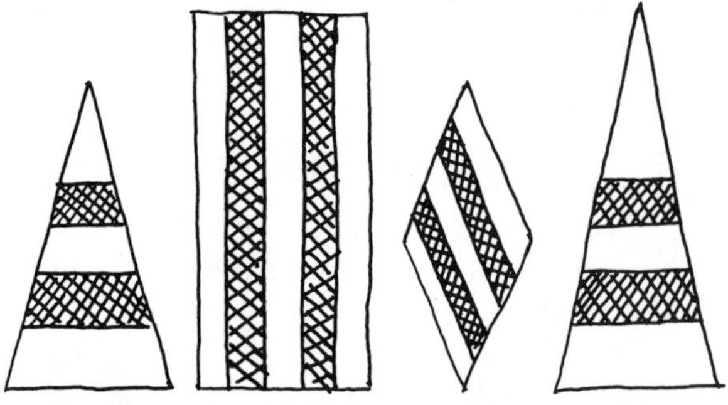

To finish slicing layer sandwiches, vary shapes by trimming as illustrated.

spreads as butter spreads keep moisture from getting into bread and making canapes soggy.

5. Arrange main meat or seafood item on the buttered base. If the pieces are individual items like sardines, shrimp or salami rolls, be sure to space properly for cutting.

6. Decorate and garnish.

7. If time allows, chill before cutting. Then cut into desired shape with slicer. Canapes can be square, long rectangle, triangle or diamond-shaped—but they cannot be round.

8. Transfer to serving platter, cover with foil or transparent wrap till time to serve.

Canape Base from Lengthwise Slice of Pullman Bread

The thick slice of pullman bread is placed in a hot oven until it is medium brown on both sides. When slice is properly browned, remove from oven and place weight on slice. This will prevent its curling or will straighten slice out if it has started to curl.

The following canape combinations can be placed on long toasted slices:

1. Egg-Paste—spread egg-paste on entire slice and top with a layer of smoked salmon.

2. Caviar—place caviar in bowl; soften with oil if needed and sprinkle over entire slice.

3. Cream Cheese and Salmon—spread cream cheese on top of long slice, top with layer of salmon.

4. Sturgeon—spread butter over entire slice; top with smoked sturgeon.

5. Sardine—spread egg paste over entire slice; slice boneless sardines in half and put on next, then place a sliver of pimiento on top of each sardine half. Use Norwegian briesling sardines.

6. Salmon Roe—mix salmon roe with soft butter and spread over slice.

7. Cheddar Cheese—spread cheddar cheese butter over entire slice and top with layer of sliced ham.

8. Tongue—spread cheddar cheese butter over slice; top with layer of boiled tongue slices.

9. Chicken—make as above, substituting chicken for tongue.

After completing toppings for long slice of bread, refrigerate until time to serve, then cut into desired canape shape and add any decorations.

Aspic Glaze

A neutral aspic glaze is sometimes applied to cold canapes. The aspic adds sheen to canapes which makes them more eye appealing; however, care should be taken to keep the glaze from penetrating the bread base and making it soggy.

Layer and Pinwheel Canapes

Both of these canapes can be made from pullman bread and are especially well suited to mass production since they are not open faced and can be kept longer under refrigeration or frozen.

To Make the Layer Canape: Yield—about 120 canapes from one pullman loaf.

1. Slice 2-day-old pullman bread lengthwise about ⅛-in. thick; leave crusts on.

2. Spread bread with butter spreads or cream cheese spreads. If sliced meats are used, both sides of middle slices must be buttered, as there must be butter on either side of filling.

3. Assemble four slices that have been spread into a block.

4. Wrap blocks in aluminum foil and refrigerate; they can be held for 2 to 3 days. They can also be frozen.

5. When ready to serve, trim crust from around each block and slice into about 24 rectangular shaped canapes. Blocks can also be sliced into pyramid shapes or triangles.

Although colored pullman bread is available, the colors of the fillings are usually appealing enough and show off best when contrasted with white, whole wheat or rye bread.

Note: The devilled egg paste referred to above is made by putting egg yolks through a sieve, then mixing with soft butter and seasoning with mayonnaise, worcestershire sauce, salt, pepper and english mustard. It is a good spread for layer canapes.

Layer Canape Combinations: These are made from pullman bread as described above.

(a) Two slices of rye, two slices of white bread, sliced American cheese, sliced pullman ham, various butter spreads.

(b) Pullman rye bread, sliced corned beef, horseradish butter.

(c) Pullman white bread, curry butter, sliced turkey breast.

(d) Pullman rye bread, green butter, swiss or muenster cheese.

(e) Pullman rye bread, anchovy butter.

(f) Pullman rye bread, sardine butter made with boneless and skinless sardines.

German Pumpernickel Based Combinations: This dark brown, very firm bread comes thinly sliced and is available in triangles, squares and rounds, imported and wrapped in air tight foil. Domestic pumpernickel comes in pullman size slices in transparent wrap. The larger slices are more suitable for layer canapes, while the fancy shapes lend themselves best to open face canapes. Suggested spreads for pumpernickel layer canapes assembled five slices to a block:

(a) Blue cheese butter.

(b) Chive butter with slices of gruyere or muenster cheese.

(c) Cream cheese combinations—blue cheese, chopped pickles, chives, etc.

Boston Brown Bread Layer Canapes: This dark brown, slightly sweet, moist bread comes from a small round can. Cut into slices and spread with cream cheese or a mold ripened cheese, boston brown bread is assembled in five-slice rounds, then cut into tiny sections and decorated with garnishettes.

Brown bread cannot be sliced in a machine as the molasses in it creates a film on the blade which makes the slices crumble.

Pinwheel Canapes (Also Called Tea Sandwiches)

These canapes can also be prepared several days before they are to be used and then refrigerated. Some pinwheel canapes can also be frozen. The pullman bread to be used in pinwheel canapes should not be more than 1 day old as it must roll easily without breaking. Fresh pullman bread is too fragile.

To Make Pinwheel Canapes: Yield—each roll yields 6 canapes; one pullman loaf will make 120 to 140 canapes.

1. Slice pullman bread (with crust on) lengthwise, about ⅛ in. thick.
2. Place bread slices in rows on work table.
3. Apply all spreads and fillings. Slice off crusts.
4. Roll slice up tightly, rolling the long way.
5. Wrap three rolled slices together in aluminum foil or waxed paper and refrigerate.
6. If rolls are frozen, they will be solid in about 15 minutes.

Pinwheel Canape Combinations: (a) Pullman white bread, parsley butter, sliced pullman ham, cream cheese spread, one asparagus stalk through center.

(b Pullman white bread, anchovy butter, dark breadstick through center.

(c) Pullman rye bread, horseradish butter, thin sliced corn beef.

(d) Pimiento butter; American cheese (sliced very thin lengthwise from a whole block); pullman ham. Make sure butter spread goes between ham and cheese and pullman white or rye bread, whichever is used for pinwheel.

(e) Pullman white bread, mustard or tomato butter, sliced roast beef, dill pickle through center.

(f) Pullman white bread, tuna butter, pimiento strip through center.

(g) Pullman rye bread, blue cheese butter, pumpernickel bread-stick through center.

Cheese-Filled Pinwheels: (a) For cream cheese and jelly pinwheels, choose jellies with deep color for effective contrast. Prepare the jellies by placing 1 tbsp. unflavored gelatin in a shallow pan. Dissolve gelatin with 2 tbsp. water. If gelatin does not dissolve, heat slightly. Add 1 cup jelly, stirring in with whisk. Cool. If color is not deep and rich, add food coloring. Red currant, apricot and mint jellies may be prepared by this method.

(b) For American cheese pinwheels, mix two parts cheddar with one part cream cheese, add worcestershire sauce and a drop or two of liquid pepper sauce.

(c) Cream cheese for pinwheels can be mixed with soft butter. To this basic spread may be added:

Chopped nuts topped with chopped pimiento and parsley bits; chopped olives; chopped chives; a lox topping.

Rollatinis

Rollatinis are pinwheels in which meat replaces the bread and is spread with any one of a variety of cream cheese or butter spreads. Rollatinis may be sliced and served on canape bases or served alone as a bite-size canape.

Rollatinis may be made from: pullman ham, westphalian ham, prosciutto and virginia ham, pastrami, mortadella sausage, genoa salami, corned beef, roast beef, smoked beef tongue sliced lengthwise, bologna, and smoked salmon. Rolls should be refrigerated until they are solid and will slice neatly. For extra garnish, pickles or olives can be placed inside the rolls.

Rollatini Combinations: (a) Mortadella sausage with cream cheese and chive filling.

(b) Pullman ham with liver spread made of equal parts liver puree and butter.

(c) Westphalian ham with egg spread made of equal parts devilled egg spread and butter.

(d) Pastrami with green butter.

(e) Corned beef with horseradish butter.

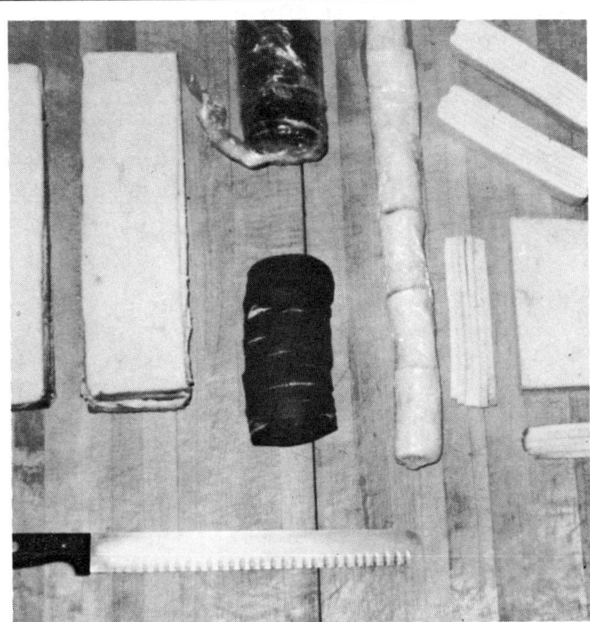

Above, square and round layer and pinwheel sandwiches just out of refrigeration are ready to be unwrapped and sliced. Thin round slices of boston brown bread spread with cream cheese and stacked four slices high, are chilled, then cut into triangles. At right, working from an assortment of layer sandwich shapes and variously decorated pinwheels, mosaic-like arrangements of tea sandwiches capitalize on color and ingredient contrast. Designs in red pimiento, ripe olive, truffles or green olives add spark to pinwheels.

Top row: Heart-shaped sandwiches of chicken spread; pinwheels of cream cheese and currant jelly on white bread; half moons of white bread with seafood spread and mayonnaise. Row 2: Pinwheels of cream cheese and mint jelly on white bread; pinwheels of cream cheese and chopped nuts on whole wheat bread. Row 3: Layer sandwiches with ham and American cheese fillings, cut in triangles. Row 4: Checkerboard sandwich with deviled egg paste, ham spread filling on white and whole wheat bread; more currant jelly and cream cheese pinwheels on white bread. Row 6: Layer sandwiches of white bread with chicken spread and chopped ripe olives. Bottom row: Pinwheels of white bread spread with cream cheese and bits of red pimiento; more heart-shaped sandwiches with chicken spread. Napkins specially folded at corners of tray garnished effectively with bunches of fresh green parsley.

TOOLS OF THE CANAPE TRADE

For professional performance, a canape maker needs these tools: 1. Small pastry tubes. 2. Large french vegetable cutters. 3. Large french slicing knife. 4. Serrated bread knife. 5. Small pair of scissors. 6. Diamond-shaped cookie cutter. 7. Large and small star cookie cutters. 8. Set of 24 vegetable cutters in assorted shapes and sizes. 9. Channel knife for marking oranges, lemons, cucumbers and similar small items. 10. Decorating tool for marking watermelon. 11. Oval food and vegetable cutter. 12. Small oblong vegetable timbale that is shallow. 13. Parisienne cutter for melon, pineapple and similar ingredients. 14. Small parisienne cutter for vegetables. 15. Small timbales with high sides for aspic and vegetables. 16. Apple or radish rose cutter. 17. Flying bird design. (Use chart below to match description with tools.)

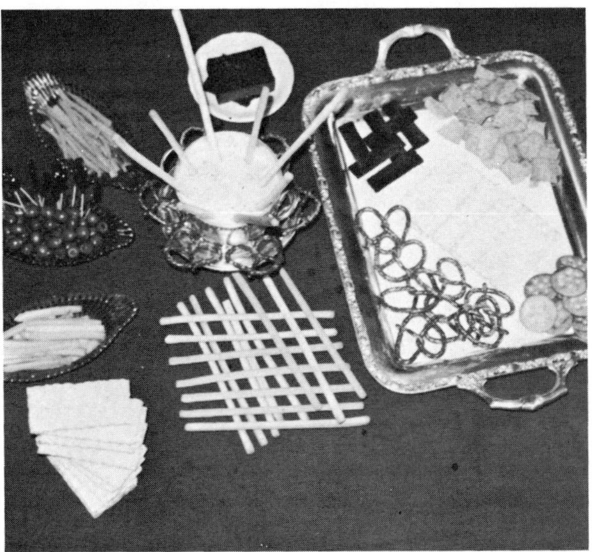

At left, from top: butter curls, dark pumpernickel, cheese choices; on platter, pretzels, crackers; cheese hedge hog; bottom, cream cheese balls rolled in chopped nuts, ripe and green olives, bread sticks. Above, dips and dippers: from top, carrot sticks, olives, celery sticks, rye crackers, bread sticks; tray, pumpernickel, pretzels, assorted crackers.

Dips for Parties

Another do-it-yourself system of canape service is the presentation of dips and dippers. Most dips are made with cream cheese and sour cream as the basic ingredients. To heighten the flavor of either of these, use one of these suggested additions:

Chopped clams, sauteed onions, garlic. Mashed portugese sardines, chopped olives, lemon juice. Chives, chopped hard cooked eggs, prepared mustard. Bacon crumbs, chopped watercress, grated onion. Chopped smoked oysters, grated onion, chopped olive pieces. Crumbled blue cheese, and chives. Chili sauce, mayonnaise, cheddar and cottage cheese may also be combined into dips.

The consistency of a dip should be about that of mayonnaise. To thicken a dip, use cream cheese; to thin one, use sour cream, bouillon or milk.

The "dippers" should be dry, crisp and within easy reach of the bowl of dip. Popular dippers are: potato chips, corn chips, pretzels or pretzel sticks, crackers, croutons, french bread rounds, miniature pumpernickel or rye, celery sticks, carrot sticks, cauliflower buds, whole shrimp, ham or turkey chunks, french fried potato sticks, or pineapple chunks.

Caviar for Canapes

Prime caviar is the salted roe or fish eggs from the female sturgeon in the Volga River and its tributaries in Russia. There are several types of sturgeon and imported caviar is named for the type of fish it comes from; beluga caviar is the most commonly used imported caviar. Imported Russian caviar is packed in various sizes of containers, is large and black and is a luxury item.

Imported skandinavian caviar from whitefish and salmon is less expensive and is used on smorgasbord tables. Red caviar comes from salmon while whitefish caviar is smallgrained and cured with black food coloring.

In some domestic caviar, too much food coloring is used, so when it is blended with butter, the combination gets too black, and is unappealing as a spread. Domestic salmon caviar can contain too much liquid which makes canapes unappealingly soggy soon after they are spread. The domestic varieties are best served to be eaten at once.

Caviar on an Ice Carving: The service arranged for caviar should properly set off this luxury item. An ice carving is the ideal pedestal for imported caviar. The carving should have a tub on its base to hold the original can. Alongside the ice carving, place bread croutons in a folded napkin, a small glass dish of chopped onions and a small glass dish of chopped hard cooked eggs. Guests should be encouraged to fix their own caviar canapes "a la minute." This method of serving is more fun for the guests and less work for the chef.

(See arrangement below of "fix-it-yourself" caviar, lemon wedges, croutons, chopped onion, hard cooked eggs.)

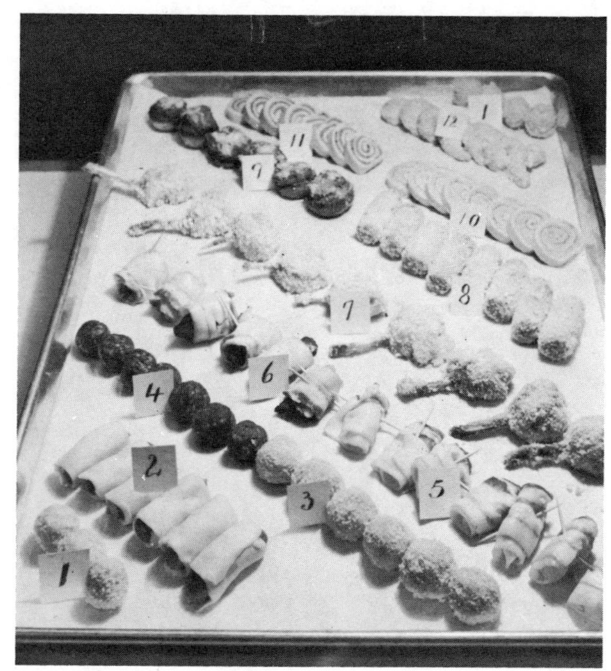

These canapes are ready to be heated: 1. Cheddar cheese balls, breaded to be deep fried. 2. Baby franks in blankets, rolled in puff paste and baked. 3. Seafood balls, deep fried. 4. Well-seasoned, sauteed meat balls. 5. Pineapple chunks rolled in bacon and baked or fried. 6. Chicken liver bits rolled in bacon. 7. Small-boned chicken wings for deep frying. 8. Curry-flavored chicken croquettes. 9. Mushrooms stuffed with chicken livers. 10. Smoked salmon rolled in puff paste for baking. 11. Cheddar cheese mix rolled in puff paste for baking. 12. Breaded fried shrimp with cocktail sauce.

Hot Canapes for the Buffet

To make sure that hot canapes are served hot, preparation should be planned so that bread-based canapes are assembled on a buttered sheet pan or cookie sheet. Canapes so prepared can be frozen or baked immediately.

Canapes to be frozen should be wrapped tightly in foil. They will not be soggy after baking as heat will crisp any bread base. To avoid staleness, hot canapes should be served immediately after baking. Baking time averages about 5 to 8 minutes. Using frozen canapes simplifies finishing off and cuts down on last minute preparation when they are scheduled. Further assortments of hot canapes can be made up from these selections and passed on small trays while the canapes are

ASSORTMENT OF HOT CANAPES FOR BAKING

	Base	Spread and Topping
Canadian	Pullman white bread 2-in. circle	Thin round slice of small white onion, dab of mayonnaise with grated parmesan and paprika over top.
Swiss Cheese	French bread square, ¼-in. thick	Plain butter spread, grated swiss cheese, caraway seeds, paprika.
Clam and Cheese	Pullman white bread lengthwise slice	Mixture of 1 cup grated cheddar cheese, onion, ½ cup minced clams with juice enough to make spreading consistency, cayenne, chopped parsley. Spread on bread slice, then cut slice into small shapes.
Curried Shrimp	Pullman white bread lengthwise slice	Mixture of 1 cup shrimp pieces, hollandaise and cream sauce, chopped dill; keep mixture thick, adding bread crumbs to thicken if necessary. Spread as above.
Tuna and Cheese	Pullman white bread lengthwise slice	Mixture of 1 cup grated cheddar cheese, ½ cup canned tuna (flaked), ground black pepper, dash of dry vermouth. Spread and cut as above.
Anchovy Roll	Pullman white bread sliced as for pinwheels	Mixture of 1 lb. cream cheese mixed with raw egg yolk and chives. Spread on bread, place one anchovy fillet through center. Roll bread and slice for pinwheels. Bake.
Pizza	French bread circle, ¼-in. thick	Spread with tomato butter. Add small slice tomato, thin slice pepperoni, cover with sliced mozzarella cheese.
Mushroom	Pullman white bread lengthwise slice	Mixture of cream cheese, chopped mushrooms, chopped chives, raw egg yolk and seasonings. Spread on bread slice, then cut slice into small shapes.
Liverwurst	Pullman white bread sliced as for pinwheels	Mashed skinless liverwurst or liver puree mixed with chopped mango chutney. Make into pinwheels and bake.
Spicy Ham	Pullman white bread or rye lengthwise slice	Spread with butter, chopped ham and hard cooked eggs, horseradish, chopped parsley and worcestershire mixed into paste.

Note: As a rule hot canapes do not have to be garnished or decorated like cold ones, as the combinations of ingredients provide eye appeal. Serve them freshly baked and piping hot.

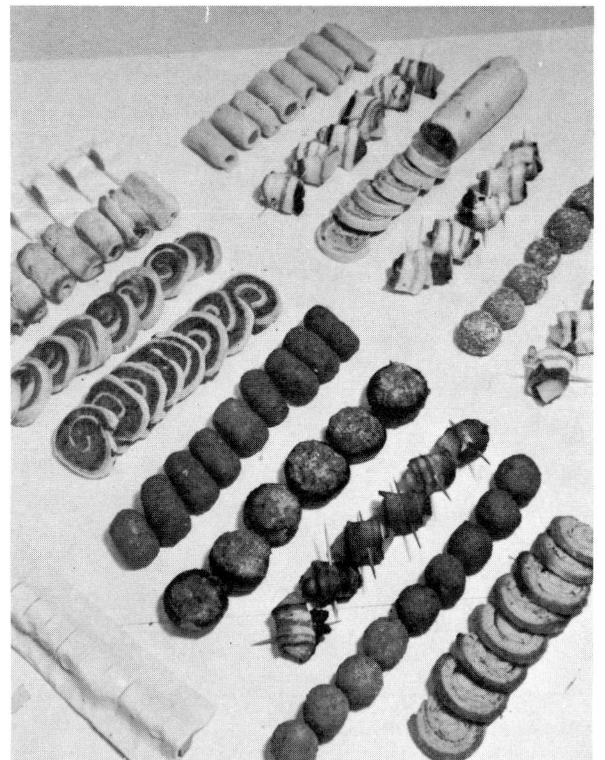

Unbaked canapes at rear; finished products from left to right —baby frankfurters baked in puff paste; cheddar cheese rolled in puff paste and baked; chicken livers rolled in puff paste; deep fried, curry-flavored chicken croquettes; mushrooms stuffed with chicken livers and baked; chicken livers rolled in bacon, anchored with toothpicks; breaded deep fried cheddar cheese balls; smoked salmon rolled in puff paste. In front, raw puff paste in position for wrapping around filling.

still piping hot:

Cheese straws made from puff paste to which parmesan cheese has been added.

Anchovette puff paste made into diamond shapes and topped with anchovy fillet.

Pate squares or pockets filled with chicken livers.

Miniature hot frankfurters wrapped in puff paste.

Quiche Lorraine, pastry base topped with cooked crisp bacon, swiss cheese, eggs and cream.

Ham on toast diable, ham, sweet pickle, dry mustard and cream sauce topped with parmesan and baked on toast.

Light meat balls made of finely chopped meat, onions, mustard, bread crumbs and bouillon, well seasoned and fried or oven fried.

Cheddar cheese triangles made by placing smooth cheese paste on crisp toast, add tomato slice and broil.

Deep fried curried chicken croquettes.

Stuffed mushrooms made by broiling mushrooms till half done, stuffing with preferred filling and finishing off in oven.

Miniature Monte Cristo sandwich.

Miniature pizza.

Hot cheese balls.

Hot Canapes Made from Puff Paste

Puff paste can be made on premise or purchased from a pastry shop. It can be filled with leftovers and the canapes can be frozen after assembly is completed. They should be brushed with egg wash before freezing and will come from the freezer ready for baking.

Piroques: (a) Cut puff paste in long strips about 2 in. wide and roll thin.

(b) Use one strip for bottom of canape and one for top. Cut slits into the top strip every inch.

(c) Pipe filling down the center or apply with a spatula on bottom strip. Put egg wash around the filling and press on top strip.

(d) Place on sheet pan and bake 15 minutes at 350°F.

(e) When golden brown, cut through slots for bite-size pieces.

To fill piroques, use:

1. Diced creamed mushrooms with shallots and vermouth in a rich, thick cream sauce.

2. Minced smoked ham in a rich paprika sauce finished with cream. Other cooked meats can also be used.

3. Diced end pieces of smoked salmon and chopped onion, sauteed and combined with julienne of cooked cabbage, chopped hard cooked eggs and capers to make russian salmon filling.

Cheese Puffs: Mix 1 cup parmesan cheese with ½ cup egg whites, nutmeg and paprika to make a paste. Spread on rolled out puff paste, cut into various bite-size shapes and bake in oven.

Salmon Snails: Combine canned or leftover cooked salmon with rich thick cream sauce. Add sauteed chopped onion, a dash of cayenne pepper and 1 egg yolk to each pound of salmon.

Spread cool filling on a square piece of puff paste. Roll square into a stick 1½ in. in diameter and freeze. When solid, cut or saw into pinwheel size pieces. Apply egg wash and bake.

Pockets: Puff paste is cut in circles with 3-in. cutter, filled with any type of meat farce that has been heavily spiced. Fold circle in half and bake. When baked, seam opens like a pocket.

Pigs or Sardines in Blanket: Roll cocktail franks or boneless and skinless sardines into small puff paste strips. Secure with egg wash and bake at 375°F. for 10 minutes.

Petite Patty Shells: Use small round cutters to make shells of puff paste. These shells are an excellent accompaniment for such hot fillings as: Sweetbread Financiere, Seafood Newburg, Kidney Ragout in Madeira Sauce, Ragouts of Curried Chicken, Creamed Ham, and other meats. In making fillings for petite patty shells, be sure all ingredients are diced fine.

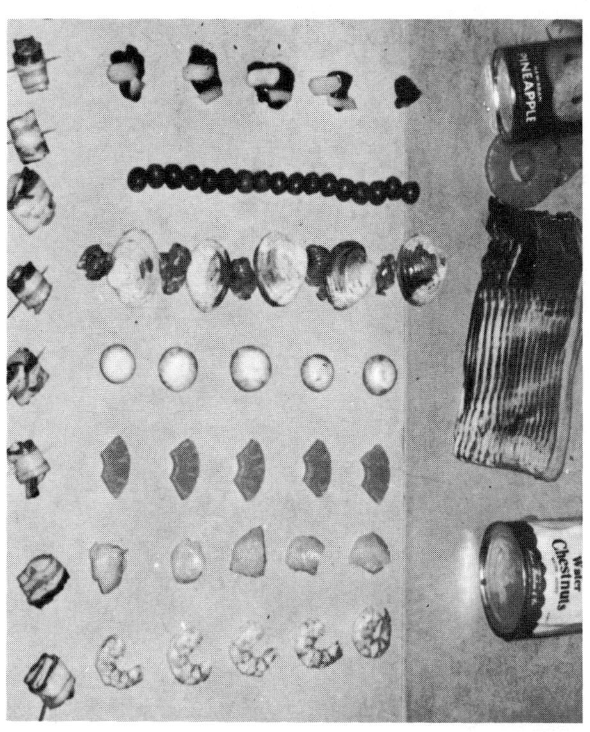

Suggested filling for bacon wrapped tidbits: top to bottom, chicken liver, water chestnut and pineapple; stuffed green olives; oysters; mushroom caps; pineapple; scallops; shrimp; front row, ramaki.

Bacon Wrapped Tidbits

These gourmet items should be served in chafing dishes. If no chafing dishes are available, bacon wrapped items can be passed around in small enough quantities so they will stay hot until eaten.

Most of these items can be frozen in the wrapped stage, but not after they have been marinated. Since wrapping them is the most time-consuming part of their preparation, it should be scheduled during slack periods. The chart below includes basic preparation methods for several of the most often requested items:

BACON-WRAPPED TIDBITS

	Bacon Slices	Other Ingredients, Marinades	Finishing Step
Green Stuffed Olives	Strip, cut six per bacon slice	Roll bacon around olive; fasten with plain toothpick; bread. Can be frozen after breading.	Deep fry at 400° for 2 to 3 minutes
Chicken Liver Rumaki	½ bacon slice	Marinate ½ chicken liver in soy sauce, lemon juice, white pepper, ginger. Roll bacon strip around liver, an onion leaf and half a water chestnut.	Oven-broil
Pineapple Chunk, canned or fresh	⅓ bacon slice	Same marinade as for Rumaki. Roll bacon strip around pineapple.	Oven-broil
Scallops	⅓ bacon slice	Pre-cook scallops. Marinate in sherry wine, soy sauce, ginger and garlic. Wrap with bacon slice.	Oven-broil
Oysters	⅓ bacon slice	Marinate in lemon juice, white pepper, white wine. Wrap in bacon slice.	Oven-broil
Smoked Oysters	Strip, cut four per bacon slice	Wrap bacon slice around smoked oyster. Bread.	Deep fry
Mushrooms	⅓ bacon slice	Marinate in soy sauce, lemon juice, ginger, white pepper. Wrap in bacon slice.	Oven-broil
Shrimp	⅓ bacon slice	Dip shrimp in batter made of eggs, garlic, chopped parsley, salt and pepper.	Deep fry or saute

Note: Many other combinations can be used, but when making bacon-wrapped items be sure to use plain toothpicks to hold wrapping tight. Oven-broil all items because toothpicks will burn if placed under an open flame of 500° F. Miniature kebobs can also be created with these items using short metal or wooden skewers.

SAUERKRAUT BALLS

Ingredients

Sauerkraut	2 lb.
Smoked Ham	1 lb.
Hard Cooked Eggs	4
Raw Egg Yolks	2
Bread Crumbs	1 cup
Onion, medium	1
Chives	to taste
Black Pepper	to taste
Garlic	to taste

Method

Put all ingredients except egg yolks, bread crumbs and spices through fine blade of meat grinder or a blender. Mix in remainder of ingredients and make into a rather firm paste.

Pipe mixture in small balls on waxed paper and freeze. Remove frozen patties from freezer and bread. Deep fry for a few minutes at 400°F. Serve hot with dip.

Celery and Endive Canapes

Stuffed Celery: Slice celery lengthwise into narrow short pieces. Blend equal parts cream cheese and roquefort with dash of worcestershire sauce, salt and pepper. Place mixture in pastry bag and fill celery. Sprinkle with paprika and refrigerate.

A source of supply for chicken wing snacks are the 2-lb. broilers featured regularly in many operations. Wings are removed as at right, then outer bone and inner bone are cut apart. Parts are collected in freezer until time for use. Chicken wings can also be purchased. At left in picture below, bone from inner wing is shown with loosened meat pushed into ball at one end of bone. At right below, bones have been removed from outer wing section, except for wing tip. Water chestnuts, previously marinated in soy sauce, go into pocket made by boning. Other items may be used to fill pocket. In picture below right, breading and mustard-flavored egg wash are shown. Snacks made from outer bone are broiled; inner wing sections are deep fried.

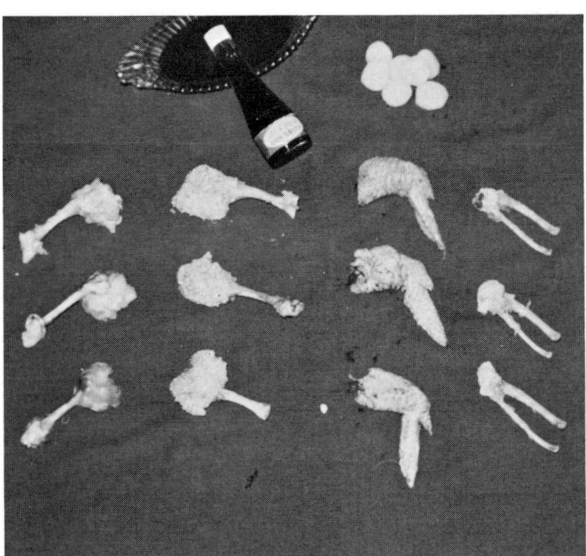

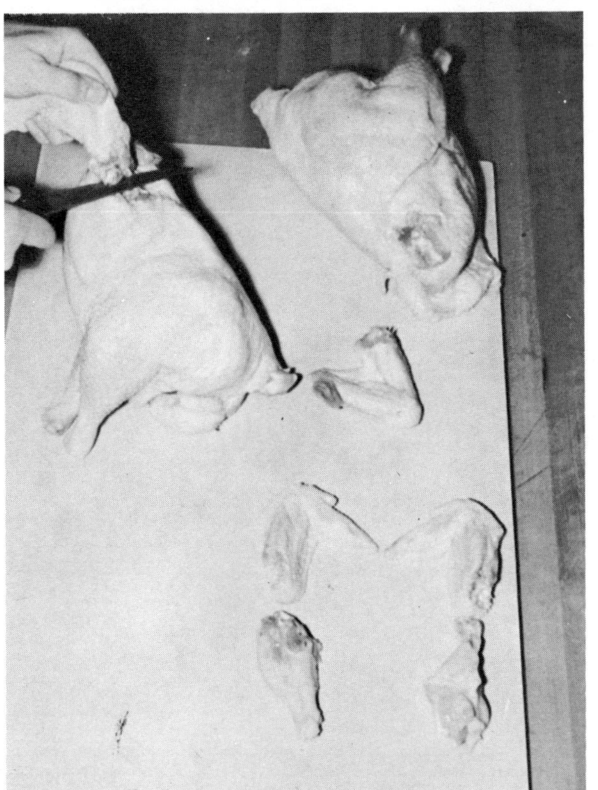

Belgium Endive Canapes: This crisp vegetable with its pale leaves is popular served as a dipper or a canape. For a dipper, cut fresh heart of endive in six wedges lengthwise and arrange neatly around a bowl of dip; blue cheese, sour cream, clam, lemon or curry mayonnaise are good complements.

To make canapes, cut whole heart of endive crosswise. Pipe shrimp or crabmeat butter on one-half of leaf, cover with other half and push a toothpick through both halves.

Chicken Wings as Snacks

By using a special boning technique, both the outer and inner bones of the chicken wing can be made into interesting party snacks. Chicken wings can be accumulated from 2 lb. broilers used in regular food operation and stored in the freezer or they may be purchased in 5 to 10 lb. quantities.

To Make Stuffed Chicken Wings: Instructions here are for both the outer and inner bone section.

Outer Bone: Bone outer wing section leaving wing tip. Loosen meat around joints and then push it toward the wing tip. Pull out thin bones and in the remaining pocket place water chestnuts which have been marinated in soy sauce. Broil. During broiling the wing will stiffen and the tip will serve as a handle for the cooked chicken wing. Other fillings can also be used.

Inner Bone: The inner wing section has a heavier bone. Loosen meat around joints and push it in a ball toward one end of the bone. Bread in egg wash made with prepared mustard. Deep fry. Finished piece will look like a lollipop with the exposed bone for a stick.

Pancake Finger Food

In this practical method for using crepes or french pancakes as finger food, the filled pancakes are frozen ahead of serving time. Use large round pancakes 8 to 10 in. in diameter split in half, small crepes or pancake batter baked on a small cookie sheet. For large quantity production, baking on a cookie sheet or sheet pan is most efficient.

To Make Pancake Finger Food: For about 25 large pancakes, or 6 to 8 squares baked on a cookie sheet combine the following:

CANAPE PANCAKE BATTER

Ingredients

Whole Eggs	5
Milk	1 qt.
Cornstarch	½ cup
Flour	¾ lb.
Salt	½ oz.

Method

Mix and blend eggs. Add salt. Gradually add cornstarch and flour. Blend well.

To Bake

Do not pour as thin as a crepe. Bake on a buttered cookie sheet in a 500° oven for 5 to 6 minutes. Press down after baking.

Fillings

These should be paste-like in consistency, made of cooked meats, poultry or seafood, minced or ground and heavily seasoned with onions added, then mixed with a rich cream sauce as a binding agent.

Combinations for Pancake Canapes—(a) Smoked ham and mushrooms.

(b) Canned tuna and canned clams, onion.

(c) Canned cooked salmon and mushrooms.

(d) Beef and sausage.

(e) Crabmeat, with or without mushrooms, chopped dill.

(f) Turkey or other poultry with mushrooms, green pepper.

Assembling and Finishing Pancake Canapes—

1. Lay out cooled pancake flat on table.
2. Spread filling over it and roll tightly.
3. Arrange rolled pancakes on tray and freeze halfway through.
4. Remove solidified rolls from freezer and cut into 1-in. pieces.
5. Bread pieces in flour, eggwash and crumbs.
6. Deep fry at 400°F. for about 2 minutes until golden brown.

Serve with cocktail sauce or with a dip from a chafing dish. Supply picks.

Finger Sandwiches for Teas, Receptions

Sandwich assortments for afternoon teas may be arranged from bread cut in long slices, triangles, squares, hearts, diamonds, ovals, rounds or elongated triangles.

Popular combinations for finger sandwiches include:

1. Cream cheese with chopped olives on dark bread.
2. Puree of chicken with almonds on white bread.
3. Peanut butter and bacon on white bread.

Ingredients for assembly of pancake canapes are pictured above. Tightly rolled pancakes can be frozen.

4. Pinwheel of cream cheese, mint jelly with gelatin added rolled in white bread.
5. Blue cheese mixed with cream cheese on pumpernickel bread.
6. Puree of ham and dill pickle on rye bread.
7. Pinwheel of cream cheese, currant jelly with gelatin added, rolled in white bread.
8. Fine chopped tuna salad on whole wheat bread.
9. Pinwheel of pureed chicken and truffles.
10. Cream cheese with chopped walnuts on crackers.
11. Shrimp and tuna salad on white bread.
12. Layer of ham and swiss cheese on pumpernickel bread.
13. Layer of cream cheese and chives on pumpernickel bread.
14. Puree of beef tongue mixed with chopped chutney on rye bread.
15. Mousse of chicken with curried mayonnaise on white bread.
16. Puree of sardines with red pimientos on rye bread.
17. Chicken salad with diced celery and mayonnaise on white bread.
18. Cream cheese and pimientos on whole wheat bread.
19. Pinwheel of cream cheese, apricot jam with gelatin added, rolled in white bread.
20. Puree of chicken liver with raisins and chopped nuts.

Costing Canapes

Listed here are three sample assortments of canapes. The number of canapes allowed per person is based on service of four or five different items in the assortment offered. For a two-hour cocktail party or similar gathering, 8 to 10 canapes per person is the average consumption.

Prices for each canape have not been set because of

the fluctuation of food prices. The cost of the base for canapes is only a fraction of a cent with the major cost set by the topping used. Caviar is probably the most costly canape ingredient while margarine or cream cheese mixtures used in pinwheel or layer canapes are the least expensive. Selections can be adjusted to control cost.

CANAPE PRICE LIST

I. DELUXE ASSORTMENT (priced at $2.00 to $3.00 per person)

Item	Allowance Per Person	Your Cost Per Person
Russian Caviar	1 to 2	
Pate de Foie Gras	1 to 2	
Shrimp	1 to 2	
Smoked Salmon	1 to 2	
Anchovy Rings	1 to 2	

II. MEDIUM ASSORTMENT (priced at $.50 to $.60 per person)

Item	Allowance Per Person	Your Cost Per Person
Cheese Checkerboard	2 to 3	
Domestic Caviar	2 to 3	
Smoked Oyster	2 to 3	
Anchovy Butter	2 to 3	
Salami	2 to 3	

III. ECONOMY ASSORTMENT (priced at $.25 to $.30 per person)

Item	Allowance Per Person	Your Cost Per Person
Layer Canapes	2 to 3	
Pinwheel Canapes	2 to 3	
Party Picks	4 to 6	

CHAPTER III

Hors d' Oeuvres

Classical hors d'oeuvres differ from canapes mainly in that they are served on plates to be eaten with a knife and fork. Frequently, the same ingredients presented in hors d'oeuvres can be served as canapes, just by putting them on the kind of base that can be picked up for out-of-hand eating.

The knife and fork hors d'oeuvre fulfills the same role on the menu as the canape or appetizer. It is designed to be served as a first course that will stimulate the appetite and get the meal off to a good start. The hors d'oeuvres must be planned for this purpose whether presented on the buffet table or as the first course of a dinner served at a table. Eye appeal and flavors in zesty combination are essential to successful hors d'oeuvres.

At buffets planned for large groups, the hors d'oeuvres are often arranged on a separate table, although they may also be placed on a special section of the main table. Carts, with crushed ice wells to keep these specialties chilled, are sometimes used for rolling service.

Oblong or square glass dishes are most often used to present hors d'oeuvres. China, earthenware, wood or plastic containers may also be used; but metal should be avoided, since many of these dishes contain acid which will tarnish silver or metal dishes. Small forks are usually offered with the dishes.

An assortment of 5 or 6 small portions of these classical hors d'oeuvres can be an appetite-stimulating alternate to the more-often served shrimp cocktail or fruit cup. Properly selected, the assortment can be impressively less costly, too.

From the 20 cold hors d'oeuvres listed here 6 to 8 assortments can be selected:

1. Brussels sprouts stuffed with smoked tongue mousse.
2. Standing sardines (small briesling sardines) on tomato slices. (Hold upright with onion rings.)
3. Salami cones stuffed with egg or cheese spread.
4. Rollatini of mortadella sausage with cream cheese filling.
5. Cherry tomatoes stuffed with ham or poultry puree.
6. Cucumber boats filled with shrimp salad.
7. Artichoke bottoms with smoked salmon roulades, filled with hard cooked eggs, dill, capers.
8. Blanched pear onions stuffed with beef farce.
9. Avocado balls in blue cheese dressing.
10. Tartar steak balls rolled in chopped eggs.
11. Artichokes or leeks vinaigrette; leeks rolled in prosciutto ham slices.
12. Liver pate in aspic.
13. Small pickled eggplants with salami.
14. Virginia or prosciutto ham with fresh figs or melon.
15. Half radishes stuffed with egg spreads.
16. Anchovy rings on tomato slices with onions and olives.
17. Smoked oysters with eggs.
18. Blue cheese balls rolled in parsley with dark bread, radishes.
19. Russian salad (See recipe section.)
20. Marinated vegetables and mushrooms.

The following may also be presented as knife and fork hors d'oeuvres. Plan to use lettuce leaves as a pleasing frame or radish roses, green pepper rings, pimiento strips and olives to add decorative notes of color to the hors d'oeuvres.

Stuffed devilled eggs with caviar; smoked nova scotia salmon with capers; jumbo shrimp, russian dressing; pate de foie gras and truffle in madeira jelly; marinated fillet of herring in sour cream; rolled smoked salmon and cream cheese; sliced lobster on hard cooked egg slices with mayonnaise sauce; smoked eel on lettuce leaf; cornets of virginia ham with liver pate; stuffed green pepper wedge with devilled egg paste; green asparagus tips, sauce piquante; artichoke bottom with goose liver pate and truffle; smoked sliced lake sturgeon; small fresh poached salmon steak, sauce vert; cucumbers in sour cream sauce.

Smoked Salmon

Many of the hors d'oeuvres for which the Scandinavians are noted are based on smoked salmon. Smoked salmon available in this country may be either imported or domestic and can be purchased in the slab or canned, either in one piece or in thin slices.

Smoked salmon for hors d'oeuvres needs to be thinly sliced; the more heavily smoked salmon is easier to slice. Canned sliced smoked salmon is packed in oil with parchment placed between slices. The color of smoked salmon varies from pale pink to brick red.

To Slice a Slab of Smoked Salmon:

1. Place well chilled salmon skin side down on long wooden board or piece of marble.
2. With an 8 to 10 in. stainless steel slicer, dipped in oil, slice salmon on the diagonal, starting below the head.
3. Do not cut through the skin but keep moving the knife across the bottom of each slice so that skin is left on the cutting surface.

Note: Half of a smoked salmon makes an impressive buffet presentation.

Smoked Salmon Hors d'Oeuvres: These items should always be served chilled on non-metal platters:

1. Smoked salmon slices accompanied by capers, sliced onions and quarters of hard cooked eggs can be placed on lettuce leaves, garnished with fresh dill sprigs, and with slices of pumpernickel bread or rye crackers with capers. Oil and vinegar should also be available.
2. Rolled salmon slices slipped through onion or cucumber rings served with the above accompaniments.
3. Salmon slices spread with a mixture of cream

Right, a selection of knife and fork hors d'oeuvres served from oblong glass dishes. Starting at top left the colorfully garnished dishes contain: shrimp in marinade; pickled mushrooms, anchovy rings on tomato slices; sardines with lemon slices; deviled eggs with mushroom caps in aspic; salami cones stuffed with egg spread; liver pate in aspic; marinated vegetables; smoked, sliced lake sturgeon; stuffed celery. Decorated timbales add color to the tray; radish roses and parsley are highlights for the dishes. *For more knife and fork hors d'oeuvres suggestions, see preceding page.*

Highlight the hors d'oeuvres section of the buffet table with a dramatic display. Below, shrimp tower above a brilliant circle of jellied first course offerings.

cheese and chopped dill and rolled up for slicing into rouladen. Other cream cheese spreads also combine well with salmon in rouladen.

4. A block of cream cheese made into a colorful checkerboard with salmon squares. The combination goes well on pumpernickel bread.

5. Salmon slices rolled around hard cooked egg quarters; around firm yellow asparagus stalks or around dill pickles.

6. Leftover bits of smoked salmon chopped fine and mixed with cream cheese or egg spread, with chives and dill for added seasoning.

To Make Pickled Salmon: Gnavad Lax: Allow 2 to 3 days for the curing process when using fresh salmon.

1. Place one-half boneless fresh salmon, (about 5 lb.), skin side up in a stainless steel hotel pan. Rub with sliced lemon. Add the following spices: ⅓ cup salt, ¾ cup sugar, 2 tbsp. crushed black pepper and fresh dill. If desired, juniper berries and crushed white pepper may also be added. This spice mixture is rubbed into the raw salmon which is then covered with foil and placed in the refrigerator for 2 to 3 days.

Pickled salmon, a popular specialty in the Scandinavian countries, can be presented in the same dishes as smoked salmon.

Herring and Other Smoked Fish

The herring in sour cream most often served in the United States is stronger in flavor than the Scandinavian herring specialties which are a basic offering on smorgasbord tables. These mild yet spicy dishes are excellent as knife and fork hors d'oeuvres.

To duplicate these more delicate dishes, cured herring must be given special treatment. To cure herring, the fresh-caught fish is deveined and the head is removed; then the fat, foot-long fish is immersed in a heavy salt solution. This method of curing or preserving makes it possible to ship herring without refrigeration, but also makes herring inedible as it comes from the barrel.

To Prepare Cured Herring:

1. Bone and skin herring, then rinse under running water for a day. The rinsing eliminates the excess salt in

Boneless fresh salmon, left, is ready to be pickled. Fresh dill and juniper berries are at hand to add authentic flavor to this scandinavian hors d'oeuvres. Below left, hand and knife position for slicing smoked salmon; directions detailed on page 35.

A leafy stalk of celery is the simple yet eye-catching centerpiece for this small selection of classical hors d'oeuvres. From upper right—shrimp, liver pate, salmon, cornets of salami, stuffed deviled eggs, sardines, rolled filets of anchovy with russian dressing, cocktail sauce.

which the herring has been cured and will make the meat turn from light brown to off-white, though retaining its original firmness.

2. Marinate rinsed herring for another day.

MARINADE FOR CURED HERRING

Yield: enough for 10 to 15

Ingredients

White Vinegar	1 qt.
Sugar	1 cup
Fresh Dill	3 stalks
Parsley Stalks	as needed
Pickling Spice	1 tbsp.
Raw Carrot, diced	1
Fresh Horseradish	small piece
Red Onion	1

Method

Combine ingredients and bring to a boil. Cool before pouring over herring which has been placed in crock or jar. Marinate for at least one day.

To Serve

Keep a quart or two of this spicy essence on hand to add when serving herring that has been marinated. Fresh sliced onions, julienne of leeks and crushed black pepper should also be added.

Note: This marinade and service can be used for any cured herring except matjes herring and kippers or smoked herring.

Matjes Herring: These canned, skinless fillets are marinated whole in red wine, mustard seeds, dill stalks and bay leaves. The red wine marination gives the fillets a reddish brown color and makes their flavor stronger. The most suitable sauce to serve with matjes herring is plain sour cream mixed with onions and chives. Sauce should be served separately, never mixed in.

Smoked Herring: Usually packed in wooden crates, smoked herring is butterfly cut with the pairs wrapped in cellophane. The fairly dry fish have an appealing smoky aroma and golden color. Be sure to remove smoked herring skins before serving.

Serve smoked herring with these accompaniments for knife and fork hors d'oeuvres:

1. Sliced tomatoes, sliced hard cooked eggs and onion slices.
2. Sliced cucumbers and egg salad.
3. Swedish horseradish sauce made by blending 1

Smoked salmon rouladen slices circle decorated timbale. Rouladen were made by covering salmon slices with cream cheese blended with chopped fresh dill, rolling them tightly, chilling and slicing.

part mayonnaise, 2 parts whipped cream and fresh grated horseradish to taste.

Bismarck Herring: The baby herring is not skinned, but preserved in a boneless butterfly cut. It is used to prepare:

1. Rollmops using one half fillet to roll around raw carrot sticks, chopped onions and dill pickle strips. Fasten with toothpick.
2. Fillets in Aspic. Bismarck herring fillet strips are arranged criss-cross fashion on a china or glass platter, then decorated with cooked carrot slices, pickles and onions and the whole covered with a light aspic. Mayonnaise is the accompaniment for this dish.

Herring in Wine Sauce: Frequently served in the U.S., herring is marinated in sauce described above with white wine substituted for vinegar. This herring, available both in tidbits and fillets, can be served with sour cream, swedish horseradish sauce, mustard sauce and apple cream.

Schmaltz Herring: Kosher herring, usually whole, neither skinned nor boned, comes in a special vegetable oil with onions and bay leaves.

Herring Salad: Leftover pieces of herring of any kind (except Matjes herring) can be used in this salad-like hors d'oeuvre.

HERRING SALAD

Ingredients

Potatoes, cooked Red Beets, cooked and pickled Apples, peeled and diced Red Onions and Pickles Hard Cooked Eggs, chopped	equal parts
Mayonnaise Sour Cream Whipped Cream	as needed
Pickled Beet Juice	for moistening
White Pepper	to taste
Chopped Parsley	to taste

Method

Blend first five ingredients. Bind together with mixture of mayonnaise, sour cream and whipped cream. Moisten with beet juice and add seasonings. Be careful not to add too much beet juice as salad should not be runny.

Other Smoked Fish: The following smoked fish can be substituted for herring in the dishes described above. All smoked fish should be refrigerated.

1. Smoked sturgeon. (The most expensive).
2. Smoked eel.
3. Smoked mackerel.
4. Smoked chubs or whitefish.
5. Smoked codfish.
6. Smoked butterfish.

Fancy Hard Cooked Eggs

Decorated in numerous imaginative ways, hard cooked eggs are basic to buffet presentation. With a spiced-up stuffing, these eggs are a decoration that rates as good eating, too.

First step in the creation either of fancy egg figures or the more usual patron-pleasing deviled eggs is to produce perfect hard cooked eggs. Eggs that are cooked right, peel right; if eggs don't peel right, they can't be used on the buffet.

These variously decorated deviled eggs combine cream cheese, butter, mayonnaise and seasonings with hard cooked egg yolks. Decorations were cut from green peppers, pimientoes, carrots, olives.

When preparing hard cooked eggs for the buffet, be sure to:

1. Use fresh refrigerated eggs.
2. Bring water to a boil, add salt, then eggs. (If boiling large quantities of eggs, place eggs in the empty pot, add water and salt and boil.)
3. Do not bubble-boil eggs, instead turn heat down and simmer eggs slowly.
4. Approximately 10 minutes boiling time will coagulate the eggs; time the actual boiling time, not the time eggs are on the stove.
5. Pour off all boiling water and chill eggs immediately in cold water and ice. If this step is not followed correctly, the best hard cooked eggs will not peel properly because the steam jacket that causes the shell to come off easily will not form.

The steam jacket is the space produced by steam action between the shell and the coagulated egg white. The steam jacket makes membranes of egg adhere to shell, so when the egg is peeled, membranes come off easily with the shell in one piece.

Note: Green egg yolks result from overcooking eggs. Sulphur, which is a component of the egg yolk, will deposit on the surface of the yolk ball during violent boiling.

Egg Yolk Cream: Egg yolk cream, also called egg paste, is prepared with minced egg yolks (put through a sieve). Add a little butter and mayonnaise, dry mustard, lemon juice and hot seasoning. Use ¾ egg yolk and ¼ creamed butter in mixture. Egg yolk cream is used for most deviled egg preparations. It should always have a very firm and fluffy consistency so it can be piped with a pastry bag.

Note: Adding butter to egg yolk spread, gives it greater storage quality and firmness when refrigerated.

In most instances today, fancy hard cooked eggs are used as decorative additions to buffet foods such as salads, hors d'oeuvres, cold salmon displays, cold lobsters, smoked hams and pates. Color can be added to hard cooked eggs by blending tomato paste or green herbs with yolks. Hard cooked eggs are not often displayed as a separate dish because they are time-consuming to prepare and cannot be made more than a half day in advance since they deteriorate quickly.

Egg Figures: Slice off both ends of hard cooked egg with paring knife so the egg ends are flat. Use ripe olive for head, arms, buttons, bow tie, and a radish or carrot for hat. Pipe features on with egg yolk cream.

Eggs Made into Mushrooms: Slice off both ends of hard cooked egg; remove pulp from one-half small tomato to use as cap; pipe on an egg yolk collar to hold cap in place, then pipe dots of egg yolk cream on tomato cap.

Egg Heads: Place whole hard cooked egg on cracker or crouton base, using egg yolk cream to hold it. Add carrot piece for nose, radish strip for mouth and capers for eyes. Make hat with circular piece of pumpernickel bread with salami cone on top; attach hat with egg yolk cream. Truffle bits can also be used to make face.

Eggs Made into Frogs: Slice off end of whole hard cooked egg, cutting at an angle. Coat egg with light green chaud froid sauce which has been mixed with parsley. (Green effect can also be obtained by soaking in green colored water for a few hours.) Use two paring knives to cut wedge out for mouth. Use bits of radish skin for eyes, cooked carrots for feet and a slice of radish with skin showing for mouth.

Egg Drums: Slice off ends of whole hard cooked eggs. Put pimiento strip in a circle around top and use green and yellow leek strings to outline sides of drum. Glaze with aspic.

Eggs Stuffed with Smoked Oysters: Remove yolk from one half egg. Place smoked oyster inside. Pipe on border of egg yolk cream.

Eggs with Caviar: The salty crisp note of caviar can be added in several ways:

1. Mix russian caviar with minced onions and egg yolk cream. Pipe mixture into egg halves and garnish with small onion rings.
2. Top deviled egg with caviar.
3. Garnish deviled egg with smoked salmon strip and put a border of caviar around strip. Top with fresh dill.
4. Top plain hard cooked egg half with caviar. Remove pulp from cucumber slice with fancy cutter and put caviar in center of cucumber slice.
5. Spread caviar on strip of salmon. Roll up, then

Utensils and ingredients assembled (mise en place) for deviling eggs. Note eggs cut two ways; sieve for yolks; bowl of creamy butter; dishes of pureed liver, mayonnaise, pureed tuna; pastry tubes. Use purees to vary egg yolk cream.

A contrast of hors d'oeuvres flavors first served in Italy: honeydew melon sections covered with thin slices of prosciutto ham. The pale green of the melon sets off the rosy covering of meat. Lemon or lime sections are popular with melon lovers. This knife and fork hors d'oeuvres is especially refreshing as a first course for summer dinners.

slice into small snails and put one snail on top of deviled egg.

Eggs with Anchovies: Place anchovy rolled around caper on plain hard cooked egg half or on deviled egg. Circle anchovy with ring of red pimiento for eye appeal.

Eggs with Smoked Salmon: Pull strip of smoked salmon through pitted ripe olive, shape into bow tie and place on whole hard cooked egg.

Eggs with Tarragon and Rollatinis: Place any smoked meat rollatini on half hard cooked egg, decorate with tarragon leaves.

Variations for Egg Yolk Cream

Smoked tongue, tuna, goose liver, smoked salmon, sardines, (all in pureed form,) green herbs (dill, parsley, tarragon, etc.) and tomato paste can be added to egg yolk cream or piped onto plain hard cooked eggs.

Relishes for Hors D'Oeuvres

A lazy susan arrangement of relishes served with rolls or crackers and cottage cheese has gained wide acceptance in America as a first course. Many of the relishes to be used can be purchased ready to serve.

The arrangement of the relish assortment should make the most of the contrasting colors and shapes of the basic ingredients. Among the many purchasable relishes:

Corn Relish	Green Tomato Relish	Spiced Fruits (mixed)
Sweet Pickle Relish	Chow Chow Relish	Mixed Pickles
Candied Watermelon Rind	Sweet Onion Relish	Pickled Pygmy Egg Plants
Cherry Peppers	Mustard Relish	Green Tomato Relish
Cranberry Relish		
Jamaica Relish		

Some relishes can be made up economically during the periods when fruits or vegetables used in them are in season. Recipes for two relishes that can personalize an assortment, made primarily of ready-to-serve items, are suggested for preparation during slack periods.

CRANBERRY RELISH

Ingredients

Fresh or Fresh Frozen Cranberries	1 lb.
Apples	2
Oranges	2
Lemon	1
Walnuts, chopped	½ cup
Sugar	½ lb.
Brandy or Madeira Wine (optional)	1 oz.

Method

Remove seeds from apples and oranges; however, leave skins and rind on. Put fruits through medium blade of meat grinder or buffalo chopper. Place mixture in crock or jar, add sugar and stir thoroughly. Marinate for 24 hours. Add brandy or wine before serving. When refrigerated, this relish will keep for several months.

CORN RELISH

Ingredients

Frozen Kernel Corn or Fresh Corn Taken from Cob	3 cups
Green Pepper, diced	1
Onion, chopped	1
Tomato Concasse	½ cup
Cucumber, diced	1
Pimientoes, chopped	½ cup
Sugar	1 cup
Cider Vinegar	1 cup
Salt, ground black pepper, Turmeric and Mustard Seeds	to taste

Method

Put all vegetables except corn through coarse blade of food grinder.

Blanch corn for 10 min. Add ground vegetables, spices and sugar to corn with enough corn water to simmer for 30 min. Pour mixture into jars and seal.

Can be served after 24 hours.

ATTENTION GETTING
HARD COOKED EGGS

NOTES

CHAPTER IV
HAM

A ham, properly decorated, emphasizes the beauty and bounty of the buffet table. It may also dramatize the color scheme or the theme selected for a buffet. A whole ham is usually served with accompanying slices or cones, sometimes prepared from a second ham, to make it easy for patrons to handle.

Hams are available in several types and sizes. Regular smoked hams, weighing 10 to 18 lb., come fully cooked with the shank, aitch and part of the thigh bone still in. These hams should be refrigerated. Semi-boneless fully cooked hams, weighing 8 to 12 lb., have only the thigh bone.

The virginia or smithfield ham weighs 10 to 15 lb., has a black pepper coating, a distinctive aroma, and is high priced. It is usually served raw, though it may be baked or boiled, and is always sliced paper thin.

Prosciutto ham is similar to smithfield ham, but the spice mixture rubbed into the surface is different. A special ham holder mounted on a platter makes it easier to slice this uncooked ham paper thin. Melon slices usually accompany it.

Country style ham, weighing 10 to 15 lb., is heavily smoked and comes with the bone in.

Formed boneless ham, in various sizes up to 10 lb., is round and fully cooked. It is especially adaptable for cones and slices.

Westphalian ham is an imported german ham, weighing 6 to 8 lb., which comes in a roll. From young pork, this ham is very firm and is served uncooked in paper thin slices. Slices hold together well when made into rolls or cones.

Oval canned hams range in size from 2 to 10 lb. and are especially adaptable for display pieces on the buffet. These hams are packed with special flavors, in some instances. To prevent them from coming apart during slicing or carving, keep canned hams well refrigerated.

Pullman canned hams, which come in long rectangular shaped cans, are best utilized on the buffet as extra slices, or in canapes.

Other smoked pork products that are used to augment display (grosse pieces) include: rolled ham, ham loaf, canadian bacon, smoked pork loin, smoked picnic shoulder.

The same procedure can be used to prepare (1) regular bone-in smoked ham, (2) semi boneless ham, (3) smithfield ham, (4) prosciutto ham and (5) country style ham for decorating as a display or grosse piece on the buffet table.

A decorated ham is the crowning touch on this platter which also presents stuffed, roasted cornish game hens, sliced galantine of chicken (recipe on p. 146), artichoke bottoms filled with carrots and peas and in front a row of small vegetable timbales with a larger heart-shaped timbale in the center. Entire display is covered with a sherry wine flavored aspic.

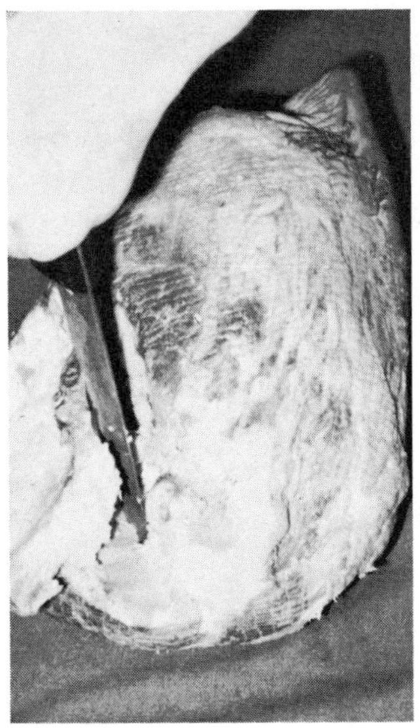

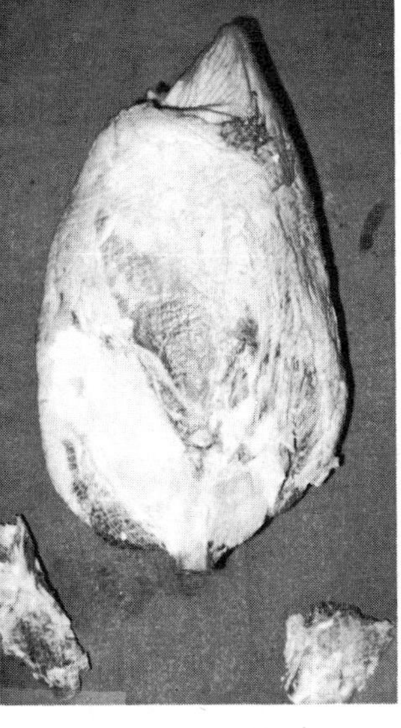

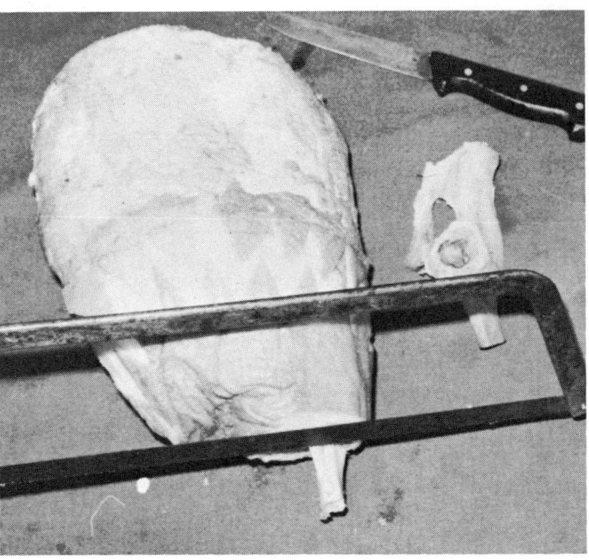

Starting with fully cooked whole ham, prepare ham for display by first removing piece of aitchbone with boning knife, at left above. Uncover end of shank bone by cutting away about 2 in. of rind and meat around the bone, above right. Shave end of shank bone clean after cutting away meat.

Use a meat saw to sever the thin bone that extends beyond the shank bone. Several types of ham are available fully cooked with the bone in. These include: regular smoked hams weighing from 10 to 18 lb.; virginia or smithfield hams weighing from 10 to 15 lb.

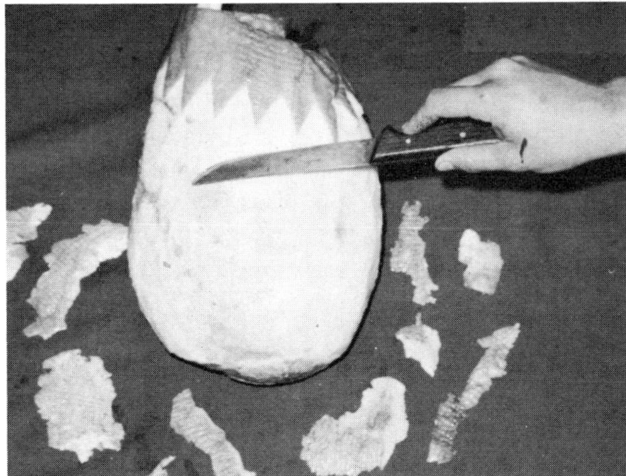

Cut the ham rind in scallops about 4 in. down the shank bone and discard excess rind. Trim all excess fat off the surface, leaving only about ¼ in.

Fat on ham should be sliced as smoothly as possible so coating will also be smooth. If ham is to get a chaud froid coating, apply a coating of basic aspic over the smoothed fat layer first. The coating of aspic helps hold the chaud froid coating in place. Be sure to apply aspic with a pastry brush to the scalloped ham rind. The aspic will give it a shiny edge to contrast with the white chaud froid.

This fruit-decorated ham has a design combining pear slices, pineapple wedges for the outer edge and a pineapple circle for the center; peach slices, cherries and prunes, all held in place with an aspic coating. Toothpicks hold fruit slices in position until total design is completed and ready for coating of aspic. Design should be planned in advance so that color and shape balance can be perfected.

Ham slices give unique shape to this presentation. Band of decorated chaud froid is eye-catching.

Important step in preparation of Chaud Froid Ham Classical is coating of ham with white chaud froid sauce. Ham is placed on rack over pan so that excess chaud froid sauce can be re-used, above. Decorations are carefully placed on coated hams after they have been chilled, right. Chef Waldner, center, works with buffet students on ham decorations.

To Prepare Ham for Display

1. Remove the piece of aitchbone with boning knife.
2. Uncover the end of the shank bone by cutting away about 2 in. of rind and meat around the bone. The end of the shank bone should then be shaved clean.
3. With a meat saw, sever the thin bone that sticks out beyond the shank bone.
4. Cut the ham rind in scallops about 4 in. down the shank bone and discard the excess rind.
5. Trim all excess fat off the surface, leaving a layer only about ¼ in. thick. Slice the fat as smoothly as possible and round off neatly.
6. For standing ham, flatten the bottom by removing a slice about 2 or 3 in. thick.
7. If the ham is to be given a chaud froid coating, first apply a coating of basic aspic over the fat. This will make the chaud froid adhere better.
8. If fried bread socles are to be used to tilt a ham upward, use a double socle to provide the necessary support.
9. Apply aspic with a pastry brush to the scalloped ham rind to give it a shiny edge.
10. After ham is completely decorated, a large paper frill should be used to conceal the exposed end of the shank bone.

Basic Procedure for Ham Buffet Display Pieces

Method I—Chaud Froid of Ham Classical: Follow the procedure given here:

1. After preparation steps for ham outlined above have been completed, cut off the lower third of the ham, using a meat saw to sever the thigh bone.
2. Bone the piece you cut off and slice uniformly in slicing machine. Each slice should have a neat rounded edge with about ¼ in. of fat. Stack slices; refrigerate.
3. Place remaining piece of ham on wire rack and apply an undercoat of aspic flavored with ham or other meat. Next, cover with a white chaud froid sauce; a cream cheese based chaud froid makes a good covering.
4. Decorate. Ideas for ham decoration are outlined in Chapter XIV.
5. Prepare a base for the decorated ham on an oval platter. Use a fried bread socle as the base, then cut two wedges of unsliced pullman bread to use under the socle to tilt the ham upward after placing on base.
6. Use liver mousse or russian salad to build up a ledge around the entire base of the ham.
7. Place ham slices in a circle over the mousse or salad. Slices should overlap and a thin edge of fat should show on each slice. Two overlapping rows can be arranged; a boneless rolled ham can be sliced if more slices are needed. Do not cover up any of the chaud froid coated area with the ham slices.
8. Glace the ham and the added slices with clear aspic. For ham garnishing ideas, see Chapter XIV.

Note: To speed preparation of this ham, the chaud froid coating can be put on after Step 6 (the buildup of the mousse or salad).

Below, ham slices are made into three types of rouladen: (1) back row, wedges of melon rolled inside ham slice, roll decorated with small fluted mushrooms and truffle pieces; (2) center row, cornets made from ham slices stuffed with liver pate and decorated with truffle stars; (3) front row, spears of asparagus rolled inside ham slices which are decorated with ripe olives. All three types of rouladen are finished with a coat of clear aspic.

Above, small platter of rouladen has vegetable timbale in center and mound of asparagus spears at front. Rouladen are easy for guests to handle and, as portions are removed, arrangements can be quickly replaced with fresh trays. Trays this size are effective addition on large buffet and help in narrowing gap between portions and patrons.

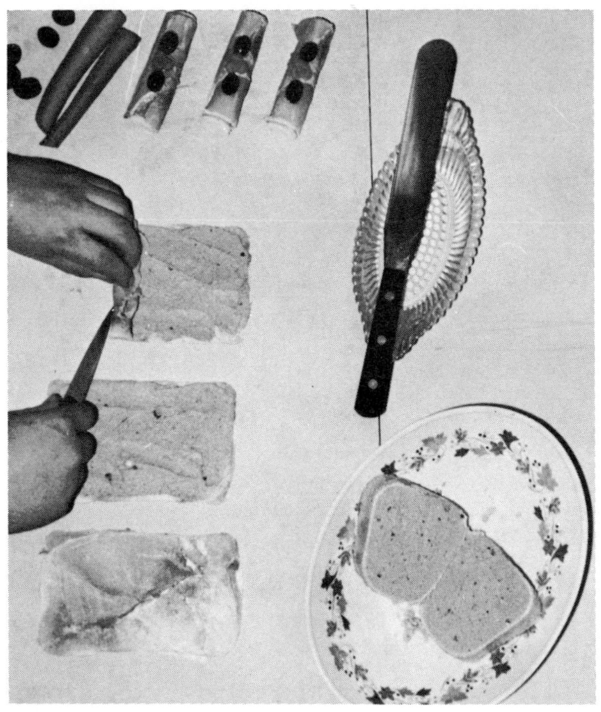

Easy working arrangement for preparation of Ham Rouladen includes stack of pullman ham slices, slices of liver pate for spreading on ham, spatula to spread pate with, truffle circles to use in decorating finished rouladen. Worker is shown making tight rolls of ham slices after pate has been spread over them.

To Prepare Ham Rouladen

Ham rouladen—thin slices of ham rolled around a filling of liver mousse, are an excellent addition for both large and small ham displays. Mise en place for preparation of ham rouladen is pictured above.

To make ham rouladen:

1. Cut thin slices from pullman ham. Pullman ham is the most efficient type for use in preparation of rouladen.
2. Use spatula to spread liver mousse filling over ham slice.
3. Roll ham slice tightly around filling.
4. Decorate rolls with circles of truffle sheet or ripe olives.

Note:

Thin slices of ham can also be rolled into cornets and filled with liver pate.

Method II—Chaud Froid of Ham Moderne:

1. Select two 12 to 14 lb. ready-to-eat hams. Trim skin and excess fat off carefully, leaving smooth surface. Bake in a moderate oven for one hour. Cool.
2. Slice one-half of one cooled ham and replace slices.
3. From the second ham, cut enough slices to go around first ham. Slices should be overlapped with thin edging of fat showing.
4. Take a decorated oval of chaud froid sauce which has been made to fit the center of the ham and put it in place on ham. Next, cover decorated ham with clear meat aspic.
5. Arrange additional ham slices around decorated ham. Artichoke bottoms stuffed with cherry-flavored goose liver pate and topped with truffle decorated mushroom caps are an attractive accompaniment.

Above, initial steps in preparation of Chaud Froid of Ham Moderne include careful placement of slices around ham. Truffle sheet cut-outs are inserted between slices to make border for chaud froid circle which will complete center decoration, as charted below.

Below, chart details construction of centerpiece. Instead of fruit to complete design, this presentation utilizes artichoke bottoms, topped with truffle-starred mushroom cap.

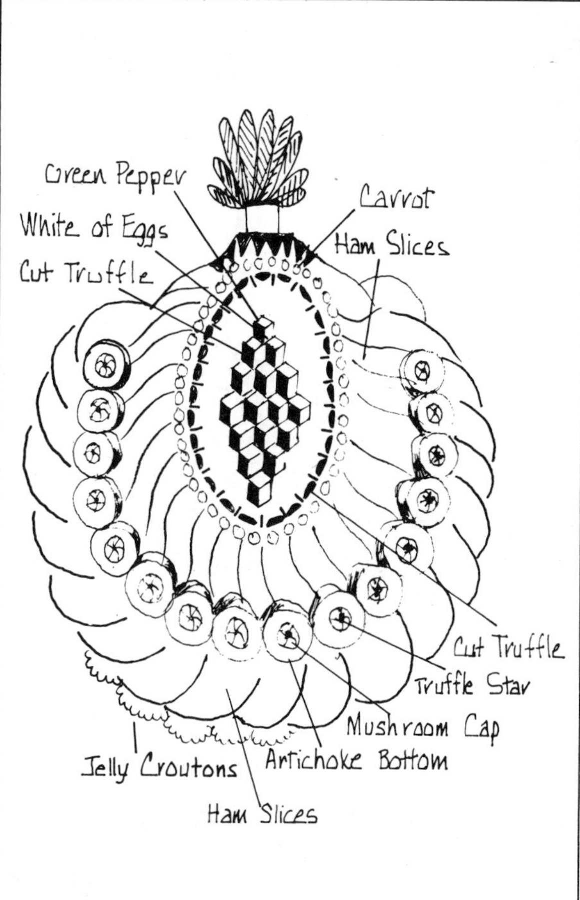

Above, cornets of ham filled with liver pate are decorative and inviting portions as positioned on this ham. Shiny coat of clear aspic heightens appeal.

The detailed directions for chaud froid decoration of this presentation of Chaud Froid of Ham Moderne are charted at left below. Preparation steps are detailed on facing page. Chaud froid circle here is bordered with pineapple half circles and sections of maraschino cherries. Pineapple halves hold ham rouladen topped by arrangement of fruits.

Canned Ham Moderne

Ham Platter with Vegetable Timbales

HAM: EVERYONE'S FAVORITE

Virginia Ham, American Beauty

Ham Moderne

Above, use a decorated ham to pinpoint the meaning of the celebration. The date of an anniversary, graduation or event of similar significance, gets extra attention when boldly outlined on a white chaud froid coated ham.

Below, ham coated with chaud froid must be protected while it is being decorated. Here ham is tilted against block of wood on tray while rolled slices are put in place.

Method III—Standing Ham Moderne:

1. Cut a 2 to 3 in. slice from the aitchbone end of ham so it will stand flat on platter.
2. Cover ham with chaud froid sauce using either of the following methods: (a) Place ham on a wire rack with trimmed, fatty side facing up and, using a ladle or small saucepan, pour chaud froid sauce over entire ham. (b) Prepare 3 to 4 gal. of chaud froid and cool in a deep stock pot. Hold ham by exposed bone and dip into chaud froid twice. The walk-in refrigerator is the best place for this method.
3. Scrape excess chaud froid sauce off the ham rind with a paring knife.
4. Chaud froid covered ham is more difficult to decorate because it must remain upright or coating will be damaged. To protect coating, place ham tilted backward on the shank bone against a block of wood or styrofoam.
5. When ham is decorated and ready to serve, move it to platter and place in upright position.
6. Slice a rolled boneless ham or a canned pullman ham into fairly thick slices and make rouladen, filling them with mousse or salad. Arrange rouladen around standing ham and glace with aspic.

Striking decorations create stand-out display of standing ham on platter. A second decorated circle of chaud froid at the front of the platter is framed with more ham slices. Ham slices also border platter.

Method IV—Chaud Froid of Ham Carnival Style:

1. Follow the procedures outlined in steps 1 to 4 for Standing Ham Moderne.
2. The head of a roasted suckling pig is used in making this figure. (Head can be held in the freezer.) To make costume, start with tuxedo jacket cut from red pimiento sheets. Outline for jacket can be traced on pimiento sheet from cardboard pattern. Use spatula to slide pimiento sheet jacket into place on standing ham. Sheets will stick to ham.
3. Use truffle sheet to make black cummerbund, bow tie and buttons.
4. Attach pig's head to ham with a skewer or wooden dowel. Shank bone should be sawed off ham used for this figure.
5. Decorate pig's head with egg whites and ripe olives for dramatic effect. Carve hat out of large turnip.

8. Arrange slices from a second ham on platter. Coat entire arrangement with meat aspic.

Ham Carnival Style is a conversation piece that is not too difficult to put together. The vividly costumed figure is placed well back on the platter which leaves room for slices cut from a second ham to alternate with fans of dill pickles and ripe olives placed for shape and color contrast at strategic intervals. The jaunty figure presiding over the tray wears a hat carved from a turnip.

Above, set-up assembled for decorating Ham Carnival Style. At left in picture, uncut red pimiento sheet used for tuxedo; next to it, pig's head and pan of brown aspic with brush. Brown aspic is used to add shine to pig's head. At lower left, pieces of red pimiento sheet are cut out to make tuxedo jacket to be placed on ham which has been coated with chaud froid and chilled. Chaud froid coated ham is tilted up on block to make decoration easier. Paper pattern for tuxedo jacket is placed over pimiento sheet and parts are traced around pattern onto sheet which is then cut. Slide pieces onto ham with a spatula. Chaud froid coating will hold pimiento sheet pieces in place. At right, black buttons and cummerbund are cut from truffle sheet and positioned to complete dinner jacket costume on ham. Right, a white chaud froid flower buttoniere is the final touch for the costume. Head is fastened into place on skewer.

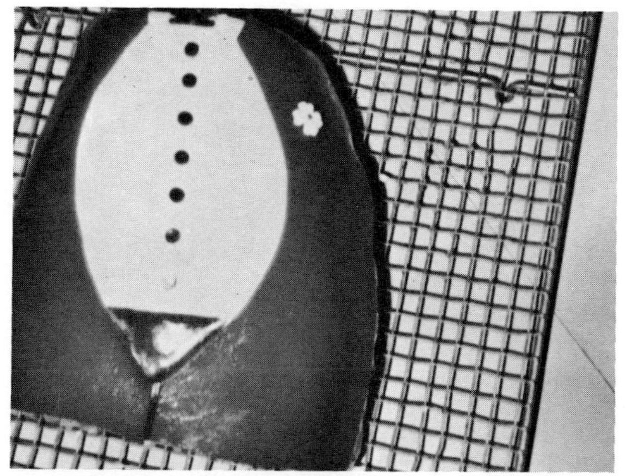

Genoa Ham

Method V—Smoked Ham Genoa Style:

1. Use prosciutto or virginia ham for this ham and prepare as follows:
   - Remove piece of aitchbone with boning knife.
   - Uncover the end of the shank bone by cutting away about 2 in. of rind and meat around bone. The end of the shank bone should then be shaved clean.
   - With a meat saw, sever the thin bone that sticks out beyond the shank bone.

A colorful accompaniment for ham prepared by any method is a tray of sliced candied sweet potatoes attractively arranged with quartered apple slices, and maraschino cherries against a background of orange half circles.

   - Cut the ham rind in scallops about 4 in. down the shank bone and discard the excess rind.
   - Trim all excess fat off the surface, leaving a layer only about 1/4 in. thick. Slice the fat as smoothly as possible and round off neatly.
   - Cut off the lower third of the ham, using a meat saw to sever the thigh bone.
   - Bone the piece you cut off and slice uniformly in slicing machine. Each slice should have a neat rounded edge with about 1/4 in. of fat. Stack slices; refrigerate.
2. Cover ham about 1/2-in. thick with a mousse or egg paste made thick enough to stick on ham and form a coating.
3. Use thin-sliced genoa salami to make cones. Press cones into mousse or egg paste, using enough to cover entire ham. When ham is refrigerated, cones will congeal in place.
4. Pipe egg yolk cream (see recipe below) into each cone; use pastry bag with fancy star tube.
5. Decorate shank bone with red or green melon balls on toothpicks.
6. To serve, arrange additional slices of ham on platter with antipasto relish.

EGG YOLK CREAM OR PASTE

Put following ingredients through wire sieve:

Hard Cooked Egg Yolks	12
Cream Cheese	4 oz.
Butter	2/3 oz.
Mayonnaise	2 tbsp.
Prepared or Dry Mustard	1 tbsp.
Salt, Pepper, Worcestershire Sauce	to taste
Hot Liquid Pepper Sauce	few drops

Two fruit-glazed arrangements on hams that offer colorful focal points on the buffet.

Method VI—Baked Fruit-Glazed Ham:

1. Use a regular ham with the bone in, prepared as outlined above. Flatten bottom of standing ham by removing slice about 2 or 3 in. thick. Before baking, sprinkle surface with mixture of brown sugar and powdered cloves. Whole cloves, inserted uniformly over ham, may be substituted for powdered cloves.
2. Place ham in hotel pan and bake for about 1 hour until sugar caramelizes and surface is evenly browned. At this point pour pineapple or orange juice into pan to dissolve caramelized sugar. Baste ham with combined liquids.
3. Chill cooked ham and follow breakdown procedures for any of the hams described in Methods I through V. It is not necessary to apply aspic or chaud froid sauce, however.
4. Prepare thick fruit gelatin, using ¼ less water than directions call for: orange or cherry flavored gelatin is best with ham.
5. Select fruit decorations for the ham from the following: canned pineapple rings, peaches, cocktail cherries, mandarin or regular orange sections, prunes or grapes or fresh melon balls. Slice fruits into uniform pieces and soak in fruit gelatin.
6. Decorate ham with pieces of fruit held in place by toothpicks. Work out appealing color contrasts.
7. Coat decorated ham with more fruit gelatin. When gelatin has congealed, pull out all toothpicks as gelatin will hold fruits in place.
8. More ham slices and gelatin-coated fruits can be used to make an arrangement around ham on platter. Orange skins filled with gelatin and sectioned are especially effective.

To Make Gelatin-Filled Orange Sections:

1. Split a whole orange in half along stem.
2. Loosen pulp from orange with handle of tablespoon. Use spoon to scoop pulp out.
3. Fill empty half orange skin with thick fruit gelatin and chill until gelatin sets.
4. When gelatin has set, cut orange half into four sections, using a stainless steel knife that has been dipped into hot water.

Gelatin-filled orange wedges are unusual yet easily prepared garnitures. Oranges are split in half as shown, hollowed out and then halves are filled with thick fruit-flavored gelatin which is allowed to set before wedges are cut.

A rack in front of decorated ham holds items to be used in finishing tray. From left, rows are: stuffed deviled eggs with pimiento and ripe olive garnish; stuffed 1-in. pieces of cucumbers filled with a mayonnaise-blended vegetable salad; stuffed half tomatoes filled with vegetable salad and capped with mushrooms; stuffed deviled eggs decorated with carrots, olive and peas; liver pate medallions covered with wine aspic.

Method VII—Oval or Pear-Shaped Canned Ham:

1. This presentation can be completed in less than 1 hour. Remove ham from can and cut off jellied liquid and most of fat.
2. Cut ham in half lengthwise and slice one half.
3. Place unsliced half on wire rack and cover with white chaud froid sauce. Place design made from truffles or ripe olives around side of ham at top.
4. Fan slices of ham around uncut portion.
5. Use pieces from red pimiento sheet, green leeks and truffle center to make decoration for top of uncut portion of ham.
6. Mandarin orange sections, square aspic croutons and stuffed tomatoes are excellent garnishes for this platter. Other items which make appealing garnishes: stuffed deviled eggs with pimiento and ripe olive decor; 1-in. pieces of cucumber hollowed out and filled with a vegetable salad blended with mayonnaise; half tomatoes stuffed with vegetable salad and capped with a mushroom; deviled eggs decorated with carrots, olive and peas; liver pate medallions covered with wine aspic.

Many vegetables lend themselves to the creation of decorative flowers to be placed on a chaud froid coated ham. Suggested for colorful floral designs:

The pear-shaped canned ham is first removed from can. Jellied liquid and most of excess fat is cut off. One half of ham is cut off and sliced.

Unsliced ham is placed on rack, covered with white chaud froid sauce and decorated around top with truffle or ripe olive V-shaped design.

Flower decorations on chaud froid coated top of ham are made from red pimiento sheet cut-outs, green leek stems and black centers cut from truffle sheets. Decorated ham is placed on tray with slices fanned as shown and garnished with mandarin orange sections. Tray is completed with squares of aspic and stuffed tomatoes. The entire arrangement is given extra sheen with a clear coat of aspic.

Leeks—blanch for 3 min., cool quickly, using green and yellow parts for stems and leaves.

Radishes—slices or skin

Tomato Skin—shaved very thin or blanched

Black or Green Olives

Lemon and Orange Peels

Cooked Carrots

Whole Pimientos—dry well before using

Watercress

Celery Leaves

Parsley Stems

Tarragon Leaves

Green Pepper Skins

Cucumber Skin

Eggplant Skin—because of the shiny coating, aspic will not adhere easily to eggplant skins.

White and Yellow Turnips

Hard Cooked Egg Whites—good material for white petals.

Thin Sheet of White Chaud Froid—also good for white petals.

Do not attempt to use red beets or pickled vegetables on a white chaud froid background as they will run and discolor the surface.

The Dummy Ham

This inedible product is used only for display purposes. The basic dummy of the ham may be manufactured of plaster of paris or plastic and must be chaud froid coated before it can be used. The dummy ham can be used as a center piece for a large platter of boneless ham slices, when setting aside a whole ham for this purpose is not feasible.

Chaud froid sauce will not stand up on a dummy ham for more than a day because of the lack of moisture.

Decorated dummy ham is a silent reminder that the star decorated rouladen are ham. Simple platter gets extra dramatic emphasis from the decorated dummy. Heart shaped timbales topped with chaud froid sheet flowers complete design for this simple yet effective round tray. Dummy hams can be decorated well ahead of time and refrigerated til time for use.

Luau Ham with Pineapple Lei

Shrimp with Waikiki Dip

Chicken Coconut Island

Hawaiian Pineapple Kebabs

Ham on the Luau Buffet

A Luau Buffet makes a centerpiece of the luau ham, then draws on the delicacies of Hawaiian, Polynesian and Far Eastern cuisine for the supporting dishes to be presented on a flower-filled table.

The luau gets its name from the young tender leaves of the taro plant (they taste like young spinach leaves). In its original setting, the luau is presented against a background of lush natural beauty. Decorations for luaus planned for American diners can follow the traditional pattern, letting flowers predominate in the decoration of dishes and tables.

The orchids in such plentiful supply in the luau areas can be used more sparingly on stateside buffet tables. Fill-in flowers to make up the lavish effect characteristic of the luau can be much less exotic. Wreaths of daisies or whatever flowers are locally plentiful will create the necessary effect.

Leis of paper flowers can also be used. Select them to circle luau platters in colors chosen to blend with the decor of the foods they will frame. Pineapple carvings —bird houses, stands or carts cut from the whole fruit can be created to hold foods attractively on the luau buffet.

Serving ideas for luau foods are also pictured on these pages; these are for dishes suggested to highlight a luau buffet. For a full luau menu, make selections from those listed under Hawaiian Buffet on page 182.

To Prepare the Luau Ham

1. Bake whole ham. Twenty minutes before ham is done, remove from oven.
2. Remove skin and score fat in diagonal grooves. Cut grooves ½ in. deep and 1 in. square, leaving strip of fat between grooves.
3. Fill grooves with crushed pineapple. Cover strips of fat with brown sugar and whole cloves.
4. Return ham to oven and bake for 20 min. or until ham has browned. Remove ham to platter.

To Decorate Luau Ham

1. Heat 2 cups of pineapple cubes in ham fat remaining in baking pan.
2. Put cubes of hot pineapple on colored picks; insert in ham. Arrange cubes of pineapple so they resemble leis. Garnish platter with cherries and mint leaves.
3. Arrange a lacy paper frill to conceal the exposed end of the shank bone for the Luau Ham.

Similar decorations can be used to repeat the luau theme on platters of ham slices or rouladen.

Pineapple and ti leaves pick up the Hawaiian theme set by the decoration of this whole ham. The hula girl is molded from mashed sweet potato mixed with gelatin diluted in chicken stock and chilled til mixture sets to rubbery consistency that will mold easily.

Decorating Ideas for Hams

Many decorating ideas for whole hams are described in easy-to-follow detail in Chapter XIV, pp. 151 to 160. In addition to the decorations worked out specifically for hams, there are also suggestions for poultry and fish that adapt well to whole hams.

Baked hams with flavorful glazes are a popular alternate to the more elaborate chaud froid coated hams. Colorful glazes can be made of orange marmalade, whole preserved cranberries, pureed apricots or guava, currant and apple jelly.

Crushed pineapple in equal proportions with white or brown sugar, pureed applesauce combined with corn syrup and dry mustard are other glazes that provide eye-catching coatings for buffet hams.

Above, conventional or informal, the decorated ham design can be equally arresting. Designs cut from black truffle sheets stand out boldly on a chaud froid background.
Right, turnip playing cards with red and black figures, made from pimiento and ripe olive cut-outs, add a gala note to a ham designed for a school farewell buffet.

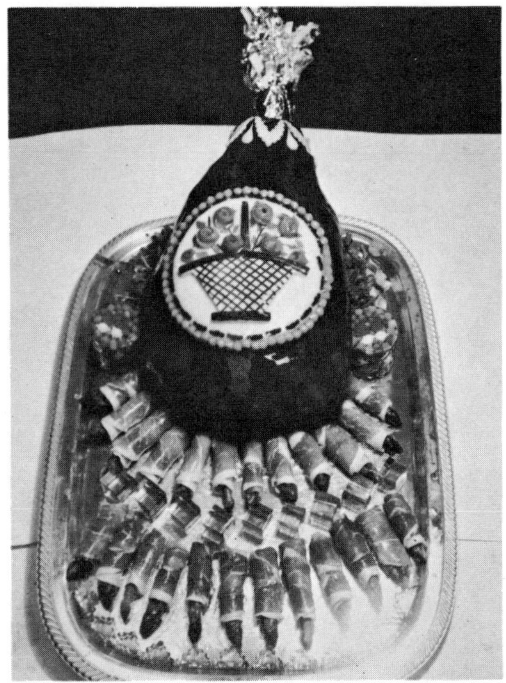

The chaud froid circle decorated on a flat surface and then positioned on the ham establishes a color scheme. The roses in the basket with their green leaves match the rosy ham slices rolled around pale green asparagus spears.

Placement of decoration heightens the impact of the unusual way the ham at right is carved. One side of the ham is cut away two-thirds of the length. Cut-away portion is sliced and slices are returned to platter. The first slice is placed against the ham and the remainder are fanned around the ham in a neatly-positioned arrangement. The panel outlined with black bits of ripe olive provides a visual center for the striking display.

NOTES

NOTES

CHAPTER V
POULTRY

The whole bird—whether turkey, capon, duckling, goose or game—is a festive food for Americans. This aura of festivity probably can be traced to the first Thanksgiving. Or it may stem from memories of Sunday dinners of chicken on the farm or tales of the quail courses consumed by Diamond Jim Brady in his unparalleled feasts of the gay '90s.

Birds for the buffet can also be decorated to carry the theme or underscore a color scheme. The larger the bird, of course, the more that can be done with it, both from the standpoint of decorating and of carving. Many decorating ideas for various kinds of poultry are detailed in Chapter XIV. Carving and boning techniques will be outlined in this chapter.

The procedures for boning, carving and presentation which follow can be used with capon and poulardes weighing 6 lb. or more; turkeys; canned or frozen turkey breasts; domestic duckling weighing 5 lb. or more; wild duck weighing 6 lb. or more; wild or domestic goose weighing 6 lb. or more; and pheasant. With any bird, the larger its size the better the results will be.

The turkey is the ideal example for carving techniques because of the amount of meat on the carcass. Slightly different approaches are necessary on domestic and wild duck. The methods used to prepare fowl, whether domestic or wild, for the table are called breakdown techniques by professionals.

A reminder that turkey was first introduced into American cuisine by the Indians is appropriate at any time of year. This Indian chief was made of white chaud froid in a plastic mold. Red gelatin in orange shells, mandarin orange sections and maraschino cherries add vivid color to the arrangement.

To duplicate this display, roast or poach 4-lb. capon; cool, remove breast and fill cavity with goose liver pate. Make individual supremes from sliced breast and beef tongue filled with goose liver pate. Place capon, supremes on wire rack; cover with white chaud froid. Place slices of capon and beef tongue over filled breast cavity; decorate with truffle design. Use small flowers made of truffles on supremes. Cover all with aspic.

Bottom right, fruit-decorated roast goose: breasts removed, sliced thin, then dipped in aspic and replaced in overlapping row around bird. Slices from a second goose in circle on tray around whole bird are decorated with mandarin orange sections and maraschino cherries. More decorated slices form V on front of tray. Rounds in center are galantine.

Right below, chicken is trimmed for tieing. Before tying, put drumsticks in parallel position and push up slightly. Tying is the surest way of keeping chicken in proper position. Bottom, string on duckling is knotted on the underside. Skewers help hold bird in desired shape. Below, duckling in position for roasting. Note compact shape of properly tied bird.

Preliminary Preparation Before Roasting or Poaching

These preparation steps are required for all types of poultry mentioned above:

1. Remove gizzards, liver and neck from cavity and use gizzards and neck to make stock.
2. Tie all birds, with the exception of turkey, so the drumsticks are in parallel position and, pushed up slightly. This can be done with butcher's twine or with a skewer. Tying is the most secure method.
3. Use large french knife to chop knuckles off drumsticks.
4. Cut outer wing sections off and add them to stock.
5. To poach poultry, put in boiling stock.
6. When roasting poultry, baste the whole bird as often as possible with a brush. This will give the bird the even golden brown color that is most eye appealing. For basting mixture use soy sauce, sherry wine and a few drops of red food coloring.
7. The stock remaining after poultry is cooked can be made into aspic. (See Chapter X.) The liquid and crusty bits left from roasting can be used to make brown aspic or brown chaud froid more flavorful.

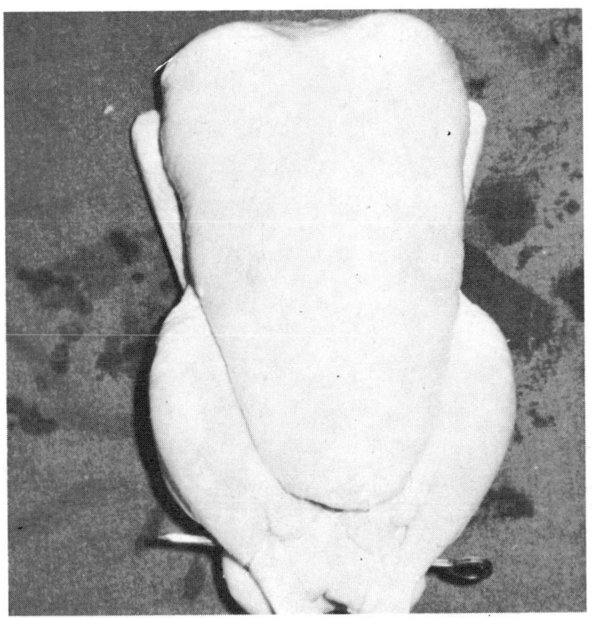

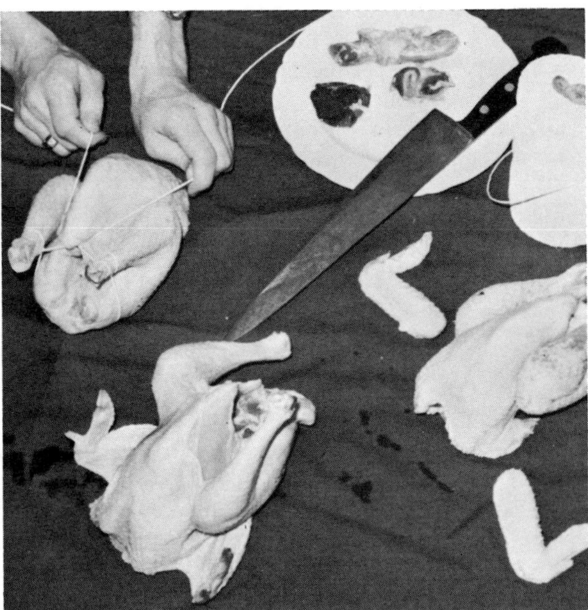

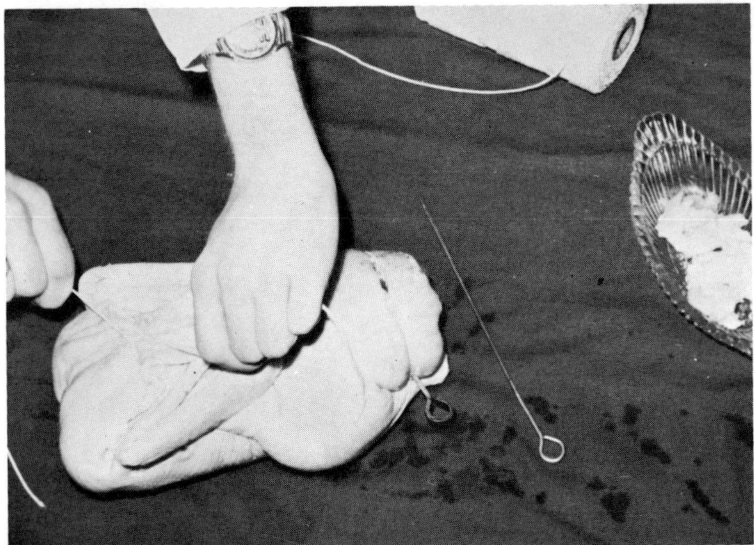

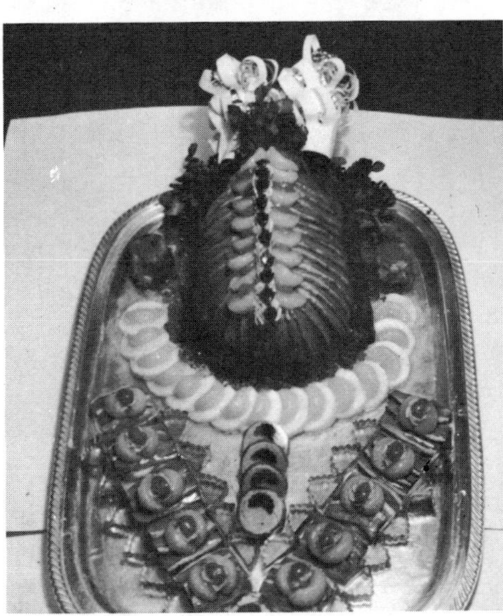

8. Slice enough meat off the back of cooked poultry so it will stay flat on the platter to make carving easier. Use a large french knife.

Preparation Pointers for Cold Turkey Breakdown

1. Have turkey well chilled before starting to bone and carve.

2. Do not over roast or over poach turkey. Over cooked poultry supremes are very fragile and are impossible to carve for a grosse piece or central figure on a buffet.

3. Use a long boning knife to remove the breasts from the carcass.

4. Carve boned turkey breasts or supremes by hand with a very sharp 10 to 12 in. slicing knife. Turkey can be sliced with a machine if each turkey breast is sliced in two horizontally and pointed ends are cut off. Slice each half separately. Machine will yield more slices. These poultry pieces should be carved thin and breast slices should be left in the order in which they fall off the knife. If this order is disturbed, the pieces are much more difficult to fan out in the arrangement common to so many turkey presentations.

5. Always plan to have at least half of the poultry breast carved and presented conveniently for serving from the buffet. The dark meat of turkey is often used under the white meat on platters for the buffet. It is also used in chafing dishes, for canape spreads, in ragouts.

6. Use only aspic prepared from poultry stock and chaud froid made from poultry stock for turkeys. (See Chapters X and XI)

7. When preparing mousse, meat puree or, in some instances, mashed sweet potatoes to use in reshaping a cooked turkey, be sure to reinforce ingredients with enough gelatin so that end product will remain stiff and hold the bird in shape throughout the buffet.

8. Apply chaud froid coating only on breasts that have been skinned. On the other hand, aspic can be applied over the skin and will give the bird a shiny golden brown coating.

9. A glace of aspic should always be applied over a chaud froid coating. The aspic will assure that decorative elements, truffle bits, etc., will adhere to the bird.

10. Before selecting a breakdown method, determine the amount of time available to do the job and choose a method that can be completed in that amount of time.

11. Choose a suitable decorating idea from Chapter XIV. Be sure it is workable in terms both of space and available raw materials.

Method I—Roast Turkey in Aspic Moderne

(See next page for how-to-do-it pictures illustrating this method)

1. Remove both turkey breasts with a long boning knife, leaving skin on.

2. Make a socle with a wedge of bread from an unsliced pullman loaf. It should be either deep fried or dried overnight in a 250° F. oven.

3. Place socle under tail of turkey so that tail end is elevated on platter.

4. Use a mousse to build up a ledge around the base of the turkey. Also build up the breast bones with mousse. The mousse will provide a base that will hold slices of breast meat when they are put back.

5. Carve both breasts into ¼ in. slices, carving through the skin. If slices are too thin, they will not hold together. Hold slices from each breast together in order they are sliced.

Roast Turkey in Aspic Classical is a dramatic centerpiece for buffets of all sizes.

6. Have aspic ready so that each slice of turkey to be used in this step, can be dipped in aspic first. Working from the tail of the turkey, take the slices from one-half of a breast and arrange them in a fan shape along one side of the carcass, then continue placing slices in a curve around the mousse ledge at the base of the bird.

7. Slices from the other breast are pushed back into their original shape, and the breast is put back into bird. Be sure breast is put back into place it came from so it will fit properly. (Put breast back in two parts, the lower part first.)

8. Chill whole bird and cover with light yellow poultry aspic.

9. Remove congealed aspic from edge of turkey. This can be reused.

10. Select a decorating idea from Chapter XIV.

11. When decoration is completed, coat finished and garnished piece with aspic. Chaud froid is not rquired for this method.

12. Insert a fancy silver skewer or a regular metal skewer topped with orange, lemon and lime slices into the tail.

13. To make drumsticks more eye appealing, add fancy papillettes or frills made from paper and foil. Be sure frills are large enough to fit the drumstick bone. For this method, knuckles at the end of the drumsticks should be chopped off before roasting.

Method II—Roast Turkey in Aspic Classical

1. This preparation starts with the first three steps outlined in Method I above. Remove drumsticks and thighs from carcass; slice thighs and use meat under breast slices. Put drumsticks back on with skewers.

2. Use mousse to build up a ledge on both sides of the carcass base as it rests on the platter. Repeat steps 5 and 6 in Method I above.

3. The slices of both breasts are overlapped, starting at the tail end of the bird and coming down over the carcass, with overlapping slices then circled out from each line toward the lower outside edges of each platter.

4. Repeat Steps 8 through 13 in Method I.

POULTRY

Right, in this presentation overlapping slices of turkey are held in place on a mousse foundation. Slices around bird are made colorful with mandarin orange slices and maraschino cherries. To prepare turkey:

1. Remove both turkey breasts with a long boning knife, leaving skin on.

2. Carve each breast into ¼-in. slices. Keep slices from each breast separate.

3. Build up breast bones on each side with mousse. Take slices from one breast and, working from tail of turkey, dip slices in aspic, then position on mousse base, working toward and across front.

4. Divide slices from second breast in half, push together and put back into place, putting lower half in position first.

1

2

3

4

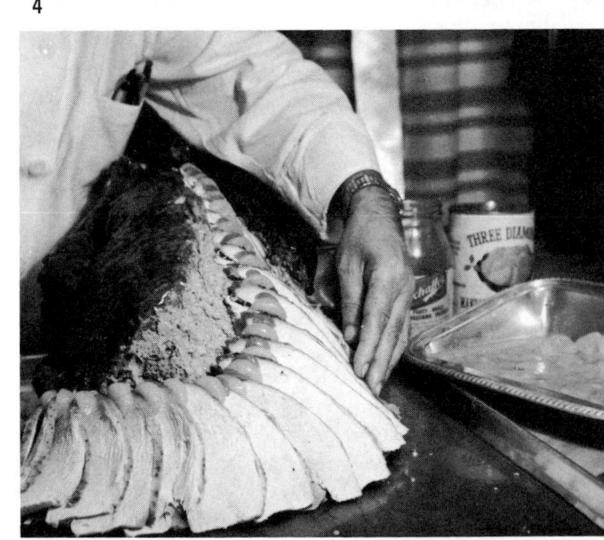

Chicken Supremes
Frozen Turkey Breast
Duckling
Pear-Shaped Canned Turkey
Roast Capon with Supremes

Poached or Roasted Turkey Chaud Froid Moderne. See preparation method at right.

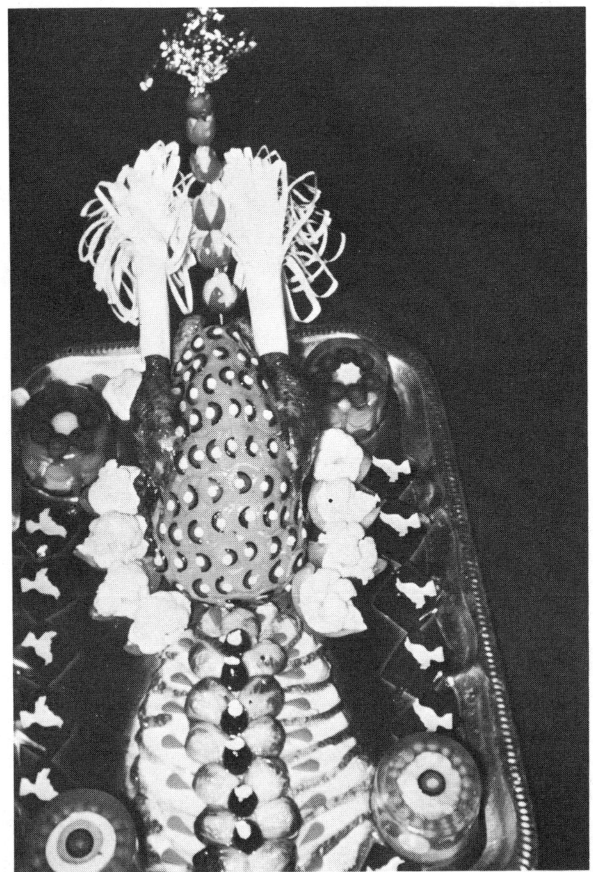

Turkey with Piece Montee. See preparation method above at right. Note frills on drumsticks.

Method III—Poached or Roasted Turkey Chaud Froid Moderne (also suitable for capons and poulardes)

1. Remove both turkey breasts with a long boning knife, leaving skin on.
2. Carve both breasts into ¼-in. slices, carving through the skin. If slices are too thin, they will not hold together.
3. Remove and skin drumsticks.
4. Place thick pieces of bread inside bird's cavity to support carcass and fill openings in the back.
5. Use a mousse to build breast up to original size. Apply mousse with a spatula dipped in hot water.
6. Place turkey on wire rack and chill.
7. Cover turkey first with aspic and then with poultry chaud froid sauce. Place a sheet pan under the wire rack to catch overflow of aspic and chaud froid sauce. These can be reused.
8. Select decorations from Chapter XIV and apply.
9. Slices previously carved from breasts are overlapped in arrangement around turkey on platter. Rouladen made from slices of canned turkey breast can also be used.
10. Decorate slices and cover carcass and slices with poultry aspic.

Note: This method can be applied to capon, but an oval bread socle should be placed under a capon if it is to be used as a centerpiece.

Method IV—Turkey with Piece Montee

1. Follow Steps 1 through 7 in Method III.
2. Arrange slices from one breast on wire rack and coat with chaud froid sauce. This step can be omitted.
3. Arrange slices from one breast in a timbale with poultry aspic and a mousse. (See Chapter XII)
4. Arrange chaud froid coated slices on the platter around the centerpiece and timbale.
5. Decorate and garnish.

Note: Smoked tongue or pimiento sheet cutouts can be used to create colorful decorative notes. Add height with skewer of lemon halves topped with foil. See picture at left below.

Turkey slices on aspic in front of decorated bird are flanked by row of galantine slices, timbales.

Method V—Poached Chaud Froid of Capon Classical

This method is most often used with 8 to 10 lb. capons because the treatment of the supreme slices enlarges them considerably. If turkey is used, the breast slices should be shaped with an oval cutter about 3-in. long. Leftover bits and pieces can be used in the mousse.

1. Remove both breasts and prepare bird as in Steps 1 through 7 in Method III.

2. Slice both breasts uniformly as in Step 2, Method III. Place them in order as sliced on a wire rack.

3. Cover each breast slice with a mound of mousse. Round mound off evenly with a spatula dipped in hot water. Keep slices in order.

4. These slices are called medallions and are coated with chaud froid sauce, decorated and then coated with aspic.

5. Place bird in center of platter and arrange finished decorated medallions in a circle or in one of several possible patterns.

Note: Plain breast slices can be coated with chaud froid and put back on reconstituted bird in one of the overlapping arrangements described above. However, all breast slices will not fit on top of the capon and some will have to be arranged on the platter.

Step 1, Poached Chaud Froid of Capon Classical—Fill oval slices of white meat with mousse; smooth mousse; cool in refrigerator.

Reshape breast cavity of whole bird with mousse; chill, then coat with white chaud froid sauce.

Designs cut out of truffle sheets are used to decorate supremes and the whole bird. Coat with aspic.

In this arrangement, medallions of pate effectively separate white-coated capon and supremes.

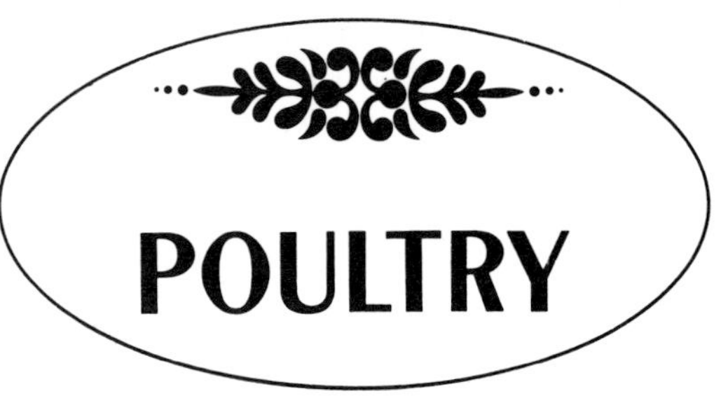

Frozen breast of turkey after thawing may be roasted or poached and prepared by any one of the first four methods described on the preceding pages. Presentation must include a substitute for the drumsticks which provide height when the whole turkey is used. Here, grapefruit, orange and lemon halves are scalloped and placed on bird-topped skewer. A kumquat and lemon slice provide a resting spot for the ornamental bird. Colors used on the skewer are repeated on the tray in the fruit garnish, aspic timbales and triangles of aspic that edge the tray.

Method VI—Frozen Turkey Breast

Whole frozen turkey breasts are a relatively new product which will reduce the time and labor required for poultry grosse pieces or displays.

Thaw breast before roasting or poaching. No tieing is necessary and there will be no dark meat to dispose of.

The frozen breasts can be prepared using Method I, II, III or IV. Since there are no drumsticks, the arrangement of slices will have to be varied somewhat.

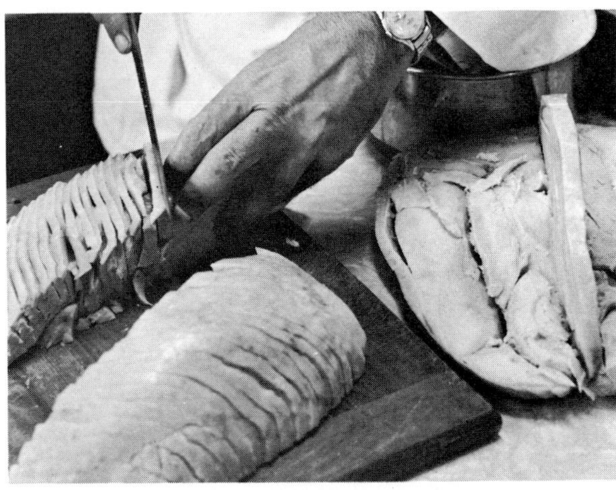

Thaw whole frozen breast of turkey. Leave ridge in center and slice to an inch of the bottom of the breast on either side of the ridge. Slice each half of breast into thin slices as shown above. Push slices from one half of breast together and return to original position at one side of center ridge.

Cover breast in original position with rich brown chaud froid sauce. Put foundation of russian salad on base to hold supremes and individual slices.

Cover supremes, slices with light poultry aspic. Place white chaud froid flower cut-outs, leek leaves on whole breast. Toothpicks help position garnish.

Within 40 minutes of opening the chilled pear-shaped can of turkey, this tray can be completed for the buffet. A 12-lb. pear-shaped canned turkey will serve 20 to 25.

Method VII—Canned Cooked Turkey Breast

An oval or pear-shaped turkey canned in aspic is used in this presentation. This is also a time- and labor-saving method and is perhaps the fastest way to create a turkey platter for the buffet.

Refrigerate the canned turkey for several hours before it is to be carved. Carve as soon as can is opened and keep in mind that if canned turkey warms up too much, the aspic seams that hold the meat together will melt and the slices will fall apart. To prepare canned cooked turkey:

1. Cut the canned turkey in half lengthwise, slicing on the diagonal.
2. Slice the outer half uniformly on a slicing machine and keep slices in order.
3. Coat remaining piece with chaud froid sauce, decorate and coat with aspic.
4. Apply some mousse on the cut edge of the piece and arrange slices alongside it and around the platter in a semi circle.
5. Decorate the slices and coat the whole piece on the platter, using a poultry aspic. Since there is no stock provided with this method, canned instant aspic is suggested.
6. The skewer with orange, lemon and lime slices described in Method I is also effective on a decorated canned ham.

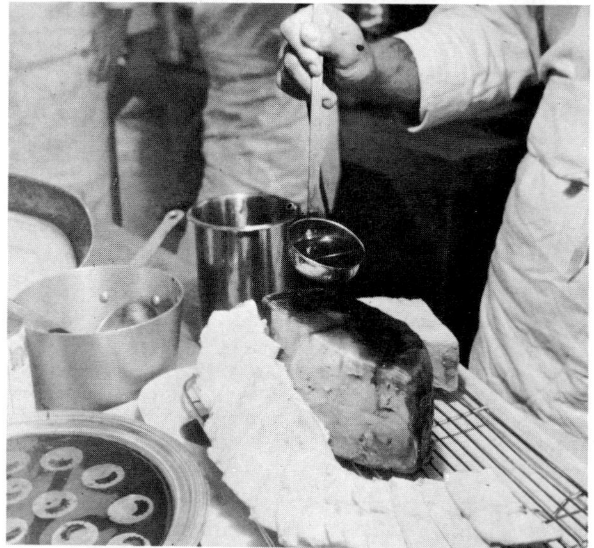

Top, half of canned turkey is sliced and fanned out alongside unsliced half. Center, above, unsliced half is covered with brown chaud froid sauce. Above, half orange shells hold cranberry sauce. Covered half of turkey is decorated with orange sections, maraschino cherries and fine julienne of orange skin. Scored, unpeeled slices of cucumber go on individual slices. Wine-flavored clear aspic covers entire piece.

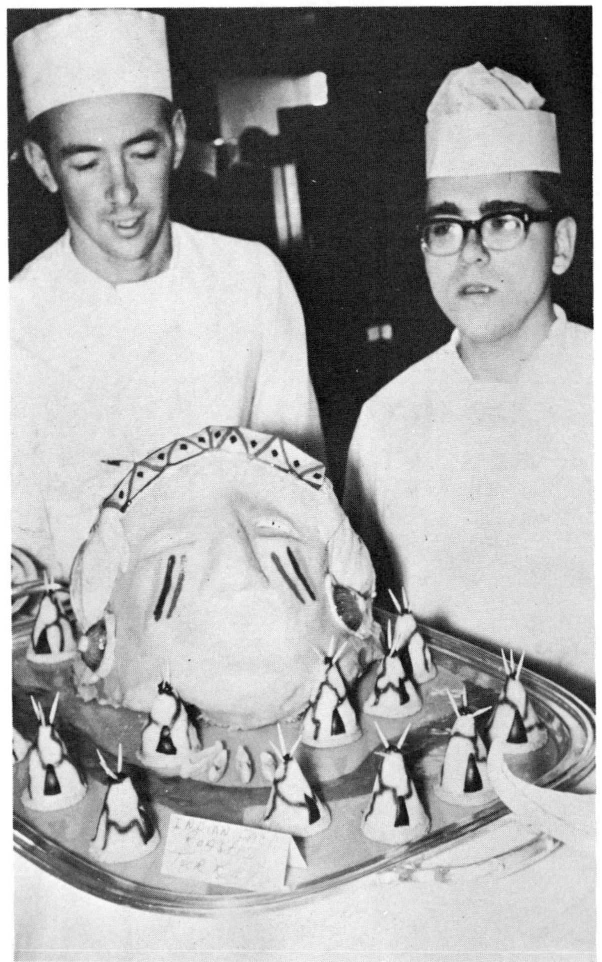

A noble Indian molded on a whole turkey using a sweet potato-gelatin base will be a dominant figure on the buffet. Feathers and headband come from breast slices. Colors for the headband are supplied with designs of pimiento, leek, and ripe olives.

An indian face, traditional motif for turkey, can be carved from a raw carrot. Feathers and headdress are made from white chaud froid sheets, cut to desired shape around cardboard patterns.

Method VIII—Roast Turkey Made into Head of Indian Chief with Cooked Sweet Potatoes

Before starting this piece, assemble: 20 lb. cooked pureed sweet potatoes; 1 cup granulated gelatin dissolved in 1 qt. poultry stock; pimientos; ripe olives; blanched leeks; hard cooked egg whites; fluted mushrooms; 10 to 15 round croutons; glace de viande; plain toothpicks.

1. Remove both breasts from roasted turkey.
2. Add gelatin that has been melted in stock to pureed sweet potatoes to thicken them so they can be used in making Indian face. To speed the thickening process, sweet potato-gelatin mixture can be put in freezer. Stir occasionally until mixture becomes rubbery. It will then be ready for sculpture.
3. Place turkey carcass on tray and apply sweet potato paste, modeling it roughly into shape of forehead and face. Build up enough paste above forehead to make a base for the Indian head dress.
4. Use small spatula or table knife dipped in water to model eyes, nose and mouth and to smooth the face. Cut scars across cheeks with knife.
5. After molding face, chill turkey till face is solid.
6. While bird is chilling, carve turkey breasts into uniform, thin slices to be used in making head dress.
7. Create head dress by using long breast slices for feathers, overlapping them, starting on one side and bringing them around the forehead to the other side. For head band use two more long slices trimmed evenly and squared at the ends.
8. Use small slices to make feathers down over the temples and cheeks.
9. Bring color into this creation by using pimientos, leeks and ripe olives to decorate the head band. Use egg whites for eyes. The red brown of the sweet potatoes is just right for an Indian face and war paint can be simulated with strips of cooked carrots, leeks and pimientos.
10. Coat entire arrangement with aspic.
11. Teepees can also be made from the sweet potato-gelatin mixture. Shape mixture on a round crouton base and use leeks, black olives and toothpicks for teepee decorations.
12. Remaining breast slices can be arranged on the platter or used on another platter.

Note: The Indian face can also be modeled on top of a whole turkey which has not been boned. However, it takes a second turkey to provide slices for the feathers. Less of the sweet potato mixture is needed here.

A Hawaiian tiki head can also be sculptured from sweet potatoes. A wooden tiki head or pictures on Hawaiian travel folders will provide a pattern for the head and ideas for decorating it. Grass houses can be created with brown dyed, hard cooked eggs and leeks.

No. of Servings from Turkey

Pounds Ready-To-Cook Turkey	*No. of Servings*
8-10	16-20
10-14	20-28
14-18	28-36
18-20	36-40
20-24	40-50

These estimates are for single servings with no allowance made for extra helpings or leftovers. Slow roasting to prevent shrinkage and expert carving will assure maximum servings for turkey.

Method IX—Indian Chief Carved from Raw Sweet Potato or Carrot

1. To prepare turkey for decorating:
   - Remove both turkey breasts with a long boning knife and remove skin.
   - Carve breasts into ¼ in. slices.
   - Remove and skin drumsticks.
   - Place thick pieces of bread inside bird's cavity to support carcass and fill openings in the back.
   - Use a mousse or russian salad to build breast up to original size. Apply mousse or russian salad with a spatula dipped in hot water.
   - Place turkey on wire rack and chill.

2. Coat chilled reshaped turkey with aspic.

3. Carve Indian face from raw, peeled sweet potato. The oblong shape of the sweet potato lends itself to easy creation of an Indian face. A carrot can also be used.

4. Place carved face in lower center of turkey and press into mousse.

5. Make eagle feathers from a cardboard pattern, cutting feathers out of extra stiff white chaud froid sauce.

6. Outline the edges of the feathers with long strips from black truffle sheet and with truffle slices.

7. Assemble feathers around face, pressing them into mousse. Chaud froid feathers should be well chilled and quite stiff for successful transfer from the sheet pan to the turkey.

8. Coat entire bird with aspic and place on tray.

9. Arrange remaining slices of turkey breast around the decorated turkey. Coat all with aspic.

Left, small indian head carved from carrot is completed with chaud froid cut-outs and truffle sheet designs. Cones of salami are used to make tepees. Raw carrot in front of tray is the size used to carve this indian face.

Pictured here (1) indian head made by filling plastic mold (2) with white chaud froid which has been colored with pimiento. Smaller Indian head (6) made by same method, using mold (4). On tray (5) white chaud froid and truffle sheets from which decorations were cut. Indian head (3) was carved from carrot, with feathers and decorations made by the above methods.

Below, large Indian with head dress was made using a carved carrot for the face. White feathers were made of white chaud froid sheets cut around a cardboard pattern. The rest of the decorations were cut from a truffle sheet. This easy decoration may also be applied to ham.

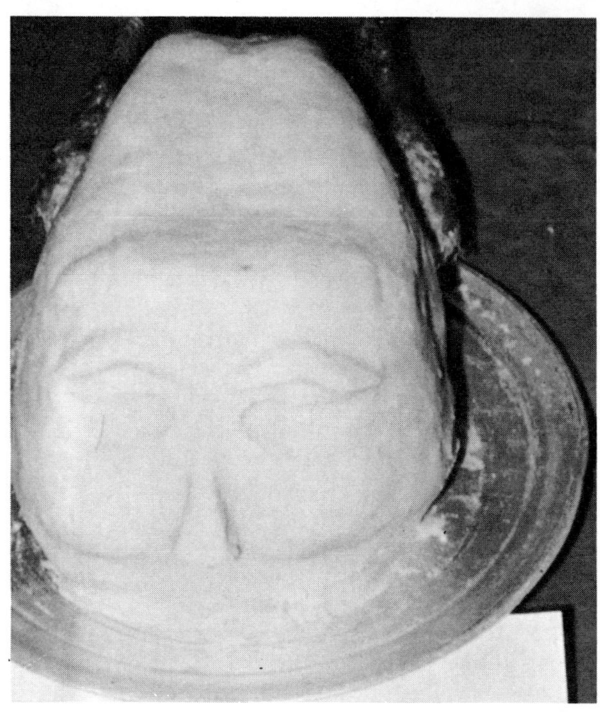

1

The Turkey Santa Claus is a great favorite with children. Directions appear on facing page; steps are pictured here: 1. Mold face on turkey carcass from potato-gelatin mixture. 2. Paint cheeks with red-tinted aspic. Eyelids are truffle strips; eyebrows and mustache, leek roots; mouth, pimiento circle. 3. Mold potato-gelatin mixture into hat on separate pan; move onto prepared base. 4. Make strip of fur on hat and the beard of chopped egg white mixed with aspic. 5. Cover all of head but hat with protective foil, then cover hat completely with red chaud froid sauce.

2

3

4

5

Method X—Roast Turkey Made into a Santa Claus

(See step-by-step pictures facing page.)

This idea is especially suited to a children's Christmas buffet table. The modeling techniques are the same as those used to create the Indian head in Method VIII. However, half sweet potato puree and half mashed potatoes are combined with gelatin to make the sculpturing material.

Before starting piece, assemble: 10 lb. cooked pureed sweet potatoes and 10 lb. mashed white potatoes; 1 cup granulated gelatin dissolved in 1 qt. poultry stock; pimiento sheet or red chaud froid sheet; green grapes; red-tinted aspic; white chaud froid sheet; turnip bells for hat; truffles; leeks.

Add gelatin that has been melted in stock to potato mixture to thicken it so that it can be molded into face. To speed thickening process, potato-gelatin mixture can be put in freezer. Stir occasionally until mixture becomes rubbery. It is then ready to be made into Santa Claus.

1. Do not bone roasted turkey but slice meat off the back so it will lie straight on the platter.
2. Chilled potato and gelatin mixture is spread over turkey breast and modeled into a smiling face.
3. Model the red and white fur hat from more of the potato mixture on a flat pan. Color the hat with red chaud froid sauce or use pimiento sheet.
4. Use a strip of white chaud froid sauce for the fur-lined rim of the hat. Place white strip around base of hat. Coat finished hat with aspic.
5. Make a base of potatoes for the hat, locating it above the face. Then transfer the hat to base above the turkey and position it properly above the face.
6. Outline the features with strips of hard cooked egg whites, use green grapes for the eyes, strips of pimiento sheet for the mouth and paint the cheeks with red-tinted aspic.
7. Arrange long slices of turkey breast (from another bird) to make Santa's beard, running them down from the chin. Cover these slices with finely chopped hard cooked egg whites mixed with aspic and the beard will be edible.
8. Arrange turkey breast slices above the head. Position bells made of raw turnip on hat. Give the whole arrangement a final coat of aspic.

Preparation Method for Domestic Duckling

Because ducklings have a good deal of fat which is lost during roasting, they shrink considerably. However, this method changes the "ugly" duckling that comes out of the oven into a "swan" for the buffet table! Two ducklings weighing at least 4 or 5 lb. raw should be roasted for this presentation.

1. Bone the breasts of both ducklings so there are four pieces of meat.

On a silver platter, place one carcass on a 1-in. high oval socle of deep-fried bread.

3. Add brandy to a liver mousse and cover the entire carcass, moulding mousse with a spatula to make a well rounded oval shape.
4. Leaving skin on, carve all four breasts lengthwise, cutting slices on the diagonal to make them as wide as possible. Since breasts are rather thin, the diagonal slice makes them twice as wide. Keep slices in order but remove end cuts.
5. Dip each breast slice in port flavored aspic. Overlap slices slightly around reshaped duck, working from the tail end. Since slices have been cut from two ducks and are extra long, they will cover mousse from top to bottom. Keep skin visible on slices for contrast.
6. The line down the back of the duck where slices meet is covered with such decorative garnishes as fluted mushrooms, orange sections or chunks of other colorful fruit.
7. Coat entire figure directly on platter using a light brown port flavored aspic. Decorate using one of the ideas suggested in Chapter XIV.

In this set-up, duckling carcass has been filled in with mousse base which will hold breast slices.

PREPARATION OF DUCK A L'ORANGE

Above, for a Cold Duckling a l'Orange, roast two ducklings and cool. Remove breast meat from both sides of one duckling; fill breast cavity with pureed chicken liver. Chill thoroughly. Slice breast meat thinly.

Left, overlap thinly sliced breast meat around duckling, putting first slices on at tail end. The chicken liver filling holds slices in place. Scalloped grapefruit shells filled with fruit should be prepared to go on tray with finished duckling.

Below left, when first duckling is decorated, carve breasts of second duckling into thin slices for medallions to go on tray with whole bird. To complete medallions, fill center hole in a small slice of canned, drained pineapple with pureed chicken liver. Cover with two overlapping slices of breast meat. Top with two orange sections and a grape. Add rosettes of puree and truffle designs. Chill thoroughly.

Below, coat duck, medallions with two or three thin layers of cool but still syrupy aspic. Coat serving platter with aspic tinted with melted red currant jelly. Chill remaining aspic to cut into croutons and triangles as garnish for platter. Arrange duckling and medallions on platter. Grapefruit baskets, aspic squares, slices of pate with truffle cut-outs can be positioned to complete display.

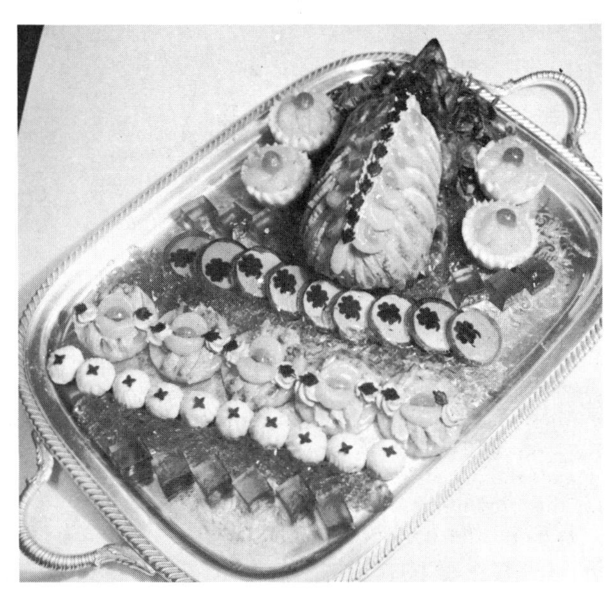

NOTES

NOTES

CHAPTER VI

FISH

Decorated Whole Small Salmon

Stuffed Salmon Trout Nova Scotia

Salmon, brook trout and turbot are delicately fleshed whole fish that can be the talk of the table. The variously flavored sauces developed to accompany them have become the trade-mark of the buffet in many food service operations.

Portions are easy to pick up from a decorated whole fish, such as salmon or turbot, and the properly planned arrangement remains attractive through many servings. Small fish, of course, are portioned out more rapidly but replacement of a single brook trout, decorated to match the ensemble, can be easily accomplished.

The salmon, counted as king when fish are ranked, merits royal treatment when destined to rule over an assembly of buffet foods.

The presentation of the whole cooked salmon should match the beauty of the live salmon's performance as it leaps upstream to spawn. It is from the amazing feats on its spawning journeys that the salmon gains flesh of the firmness and texture that make it unique among fish.

Six methods of preparing cold salmon for the buffet have been broken down into step-by-step techniques.

Classical Boneless Salmon, a whole fish coated with white chaud froid, decorated with a scene composed of bits of black truffle sheet.

Method I—Classical Boneless

If salmon is headless, mold a head from fish mousse. Prepare as follows:

1. Place eviscerated, washed and scaled salmon on board.
2. Insert sharp boning knife 2 in. behind head and run it along one side of backbone, stopping 3 in. from tail. Repeat on other side of backbone.
3. Loosen backbone completely from fish. This is not difficult as the head and tail are the only points where backbone is attached.
4. Use lobster shears to cut off backbone at head and tail.
5. Remove all other bones attached to the fins. Use these in making court bouillon.
6. Place whole fish, spread open butterfly fashion, on insert rack of fish poacher. If a wooden board is to be used, cover it first with foil.
7. Tie fish back together with strips of cloth; string will cut the flesh. Next, tie salmon onto rack; place it, together with rack, into court bouillon.
8. Have court bouillon simmering in pan. Place salmon on rack in pan with enough liquid to cover.
9. Poaching time for a 15 lb. salmon is 30 to 40 minutes; 8 to 10 lb., 15 to 20 minutes.
10. Let cooked salmon cool in court bouillon; remove with rack.
11. Reshape salmon on rack, filling with jellied russian salad or mousse.
12. Coat with mayonnaise colle de poisson and decorate, using one of the ideas in Chapter XIV.

Eviscerated, washed and scaled salmon has backbone removed this way: insert sharp boning knife 2 in. behind head and run it along one side of backbone to a point 3 in. from tail; repeat on other side of backbone. Cut backbone loose at head and tail with lobster shears and lift out.

Place whole fish, spread open as shown, on insert rack of fish poacher or on wooden board which has been covered with foil. Tie fish in place with strips of cloth.

Fill poaching pan with court bouillon and bring it to a simmer. Place salmon on rack or board in pan; be sure liquid covers it. When poached, let salmon cool in bouillon, right.

FISH

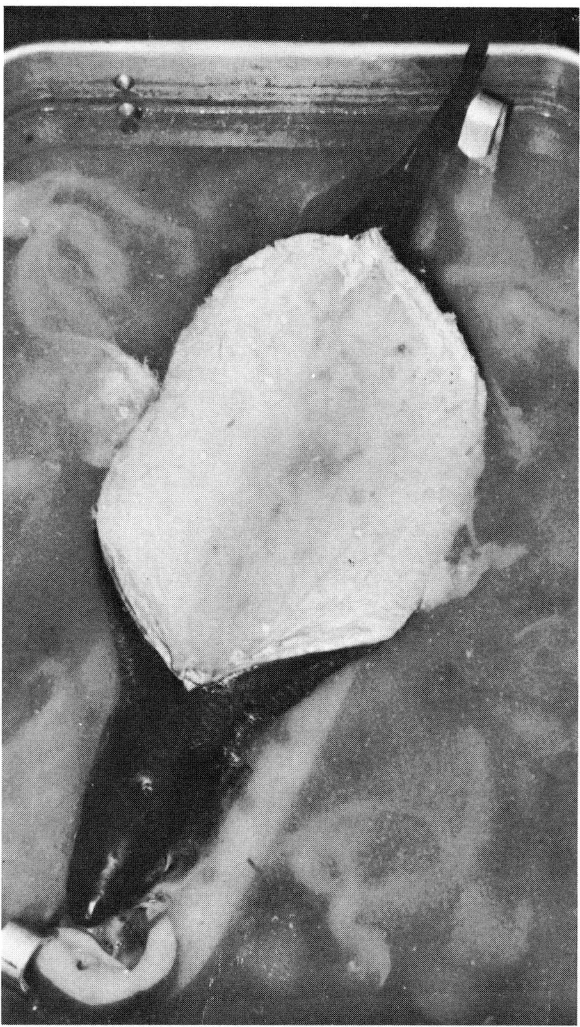

Fill cavity in salmon created when bones were removed. Use jellied russian salad or mousse to reshape fish. Coat reshaped salmon with mayonnaise colle de poisson as at left.

Equipment Needed For Preparation of Cold Salmon

The basic equipment and ingredients needed for all of the following methods include: a fish poacher with an insert rack or a large, deep stainless steel pan or steamer with wire rack; lobster shears; heavy foil; cheese cloth; large french knife and boning knife; skewers; trussing needle and twine; large fish platters or regular serving trays covered with foil; utensils for decorative work; court bouillon or fume de poisson, if available; fish mousse, russian salad and fish farce.

Before being used in any of the preparation methods detailed in this section, whole fish must be scaled, eviscerated and have gills removed with sharp shears, as at right.

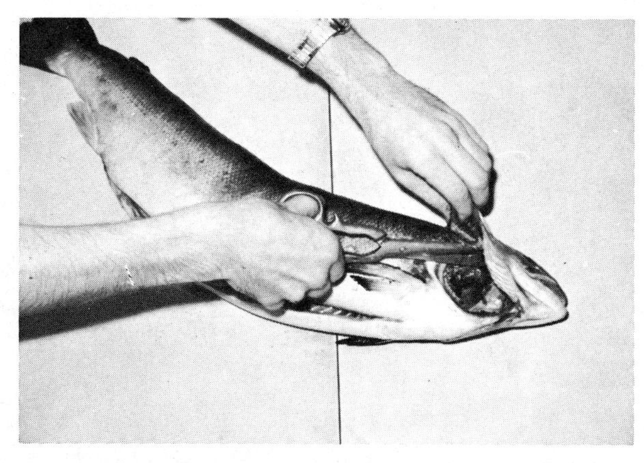

Turbot

Brook Trout

SALUTE TO SEAFOOD

Salmon Viking Ship

After salmon has had backbone removed and is eviscerated, use a previously prepared fish farce to fill entire cavity left in fish.

Method II—Viking Ship

A full color illustration of Salmon Viking Ship appears on the preceding page.

1. An uneviscerated scaled salmon with the lower part whole is required.
2. Remove backbone but do not cut through fish belly, using this method:
   - Insert sharp boning knife 2 in. behind head and run it along one side of backbone, stopping 3 in. from tail. Repeat procedure on other side of backbone.
   - Loosen backbone completely from fish. This is not difficult as the head and tail are the only points where backbone is attached.
   - Use lobster shears to cut off backbone at head and tail.
3. Eviscerate salmon from top after backbone is out.
4. Prepare fish farce.
5. Fill entire cavity of the salmon with the farce.
6. Wrap whole fish in cheese cloth.
7. Sew cheese cloth together along the back, pulling tight, to create boat shape.
8. Place boat-shaped salmon on poaching rack and tie in place.
9. Elevate ends of salmon by putting raw potato wedges under them.
10. Poach for about one hour in simmering court bouillon deep enough to cover salmon.
11. Let cooked salmon cool in court bouillon. Remove cheese cloth.
12. Coat cooled salmon with clear fish aspic. Make into viking ship using hard cooked egg halves for shields, ripe olives for viking helmets, oars piped from pate au choux, russian salad to fill across the top of salmon and a paper sail and wooden mast.

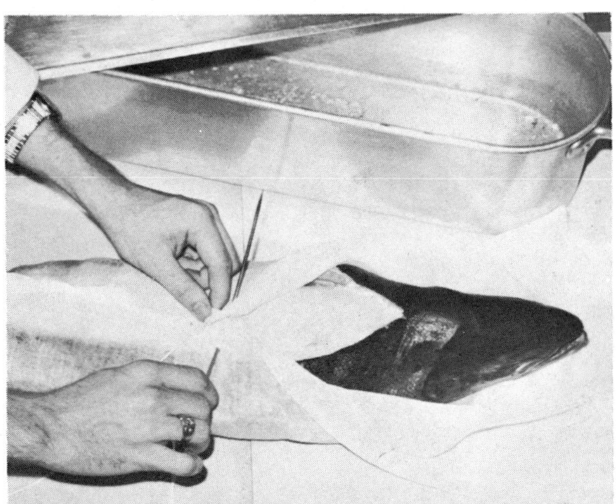

Wrap salmon in cheese cloth; sew cloth together along the back, pulling it tight to create boat shape. Place boat-shaped salmon on poaching rack and tie in place.

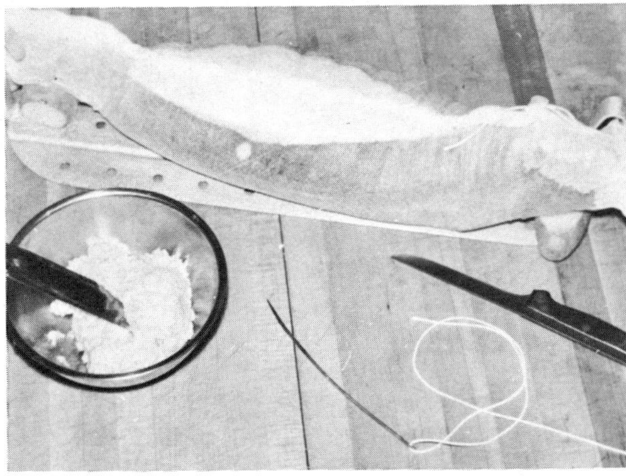

Elevate ends of cloth-covered filled salmon with raw potato wedges. Poach for about one hour in simmering court bouillon deep enough to cover salmon. Cool in bouillon, unwrap.

Sauces for these displays of salmon should be placed nearby and supply should be checked regularly to be sure containers are replenished as needed. In pictures above, Salmon Continental Style, left, is served with a spicy cocktail sauce while Salmon Artificial, right, has a mayonnaise accompaniment.

Method III—Boneless Salmon Continental Style

This is probably the most efficient and fastest way to prepare a whole fresh salmon for a buffet. The head is left on the salmon for this presentation.

1. Remove tail and head of a large eviscerated, scaled salmon, using large french knife.
2. Bone the remaining center section completely; side bones can be pulled out with tweezers or pliers. Cut center section in half lengthwise.
3. Slice each half into ½-in. slices leaving skin on. Leave slices in order as they come from fish.
4. Place slices in the same order in a flat oiled hotel pan and poach in court bouillon for 5 to 8 minutes.
5. Head and tail are poached separately for about 10 minutes.
6. On a large tray or mirror arrange slices of salmon. Place head and tail at opposite ends of platter.
7. Position a double row of decorated hard cooked eggs between the head and tail. Caviar and seafood toppings are best for hard cooked eggs used on this salmon.
8. After all garnishes are in place on tray, coat entire arrangement lightly with aspic.

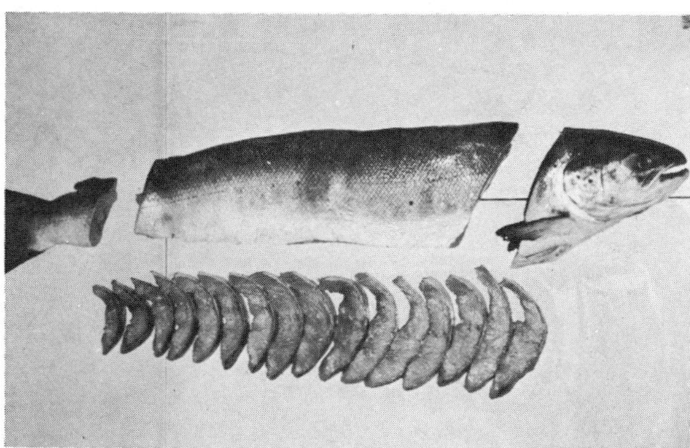

For Salmon prepared by Methods III and IV, tail and head of whole fish are removed and center section boned, then cut in half lengthwise. Each half is sliced into ½-in. slices with the skin left on and slices are left in order for poaching.

Method IV—Artificial:

1. Prepare salmon as in Steps 1 to 5, Method III.
2. Place head and tail at opposite ends of large fish platter. Use russian salad under head and tail to help keep them in place.
3. Use jellied russian salad, mousse or a dry potato salad to mold a salmon shape between the head and tail.
4. Coat salmon shape with aspic first, then chaud froid.
5. Arrange all poached slices in order around the molded salmon.
6. Coat lightly with aspic or chaud froid, but leave head and tail natural. Select decorating idea from Chapter XIV.

Method V—Scandinavian:

1. Headless, eviscerated salmon is cut in half across salmon, then center section is cut in half lengthwise.
2. Cut one half of the center section into ½-in. slices and leave the other half unsliced.
3. Roll some salmon slices into medallions and tie with string.
4. Poach unsliced piece of salmon with skin side up on rack in pan of simmering court bouillon.
5. Poach salmon slices and slices rolled into medallions in a separate pan in simmering court bouillon.
6. Cool poached unsliced piece *and remove skin.* Skin comes off more easily if scales have been left on.
7. Coat unsliced piece with chaud froid sauce or with aspic only. Decorate simply.
8. On a long china or wooden platter combine decorated unsliced salmon piece with slices and medallions in attractive design. See picture at right.

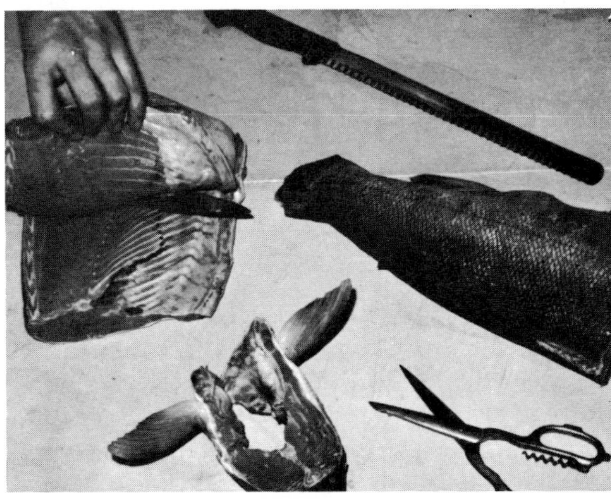

Initial steps in preparation of Scandinavian Salmon (see picture of finished dish and directions top, right): remove head; eviscerate; then cut fish in half crosswise. Cut center section in half lengthwise as shown. Slice above and below backbone with french knife to remove it easily, below.

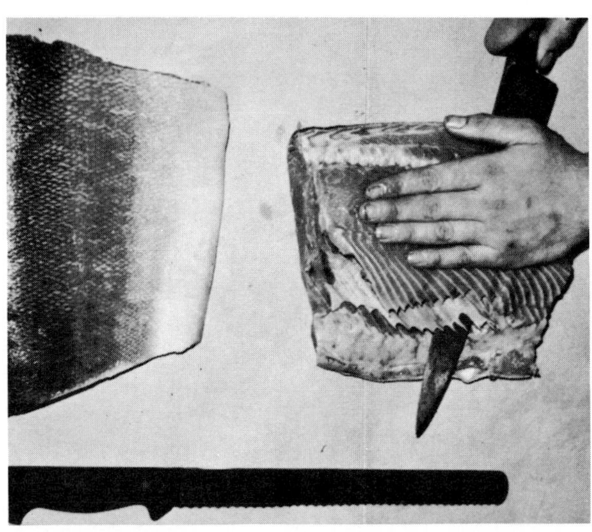

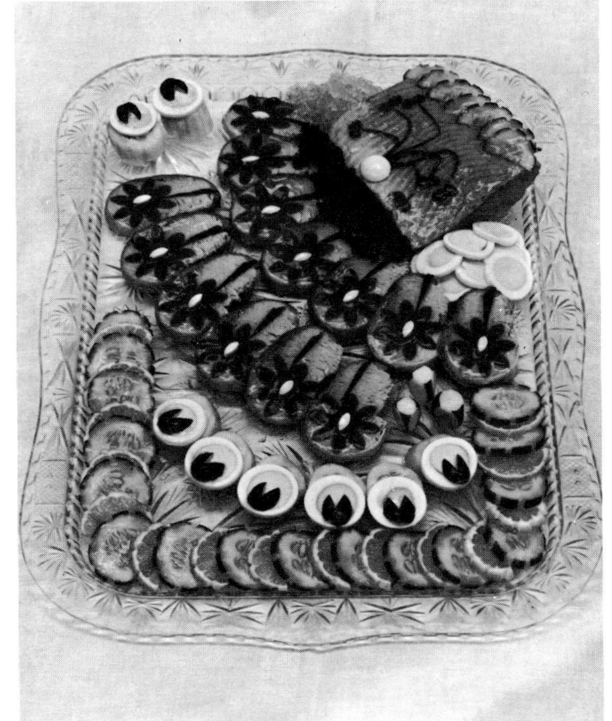

Cut one half of center section into ½-in. slices; leave other half unsliced. Poach unsliced piece with skin side up on rack in pan of simmering court bouillon. Cool, skin.

Poach individual salmon slices, and medallions if they are to be used in the arrangement, in a separate pan in more simmering court bouillon. Cool in bouillon and decorate.

Salmon Trout on Buffet

This version of a whole salmon display piece is made with medium-sized salmon trout, using a simplified procedure. The day before service is scheduled, one salmon trout is scaled, eviscerated and thoroughly washed.

To hold rounded shape of salmon during poaching, several stalks of celery are placed inside, then fish is tied together with two pieces of string. Tied fish is placed in a fish poacher, covered with court bouillon and, over a 15-minute period brought to a slow boil on top of the stove, then simmered for another 15 minutes. After cooling, salmon is placed in refrigerator overnight.

On the day of service, the whole salmon is lifted from poacher, (see below), and placed on a rack so skin can be removed. A triangle of chaud froid sheet, decorated with a sailboat cut from a truffle sheet, is centered on one side of the salmon. Flowers made of leek stems lead to blossoms cut from pimiento sheets positioned on shrimp, below right. Decorated salmon is returned to refrigerator to chill thoroughly.

From a second salmon trout, 16 small slices are cut and poached in court bouillon with white wine added. Slices are cooled, then placed on wire rack and each slice decorated, as shown at right below.

Decorated whole salmon and slices are placed on silver tray, or sheet pan covered with foil, with deviled eggs, fresh asparagus tips and sliced tomatoes. Arrangement is covered with wine-flavored aspic. Aspic croutons, chopped aspic, small vegetable timbales and outer circle of lemon slices complete platter.

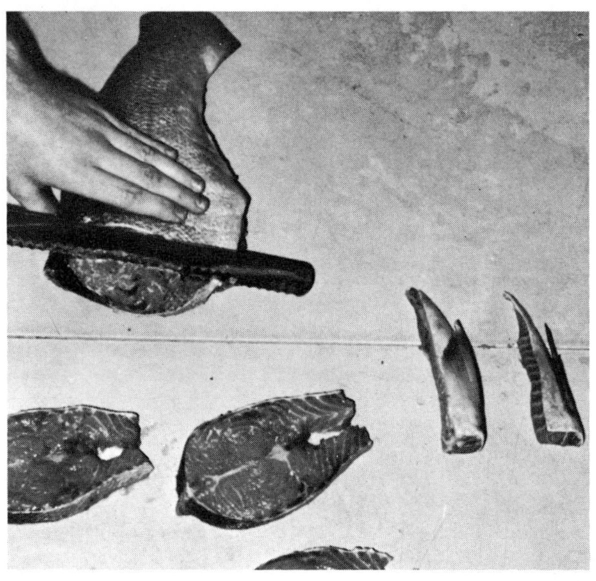

Partially thawed, eviscerated, scaled salmon tailpiece is placed on slicing board to start preparation of Salmon Modern, Method VI. Large french knife is used to cut double cutlets ½-in. thick from upper half of salmon.

Method VI—Modern, Not Boned/Frozen Tail Piece:

1. Place partially thawed, eviscerated scaled salmon tail piece on slicing board.
2. With large french knife cut double cutlets, ½ in. thick, starting at the head, from upper half of salmon.
3. Poach unsliced tail piece in court bouillon. Tying and wrapping is not necessary.
4. Poach double cutlets separately on rack in oiled pan. Cover with simmering court bouillon.
5. Cooled, unsliced tail piece is skinned and finished with aspic or chaud froid sauce. Skin can be left on, if desired.
6. Place tail piece on platter and fan cutlets around platter from the tail of the salmon.
7. These double salmon cutlets only have to be decorated on one side since they overlap and are partly covered.

Note: The methods outlined above may also be used in preparing other fish shaped like salmon such as sturgeon, lake or brook trout, sea bass, pike, carp, blue fish.

Salmon tailpiece, poached whole, carries main decoration. Double cutlets only have to be decorated on one side since they overlap and are partly covered.

Sources of Salmon

Salmon are caught in both the North Atlantic and the North Pacific oceans. The Atlantic salmon, known as Kennebec, averages 10 to 20 lb. in weight, although some individual specimens may run as high as 60 to 80 lb. The firm flesh is an orange-pink. The deliciously flavored meat is highly prized. Little of the Atlantic catch is canned as the supply has become very limited.

On the other hand, Pacific Coast salmon has become one of the most valuable fishery resources of the U. S. and Canada.

The five different species of Pacific Salmon are:

1. Chinook or King Salmon. Is the largest, averaging about 22 lb. in weight, but specimens much larger are frequently taken. It has a deep, thick body with a small head. As a rule the flesh is a deep salmon red but it may vary from this shade to almost a white among different specimens in certain fishing areas. Chinook salmon is widely distributed, but the most important geographical source is the Columbia River.
2. Red or Sockeye. Averages about 6½ lb. in weight with a maximum of 12 lb. The body is slender and the head small. The flesh is a deep orange red. Its attractive appearance and flavor keep this species in great demand; when canned it is designated a "fancy" pack.
3. Medium Red Salmon. Also known as silver salmon because of the silvery color of the body. It averages about 9 lb., with a maximum weight of about 30. Its flesh is lighter than that of red salmon but deeper than chinook.
4. Pink Salmon. Is the smallest of the Pacific salmon but the most abundant. It averages 4 lb. in weight and rarely exceeds 8 lb. Although the flesh is rather light in color, it has a delicate flavor and is high in nutritive values. Because of its abundance, it is an inexpensive source of high quality protein, minerals and vitamins.
5. Chum or White Salmon. Its average weight is about 8 lb. with a maximum of 16 lb. The flesh is light colored; when canned, it ranges from a light pink to a yellowish white. Because of this lack of color and its low fat content, it costs less than the other species. It is, nevertheless, high in food values and can be used advantageously, whether fresh or canned, in less expensive entrees.

Decorated slices are placed in S-curve on aspic coated platter. Hard cooked eggs, cucumber shells filled with vegetable salad, aspic squares, vegetable timbales and shrimp are used to fill out platter of Boned, Sliced Half Salmon.

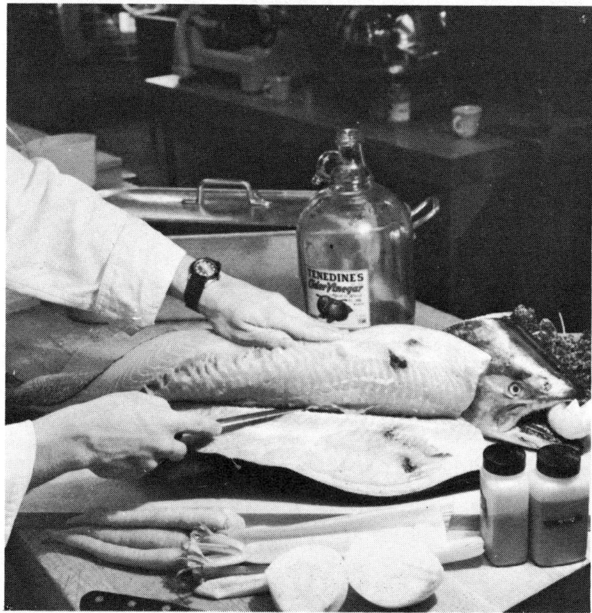

Boned, Sliced Half Salmon preparation starts on carving board where center bone and smaller bones are all removed from whole fish.

FISH

To Prepare Boned, Sliced Half Salmon:

1. Scaled eviscerated salmon is placed on carving board. Remove centerbone and smaller bones on each side.
2. Cut slices carefully and place in buttered hotel pan. Add 2 cups of cut-up vegetables, ½ cup of vinegar, 1 cup white wine, juice of 2 lemons, salt, 2 bay leaves, peppercorns to make court bouillon. Cover with buttered wax paper.
3. Poach for 10 minutes and cool well.
4. Place 16 slices cut from half salmon on wire rack. Use pimientos and leeks or tarragon to make small flower designs for decoration. Refrigerate well.
5. Make aspic of ½ gal. of court bouillon, 6 egg whites and 3 oz. of gelatin. Bring ingredients to a boil to clarify aspic.
6. Cover platter selected to hold fish with a layer of aspic ¼ in. thick. Place in refrigerator. When aspic has hardened well, place salmon slices on platter in S-curve. To complete platter, add stuffed hard cooked eggs, 1½ in. cucumber shells filled with a vegetable salad, aspic cubes, vegetable timbales and shrimps.
7. Serve with sauce verte.

Note: This presentation makes a display of salmon slices that can be as effective as a whole decorated salmon, yet is easier to prepare and serve.

Slices are carefully cut from halves of salmon. Slices are poached in court bouillon and cooled. Decorated slices are refrigerated until thoroughly chilled.

Turbot, Other Flat Fish

Turbot, a flat, white, delicate and flaky-meated fish was designated an epicurean dish by the Romans. As its use spreads across the country today, more and more Americans are coming to share the enthusiasm of the early epicures for this unique fish.

A member of the flounder family, the turbot is very discriminating about the food it eats and this is the explanation for its delicate flavor.

Described by DeGouy as a fish "with a body of almost square proportions, turbot is frequently called halibut although it is much smaller and of much more delicate flavor. This fish inhabits the rocky shores and is superior in flavor to fish which inhabit muddy shores. It has a firmer and more delicate flesh . . . is found on the Atlantic Coast from Maine to the Carolinas."

The turbot ranges in size from 18 in. to 2 ft., weighing on the average from 4 to 10 lb. However, turbots have been known to weigh 70 lb. and 25-lb. turbot are not unusual.

Note: This same method of preparation and presentation may be used for other flat fish.

To Prepare Turbot for the Buffet

1. First step in preparing whole turbot for buffet presentation is to remove fins from fish with shears.
2. Next fillet the top half with a sharp knife.
3. Remove skin from fillets cut from top half of fish. Leave bottom half of turbot in one piece.
4. Cut fillets from top half of turbot into slices and place in order in pan for poaching.
5. Disconnect vertebrae still in place on bottom half of turbot at head and tail before putting bottom half in pan for poaching.
6. After bottom half of turbot is poached and has cooled, remove vertebrae and build up fish to original size, using fish mousse made with truffles to reshape turbot.
7. Coat whole turbot with white chaud froid and center decorated panel on it.
8. Decorate slices and arrange on platter with reshaped turbot, filling in with halves of hard cooked eggs made into lady bugs, lemon slices and aspic croutons.

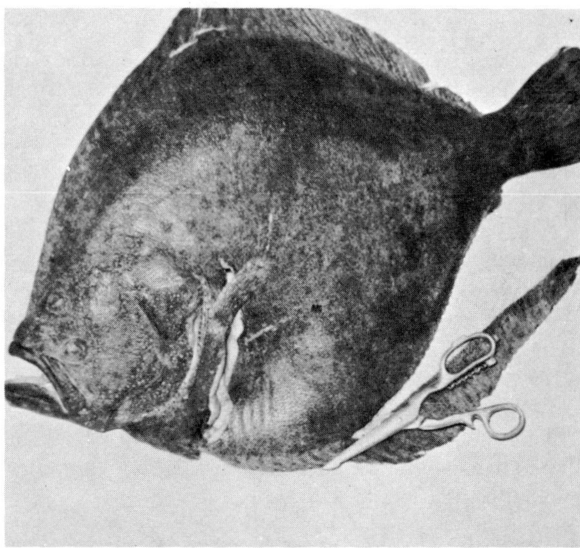

First step in readying turbot for buffet presentation is to remove fins with sharp shears.

Fillets are cut from top half of turbot with sharp knife. Flesh is slit and laid back for filleting.

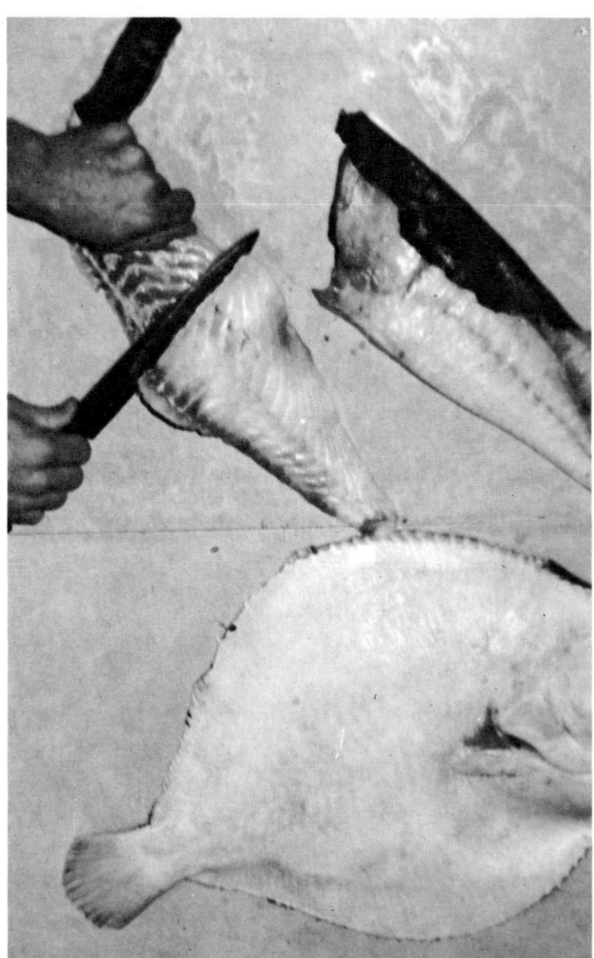

Skin is removed from fillets cut from top half; bottom half of turbot is left in one piece for this preparation.

Fillets from top half are sliced and placed in pan for poaching. Slices are kept in order as cut from fillets. Bottom half has vertebrae disconnected at head and tail before it is put into separate pan for poaching.

Unique shape of turbot is recreated on this platter with decorated slices of the fish framed by lemon circles.

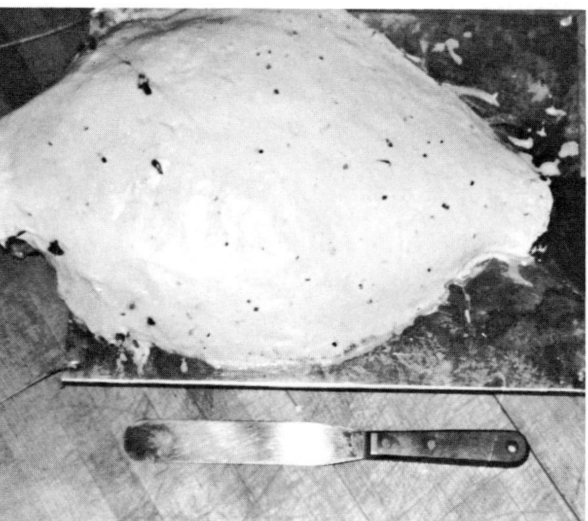

After poaching, bottom half has vertebrae removed and is then built up with fish mousse to original size. Mousse is smoothed so that chaud froid coat will adhere smoothly. Reshaped turbot is thoroughly chilled before chaud froid coat is added.

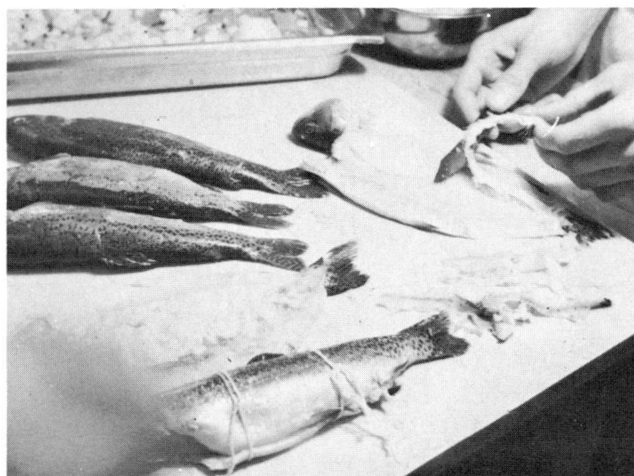

For Brook Trout Lucullus, the required number of trout to be used must be of uniform size. Cleaned, washed trout are arranged in shallow poaching pan, covered with court bouillon and poached in simmering liquid for 5 minutes.

Cool trout in bouillon they were poached in, then place in refrigerator until thoroughly chilled. *Next step above right.*

To complete decoration, put a flower at end of chive sprig. Make flower of small rounds of pimiento with truffle bit in center. Dip all decorations in liquid aspic before placing them on fish.

Place chilled trout on wire rack and, using a sharp knife, remove a panel of skin to uncover area for decoration. Dip fresh chives and some tarragon leaves into boiling water for 15 seconds. Arrange a sprig of chives and add tarragon leaves on skin-free area of trout.

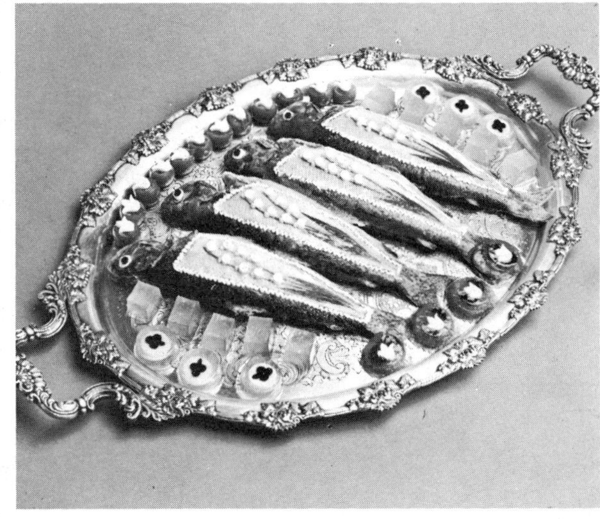

Outer edge of decorated panel is outlined with egg yolk paste. Coat decorated trout twice with aspic, chilling trout after each coating. Add aspic croutons, decorated medallions and cherry tomatoes to tray.

To Prepare Brook Trout Lucullus:

1. Select 7 or 8 brook trout of uniform size, weighing about ¾ lb. each. Clean and wash trout and arrange in shallow poaching pan.

2. Cover trout with a sheet of parchment, add court bouillon and poach 5 minutes in simmering liquid.

3. Cool fish in broth, then remove fish and chill.

4. Place chilled trout on wire rack and, with a sharp knife, remove a panel of skin. Dip fresh chives and some tarragon leaves into boiling water for 15 seconds. This will wilt them and intensify the color. Arrange a chive stem with tarragon leaves on skinless portion of trout.

5. Put a flower at the end of the chive stem. Make flower of 5 or 6 small rounds of pimiento with round of truffle for center. Dip all decorations in liquid aspic before placing on fish.

6. Outline skinned panel with an egg yolk paste made with soft butter, a little mayonnaise and flavored with dry mustard, a dash of worcestershire sauce and salt added to hard cooked egg yolks.

7. Coat decorated trout twice with aspic, chilling trout after each coating.

Brook Trout Printaniere has a decorative panel covering whole fish. Piece montee is used as focal point with smaller vegetable timbales arranged between individual trout. Two heart-shaped vegetable timbales and a semi circle of decorated stuffed hard cooked eggs fill out design.

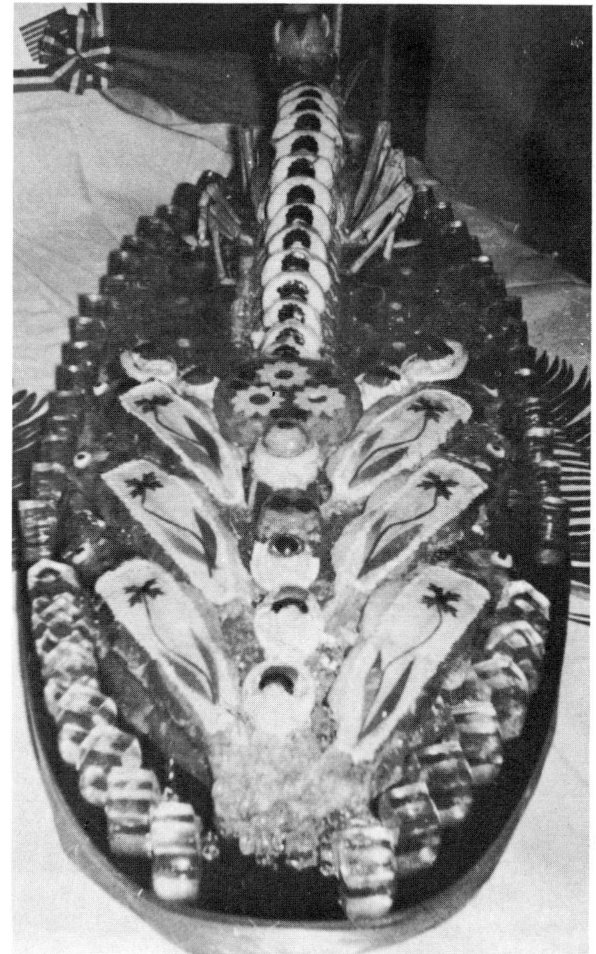

A combination platter, using a filled lobster shell for height features six individual Brook Trout Lucullus. Hard cooked eggs repeat decoration of lobster medallions; aspic croutons, small vegetable timbale and chopped aspic are added.

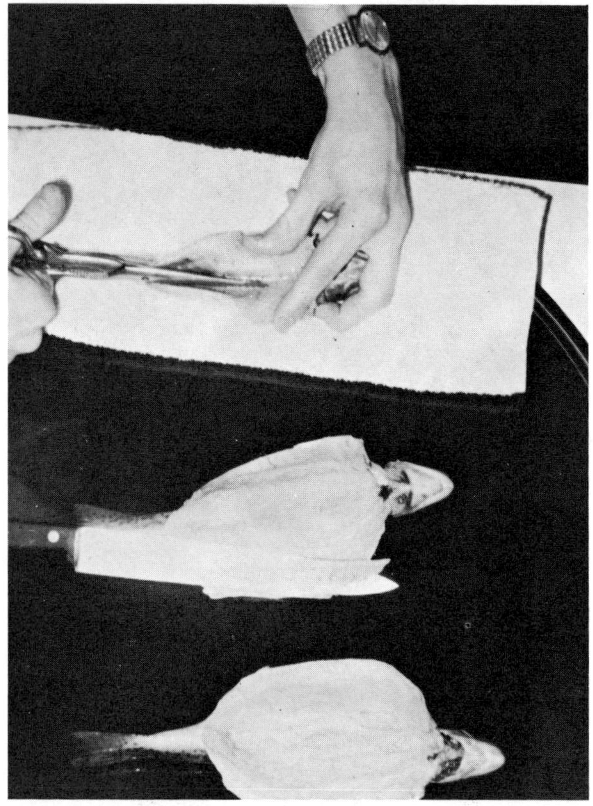

Brook trout are boned and spread butterfly fashion on work table. Scissors are used to disconnect vertebrae which is then easy to remove with sharp knife. Head and tail are left on fish. Next step at right.

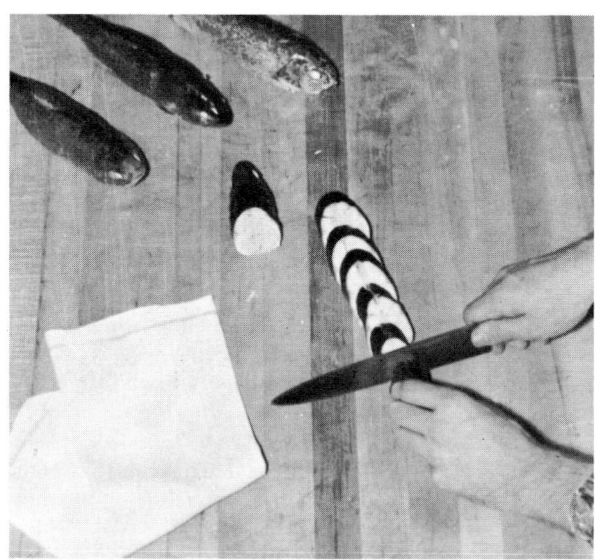

Fish farce is used to stuff trout to original size. Filled trout are wrapped in cheese cloth and placed on rack of fish poacher. They are simmered in well seasoned, wine-flavored court bouillon until cooked, then cooled in the bouillon.

After thorough chilling in refrigerator, trout are unwrapped and carved in bias slices for decoration and arrangement on bed of chopped aspic on silver platter or foil-covered sheet pan.

Decorated slices cut from each trout are re-positioned between head and tail. For maximum effect, trout slices should be kept in order for re-positioning. White asparagus spears and lemon circles add contrast to these decorated trout.

NOTES

NOTES

CHAPTER VII
Shellfish

Capitalize on the colorful shells of lobster and king crab in building seafood displays for the buffet. The delicately-flavored meat of these two crustaceans has a wide following among diners today.

Lobsters on the Buffet

Both large (5 to 8 lb.) and small (1 to 2 lb.) lobsters are used for buffet service. The large lobsters are usually cheaper because they are in less demand and require less work per pound of meat available. They also make more spectacular displays.

The smaller lobsters are sometimes split in half for less elaborate buffet displays. One-half lobster makes one serving.

Shipments of live lobsters should be checked immediately on arrival to make sure that all are alive. A dead lobster is potentially dangerous and should be removed and discarded immediately.

Preliminary Preparations for Lobster

Determine boiling time for live lobsters on the basis of weight. After boiling the required time, small lobsters are left in the broth for an additional 15 or 20 minutes. If the broth is to be used for aspic, lobsters are then removed. However, if broth is not to be used further, let it cool and then store cooked lobsters in the broth with fresh dill sprigs in the refrigerator. They may safely be stored in broth under refrigeration for 2 to 3 days.

To boil, live lobsters are placed in boiling salted water or in a steamer for a period of time, as charted below. Dill stalks, lemon slices, bay leaves and peppercorns are suggested for flavoring rather than seaweed which is much stronger.

LOBSTER COOKING CHART

1 lb. lobsters	8 minutes
2 lb. lobsters	16 minutes
3 to 4 lb. lobsters	20 minutes
5 to 8 lb. lobsters	40 minutes
10 lb. or heavier lobsters	1 hour

Cold Lobster Displays

The methods suggested for lobster presentation were worked out to ensure easy service for the patron selecting this luxury item from the buffet table. The tools required in making these displays are: lobster or poultry shears, small meat saw, large french knife.

Meat from cooked lobster tail is removed in one piece. Tail is sliced on bias in ¼-in. medallions.

Two boiled lobsters are set on a rice socle with medallions of cooked lobster meat, arranged in washed shells, making edible frame for display. Socle has been covered with white chaud froid and is decorated with a sailing ship made of pieces cut from a truffle sheet. (See directions for decorations, p. 128.) Stuffed tomatoes, artichokes, aspic croutons complete platter.

Shellfish

Above, 4-lb. lobster yields 16 oz. of lobster meat. Below, claw from 16-lb. lobster yields 25 oz. of meat. Right, tail from 16-lb. lobster yields 11½ oz.

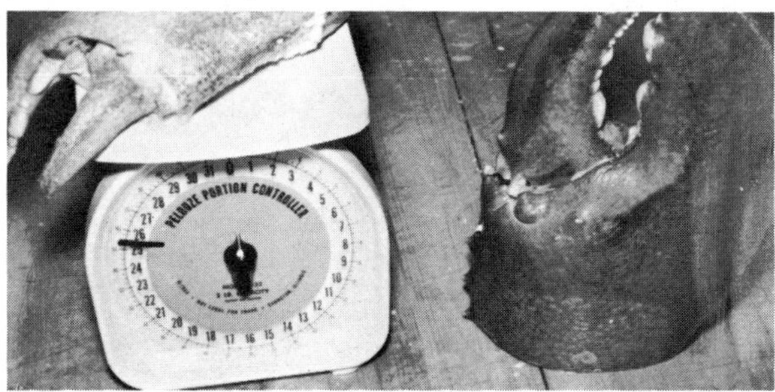

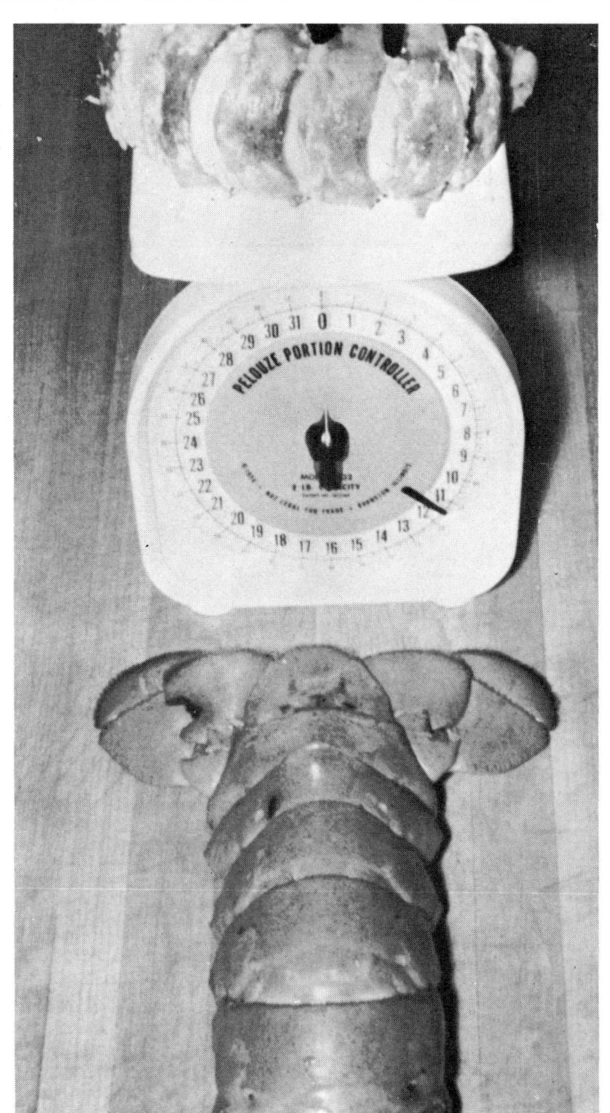

High display piece created from lobsters elevates lobster meat to area just below bowl of sauce at top of tower created from lobster shells. Lemon slices and decorated hard cooked eggs add to arrangement. Lobster meat has been removed in whole pieces in picture at right.

A spice sauce adds a piquant flavor to cold lobster. The following recipe can be varied to produce the degree of spiciness most acceptable to guests.

COCKTAIL SAUCE

Yield 1 qt.

Ingredients

Chili Sauce	2 cups
Tomato Catsup	1½ cups
Prepared Horseradish (variable)	½ cup
Lemon Juice	3 tbsp.
Salt	1 tsp.
Worcestershire Sauce	1 tsp.
Hot Pepper Sauce	1 dash

Method

1. Combine all ingredients; chill.
2. If milder sauce is desired, omit hot pepper sauce.
3. Vary horseradish according to strength and amount needed to meet guest requirements.

Method I—Regular French Method

1. Either twist off by hand or use shears to cut off both large front claws.

2. Use shears to slit back of lobster all the way, removing strip of shell; or slit at bottom of tail and remove tail meat there.

3. Pull meat from lobster tail in one piece; remove the tomalley (green liver) and save it. Clean out lobster head and rinse shell with cold water.

4. Make a straight cut on both claws with meat saw. Pull meat from claws. Crack rest of claws and remove meat. If claws are to be left on whole lobster, cut slit on underside of lobster and pull meat through opening. Save lobster juice for aspic.

5. Mix broken lobster pieces from claws with russian salad to make lobster salad.

6. Put lobster salad into empty lobster shell and spread evenly. If there is salad left, use it to fill artichoke bottoms or tomatoes.

7. Make a long incision across lobster tail and pull out veins. Slice tail meat on the bias in ¼-in. medallions. Place medallions in orderly arrangement on lobster salad in shell.

8. Decorate each medallion with a circle cut from truffle, pimiento or egg yolk sheet.

9. Use larger pieces of lobster meat taken from claws to make slices to top stuffed eggs for garnishing finished lobster.

10. Coat lobster with aspic made of lobster, fish or chicken broth. Chill in refrigerator.

11. Bread socles to be used in lobster display can be made by (a) cutting a wedge from a loaf of unsliced stale pullman bread and deep frying or (b) wrapping a long wedge of bread with aluminum or gold foil; bread does not have to be fried.

12. Place stuffed lobster on socle or tray, surrounding it with empty claws which have also been aspic-coated. Tray may also contain lemon slices and baskets carved from lemons to hold cocktail sauce and dill mayonnaise; artichoke bottoms or tomatoes stuffed with additional lobster salad; sprigs of fresh dill, aspic cubes or chopped aspic.

Note: If two lobsters are used, the socle that holds them becomes quite steep and each lobster should be anchored with a metal skewer to the bread.

Garnishes for Crab and Lobster Displays

When planning displays or platters featuring crab or lobster, keep the following in mind as possible garnishes:

Marinated fluted cucumber slices
Lemon or lime rings
Lemon or lime wedges lightly dipped in paprika or minced parsley
Mushroom caps
Celery curls
Radish roses or slices
Tomato slices or wedges
Parsley
Watercress
Beet and horseradish relish
Watermelon pickle
Tomato relish
Pickles, sweet, sour or dill
Deviled eggs

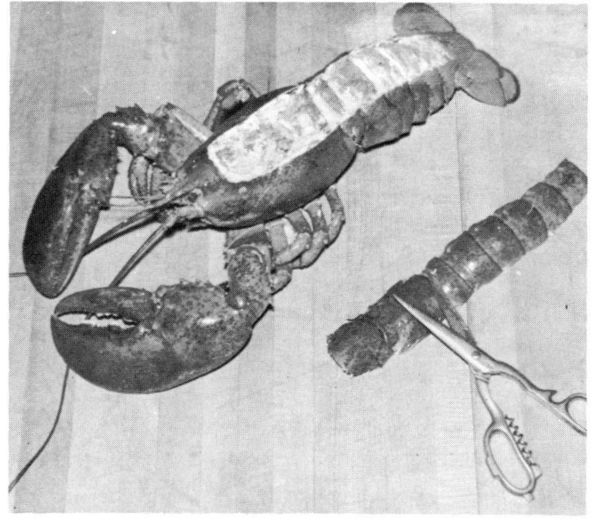

After twisting claws off lobster, by hand or with shears, use shears to slit back of lobster, removing strip of shell. Shell can also be slit at tail and tail meat removed through slit.

After rinsing shell with cold water, fill it with russian salad to which bits of lobster meat from claws have been added. Position lobster meat on salad.

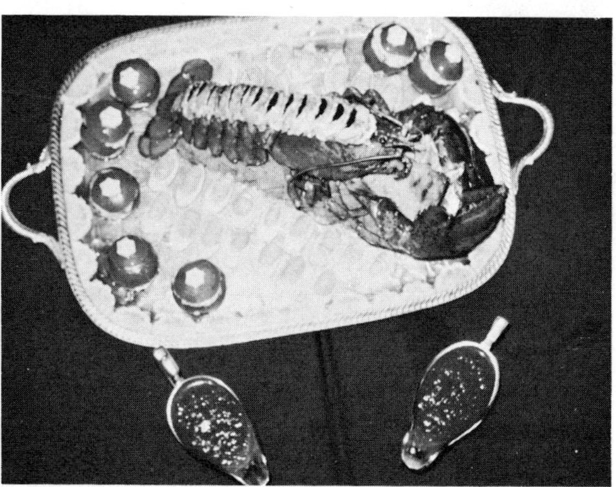

Lobster prepared by the Regular French Method is elevated on bread socle and arranged on tray with aspic timbales. Boats of cocktail sauce accompany lobster.

Method II—with Fancy Eggs (Picture below)

1. Prepare 4 to 5 lb. lobster as follows:

A. Twist off by hand or use shears to cut off both large front claws.

B. Use shears to slit back of lobster all the way, removing strip of shell; or slit at bottom of tail and remove tail meat there.

C. Pull meat from lobster tail in one piece; remove the tomalley (green liver) and save it. Clean out lobster head and rinse shell with cold water.

D. Make a straight cut on both claws with meat saw. Pull meat from claws. Crack rest of claws and remove meat. If claws are to be left on whole lobster, cut slit on underside of lobster and pull meat through opening. Save lobster juice for aspic.

E. Mix broken lobster pieces from claws with russian salad to make lobster salad.

2. Fill empty lobster shell with russian salad or with salad made by combining pieces of lobster meat with diced cucumbers, cooked rice, diced tomatoes and a dill mayonnaise. Make a long incision across lobster tail and pull out veins. Slice tail meat on the bias in ¼-in. medallions. Place medallions in orderly arrangement on lobster salad in shell. Decorate medallions with circles cut out of truffle, pimiento or egg yolk sheets.

3. Select one of the following fancy hard cooked eggs and decorate about 6 to 8 for each lobster: (Directions will be found in the chapter on Knife and Fork Hors D'Ouevres for producing these eggs.)

a. Eggs made into frogs (dyed green).

b. Half eggs made into faces with bits of truffle or radish skin.

c. Egg heads with hats.

4. Coat decorated hard cooked eggs with aspic. Arrange in a row on top of lobster. Display will have more impact if eggs are all decorated the same way.

5. Coat lobster shell with aspic. Place on wedge-shaped bread socle (see Step 11, Method I). Select a decorating idea from Chapter XIV (see salmon section of that chapter). Lemon slices and baskets, tomato wedges and more hard cooked eggs fill in on platter.

First step in preparation of Lobster Modern (directions facing page) is modeling of a wedge of jellied russian salad on silver platter selected for this display.

Lobster medallions sliced on bias from tail meat are arranged on salad wedge in between slices of hard cooked eggs topped by ripe olive slices.

Bright red lobster claws and curly green parsley accent arrangement of elevated lobster medallions flanked by decorated hard cooked eggs. Boats hold tartar sauce. Method II.

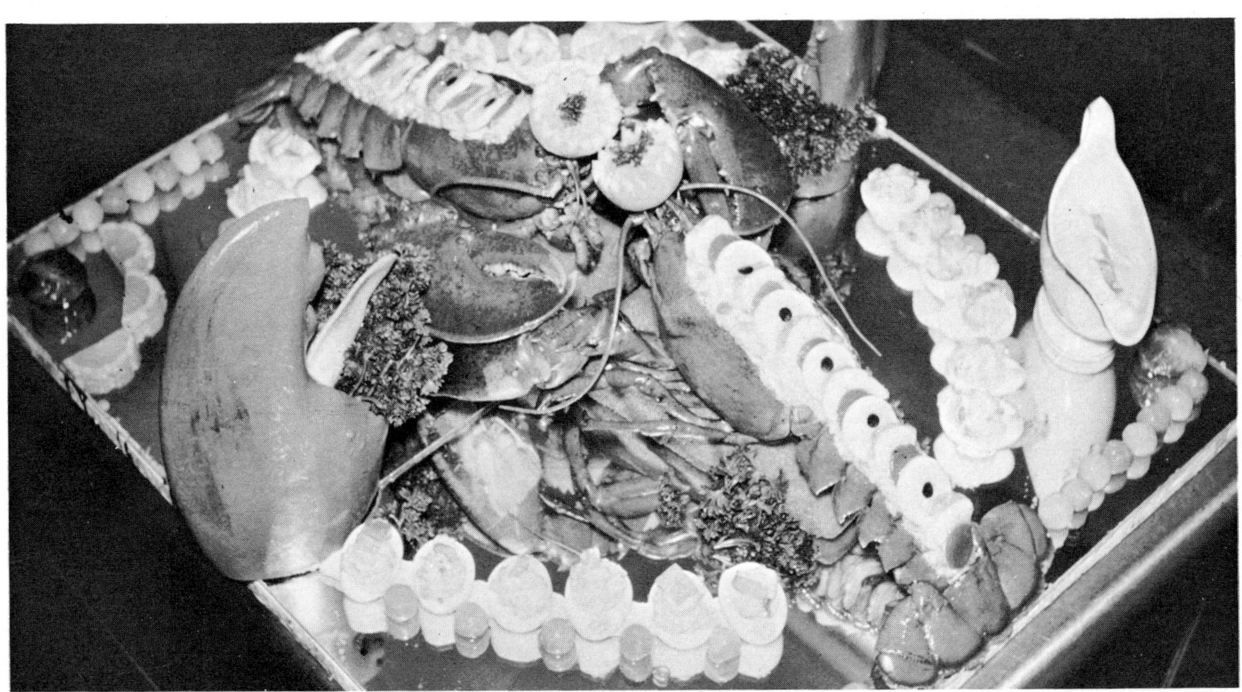

Method III—Modern

1. Take several 4 to 5 lb. lobsters apart, separating head section, tail and claws. Remove meat from claws as in Method II, Step 1 D, facing page.

2. Use shears to open up white underside of tail. Pull meat out in one piece.

3. Add gelatin to russian salad in which large pieces of lobster have been blended with mayonnaise. Salad must be quite stiff. Chill salad.

4. Shape a wedge-shaped socle of jellied russian salad and place it on platter to be used in making display. Shape one socle of salad for each lobster, making it long enough so tail meat can be displayed. Use a spatula dipped in hot water to shape jellied salad into smooth socle. Stiffen socle further by chilling in refrigerator or freezer.

5. Slice lobster tail. Alternate slices of lobster with slices of hard cooked eggs and ripe olives on top of jellied salad socle. Aspic coating may be added, if desired.

6. Add interest to arrangement with empty lobster shells and garnishes.

Note: This method is practical for cocktail parties if small forks are provided.

Method IV—with Brook Trout Chaud Froid

1. Break down 3 to 4 lb. lobsters as in Method II, Steps 1 A through 1 D. Fill with a favorite lobster salad.

2. Poach one 8 oz. brook trout for each lobster, keeping trout in upright position during poaching.

3. Cool trout, then skin with paring knife, or leave natural, and coat with chaud froid sauce. Leave head and tail uncoated.

4. Arrange lobsters on socles made of wedges of unsliced stale pullman bread either wrapped in foil or deep fried and left unwrapped. Place one decorated trout in upright position on each lobster, picking up trout with large spatula.

5. Slice lobster tails and large pieces of meat from claws in appetizing slices. Alternate these slices with sliced cucumbers and eggs on either side of the trout-topped lobster. Add other garnishes as desired. Sauce ravigotte, remoulade or similar mayonnaise-based cold sauce can be served as accompaniment.

Method V—Piece Montee

1. Remove head and tail from 3 to 5 lb. lobster. Slit tail and remove meat as in Method II, Steps 1 B, 1 C. Leave head shell in one piece.

2. Cut meat from tail and large pieces from claws into thin medallion slices. Place slices in a large ring mold or any fancy aspic timbale mold. For decorative touches, add truffles, leeks, pimientoes or slices of green vegetables.

3. Fill center of mold with lobster chunks and lobster salad, jellied russian salad or lobster mousse. Seal timbale with aspic and chill for several hours.

4. Fill tail shell of lobster as suggested above and coat with chaud froid sauce.

5. When timbale or ring mold has set, turn out on tray selected for service. Arrange filled shells on same platter.

6. Use yellow asparagus or hard cooked eggs as garnitures and offer a mayonnaise sauce as accompaniment.

Note: To add height to the mold, place a fancy brochette in the center.

Lobster with Brook Trout Chaud Froid is an easy variation of the Regular French Method of preparing lobster. It is accompanied by sauce ravigotte, remoulade or a similar mayonnaise-based cold sauce.

Shiny lobster shells provide gondola setting for lobster meat. Lemon slices add garnish and color too. Pineapple carts hold whole pieces of lobster to be enjoyed with cocktail sauce in center dish. Empty claws are colorful focal points.

A fancy brochette on a skewer adds height to the piece montee created with lobster meat in this aspic timbale mold. Mold also contains truffles, leeks, pimientoes and slices of green vegetables; has a center of lobster or russian salad.

Shellfish

Method VI—with Sole Fillets

1. Remove meat from a 2 to 3 lb. lobster from the underside. This will leave shell intact as seen from the top.

2. For each lobster, poach one sole fillet in white wine, then chill. Slice meat from lobster tail and arrange slices neatly across sole fillet, using hard cooked egg or cucumber slices or other garnishes between lobster slices.

3. Arrange 4 or 5 lobsters prepared in this fashion on platter, heads together in the center and tails spaced out evenly to complete circle. Coat all elements with lobster aspic.

4. Coat empty lobster shells with aspic and arrange with large pumpkin. Shells can seem to climb out of pumpkin or can be fastened with skewers so they lean against it.

5. An idea for decoration can be selected from Chapter XIV.

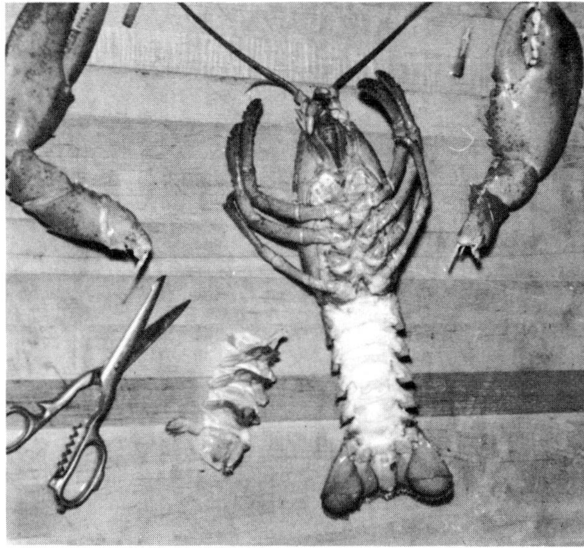

First step in preparation of Lobster with Sole Fillets is to twist off lobster claws and cut shell from underside so meat can be removed leaving shell intact on top.

All lobster meat is removed from tail and claws, shells are cleaned out and meat is sliced neatly. This arrangement requires four or five whole lobsters.

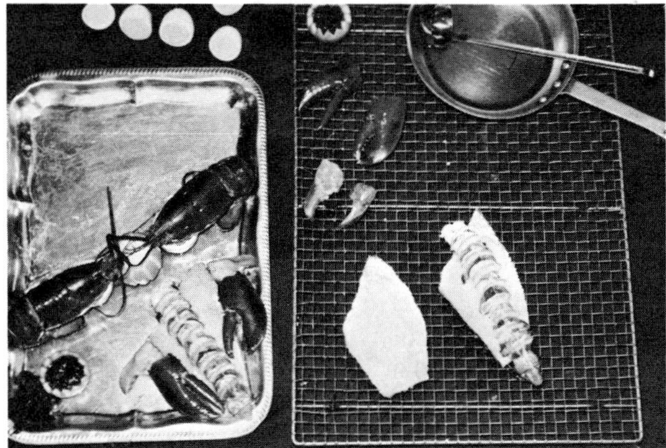

One sole fillet is poached in white wine, then chilled for each lobster. Sliced lobster meat is arranged on sole with hard cooked egg or cucumber slices.

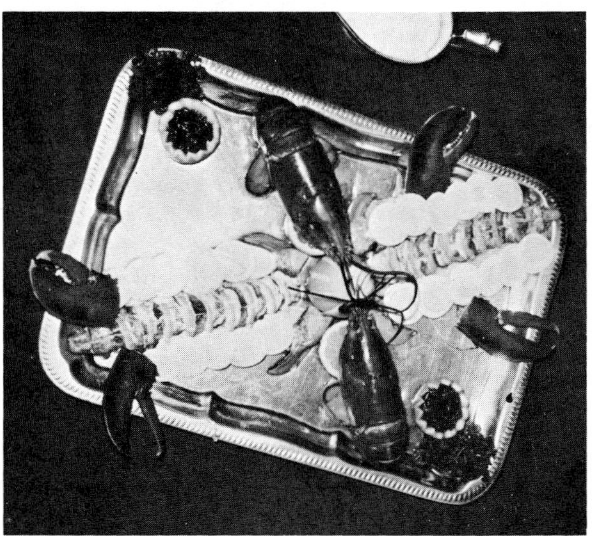

Lobster shells are arranged head to head crossed by line of sole fillets topped with lobster slices and garnishes. Hard cooked egg slices line lobster slices.

Method VII—Lobster Tower (requires 10 to 12 small lobsters weighing up to 3 lb.)

1. Remove tail meat as in Step 1, Method VI. Twist claws off.
2. Use french knife or saw to make a straight cut in large claws so meat can be pulled out in one piece.
3. A cylindrical shape 10 in. high, 8 in. in diameter at bottom and 2 in. at top should be made of one of the following: foil-wrapped styrofoam; tallow, or unsliced pullman bread (deep fried or unfried). Use gelatin to hold cylinder in place on round platter. This is the base of the lobster tower.
4. Place empty lobster shells, head down, against cylindrical base. Pull feelers back. Secure lobsters to base with toothpicks inserted under tail.
5. Place a round, slightly larger plate on the top of the base around which lobsters have been fastened. Fasten a foil-wrapped cabbage or styrofoam ball on plate with gelatin or glue.
6. Position meat of whole lobster tails against base above shells. Secure tails with toothpicks. They may also be held in place under edge of plate at top of base. Coat tails with aspic.
7. Lobster medallions or, shrimp or vegetable timbales can be used as a small piece montee at the top of this lobster tower.
8. Place open lobster claws holding lobster meat, that has been loosened so it can easily be picked up, around the base of the tower. Add to this garnishes and sauces suggested for other methods of serving lobster.

Decorated hard cooked eggs peek out between lobster shells on platter circled by lobster claws opened so meat in them can easily be picked up. Border is half lemon slices.

A whole pineapple is used to top base of this Lobster Tower. Meat is removed from tails and claws of 10 to 12 small lobsters. Shells are fastened head down against base.

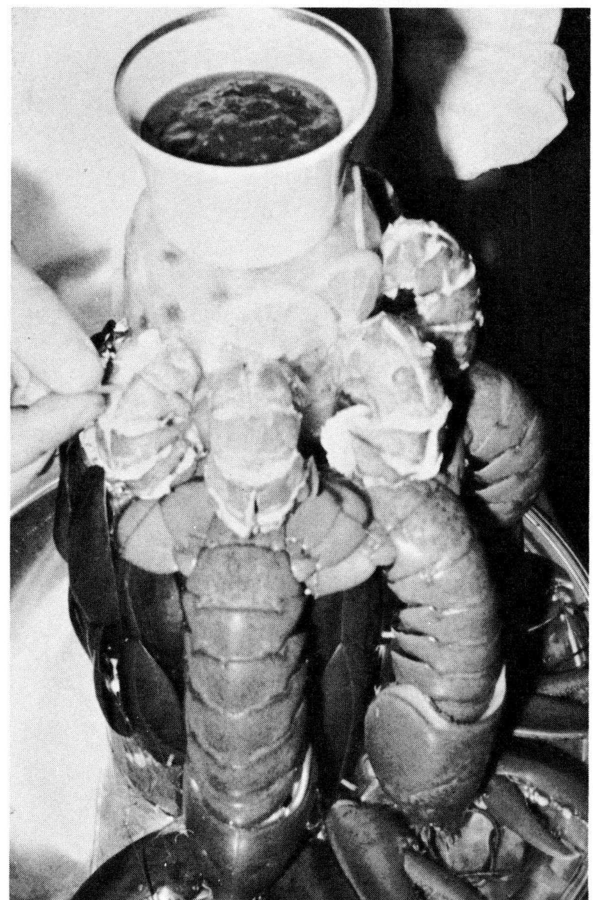

Meat taken out whole from lobster tails is fastened in place above shells with toothpicks. Plate can be placed over them or, as here, bowl of cocktail sauce can anchor empty shells.

Gay figures for a seafood buffet, these lobster men created from empty shells, plaster of paris, styrofoam and enamel paint can be used many times. Because they can be re-used the time spent in their construction can be justified where seafood buffets are scheduled frequently, or where such figures work into regular buffet table design.

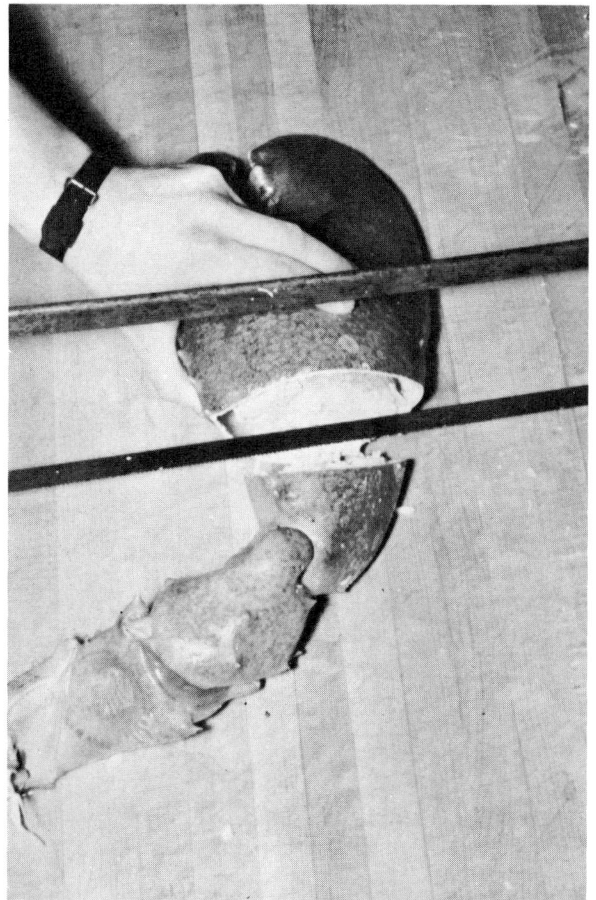

A saw is recommended to cut claws and other parts of shell into pieces that will fit into figures.

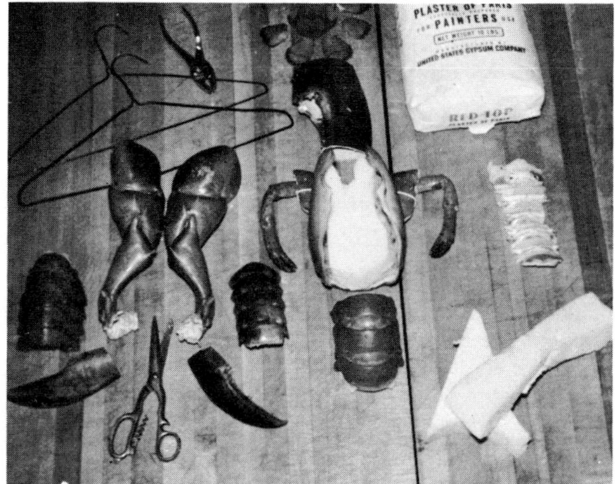

Before making any attempt to attach parts of figures, lay out all pieces cut from shells on table and arrange them in the order needed to create selected figure.

Method VIII—Creation of Lobster Figures

These figures require both time and patience as it takes from 2 to 3 hours to make a figure from a lobster shell. Part of this time is needed to permit drying of the plaster of paris used to hold the figure together. Once completed, however, lobster figures (indians, musicians, chefs, knight on horseback, hillbillies, roman chariots) can be used indefinitely as buffet centerpieces.

Each figure requires 2 whole lobsters. These lobsters should be boiled, as instructed previously.

1. Remove all meat from boiled lobster with lobster shears. Freeze meat if it is not to be used immediately.

Cut tail open on bottom; cut large claws above first joint; leave connecting inner section of claws whole; clean out entire head, removing 8 small claws.

2. Rinse all empty shells thoroughly with warm water to remove skins and remaining meat.

3. Store clean shells in water diluted with vinegar, ½ cup per quart of water.

Assembling Figures—Items needed for assembling figures include plaster of paris, styrofoam for supports, wire and wire clippers, and enamel paint; use cardinal red and burnt orange paint mixed to achieve proper color.

1. Lay out all empty lobster shells on table and arrange figure from shells so parts can be properly connected.

2. Connect pieces of shell to be used as legs and shoes with pieces of styrofoam and wire, letting the wire extend beyond shoes to be used as support on base when figure is completed. Cement parts together with plaster of paris and let dry for 20 minutes. Mix plaster of paris with vinegar, in small amounts, making new batches for each step.

3. Make upper part of body using lobster shell head and tail supported with a styrofoam cylinder. Run wire through to position arms, being sure to let ends of wire extend far enough to hold arms. Let dry for 20 minutes.

5. Cement shells for arms and hands together, using styrofoam and wire. Cement pieces of styrofoam under arms of figure. Let dry for 20 minutes.

6. After body and arms are dry and solid, attach arms to wires extending from body. Cement carefully and let dry for 20 minutes.

7. Fill base or frame to be used in supporting figure with plaster of paris.

8. Insert leg and shoe into base while plaster is wet, half submerging shoe so it will harden into the plaster of paris. Support from sides while material dries.

9. Make head by inserting end of one large claw, which has been sawed off to shorten sufficiently, into styrofoam holding body shells. Smooth plaster of paris at neck joint. Let dry for 20 minutes.

10. When shoes and legs are solid in hardened base, cement small pieces of styrofoam holding wires to upper end of legs. Wires will be inserted into body to help hold it in place on legs. Let dry for 20 minutes.

11. When both the body and the legs are completely dry, cement them together with more plaster of paris, adding as much extra as required to shape body as needed to create selected figure. Let dry for 20 minutes.

12. An appropriate hat or head-dress will help identify the figure. Easy to make are cowboy hats, head-dresses for indians or paper chefs' hats.

13. To make cowboy hats, cement all fantails from both lobster tails together to form a hat. Let dry and when dry attach on top of open claw which forms head.

14. After completed figure is dry and firm, sand exposed plaster of paris.

15. To paint figures, use a mixture of cardinal red and burnt orange enamel to simulate the color of boiled lobster on plaster of paris; use white lacquer for shirts; black lacquer for boots, hair, gloves, mustache (made from feelers), eyes, buttons, hat and bow tie.

16. Cover base with a mixture of dyed green coconut and dissolved gelatin. This will harden after a few days.

To make musical instruments: a. For drum, cement 2 tail shells together around styrofoam; use plaster of paris to complete drum shape. Paint to simulate drum.

b. For guitar, use 1 large claw, cut and 1 small claw.

c. For base, use a whole lobster head, a small claw and feelers for strings. When making lobster figures of musicians to play these instruments, be sure to position arms and hands properly for indicated instrument.

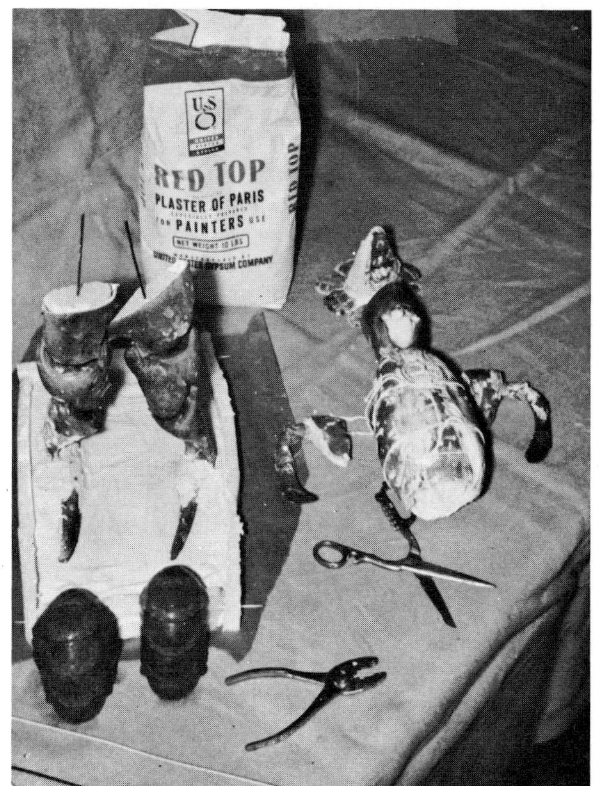

Shoes and legs are made from continuous piece of lobster shell and cemented onto base of plaster of paris. Wires run through shells are embedded in base and, at opposite end, are left extending so they can be fastened to upper part of body to help hold it in place.

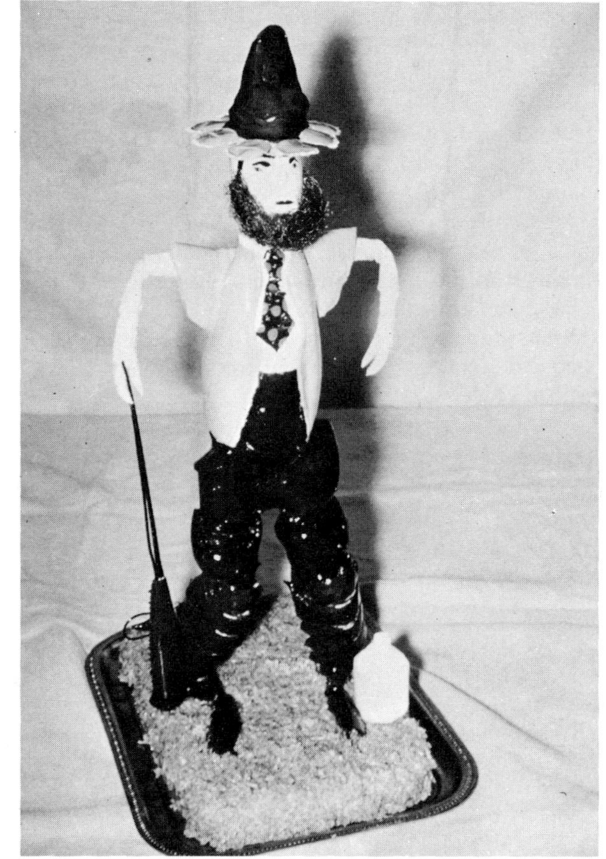

Completed figure steps out jauntily, adding action to buffet table. Figures are painted with mixture of burnt orange and cardinal enamel and lacquer; white for shirts, black for boots, hair, gloves, necktie, hat, bowtie, buttons, eyes.

Languste for the Buffet

The texture of languste meat is similar to lobster, but more closely resembles african or indian rock lobster tails. The languste does not have large front claws but, other than that difference, can easily be adapted to any of the presentation methods detailed for lobster.

When poaching a whole languste for a cold platter, tie it to a small board, or the insert rack of a fish poacher, to prevent curling. Tie the feelers in a vertical position to a wooden stick. A 50 gal. stock pot will take a languste and its 15 in. feelers easily. If one is not available, dip feelers first in boiling water til they turn red, then poach languste in bain marie or large pan.

Whole Alaskan King Crab

This large spectacular crustacean is relatively easy to prepare as a seafood display for the buffet. King crab to be displayed whole on the buffet should weigh from 10 to 15 lb. King crab is usually shipped from Alaska fully cooked and frozen. The cooked crab is light pink in color. King crab meat is a high cost item and should be handled carefully.

1. Let king crab thaw out partially.
2. With bottom of crab up, use a very sharp paring knife to open up all the claws and pull meat from them in whole pieces. Separate incisions will have to be made between the joints. This should be done carefully so that all the legs remain attached to the body.
3. Slice meat into uniform ¼-in. slices or medallions.
4. Place empty crab shell on large board or mirror with legs fanning out from body. Arrange crabmeat medallions in fan-shaped rows in between the crab legs. This makes it easy for diners to pick up. Crabmeat can be coated with aspic, if desired.

Note: The hollow crab shell can be saved and used again to create display. One-lb. packages of frozen crabmeat can be served with it. Shell must be frozen if it is stored. Since shell has a natural shine, it does not need an aspic coating.

To Garnish: Use lemon baskets filled with cocktail sauce or herb mayonnaise; opened cherrystone clams; various stuffed eggs; lemon slices; sprigs of fresh dill or parsley; stuffed tomato quarters.

Sauces to Serve: Caviar mayonnaise, russian dressing, remoulade sauce, plain mayonnaise, dill mayonnaise, cocktail sauce.

Languste is used in this display of Lobster Parisienne. Egg yolk cream holds lobster slices in place on empty shells. Lobster slices are decorated with pieces of pitted ripe olives or truffle cut-outs. Seafood salads, stuffed eggs, stuffed cucumbers, vegetable timbales and aspic croutons and chopped aspic are used to complete arrangement.

King Crab is usually available from Alaska, fully cooked and frozen. Place partially thawed crab bottom side up and use sharp paring knife to open claws and pull meat from them in whole pieces. Leave legs attached to body.

Slices of crabmeat are cut into ¼-in. medallions to be arranged in fan-shaped rows in front of empty crab shell. Lemon baskets hold spicy sauce.

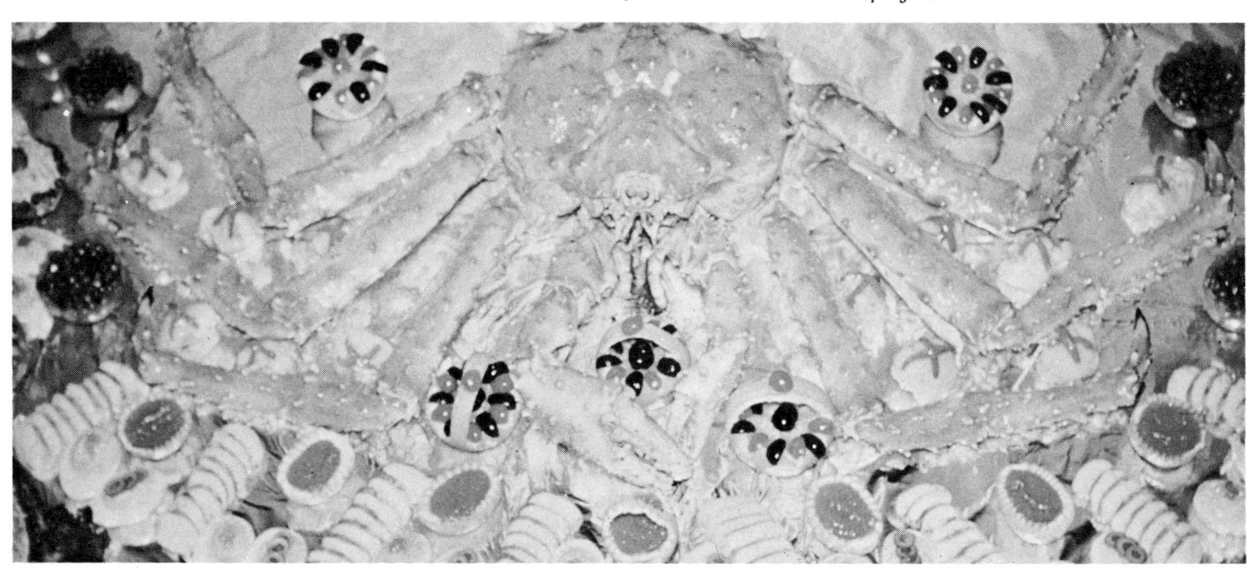

NOTES

NOTES

CHAPTER VIII Game, Game Birds

A full saddle of venison (rack and saddle) easily qualifies as the "glorious piece de resistance" on a cold buffet. In Cold Saddle of Venison Hubertus, the meat is surrounded by bartlett pear halves filled with currant jelly.

The saddle can be purchased separately for buffet preparation.

To Prepare Saddle of Venison

1. Remove skin of saddle carefully. Cut salt pork in fine strips. Use larding needle to pull strips of salt pork through venison, leaving about ¼ in. between strips.

2. Oil saddle well, season with salt and freshly ground pepper and place in a hot roasting pan in a 500°F. oven. Roast to medium rare which should take from 30 to 40 minutes depending on the thickness of the meat.

3. Cool saddle. Cut two fillets from centerbone. Remove bone.

4. Fill cavity with delicate wine-flavored liver mousse or pate and round off smoothly.

5. Slice fillets diagonally to make slices longer. Cover entire saddle with slices, placing larger slices in the center and toward the front.

6. Set covered saddle on wire rack and refrigerate for a short period.

7. Slice pate and cut circles from it with a 1-in. round cutter. Place circles on a tray or platter, decorate with a truffle cut-out and coat with a well-flavored wine aspic. Cool thoroughly.

8. With 1½ in. cutter, cut around aspic-coated pate medallions and place on top of the saddle of venison, alternating them with mandarin orange sections.

9. Place bartlett pear halves filled with currant jelly on wire rack. Add aspic decoration topped by half a maraschino cherry. Cover with sherry-flavored aspic.

10. Place saddle of venison on a large silver tray or on a gold-framed mirror; arrange pears in rows on either side. Edge tray with aspic cubes and chopped aspic.

11. Accompany saddle with cold cumberland sauce. (See cumberland sauce recipe, page 144.)

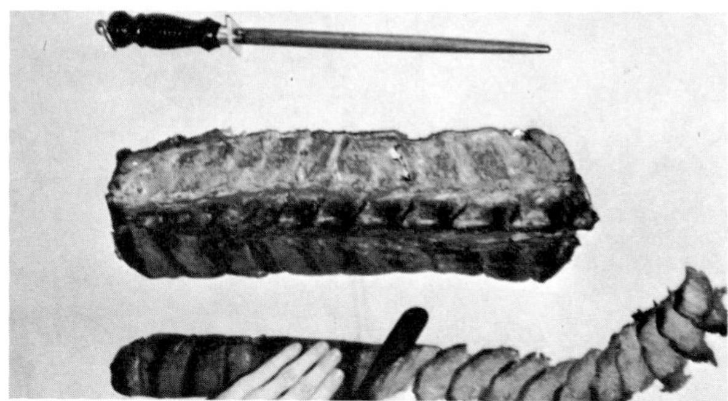

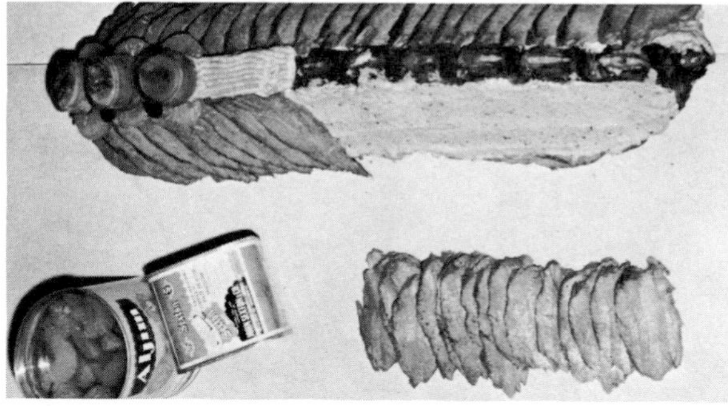

Below, Saddle of Venison for the buffet has a row of truffle-decorated pate slices edged with mushroom caps across the top. Pear halves filled with currant jelly under an aspic coating line sides of platter with timbale triangles at the front.

Left, removing loins is first step in preparing saddle of venison. Loins are sliced for later repositioning on saddle. Above, liver pate is used to cover carcass and hold slices of venison for easy service. Start positioning slices from back.

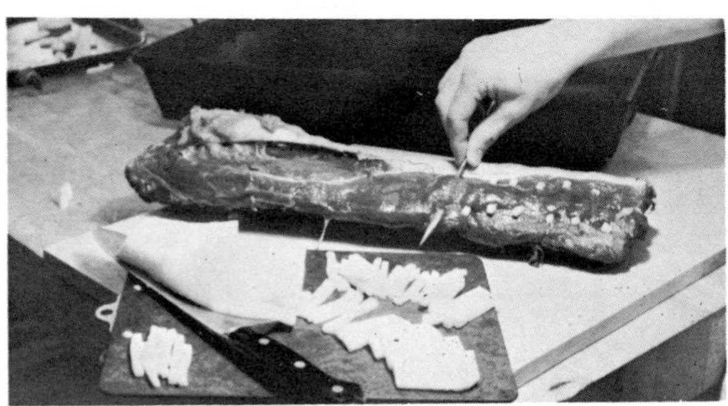

Slim strips of salt pork are threaded through saddle every quarter inch with larding needle. Saddle is oiled, seasoned and roasted to medium rare.

To Prepare Saddle of Venison Hubertus

With saddle and rack of venison available commercially, it is possible to feature this unusual roast in or out of season. First step in preparation is to remove skin carefully from saddle. Saddle is then larded with strips of salt pork. After saddle is oiled thoroughly, seasoned with salt and freshly ground pepper, it should be placed in a hot roasting pan and hot oven (500°F.) for 30 to 40 minutes only, to roast to medium rare.

When cooled, saddle is coated with pate, loins are sliced and slices replaced. *(See pictures preceding page.)* After a short period of refrigeration saddle is ready for decoration. Slices of pate, decorated with a truffle cut-out and covered with wine aspic, are placed along the center of the saddle with mandarin orange sections.

Pear halves with the colorful addition of jelly and cherries are arranged in a bed of chopped aspic to complete the platter.

Pheasant

Use the same methods to cook and carve pheasant for buffet presentation as suggested for capon and turkey in Chapter V.

Roast is cooled, then filets or loins are cut from sides and carefully sliced. Pate mousse is used to fill in bone structure and smoothed off carefully.

Here a gold framed mirror is used to set off an elegant arrangement of Cold Saddle of Venison Hubertus. Frame has interlining of aspic triangles.

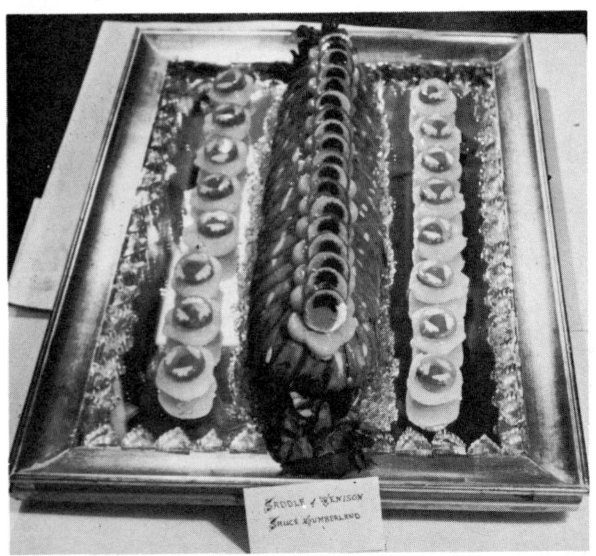

Above, saddle is re-covered with slices cut from filets. Larger, heavier slices are placed in the center and along the front of the saddle. Below, 1½-in. cutter is used to slice out pate circles for top of venison. Circles are decorated and coated with aspic.

Left, Glaced English Grouse, a rare offering, displayed in an eye-catching arrangement climaxed by checkerboard design centered on each bird.

Below, two sliced pheasants flank a centerpiece of pineapple hollowed out to hold melon balls. Small glass dishes holding more melon balls with red grapes complete platter. Aspic triangles in upright position line edge of platter. The sliced pheasants are decorated with pineapple sections and an ornament of fluted mushroom and truffle design.

Pheasants for buffet service should be as large as can be obtained. Breasts are the largest, most tender and preferred part of the bird; drumsticks tend to be tough.

To coat pheasant, prepare brown chaud froid using residue from pan in which birds are roasted.

Fried potato nests and quail (when available) are effective additions to platters of pheasant.

Pheasant with plumage is sure to intrigue buffet patrons. Equally exotic in this arrangement are quail, decorated and displayed in bread baskets. Vegetable timbales are placed between quail. Sliced pheasant is elevated on chaud froid coated socle for heightened effect. Plumage is carefully separated from food.

Other Game Birds

Small game birds, such as quail and woodcock, as well as rock cornish game hens and small chickens are served whole. Half a breast of quail usually is the portion per person when served on a cold platter.

Small whole birds can be added to presentations of larger birds for the creation of a conversation-making game display. When whole birds are used this way, they should have brown aspic or chaud froid coats. It is easy to dip small whole birds in aspic or chaud froid when they are held by the end of a drumstick.

Right, game hens are placed on their backs with a pear half positioned between the tiny drumsticks. Contributing color to the platter are orange segments and cherries placed in each pear half and red gelatin filled orange shell wedges.

Peacock, the bird in central position on this platter, is not often scheduled for American buffets. A capon would be a satisfactory substitute. Game hens elevated on potato nests surround the central bird.

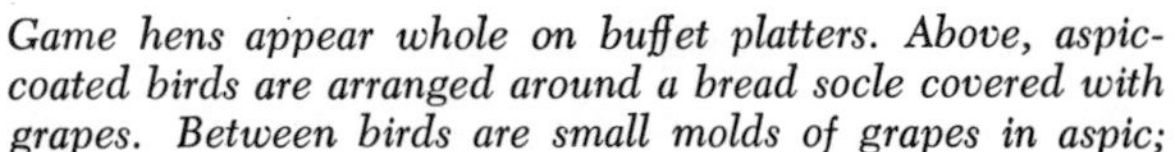

Game hens appear whole on buffet platters. Above, aspic-coated birds are arranged around a bread socle covered with grapes. Between birds are small molds of grapes in aspic; scalloped half orange slices holding mandarin orange segments border platter. Above, game hens with shiny aspic coats are placed around a noodle basket holding black grapes.

Above, trim leg bones of rock cornish game hens, then band with aluminum foil to keep legs, wings close to body, plump breasts. Left, put birds in buttered pan with chopped onion, carrot, celery, bay leaf, peppercorns.

After buttering breasts generously, roast game hens in 450°F. oven 40 to 45 minutes. Chill thoroughly in refrigerator. Coat birds with aspic and serve with tiny tarts of short pastry filled with chestnut puree and feature as Rock Cornish Perigueux. Game hens are displayed on their backs with fruit and jelly garniture between drumsticks.

NOTES

CHAPTER IX
FRUIT, CHEESE

Large watermelon baskets are the most common carved fruits appearing on buffet tables. The watermelon basket has two advantages. The fruit scooped from it in balls or cubes will provide the major portion of fruit needed to fill it. In summer, when melons are seasonal, the watermelon basket is also a low cost source of fruit. While melons can be obtained at other seasons, they become more costly.

Watermelons can be carved in several ways: as either horizontal or vertical containers, a viking ship, baby carriage, outrigger, whale or fish; they can be scored, provided with handles or made into a castle.

Watermelons destined to be carved as centerpiece-containers should be fresh, with a rich green rind and no bruises.

To Carve Watermelon

1. Cut a ½-in. slice from side or end of melon so it will rest flat on platter; it will take a large knife to slice melon.

2. Mark points to be carved on rind with pencil.

3. If outside of rind is to be scored, it should be done with paring knife before fruit is scooped from inside. Grill scoring is more time-consuming, but it gives the basket a more attractive appearance.

4. When melons are carved a day in advance, wrap tightly in transparent wrap. Do not fill melon until time for service.

To Make Vertical Watermelon Basket:

1. Cut 2 parallel slices 1½ in. apart from end of watermelon to center. Cut away 2 side sections, leaving slice for tall handle.

2. With a channel knife, score skin 1½ in. from top of basket, using string as marker. Score sides of melon with deep crisscross lines to make grill.

3. With large french ball cutter, scoop out holes in the rind edge at ¾-in. intervals.

4. Remove center of melon with a large french ball scoop, leaving a shell about 1-in. thick. Trim meat on handle close to rind and score handle.

5. Make balls of canteloup and use them to fill holes in rind at top of basket.

6. Make small watermelon balls or use blueberries to fill the holes scooped out of the side of the melon.

Fruit Filling—Sprinkle sweetened mixed fruits and berries generously with kirsch or eau de vie de framboise. Garnish top with circles of melon balls and berries and overlapping slices of strawberries and citrus fruit. Decorate center with whole strawberries and mint leaves. Cognac, rum, liqueurs and white wines may also be used.

Fruit for dessert in an eye-catching buffet arrangement. Carved watermelon baskets with handles, hollowed pineapples, with tops intact to supply lids, and grapefruit baskets hold liqueur flavored melon balls. Black grapes provide dark contrast, as placed here in front of the pale gold grapefruit baskets of pastel melon balls.

Strawberries are the accent in these fruit arrangements, topped with a sprightly touch of mint leaves. The scored and scalloped vertical watermelon basket holds fruit in a carefully patterned display. The scalloped edges of the basket are filled with pale melon balls. Blueberries fill holes carved in row just below rim of melon basket. In grapefruit baskets surrounding water melon, sliced strawberries alternate with melon balls.

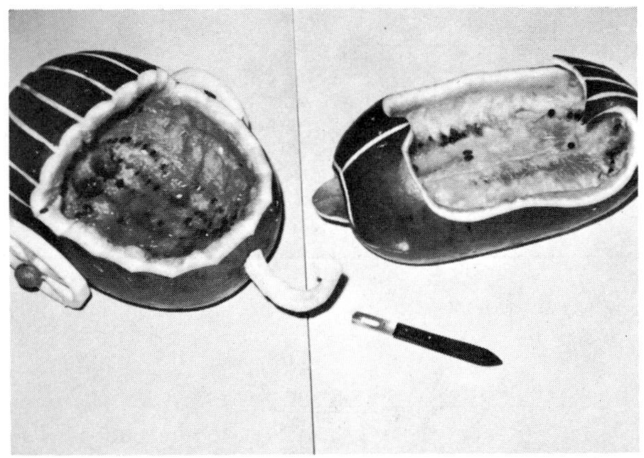

Above, watermelon cart rests on carved turnip wheels held by cherries. Cart pull is turnip too. Whale is carved with flipped-up tail. Melon skin is deeply scored for both figures. Below, peach twins with whole clove features rest on sherbet lining of this carved baby carriage. Wheels are cut from yellow turnips. Fancy picks hold grapes around edge of cart.

To Make Horizontal Watermelon Basket:

1. Follow procedure outlined on preceding page in preparing watermelon for carving into horizontal basket, except work with melon in horizontal position. Cut 2 parallel slices 1½-in. apart and from 2 to 3 in. deep in center of top half of large watermelon. Remove shallow sections of melon on either side, leaving the 1½-in. slices for the handles.

2. With a channel knife, score skin 1½ in. from top of basket, using string as marker. Score sides of melon with deep crisscross lines to make grill.

3. With a large french ball cutter, scoop out holes in the rind edge at ¾-in. intervals.

4. Remove center of melon with a large french ball scoop, leaving a shell about 1-in. thick. Trim meat on handle close to rind and score handle.

5. Make balls of canteloup and fill holes in rind at top of basket. Make small watermelon balls or use blueberries to fill holes scooped out of side of melon.

Above right, carved basket holds watermelon balls and a few blueberries for contrast. From tray around basket, whole apples, oranges, pears can easily be selected. White grapes in small bunches are massed for maximum effect with these dessert fruits. Below, still another formal pattern for fruit in a carved melon basket with dark shiny leaves as background. Fruits in basket present varying shapes; are arranged to contrast light and dark. Scalloped edges are filled with melon balls. Strawberries are used whole and as sliced row in upright position between rows of melon balls.

Hawaiian-inspired fruit arrangement combines two outriggers elevated on oranges with a plain half watermelon holding fruits arranged in a striking pattern. Outriggers each hold pineapple made into bird of paradise. These pineapple shells hold more easily picked-up fruits. Flowers fill empty spaces in the outriggers.

To Prepare Grapefruit Baskets

In first step at right, grapefruit are cut in half and sections of fruit are removed, then remaining membranes are carefully scraped loose and removed. With sharp knife, cut edge of grapefruit into scallops. Make handles for baskets from grapefruit skin.

Each grapefruit basket is placed on leaf of lettuce, romaine or chicory on salad plate and filled with whatever assortment of fruit is preferred. In picture below, baskets are being filled from bowls of such fruits as honeydew wedges, canteloup balls, orange and grapefruit sections, bits of apple, pear and pineapple and whole grapes. A selection of these fruits could be mixed first and then dipped into baskets to speed preparation.

Below right, fresh strawberries and mint leaves are centered on top of baskets. These baskets are equally popular as an appetizer or a dessert.

If grapefruit baskets are intended to be used as dessert, add a few drops of kirschwasser to the fruits.

Cantaloup, Honeydew, Spanish and Other Small Melons

Use techniques described preceding page (handles are usually not practical). Cantaloup cannot be stored for more than a few hours. Place carved melons on ice carvings to keep them chilled.

Fruit and Cheese

Platters of fresh fruit to be eaten out of hand with cheese cubes or small cheese slices are an easily prepared buffet dessert.

Grapes, pears and melon balls on picks are an excellent foil for gruyere, swiss, edam, cheddar, port salut and smoky cheese. Mold ripened cheeses (such as blue and roquefort) and semi-soft cheeses, (brie, camembert and beursault) add a piquant spread to crisp apple slices, or spiced sechel pears.

Three ways to carve small melons include shell presentation, far left, with carved turnip rose; baby carriage with watermelon handle and baby to go in it made from peach head with clove features and decorated coverlet; near right, scalloped basket with unusual handle. Small carved melons should be kept on ice carving to keep them properly chilled.

Flag markers identifying cheese on a tray make it easy for patrons to select the cheese they know and want, or to try small bits and know which to return for more of. This lazy susan fruit-centered cheese display has the glamor touch of grape shears. Extra plates and knives and packaged crackers round out the service.

It takes a sharp knife to shape a pineapple. The varied presentations possible illustrated here include: at far left, a half shell with foliage left on; pineapple with side carved out to hold canapes on picks, shown empty and filled; whole pineapple with top sliced off and cart made from two pineapples.

Cheeses are displayed separately carved for easy self service. Accompanying fruit is on pedestal as centerpiece. Each cheese is clearly identified.

To Carve Pineapple

Pineapples should be fresh and not over-ripe for carving. They can be quickly carved into stands (for picks holding ham cubes, pineapple balls, etc.); carts (using slices from a second pineapple for wheels); bird houses; and with a special cutter, one-half pineapple can be made into a bird of paradise.

NOTES

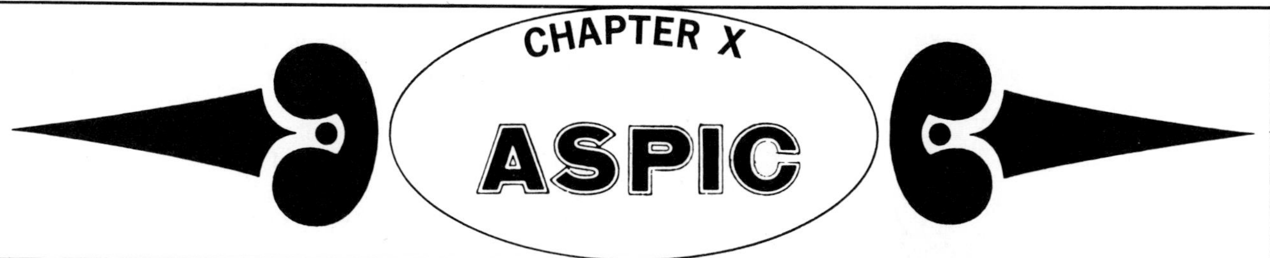

Before starting to learn the techniques of aspic making, the terms associated with aspic should be clearly understood. Jellied coatings require three kinds of product: fruit flavored gelatin, plain gelatin and meat jelly or aspic.

Fruit flavored gelatin is made by combining plain gelatin with fruits. It is available in many colors and flavors, comes packaged in granulated form. Fruit flavored gelatin is seldom used to coat meats, poultry or fish, with one exception: in preparing some fruit-decorated cold hams.

Unflavored gelatin which is colorless, is a granulated product packaged in boxes and cans which is used to stiffen meat aspic. It is the gelatin that makes meat aspic set or jell when it is refrigerated.

Aspic, rather than meat jelly, is the professional term for the coating used on many buffet displays. Since meat jelly can be any liquid or residue from the roasting or poaching process that has congealed, such jellies cannot qualify as aspics.

Aspics can be made from meat jellies, but there are additional steps required since aspic must be crystal clear and have exactly the right amount of gelatin.

A true aspic is made from a rich meat, poultry or fish stock. It is savory in flavor, clear and, after sufficient refrigeration, will become jellied, yet not rubbery.

Five methods of aspic preparation are listed in the pages that follow:

Method I—Modern Method

The five factors that are basic to modern aspic making are: stock, reduction, adding gelatin, clarification and straining. Essential information on each is given here:

Stock—A good strong stock should be prepared in advance, carefully strained and with as much fat skimmed off as possible. Stock should be kept cool.

Reduction—Wine or vinegar, whichever is indicated, is boiled with bouquet garni and shallots to produce a spicy essence for the aspic. Mixture is boiled for 5 to 10 minutes until liquid is reduced by half.

Estimating Gelatin Content—Because stock is made by boiling bits of meat and bones, it contains some gelatin to start with. How much gelatin stock has accumulated can be determined by putting about a spoonful of the stock in the refrigerator for a few minutes. The usual amount of gelatin added is 8 oz. (about a cup) per gal. of stock. If refrigerated spoonful of stock becomes quite thick in a few minutes, ¾ cup of gelatin will be enough. If it does not jell at all, add 1½ cups of gelatin. Gelatin added must be unflavored.

Clarification—To clear the stock to desired transparency, make a mirepoix to add to it. This is made of 2 lb. raw ground beef, 1 cup egg whites and juice of 2 lemons combined with 1 cup diced or ground carrots, 1 cup diced celery, 1 diced onion, 1 tbsp. parsley flakes. Mix ingredients together and chill well. Add to simmering stock. These blended ingredients will rise to the top, drawing to them all solids in the stock. The mirepoix plus the stock solids will form a raft floating on top of the simmering stock. This is easy to remove and when removed, will leave stock clear.

Straining—Clean utensils are imperative for this process. Use a china cap or sieve covered with four folds of cheese cloth or a paper strainer. Remove part of raft described above, and ladle remaining liquid slowly into strainer. Slow pouring keeps small particles from being pushed through strainer.

TO MAKE 1 GAL. STOCK FOR ASPIC

Ingredients

Chicken or Beef Stock, light	1 gal.
White Wine or Sherry	1 cup
Bouquet Garni	
Mirepoix made of:	
Egg Whites	1 cup
Ground Beef, coarse	½ lb.
Lemons	juice from 2
Gelatin, variable	1 cup approx. or 6-8 oz. weight

Method

1. Measure out 1 gal. stock. Keep cool.
2. Combine vinegar or wine and bouquet garni and boil for reduction. Watch carefully so it does not boil away too much.
3. Determine gelatin content of stock by refrigerating a spoonful for a few minutes. Add powdered unflavored gelatin to cold stock, stirring with wire whip to dissolve gelatin.
4. Heat stock and gelatin slightly to completely dissolve gelatin.
5. Add reduced wine or vinegar-spice liquid.
6. Add mirepoix (the mixture that clarifies stock by drawing all solid bits and foam to it). Stir mixture into stock.
7. Let stock simmer for 45 to 60 minutes until stock is clear. Do not stir after raft of mirepoix forms on the top. Stock burns easily; simmering in double boiler will prevent this.
8. Strain through wire cap or sieve containing four folds of cheese cloth or paper strainer insert. Ladle stock into strainer slowly. Remove fat globules from stock with absorbent paper. Fat left in aspic causes cloudiness and makes it difficult to use aspic for coating. Remove additional fat next day by rinsing top of solid aspic quickly with boiling water.

To Make Fish Aspic:

1. Substitute court bouillon for stock mentioned above, but follow method given above with these exceptions—(a) use 8 oz. of powdered unflavored gelatin since fish stock has little natural gelatin content; (b) always use a good white wine in the reduction, never vinegar; (c) do not use ground meat in the mirepoix—use 2 cups of egg

In this set-up arranged for aspic making are: top center-stock; center—plain gelatin, egg whites, ground vegetables; bottom—ground beef, pepper.

whites for each gallon of court bouillon, add white onions, lemon slices and sprigs of parsley and dill.

COURT BOUILLON

Yield: 1 gal.

Ingredients

Water	7 pt.
Vinegar, cider	1 cup
Onions, fine dice	¾ cup
Celery, fine dice	½ cup
Carrots, fine dice	½ cup
Salt	1 oz.
Peppercorns, crushed	1 tsp.
Parsley Sprigs	to taste
Whole Cloves	½ tsp.
Bay Leaf	1
Lemon, cut in thin slices	½

Method

Combine all ingredients and bring to boil. Reduce heat and simmer ½ hr. Strain and adjust seasoning.

Method II—Short Cut

Using this short cut method, an acceptable meat aspic can be prepared in 10 minutes to take care of emergency situations: Take 1 qt. can of jellied consomme warmed up to room temperature and mix with it 1½ oz. unflavored gelatin. Whip till foamy, then place in bain marie until clear. Using the same method, jellied madrilene can be prepared for use as pink tomato aspic.

Method III—Old-Fashioned Procedure

Before powdered or leaf gelatin became available, the procedure for making aspic was more complex. While aspic is rarely made this way any more, it is described here to familiarize users of this cookbook with the procedure.

Stock, made of pig's and calf's heads, pig's and calf's feet, pig rind, veal bones as well as other bones, vegetables, vinegar and spices, is simmered for about 2 days. During the long simmering, the natural gelatin from the pig's feet is dissolved into the stock. Stock is reduced by about one-third and is then usable as aspic. Stock will be very cloudy and clarification is essential.

Method IV—Artificial or Mock Aspic

The product is not designed to be eaten. Instead, it is for use: with dummy hams in teaching students how to apply aspic; for coating dummy hams for buffet display; for coating foods for culinary exhibitions which are not to be judged for flavor.

TO MAKE MOCK ASPIC

Combine 1 gal. of cold water with 8 oz. unflavored gelatin. Whip until foamy and hold in bain marie until clear. This will not be crystal clear, but will be satisfactory for specific uses listed above.

Method V—Instant

An aspic powder, imported from Switzerland, can be made up into a neutrally flavored aspic which can be applied to both meat and seafood products. This is a speedy method for preparing a crystal clear aspic.

TO MAKE INSTANT ASPIC

Mix 8 oz. of powder with 1 gal. cold water, using wire whip. Add sherry or other wine for aroma. Place in bain marie for about 10 minutes at which time it will be clear and ready to apply. It can be applied like any other aspic.

Points To Remember

1. Meat aspic can be stored up to 3 weeks in a refrigerator or walk-in box when placed in a covered stainless steel container. Always use a ladle or container when dipping aspic out of container it is stored in; never touch refrigerated aspic.
2. Only light shade of food coloring should be added to aspic; greens or blues are not good colors for meat aspics.
3. Never use a fish aspic to coat meat or poultry items; however, chicken aspic can be used to coat tuna or salmon and the flavor will be excellent.
4. If leaf gelatin is specified for aspic making, add 48 leaves of gelatin for each 1 gal. of stock. Soak leaves in a small amount of cold stock before dissolving in the gallon container.

Aspic Applications

Buffet foods which are usually coated with aspic include all fresh salmon and other whole fish, turkey, capon, pheasants, ducks, quail, pates, smoked tongue, lobsters, suckling pig, galantines and molds used as piece montee which are lined with aspic. There are also certain canapes usually coated with aspic.

Aspic is added to these foods to (a) preserve the appearance and flavor of the cold meat or fish; (b) add a glossy sheen that makes these focal pieces on the buffet as attractive and appetizing looking as possible, an effect heightened by proper illumination; (c) preserve cold platters which have a storage life, when refrigerated after being coated, of up to 2 days; (d) preserve foods coated with chaud froid. Any chaud froid coated piece has to have a final coat of aspic.

To Apply Aspic to Decorated Capon (or Other Food)

1. Capon, and any other food item to be coated with aspic, should be thoroughly chilled. If space in a freezer is available, put capon in for 8 to 10 minutes. Be sure to remove it at the end of that time as a bird or other food item that stays in the freezer too long will no longer have a presentable surface.

If freezer space is not available, chilling to the desired temperature will take three times as long in a refrigerator. Aspic adheres to a chilled surface much better than to a warm one.

2. Place chilled capon on wire rack with a clean pan beneath rack. Pan is to hold aspic overflow which can be re-used. Also arrange all decorations and garnishes for the capon or other food item on a wire rack with pan underneath. This second rack should be conveniently located so that it is easy to add garnishes and decorations.

Skilled workers can do aspic coating of foods after they are assembled on platters or trays for service. The inexperienced worker is apt to have too much aspic running onto the platter which will spoil its appearance.

3. Dip a small quantity (about 1 qt.) of chicken aspic from container in refrigerator and place it in bain marie to heat and melt from the solid state resulting from refrigeration. Since aspic must be cool for application, place container (preferably a stainless steel bowl, never plastic) in crushed ice or in freezer and stir slowly with ladle until it reaches a syrup-like consistency.

4. Carefully ladle syrup-like aspic over capon; do not pick up any bubbles that appear in the liquid aspic. Be careful not to splash aspic on; work slowly, carefully coating the entire bird.

5. The moment aspic starts to congeal, stop applying it to bird as it will become lumpy. Aspic melting procedure should be repeated, then chilling and application started again.

If Aspic Will Not Stay On:

Check these four possible reasons for runny aspic:

1. The aspic is too warm, not syrupy enough.
2. The capon (or other food) is not chilled enough.
3. Not enough gelatin in aspic.
4. Fat in the aspic.

How Many Coats?

The first coat may be all that's needed. Check to see if capon or other food item is well covered. If it is, no more aspic coats need to be applied.

Decorating Pointers

1. When slices of capon breast or other meats are to be placed on a carcass or base, dip each slice in aspic so it will stick to the carcass. This cannot be done with fish.

2. Tiny decorations made of truffles, leeks, bits of vegetables or fruit, should also be dipped in liquid aspic before they are placed on meat, poultry or fish displays.

Note: Coating items with aspic is sometimes criticized as a costly, time consuming procedure. Actually, aspic (and chaud froid sauce as well) is only pliable for 30 to 60 seconds and procedure should be speedy to get most use from coatings while at proper temperature.

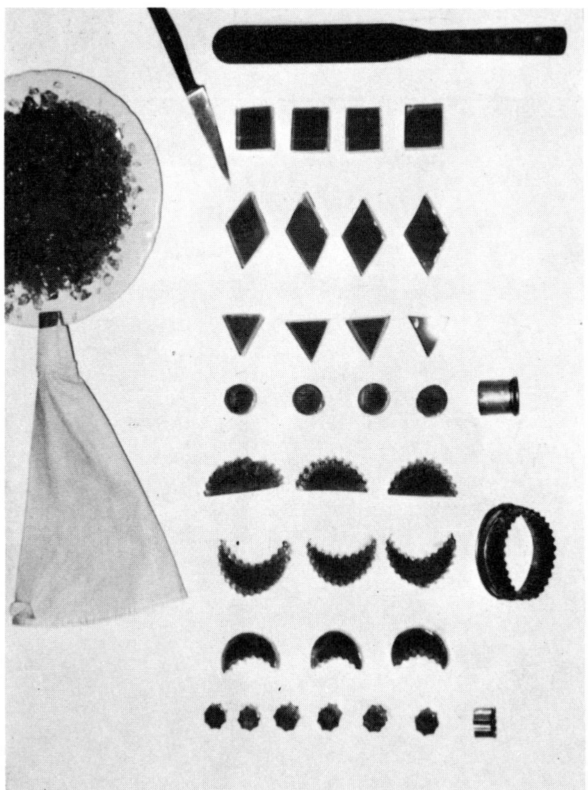

Above are shapes cut from solid aspic sheets. These make excellent borders and background for platters.

Aspic is used to make vegetable timbales like these, with a clear coating of aspic covering the finished arrangement. For directions, see Chapter XV.

Cutting Aspic to Use as Decorative Garnish

Pour liquid aspic about ½-in. thick into a flat, level pan. Refrigerate until solid aspic sheet is formed. Aspic can then be cut into a variety of shapes for decorative borders or garnishes on platter for buffet display.

Dip paring knife or metal cutters in hot water before cutting aspic with them and edges of aspic shapes will be neat and smooth. Geometric shapes, half moons, flowers can all be cut out of aspic sheets. To lift aspic shapes from pan, use a flexible spatula.

Finely chopped aspic mixed with water in a pastry tube, can be piped around the bases of display pieces.

NOTES

CHAPTER XI Chaud Froid

Chaud froid sauce conceals when it is used as a coating, unlike aspic which adds a see-through layer to whatever it covers. Chaud froid provides a rich covering that is smooth and glossy to meat, poultry and seafood arrangements.

A chaud froid coating will:

1. Spark up the appearance of what would be a drab food item. (Poached capon becomes bright, smooth and glossy when coated with chaud froid.)

2. Preserve basic flavors and prevent drying. (Turkey slices gain moisture and flavor when coated with chaud froid.)

Meat chaud froid sauce should be used only on meat; seafood chaud froid only on seafood.

WHITE CHAUD FROID SAUCE

Yield 5 pt. sauce, enough to cover several display pieces i. e., 1 large chicken or turkey, 2 hams, 1 tongue with sauce left over

Ingredients

Butter or Shortening	1 cup
Flour	¾ cup
Hot Milk	1½ pt.
Hot Strong Chicken or Veal Stock	1½ pt.
Gelatin	3 oz.
Cold Chicken Stock, to dilute	1 cup
Light Cream	1 cup
Mayonnaise	¾ cup
Salt	2 tsp.
Sherry Wine	½ cup
Liquid Pepper Sauce	few drops

Method

Melt butter over slow fire, add flour and make roux. Cook for 10 to 15 min. Cool. Slowly add hot milk, chicken stock and diluted gelatin, stirring to a smooth consistency. Bring mixture to boil, then cool. When cool, add cream, mayonnaise, salt, sherry wine and liquid pepper sauce.

When cooled well, sauce is ready to use. This sauce does not need to be placed on ice, it will work well if it is kept in a cool place. Items to be covered, chicken, ham, tongue, etc., should also be very cold. Use several light thin coatings.

If this chaud froid sauce is to be used for covering fish, substitute fish stock or court boullion for the veal or chicken stock.

Method I—Mayonnaise Chaud Froid or Colle:

This is the original chaud froid sauce discovered by the ancient Romans and refined in classical French cuisine. It has superior storage quality especially when compared to more starchy chaud froids which tend to discolor around the edges within 24 hours.

Formula:

1. Two parts regular mayonnaise and 1 part heavy aspic (with extra gelatin) from poultry, seafood or lobster.

2. *Alternate Formula:* One part aspic, one part mayonnaise, one part heavy cream.

Method: Keep aspic liquid at lukewarm temperature.

In a stainless steel bowl, mix mayonnaise and aspic together with a wire whip. Whip until all lumps have disappeared and mixture is smooth. Air bubbles will disappear and should be of no concern.

Strain mixture through cheese cloth into a second stainless steel bowl. Stainless steel bowl permits ingredients to cool faster than plastic.

Since bubbles form very easily in this chaud froid, do not whip violently close to time for using it. Let sauce settle at room temperature and if air bubbles appear as sauce begins to congeal, remelt chaud froid before continuing application.

White chaud froid coating on display pieces provides background that sets off designs planned as focal point or to set theme for the buffet. Below left, scene on whole salmon is made from truffle sheets. Below right, ham mousse displays name of honor guest spelled out in truffle sheet letters inside wreath of green leaves.

Note: Mayonnaise colle de poisson is made by the same method but uses court bouillon or fish fume for aspic.

Method II—Brown Chaud Froid Sauce

Combine 1 part glace de viande (reduced brown stock) and 1 part tomato sauce or catsup. Add gravy color booster and red food coloring to secure desired color; add sherry wine for flavor. Add gelatin if chaud froid is not jelling.

Make sure glace de viande (brown stock) used does not have excess fat in it; if it does, it will not congeal. Handle as in Method I.

Method III—Cream Sauce Chaud Froid

This is not as appealing a coating, but can be used for hams and poultry; it works well on dummy hams.

Combine 1 gal. medium cream sauce, 1 cup gelatin dissolved in 1 qt. water or white stock and 2½ cups mayonnaise.

Handle as in Method I.

Method IV—Cream Cheese Chaud Froid Sauce:

This recently developed version does not require any of the conventional bases and can be prepared in a very short time. This coating can only be used on smoked meats and fresh or smoked salmon to which it adds an intriguing flavor.

CREAM CHEESE CHAUD FROID

Ingredients

Cream Cheese	2 lb.
White Stock or Water	1½ qt.
Gelatin	⅓ cup

Method

Soften cream cheese in stainless steel bowl in steamer or bain marie. Do not attempt to soften cheese in oven.

Dissolve gelatin in stock or water in bain marie. When cream cheese has softened sufficiently, add gelatin dissolved in stock or water. Work into cream cheese with wire whip till smooth; to thin add more liquid. Strain through cheese cloth.

Note: Do not mix milk or sweet cream with this sauce. The acid in the cream cheese will cause a breakdown and consistency of final product will be too coarse. An aspic enforced with extra gelatin could be substituted for the gelatin in this formula.

To Apply Chaud Froid Sauce

The consistency of the chaud froid is vital to success in using it. Immediately after preparing a large quantity of chaud froid, test it by placing a spoonful in the refrigerator or freezer. Check in 3 minutes. If chaud froid is slightly rubbery, consistency is correct. If it is too thin, add more dissolved gelatin and test again.

When chaud froid reaches desired thickness, the next key point is melting it to masking consistency. Place chaud froid in bowl in crushed ice and stir constantly with a ladle or wire whip. When sauce has cooled but not congealed, remove from ice. Check to see that no lumps have formed on the sides of the bowl. Let sauce stand at room temperature until smooth.

When masking, (or nape) consistency has been reached, chaud froid will cover back of ladle. In summer, room temperature will melt chaud froid rather than thicken it; and, therefore, chaud froid will have to be kept in ice. In summer, especially, the most satisfactory place for chaud froid work is in a roomy walk-in refrigerator.

To apply chaud froid sauces:

1. Have item to be coated well chilled. Place on wire rack with clean pan under it. Make sure surface to be coated is smooth.
2. Move ladle swiftly, but steadily, across surface of item to be coated, being careful not to let ladle touch surface. When sauce starts to become lumpy, stop and remelt it before continuing application.
3. Cover surface completely, but do not make coating too thick. Chaud froid which runs off into underliner can be reused.
4. Refrigerate coated item immediately. If put in a freezer, chaud froid coating will solidify in 5 to 6 minutes; in a refrigerator, it will take 15 to 20 minutes.
5. Chaud froid items are usually decorated and given 1 or 2 final coats of aspic.

To Repair Mistakes

A lumpy chaud froid coating cannot be repaired; instead, it must be removed and a new coating added.

If the aspic coating over the chaud froid is lumpy, it can sometimes be repaired by holding a hot spatula over the lumpy spot to level it. Somtimes hot aspic can be ladled over the lumpy area. This has to be done very carefully so that it does not melt the chaud froid underneath, thus ruining the entire piece.

Note: Perfection in chaud froid work is perhaps the most difficult of the culinary skills. When doing chaud froid work, the ultimate artistry with food can be achieved.

Variations of Chaud Froid Sauces

Formulas for well known combinations made from basic chaud froid:

Finished Product	Base	Addition
Andalouse	Poultry or meat chaud froid	Julienne of orange poached in sherry
Fines Herbes	Fish, cream cheese or poultry chaud froid	Chopped parsley or other green herbs
Perigourdine	Brown or white chaud froid	Chopped truffles, madeira wine
Ecco ssoise	Cream cheese chaud froid or other	Brunoise of smoked tongue

To Prepare Display Designs in Advance

Scheduling elaborate designs for display pieces is now possible for even a small food service operation. A new technique which takes advantage of the freezer can be used to prepare decorative circles during slack periods.

First step in preparation of freezer decorations is to pour chaud froid sauce on a round plate. Place plate in refrigerator until chaud froid is cool and firm.

When chaud froid has set, place suitable decoration on chaud froid and arrange a border around edge of circle. An attractive decoration can be put together by this method in less than a half hour.

Chilled decorations can be lifted from plate and will slide easily onto ham, turkey, galantine or other display pieces for the buffet. When chaud froid design from freezer has been positioned on display piece, it should be given a coat of clear aspic.

Decorations on chaud froid which can be made by this method are pictured above; these are only a fraction of the designs that can be created.

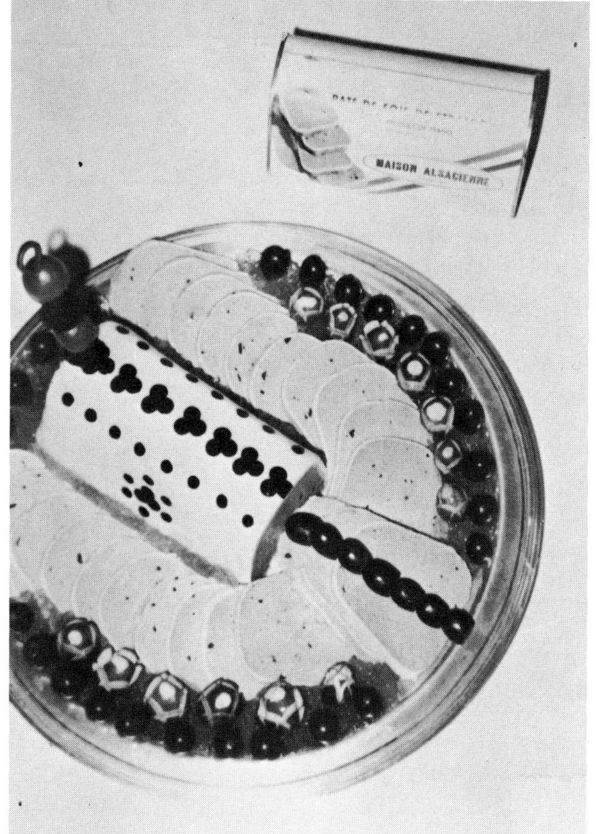

Above left, foundation of white chaud froid is first step in preparation of decorative circles to be held in freezer. Advance preparation during slack periods is bonus offered by this method.

Left, when chaud froid sauce on plate has chilled and is firmly set, decorations may be placed on it. Borders should also be arranged around circles. Completed decorations can be held in freezer.

Top, designs like those pictured can be made of ripe olive skins, radishes, pimientoes, celery slices, orange peels, leeks. Decorated circles can be created in 20 to 30 minutes when workers have mastered techniques.

Above, black decorations on white chaud froid coating make impressive buffet platter from roll of canned liver pate. Skewer of red cherry tomatoes at end of roll and border of radish flowers spark predominantly black and white motif.

To Make Chaud Froid Sheets for Decorative Purposes

Add extra gelatin to regular chaud froid sauce and pour ⅛ in. thick on a shallow pan or platter to jell. Congealed chaud froid sheet can be cut into a variety of shapes. Use fancy cutters to increase design variety.

Bright red or green food coloring added to chaud froid is not desirable since color will bleed onto white areas and display will become messy looking. However, three natural colors can be produced by using (1) truffles; (2) egg yolks and (3) pimiento.

Truffle Sheets—To make a black truffle sheet, combine:

TRUFFLE SHEETS

Ingredients

Truffle Peelings or Trimmings	4 tbsp.
Unflavored Gelatin	2 tbsp.
Aspic	¾ cup
Sherry	1 tbsp.

Method

Dissolve gelatin in aspic and combine with all other ingredients in electric blender. Blend on high speed for 2 to 3 minutes. Heat mixture for approx. 10 minutes in a bain marie to intensify black color:

Pour liquid onto a slightly oiled platter. Liquid will be very thin and should be spread in thin layer. Refrigerate until sheet sets. A freezer will speed process as sheet will set in about 3 minutes in freezer.

Note: A pinch of charcoal powder or charcoal tablets will intensify black color.

Pimiento Sheets—This will provide an orange to red sheet; for a deeper red, add red food coloring.

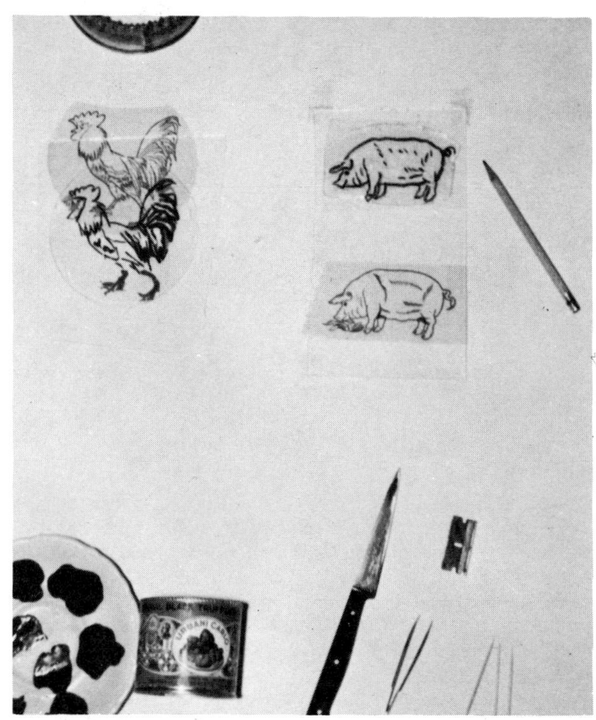

Elaborate decorations made from truffles or truffle sheets can first be assembled on circle of congealed chaud froid. Chaud froid circle can be transferred to the display piece with a spatula when design is completed. Tweezers and a sharp knife are essential to creation of complicated designs. A sketch of the design is also necessary.

PIMIENTO SHEETS

Ingredients

Tomato Paste	2 tbsp.
Pimiento Scraps	1 cup
Gelatin, unflavored	2 tbsp.
Aspic	½ cup

Method

Dissolve gelatin in aspic and combine with other ingredients in blender. Blend on high speed for 30 seconds. Heat mixture for approximately 10 minutes. This will bring out a darker red color.

Pour liquid in thin layer on platter which has been lightly oiled. Liquid will be thin. Refrigerate until sheet sets or put in freezer for 3 minutes to set.

Egg Yolk Sheet—This produces a bright yellow sheet.

EGG YOLK SHEETS

Ingredients

Hard Cooked Egg Yolks	5
Aspic	¾ cup
Gelatin	3 tbsp.

Method

Dissolve aspic in gelatin and blend with egg yolks for 25 seconds on high speed of blender.

Pour liquid in thin layer on platter which has been lightly oiled. Liquid will be thin. Refrigerate until sheet sets or put in freezer for 3 minutes to set.

These sheets are cut into various designs for application to chaud froid base. They can be used for silhouettes, profiles of faces, vases, lettering and numbers (cutters are available), butterflies, three dimensional designs, flower carts and many other decorative ideas. Suggestions and directions for these in Chapter XIV.

Round platters hold chaud froid, pimiento and truffle sheets from which design elements can be cut. Cutters were used to create most of the designs shown. If cutters are not available, simple designs can easily be made with a sharp knife. Elements cut from the white, black and red sheets can be used in effective combinations.

To Make More Elaborate Decorations

With Whole Truffles and Truffle Sheets—It takes skill and patience to work out a design using these materials. The sheets can be used to make large elements such as sailboats, mountain outlines, fish or profiles which can be cut from the sheet in one piece.

For more intricate designs created from several pieces of material, whole sliced truffles are needed.

1. It takes a machine to slice whole truffles thin enough to use in reproducing an intricate design. Truffle pieces are too small to hold onto properly to slice uniformly with a paring knife. Slices coming from the machine should be dipped into liquid aspic at once.

2. Cutters are available to cut out many desired decorative pieces.

3. These elaborate designs can only be carried out if enough time is allotted. Some designs will take 5 to 6 hours to complete. Work should be done sitting down. Before starting on a design, the worker should find a satisfactory sketch or photograph which he can follow. This should be the same size as the finished design.

4. If a design is expected to take more than 2 hours, do not attempt to assemble it directly on the chaud froid coated display piece. Such long exposure of the chaud froid coating in the kitchen would make it deteriorate.

Instead, put a thin coating of chaud froid on a round or oval plate, sized for the grosse or display piece that you plan to decorate.

5. Tweezers are essential in assembling a design made from slices or bits of truffle sheet.

6. When the design on the plate is completed, seal it immediately with a coat of aspic and cover it so air cannot contaminate it. If this method is followed, decorated chaud froid pieces can be stored in refrigerator up to 1 week. Be sure no warm air touches piece during storage period, as aspic and chaud froid will discolor and design will have to be abandoned.

7. When time comes to place the decorated chaud froid on the grosse piece, poultry, ham or salmon, loosen chaud froid from plate with a spatula, then lift up and slide onto surface to be decorated. Never put plate over heat to loosen chaud froid; the entire design will melt.

Note: Less elaborate designs made using whole truffles and completed in about 1 hour can be placed directly on the grosse piece.

Thread Designs—These can only be used on dummy hams which will be kept well separated from any edible food. To make them, black thread is cut into lengths needed to copy the picture of sketch that is serving as a guide for the finished decoration. The thread is dipped into hot aspic to make it more manageable and placed on the chaud froid base with tweezers. The chaud froid will hold it in place. Making such a design requires a high degree of patience and a steady hand.

This clock is made from a circle of ham salad coated with white chaud froid. Hours are numbered in black truffle sheet letters on chaud froid coated hard cooked egg halves. Clock hands and day are also cut from truffle sheet. Border is made of cherry tomatoes.

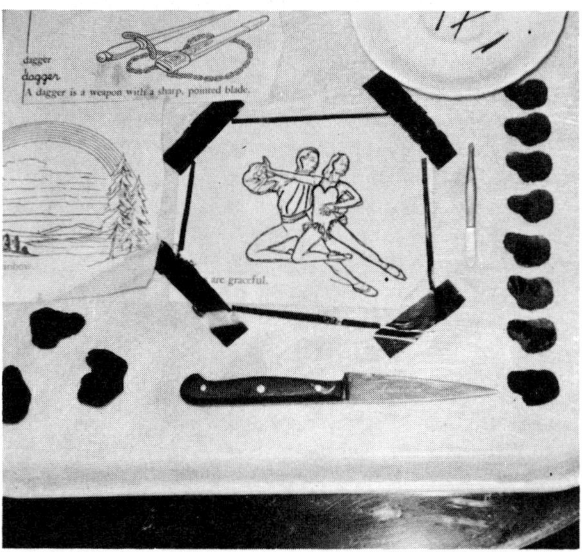

Above, truffles ready for use in design on tray set-up have been sliced on machine, then immediately dipped in aspic. Pieces cut from truffle slices will be put in place on design with tweezers. Below, machine must be used to slice whole truffles thin enough to use in reproducing intricate designs.

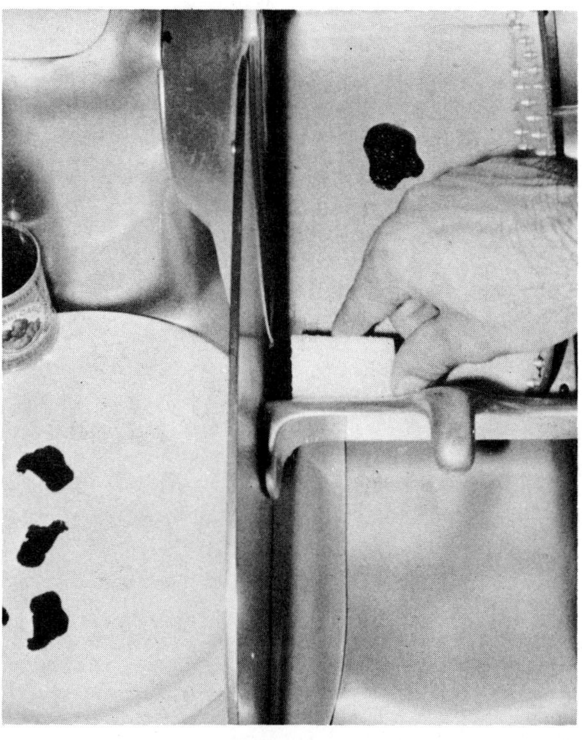

Aspic and Chaud Froid Painting—Talent as a painter in a greater than average degree is required for this type of decorative work. The technique is used to produce tropical scenes, landscapes, sunsets, seascapes or forest scenes.

1. As mise en place (or equipment arrangement), the worker needs a number of aspic portions which have been appropriately tinted with food coloring. Tinted aspic can be portioned into muffin cups. Small paint brushes can be used to apply the tinted aspic.
2. Aspic must be kept at room temperature in liquid form if it is to be applied with a paint brush.
3. Item to be painted must be chilled, then coated with chaud froid before painting. Care must be taken during painting that colored aspic does not run.
4. When painting is finished, apply a final coat of clear aspic.

Vegetables Decorations for Chaud Froid Base

Flowers created from vegetable bits do not have to resemble real varieties; vegetables that can be used to make floral decorations for chaud froid include:

Leeks: blanch for 3 minutes, cool quickly, using green and yellow parts for stems and leaves.
Radishes: slices or skin.
Tomato Skin: shaved very thin or blanched.
Black or Green Olives
Lemons and Oranges, peels
Cooked Carrots
Whole Pimientos: dry well before using.
Watercress
Celery Leaves
Parsley Stems
Tarragon Leaves
Green Pepper Skins
Cucumber Skin
Eggplant Skin: because of the shiny coating, aspic does not adhere easily to eggplant skin.
White and Yellow Turnips
Hard Cooked Egg Whites: good material for white petals; equally good is thin sheet of chaud froid.

Note: Red beets and pickled vegetables should never be applied on chaud froid as the juices may run and spoil the decorations.

A muffin tin provides the palette for the aspic artist. Each cup holds liquid aspic tinted in one of the shades needed to create the scene the aspic painter has selected. Small paint brushes are used to paint the scene and it takes above-average artistic talent for this type of decoration.

Above, the raw materials for vegetable flower decorations are assembled with the tools used in preparing them. Right, raw vegetable pieces have been arranged as blossoms, flowers on stems or in basket. These flowers are easy to create and position on white chaud froid coated display pieces.

NOTES

NOTES

The grosse piece or display item, made from meat, poultry or fish as the dominant dish among buffet foods, depends in large part for its success on the mousse, farce or salad used to re-shape it after boning or other preparation.

Since portions cut from re-shaped buffet display pieces will always contain part of the mousse, farce or salad, it is important that they contribute maximum flavor and appealing texture. The difference between mousse and farce is that cooked meat, poultry or seafood is used in making a mousse while for the farce, the ingredients are raw at the start of the preparation.

To Make a Mousse

Cooked ingredients, such as leftover roast or poached turkey, chicken, sauteed chicken livers, other liver, roast veal, roast beef, smoked tongue, poached or broiled fish fillets of any kind, crabmeat, canned salmon, all can be used in a mousse. Ingredients must be fresh from cooking or proper refrigeration or the final flavor of the mousse will suffer.

Mousse-making has been greatly simplified since the development of the electric blender, the dicer-chopper and the vertical cutter/mixer. These machines have done away with the hours of pounding formerly required to mash the meat, poultry or seafood into the necessary fine texture of a satisfactory mousse.

From being one of the most elaborate, time consuming procedures in the garde manger's bag of tricks, mousse making now can be done in minutes. The mousse must be smooth, especially when it is to be coated with chaud froid, but this smooth consistency is easily achieved with today's machines.

Machines for Mousse-Making

If an electric blender, dicer-chopper or vertical cutter/mixer is not available, it is possible, though more time-consuming, to prepare a mousse by grinding ingredients first in a meat grinder and then pressing them through a wire mesh sieve. There is an attachment available for mixers that can be used to strain the ingredients after they come from the meat grinder. In this attachment, meat is pressed through the sieve but unwanted fibres and tissues are left behind.

Electric Blender. Blenders are usually used to prepare mousse in quantities of 1 qt. or less. If meat is to be the principal ingredient of the mousse, it should be put through the finest blade of a meat grinder first.

To keep the blender working properly, there must be sufficient liquid added to the solids being blended. If this is not done and the mixture gets too thick, the blender blade will only operate effectively on the bottom or will get stuck. Liquid aspic or bouillon with gelatin added can be used to thin ingredients in blender. Usually more aspic is needed when making mousse with a blender than for any other method.

Dicer/chopper. This will mash meat or other ingredients just as well as the blender, but it will take more time. However, it will also handle larger quantities (5 lb. or more). Liquid should be added sparingly; but if ingredients are kept lightly moist, mashing action will be speedier.

Vertical cutter/mixer. This piece of equipment can handle ingredients in quantities of 10 lb. or more and works similarly to a blender. Ingredients will need to be thinned with aspic to assure the desired consistency.

A mousse when served should be spongy but fluffy, not rubbery in consistency. If it does have a rubbery texture, it can be traced to too much gelatin added to the aspic. Seasoning is all-important; if a mousse contains too little seasoning, it becomes flat and tasteless. If there is too little gelatin in the mousse, and it is to be used in a timbale or mold, the timbale will collapse after it is unmolded because the mousse will not be sufficiently solid. This is why it is important to test the mousse before using it. Directions for testing are given below.

After adding whipped cream to a mousse, do not attempt to remelt it. The whipped cream is apt to sour during remelting process. If the mousse is to be used in re-shaping capons or turkeys, the whipped cream can be omitted, giving the mousse a more solid consistency.

The three recipes which follow can be used with any of the ingredients suggested above as appropriate for mousse preparation.

HAM MOUSSE

(Can also be used for all smoked meats and tongue)

Ingredients

Ham Trimmings	2 lb.
Liquid Aspic, meat or poultry	4 cup
Gelatin, unflavored	2 tbsp.
Cream Sauce	2 cups
Medium Cream	1 cup
Madeira Wine	½ cup
Cayenne Pepper	to taste
Salt	to taste
Red Food Coloring	as needed

Method

Remove all fat, veins and rind from ham trimmings. Dissolve gelatin in aspic. Puree ham in blender. Add gelatin-aspic mixture. (If blender is used, aspic must be added with the ham; if other equipment is used, aspic should be added gradually.) Add seasonings and wine. Blend to paste consistency.

Remove blended ingredients to a stainless steel bowl and stir in cream sauce, using wooden spoon. Be sure to mix thoroughly. Cool on ice. Test a spoonful of the mixture in the freezer. When it has jelled, mixture should be lightly spongy.

As mousse begins to get stiff, fold in cream which has been whipped. Use a wire whip. At room temperature

mousse will maintain consistency for use as an ingredient that can be molded and smoothed properly for a chaud froid coating. Under refrigeration the mousse will set and become more solid.

To Use

For timbales or molds and piece montee; as a base around virginia ham or regular whole ham; to build up slices of ham; to re-shape the carcass of capon or other poultry; to fill individual slices of capon breast or pheasant breast; to fill ham rouladen, cones or other sausage slices; to level out uneven areas on meat and poultry grosse pieces to be covered with chaud froid for buffet display.

LIVER MOUSSE

(For chicken, duck, goose or pork liver)

Ingredients

Liver	2 lb.
Onion, large, diced	1
Chicken Fat	to saute
Liquid Chicken Aspic	4 cups
Unflavored Gelatin	2 tbsp.
Cream Sauce	2 cups
Medium Cream, to whip	1 cup
Brandy	3 oz.
White Pepper	to taste
Nutmeg	to taste
Thyme	to taste
Salt	to taste

Method

Remove sinews, veins, skin or muscle from liver.

Saute diced onion in chicken fat. Saute liver and onions till done, then mash. Combine gelatin with aspic. Add some of the aspic, brandy and seasonings to other ingredients and blend to desired consistency.

Put blended mixture, now a smooth paste, into a stainless steel bowl and combine with cream sauce. Stir well with a wooden spoon, then cool on ice.

Test a spoonful of mousse in freezer. If the gelatin ratio is correct, the mousse will be slightly spongy after it congeals.

When mousse begins to jell, fold in whipped cream, using wire whip. If mousse is to be used for filling out poultry, it should have an easily spread consistency. If kept at room temperature, mousse will maintain this consistency. If it is refrigerated, it will become solid.

To Use

For timbales or piece montee, to re-shape carcass of duck, capons, other poultry, pheasant and quail, to fill individual slices of capon or pheasant breast, to level out uneven spots on meat and poultry display pieces to be coated with chaud froid.

If liver mousse is poured 1-in. thick into hotel pan and left to solidify, it can be used as an imitation pate, coated with clear aspic, decorated and cut into geometrical shapes as a garnish for meat and poultry grosse pieces.

Liver Mousse can also be piped from a pastry tube into profiteroles, eclairs and other shells for use as canapes. Mousse will also provide a base for whole game birds that will hold them in place and can be used to fasten bread socles onto a tray.

SALMON MOUSSE

(Can also substitute other fish, such as cod, haddock, sole, turbot, pike, etc.)

Ingredients

Salmon, canned or cooked	2 lb.
Celery, diced	1 cup
Liquid Fish Aspic, or Chicken Aspic	3 cups
Unflavored Gelatin	2 tbsp.
Cream Sauce	1 cup
Mayonnaise	1 cup
Medium Cream, to whip	1 cup
Dry White Wine	½ cup
White Pepper	to taste
Cayenne Pepper	to taste
Chopped Chives	to taste
Liquid Pepper Sauce	to taste
Dry Mustard	to taste
Worcestershire Sauce	to taste
Chopped Parsley	to taste
Chopped Dill	to taste

Method

Remove skin and bones from salmon and blend with celery. Dissolve gelatin in fish aspic. Add gelatin-aspic mixture as needed to blending mixture. Add seasonings. Blend mixture until of paste consistency.

Put blended ingredients into a stainless steel bowl and add cream sauce and mayonnaise. Stir well with wooden spoon, then cool on ice.

Test mixture by putting spoonful in freezer. If gelatin ratio is correct, the mousse will be slightly spongy after it congeals.

When mousse begins to jell, whip cream and fold it in, using wire whip. If mousse is to be used for molding or shaping, keep it at room temperature as this will maintain the easily spread consistency. If it is refrigerated, it will become solid.

To Use

To re-shape whole poached salmon, sea bass, trout and other fish mentioned in the chapter on salmon; for fish-shaped molds, timbales; to stuff cucumbers, artichoke bottoms, mushroom caps, barquettes or tiny tart shells made from pie crust; to fill tiny patty shells; to fill slices of smoked salmon and hard cooked egg halves.

Mousse Combinations—Ingredients for mousses may be combined as indicated below. In working out such combinations, be sure that seasonings are adjusted and that the right aspic is selected for use in the blending process.

In scheduling mousses, be sure to plan on matching a seafood mousse with seafood and meat mousses with roast meat or poultry.

Vary mousses by combining:

a. ⅓ salmon mousse, ⅓ crabmeat mousse, ⅓ mashed russian salad.

b. ½ poultry liver mousse, ½ ham mousse.

c. ½ smoked beef tongue mousse, ½ liver mousse.

d. ½ halibut or sole mousse, ½ hard-cooked egg yolk paste.

e. ½ lobster or shrimp mousse, made from claws and pieces, ½ crabmeat mousse.

f. rainbow trout mousse (it will take about a dozen

rainbow trout for a mousse)

g. ½ dark meat and ½ light meat of chicken or turkey combined for mousse

h. ½ chicken mousse, ½ poultry liver mousse.

Note: The various molds or timbales that are filled with mousse are described in Chapter XV.

To Make a Farce

The farce is always prepared from raw meat, poultry or fish. The preparation of a farce is similar to a meat loaf, and the farce is used primarily as a filling to be cooked after preparation. The farce does not have to be as fine-textured or as smooth as a mousse; it is more the consistency of mashed potatoes. This consistency makes it easier to fill a salmon, trout or capon, using a rubber spatula or spoon.

A fish farce is used as a filling for fish or seafood and the meat farce works equally well with meat or poultry.

FISH FARCE

Yield: Will fill a 10 lb. salmon

Ingredients

Raw pike or other fish fillet, skinned	3 lb.
Whole Eggs	3
Heavy Cream	½ cup
Rendered Chicken Fat	4 oz.
Onion, chopped	1
Flour, sifted	1 cup
Salt Nutmeg White Pepper Dry Mustard Lemon Juice	to taste

Method

Saute chopped onion in chicken fat. Dry fish fillets; be sure fish is fresh. Grind fish fillets and sauteed onions in dicer-chopper to make a paste. Add eggs, flour, cream and seasonings.

Test farce by forming a small ball and poaching it in simmering water. If ball remains whole after 10 minutes, farce mixture is of proper consistency.

Remove farce from chopper and refrigerate until it becomes as stiff as it needs to be for intended use.

To Use

Stuff a whole salmon (see Viking Ship, Chap. VI); poach farce in mold and hold in bain marie; stuff trout, sea bass and other fish; stuff squid.

MEAT FARCE

Yield: 3 qt.

Ingredients

Fresh Pork Fat	1½ lb.
Boneless Veal	1 lb.
Boneless Pork Shoulder	1 lb.
Ham	1 lb.
Chicken or Pork Liver	½ lb.
Whole Eggs	3
Flour	½ cup
Heavy Cream	¼ cup
Garlic, variable	8 cloves
Cognac	½ cup
Salt White Pepper Allspice Cinnamon	to taste

Method

Grind all meat, pork fat and liver in dicer-chopper until smooth. Put through meat grinder if blender is to be used.

Add eggs, flour, cream and seasonings.

Test farce by forming a small ball and poaching it in simmering water. If ball remains whole after 10 minutes, farce mixture is of proper consistency.

Remove rest of farce from chopper or blender and chill till ready for filling.

Note: This farce can be varied by substituting venison, wild duck, or other meat for veal and pork.

To Use

Stuff a whole, boned suckling pig; stuff capons, turkeys and other poultry and game birds by removing both breasts plus breast bones and ribs so a large cavity is ready for the farce, fill, then re-shape bird to its original size and bake; poach farce in mold in bain marie or steamer to make terrine.

Special Salads for Buffet Display Items

Handled in much the same way as the mousses, certain finely diced, gelatinous salads can also be used to re-shape display items for the buffet tables. The three salads listed here combine readily with meat, poultry, fish and seafood; however, any other neutral salad that will retain stiffness for the necessary period of time can be substituted.

Russian salad. This mixed vegetable salad, serves as a standby under different names in various cuisines. In Vienna, it is known as the french salad; in France, it is the Macedonian salad (and in Russia, it may well be the American salad since it is called the Russian salad here).

RUSSIAN SALAD

Yield: Depends on proportions set

Ingredients

Cooked Potatoes Cooked Carrots Cooked Green Peas Cooked String Beans Raw Apples, peeled Fresh Stalk Celery or Cooked Root Celery	EQUAL PARTS ALL FINELY DICED
Sour Pickles	to flavor mildly
Mayonnaise	to bind
Prepared Mustard, optional Salt Pepper Lemon Juice	to taste

Method

It is important that vegetables be finely diced so there will be no lumps if chaud froid coating is used.

Combine all vegetables in bowl with enough mayonnaise to blend all ingredients into a stiff mixture. Keep lemon juice or any other liquid to the minimum so salad does not dilute. Also make sure that all vegetables are completely dry so they do not add to liquid.

On occasion, a mayonnaise colle (mayonnaise to which gelatin has been added) or mayonnaise to which aspic and gelatin have been added is used to bind the salad. Mayonnaise prepared this way will serve as a jelling agent for the salad. Be sure to test mayonnaise before adding to the salad to make sure that the jelling consistency is what it should be.

Note: Russian salad can be varied by adding any diced smoked meat, turkey, herring, cooked fish fillets, lobster or shrimp pieces, beef and similar ingredients.

Fine Diced Potato Salad—Any basic potato salad recipe will be satisfactory for this use providing potatoes are diced fine. Salad should be stiff and mayonnaise should be used to make the salad. Using potato salad as filler has several advantages; it is easy to prepare and leftover baked potatoes are usually available.

Egg Salad—Hard cooked eggs, put through an egg slicer can be combined with finely diced celery and mixed with mayonnaise, then properly seasoned. Chopped chives, parsley or other green herbs add piquant aroma. Be sure to keep salad mixture stiff enough to hold its shape well.

Note: Both potato and egg salad can be made gelatinous by adding gelatin to mayonnaise for a mayonnaise colle.

Russian salad is available ready-prepared in cans. For another short cut, frozen mixed vegetables can be used although salad is better without kernel corn. If frozen mixed vegetables are used, pickles and apples must be added to insure that the finished salad has the traditional flavor associated with Russian Salad.

To Use Russian, Potato and Egg Salad

These three salads can be used interchangeably to create display pieces. Suggestions include: salmon grosse pieces; stuffed cold lobster and king crab; molds, timbales and piece montee; to accompany any type of smoked ham or beef tongue; with capon and turkey, Chapter V.; for classical hors d'oeuvres, Chapter III.; to stuff such vegetables as tomatoes, cucumbers or artichoke bottoms.

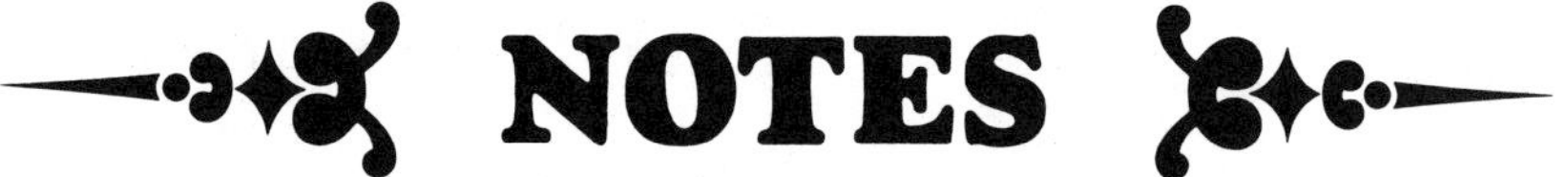

CHAPTER XIII
Pates, Galantines

"Paté maison" are among the most elegant words a menu can display. By the same token, paté maison is one of the most costly items on the food production schedule. However, the cost of paté making has been reduced enough by modern labor-saving equipment to bring it into reach for many more menus.

Paté appears in one of two forms for buffet display: (1) the paté natural which is a whole paté in aspic, or (2) paté en croute, a paté baked in a special crust. Paté may be served sliced on a cold meat platter or in small portions, sometimes individually shaped, as a cold hors d'oeuvres.

Do not confuse paté natural with chopped chicken livers, an entirely different liver preparation, or paté en croute with meat pie, as there is no resemblance.

The paté is similar in consistency to a mousse, but paté is always made from uncooked materials in contrast to the mousse which utilizes cooked ingredients.

The ingredients for a paté must have a very fine and smooth texture. This texture can be achieved by putting the meats through the finest blade of the meat grinder and then through a dicer-chopper or vertical cutter/mixer or by putting the meat through the finest blade of the meat grinder three times and then through a sieve attachment on a mixer. There are also some liver patés that can be made in an electric blender.

The finest paté in the world is the paté de fois gras, a goose liver paté imported from France or Switzerland. This canned paté, made with chopped or whole black truffles, from the livers of geese raised especially for this purpose, is prohibitively expensive, costing from $40 to $50 per lb.

Geese cannot legally be force fed in this country, nor do we have the French or Swiss secrets of paté making. Therefore, classical paté de fois gras cannot be duplicated in this country. In some areas, goose livers are obtainable and will contribute a unique flavor to paté recipes, though they do not duplicate the taste of

Slices of Pate Maison frame a decorative centerpiece topped by a vegetable timbale.

Above, aspic coated slices of pate provide outer circle for platter.
At left, flat V of overlapping pate slices gets height from pineapple shell holding mounded grapes. Aspic fills out platter and single dark grapes add to border.

Above, ingredients assembled for preparing Pate Maison using blender. Right, facing page, blended pate ingredients are poured into small individual muffin tins. Large muffin tins, rectangular pate pans, stainless steel bowls or variously shaped metal pudding molds may also be used. Grease molds with butter or hydrogenated shortening. Cover filled mold with foil and place in pan of water in oven. Poach at 400°F. in oven.

imported patés.

Fresh truffles, required by some paté recipes, are also not readily available in the U. S. Canned truffles are usually substituted.

To Make Chicken Liver Paté

This is a paté that can be made in an electric blender.

CHICKEN LIVER PATÉ

Yield: About 40 small individual portions

Ingredients

Raw Chicken, Duck or Goose Livers, deveined	2 lb.
Medium-Sized Onion, quartered	1
Whole Eggs	3
Heavy Cream	1 cup
Flour	½ cup
Brandy	1 oz.
Salt	5 tsp.
White Pepper	2 tsp.
Allspice	1 tsp.
Ground Ginger	1 tsp.
Monosodium Glutamate, optional	½ tsp.

Method

1. Devein livers and place in blender with onion, chicken fat, eggs and spices. Blend at high speed for about 5 minutes.
2. Add brandy, flour and cream and mix on low speed until mixture is blended, about 1 minute.
3. Select mold to be used; paté may be poured into small individual muffin tins, large muffin tins, rectangular paté pans, stainless steel bowls or into variously shaped metal pudding molds. Grease mold with butter or hydrogenated shortening. Pour liquid mixture from blender into mold.
4. Cover filled mold with foil and place in a pan of water in oven. Poach at 400° F. in oven. Small individual molds will take about 20 minutes; a mold large enough to hold the total mixture will take about 1½ hours. The cooked paté will have a light, spongy, consistency.
5. Unmold paté while it is still warm as it will come out easier when it is warm than after it cools.
6. Chill paté and cover with chicken aspic to which brandy has been added.
7. Decorations for paté can be made from seedless grapes, truffle slices, hard cooked egg slices, ripe olive halves or slices.

Note: Paté, properly covered with aspic, can be stored in the refrigerator safely for up to 10 days.

To Make Swedish Liver Paté

This paté can also be made in an electric blender. It has a distinct aroma if Scandinavian anchovies are used in it; however, matjes herring can be substituted and the nordic flavor of the dish retained.

SWEDISH LIVER PATÉ

Yield: About 40 small portions

Ingredients

Pork Liver, membranes and tubes removed	1 lb.
Fresh Pork Fat	½ lb.
Scandinavian Anchovy Fillets in Oyster Sauce	6
or	
Matjes Herring Fillet	½
Onions, diced and sauteed	½ cup
Whole Eggs	5
Heavy Cream	1 cup
Flour	½ cup
Salt	4 tsp.
White Pepper	2 tsp.
Black Pepper	2 tsp.
Allspice	1 tsp.

Method

1. Cut raw pork liver into cubes and soak in cold milk overnight in the refrigerator. Make sure pork fat is fresh; otherwise it will completely ruin the flavor of the paté. If pork fat is not available, substitute chicken fat or smoked bacon fat.
2. Remove liver from milk and put through fine blade of meat grinder or chopper with pork fat, anchovy or herring fillets and onions.
3. Transfer mixture to electric blender and add all other ingredients. Blend for about 10 minutes until mixture achieves fine texture.
4. Line a paté mold with bacon strips and pour mixture into mold.
5. Bake paté in pan of water in oven at 400° F. for about 2 hours.
6. Chill and serve with fresh cucumber slices or pickles and onions.

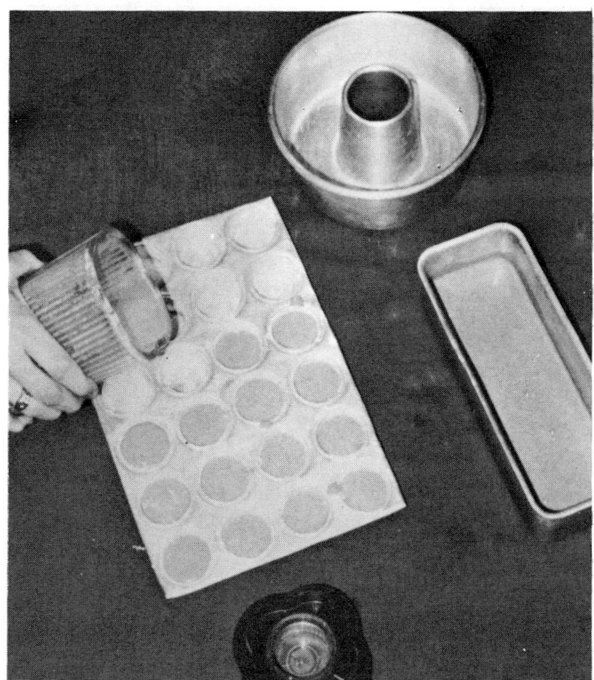

Above, small individual molds like these muffin tins will take about 20 minutes to cook; larger molds take longer.

Above right, cooked pate has light spongy consistency; is unmolded while it is still warm as it comes out easiest when warm. Individual pates are placed in pan and refrigerated to chill. At right, chilled pate is coated with chicken aspic that has been flavored with brandy. Garnish circles with seedless grapes, truffle slices, hard cooked egg, ripe olives.

Above, round silver tray, below, square tray hold crackers spread with goose liver and garnished with croutons of sherry wine-flavored aspic. Imported goose liver terrine is kept very cold and scooped out with a teaspoon kept in hot water when not in use.

Petite Patés in Aspic for Hors D'Oeuvres: Patés made using the recipes in this section—except paté en croute, can be made into small hors d'oeuvres. A loaf shaped paté maison or a liver paté baked in a hotel pan can be cut into small rounds, rectangles, triangles, half moons or similar small shapes. Trimmings can be saved for a mousse or used as an ingredient of other meat fillings. Patés can also be poached in small muffin cups, eliminating the necessity for re-shaping them.

Paté portions for individual service are placed on a sheet pan or a cookie sheet for decorating. Suggested decorations follow. Decorated portions of paté to be used as hors d'oeuvres should be coated with a full-flavored wine aspic. They can be held in a refrigerator, covered with transparent wrap for over a week.

Suggested decorative designs for hors d'oeuvres made of aspic-coated paté:

1. Liver paté on poached apple rounds, topped with half grape on walnut half.
2. Liver paté on cucumber slice with truffle cut-out or slice.
3. Paté on crouton with hard cooked egg slice and red pepper strips.
4. Paté maison with pineapple segment and mandarin orange section.
5. Paté maison with chopped pistachio nuts and truffle slivers.

Pates, Galantines

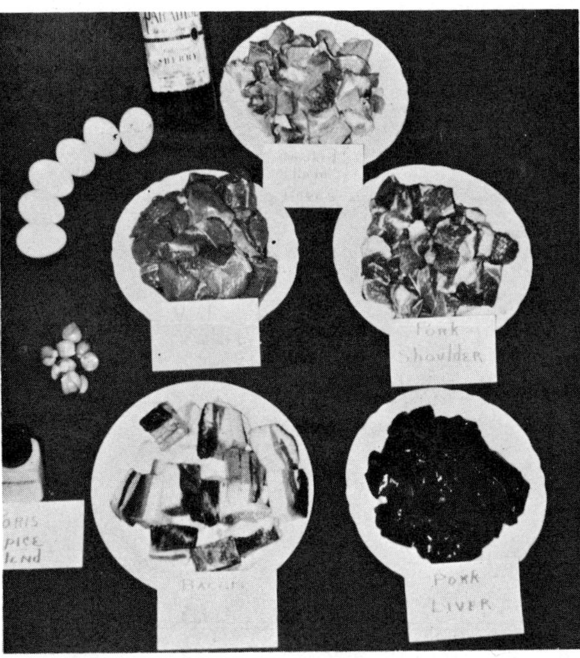

1. Ingredients assembled for Pate Maison include, from top: sherry, eggs, smoked ham cubes, veal shoulder, pork shoulder, special spice blend, bacon cubes and pork liver.

2. Cubed veal, pork and ham are placed in bowl and a mixture of sherry and brandy poured over them. Bowl with meat and marinade is held over night in refrigerator. Next day, meat is combined with pork fat, liver before grinding.

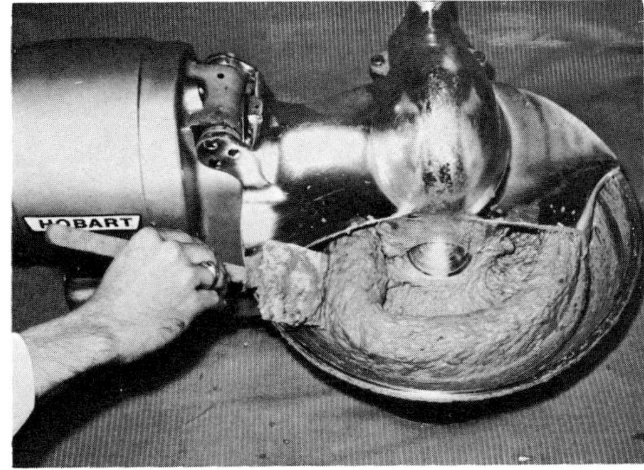

3. After meat, liver and pork fat have been ground to finest consistency, mixture is placed in bowl and special spice blend, eggs and flour are combined with it. Meat may have to be ground several times to reach desired fine consistency.

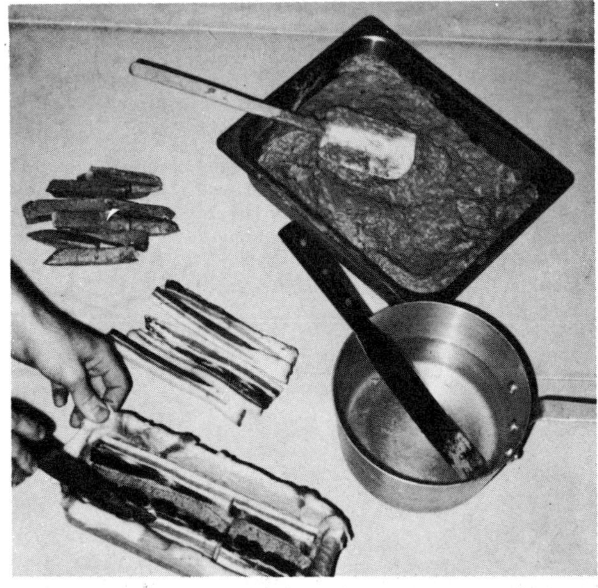

4. Smoked bacon strips are used to line pate mold. Add garnishes to pate before packing it in mold. Suggested garnishes: cubes or strips of smoked beef tongue or ham, diced truffles, pistachio nuts, cubes of smoked bacon, pork or veal tenderloin, goose livers, diced pimiento or ripe olives.

5. After garnishes are arranged for maximum eye appeal, cover filled mold with foil and bake. After pate is baked, it should be chilled, then coated with aspic. Before serving, loaf of pate can be coated with chaud froid and decorated. It may also be sliced and served without further decoration.

6. Any paté topped with fluted or plain mushroom cap, asparagus tip and truffle bits.

7. Paté maison with ripe olive slices, mandarin orange section, pistachio nuts.

8. Any paté topped with sweet gherkin, mushroom slice and truffle slice.

9. Liver paté with smoked tongue strips and seedless grape halves.

10. Fill Virginia ham rollatini with paté; put pickle strip in center.

11. Paté Gnocchis—with a tablespoon dipped in hot water, scoop out uniform balls and coat with aspic.

The petite patés described above can be used as cold hors d'oeuvres and arranged with aspic cubes on a platter for buffet presentation. They can also be placed on a crouton or toast base and served as canapes.

In addition, they can be used as components or decorative additions for display or grosse pieces designed for the buffet. They are an impressive addition to displays of turkey, capon, smoked ham, duck, pheasant, game hens, other game birds, saddle of venison.

Note: A number of canned liver paté products are available.' Using the canned product cuts down on labor and assures uniformly high quality. They are especially desirable where equipment is not available for efficient production of paté.

To Make Paté Maison

This paté can be made with a meat grinder only, if mixture is put through the grinder five times. However, the preferred preparation method is with a meat grinder, dicer-chopper and the sieve attachment of a mixer.

The paté calls for a french paté spice blend which is difficult to obtain in this country. The spice mixture can be duplicated by combining equal parts of white pepper, black pepper, paprika, nutmeg, ground ginger, sweet basil, thyme, marjoram, allspice, garlic powder with one-half part of powdered cloves. Mix spices in container and shake well. Mixture can be stored in spice jar. The recipe for Paté Maison which follows calls for 5 tsp. of the spice blend.

PATÉ MAISON

Ingredients

Fresh Pork Fat or Smoked Bacon Fat	1½ lb.
Boneless Veal	1 lb.
Boneless Pork	1 lb.
Smoked Ham	1 lb.
Poultry or Pork Liver	1 lb.
Whole Eggs	3
Shallots, diced, sauteed	6
Flour	½ cup
Sherry Wine with Brandy	1 cup
Salt	4 tsp.
Spice Blend (see above)	5 tsp.

Method

1. Cube veal, pork and ham and marinate overnight in sherry wine and brandy.

2. Put cubed meat, liver and pork fat through finest blade of meat grinder three times. Put in dicer-chopper, if available, after grinding. Next put mixture through sieve attachment on mixer. If mixer does not have sieve attachment, do not try to put mixture through sieve by hand; it is too difficult. Instead run the mixture through the grinder two more times.

Four decorative designs for galantine of poultry or pork range from easy to elaborate.

3. Place meat mixture in bowl; add spices, eggs, sauteed shallots and flour.

4. Line a paté mold with smoked bacon strips or, if fine quality salt pork is available, sides and bottom of mold may be covered with it. Poor quality salt pork may be rancid and spoil the flavor of the paté.

5. Before placing paté mixture in mold, garnishes should be added. Among possible garnishes: cubes or strips of smoked beef tongue or ham, diced truffles, pistachio nuts, cubes of smoked bacon, pork or veal tenderloin, goose livers, diced red pimiento or diced black olives, sometimes substituted for truffles.

6. Pack paté mixture, sometimes referred to as force meat or meat farce, into mold. A pork or veal tenderloin can be centered in the mold with the paté around it. Garnishes such as smoked beef tongue strips should be added with an eye to maximum decorative effect.

7. Cover filled mold with foil and bake in pan of water in oven at 400°F. for 3 hours.

8. Chill paté and coat with aspic. Store in container it was baked in to preserve the superb aroma of the paté.

To Serve

Dip a french knife in hot water to slice paté. Serve with any salad, relish or with pickled condiments.

Note: Other meat combinations may be substituted for the one listed in the recipe. Rabbit, venison and game birds can replace the pork or veal; however, the amount of pork fat and smoked ham should always remain in the same proportion as given in this recipe.

To Make Paté en Croute

This paté, probably the most elaborate paté presentation, is a raw meat or force meat mixture, similar to that in paté maison, baked in a special crust. The crust preserves the paté flavor at its finest during refrigeration.

This paté is easiest to handle when baked in the special hinged, bottomless molds designed for its preparation. However, copper molds with zinc lining and patterned sides can also be used. The regular square mold used for paté maison is also suitable although it is quite difficult to remove the paté from it.

DOUGH FOR PATÉ EN CROUTE

Yield: Crust for 4 to 5 lb. paté

Ingredients

Bread Flour	3 lb.
Lard or Hydrogenated Shortening	¾ lb.
or	
Shortening	8 oz. with
Chicken Fat	4 oz.
Lukewarm Water, variable*	1 to 2 pt.
Egg Yolks	2
Salt	1 oz.

* If chicken fat is used, less water is needed.

Method

With mixer, combine all dry ingredients, add egg yolk mixed with water and turn on slow speed until a ball forms. If no mixer is available, put dry ingredients in a bowl, make a well in the ingredients and add fat and liquids. Work until a smooth ball will form. Dough must be rather firm and elastic.

Place ball of dough on plate; oil lightly and wrap in transparent wrap. Place in refrigerator for about 5 hours.

Filling for Paté en Croute

Use recipe for paté maison to make filling for crust. It will take about 5 lb. of meat mixture (or force meat) for the dough recipe given here. Recipes can be multiplied if size of mold requires it.

Recommended garnishes for the filling are whole pistachios, chopped pimientos, truffles, cubes of smoked tongue or ham. One or two whole tenderloins of pork or veal may be embedded in the meat mixture. Fresh goose livers may also be inserted.

Assembling Paté en Croute

1. Take dough from refrigerator and roll out about ¼ in. thick. If using conventional Croute mold, cut and trim bottom, top and sides to size of mold with about ½ in.

PATE EN CROUTE

Essential steps in the preparation of Pate en Croute are pictured on these two pages. Successful production of this dish depends on careful preparation.

1. Utensils and ingredients assembled for preparation of Pate en Croute. Bowl contains Pate Maison to be used for filling. Filling will have garnitures inserted before it is packed into mold.

2. Dough for Pate en Croute mold is taken from refrigerator and rolled out about ¼ in. thick. Separate piece of dough is cut to fit bottom of mold. Other dough is shaped to line sides of hinged mold.

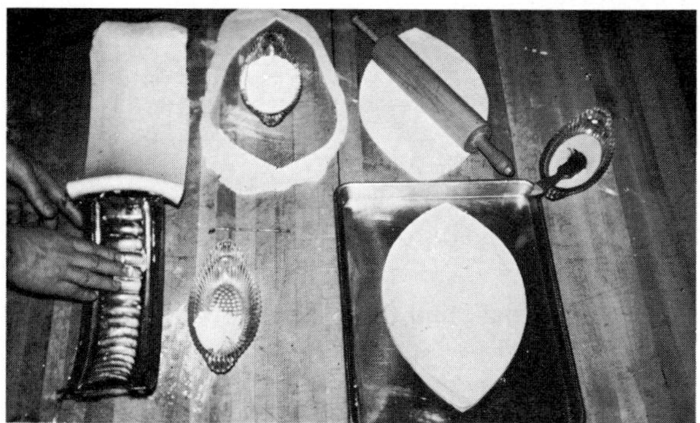

3. Dough to go underneath mold is placed on cookie sheet or sheet pan that has been greased with shortening or lard. Edges of dough at bottom part of mold are given egg wash.

4. Mold sides are also greased with shortening or lard, lined with dough, then placed on bottom crust. Seam is sealed with egg wash. Strips of salt pork or bacon next go over dough lining mold.

5. Pate Maison or forcemeat is packed tightly into mold. Build mixture up to mound slightly higher in center of mold. Garnishes should be positioned when mold is filled.

6. Cover for mold is shaped from dough, put in place and sealed with egg wash at edges. Chimneys are placed in cutouts to release steam and pressure during baking. Chimneys are made from aluminum foil. Bake Pate en Croute in 325°F. oven for 1 hr.; then turn temperature down to 275°F. If crust seems to be getting too brown, cover with aluminum foil until pate has baked required length of time.

7. When Pate en Croute is done, take it from oven and chill well. During baking, filling shrinks leaving a cavity under crust. Crust will not sag so cavity remains to be filled. A wine flavored aspic is poured into mold until cavity is completely filled. Holes in crust, which served as steam vents during baking, do double duty as opening through which aspic can be ladled.

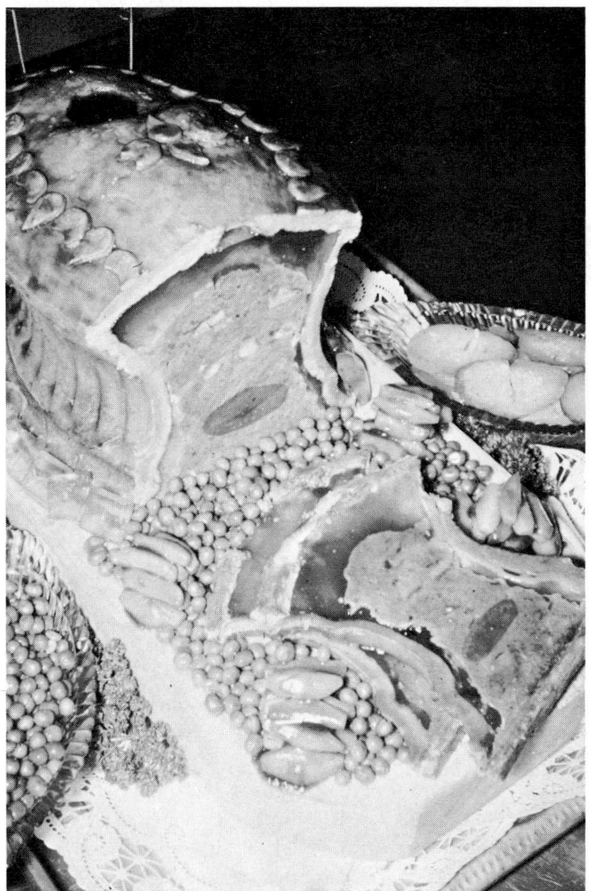

8. After mold is unhinged, and aspic has congealed, Pate en Croute is ready to be served. The crust of the pate will be quite firm but will slice easily with an electric knife or a bread knife with a scalloped or serrated edge. In this arrangement, the rich brown of the Pate en Croute contrasts nicely with the background of bright green peas. A boat of Cumberland Sauce is a popular accompaniment.

overlap for each part.

2. Grease inside of mold well with shortening or lard.
3. Line sides of mold with dough and press into place.
4. Place crust piece for bottom of mold on sheet pan and egg wash the edges of the crust dough.
5. Close mold on hinges and place on crust prepared on sheet pan. Seal seam with egg wash.
6. Cover inside of crust-lined mold with thinly sliced salt pork or bacon strips.
7. Pack paté meat mixture (force meat), to which garnishes have been added, tightly into mold. Mound mixture slightly higher than edges of mold.
8. Cover mold with prepared section of crust dough. Seal at edges with egg wash and decorate with ornamental cut-out design.
9. Place chimneys in cut-outs to release steam and pressure during baking. Chimneys can be made of aluminum foil cones.
10. Start baking in 325°F. oven; after 1 hour at this temperature, turn oven down to 275°F., cover paté en croute with foil if crust is getting too brown, and continue baking. It takes about 1 hour per pound of force meat or paté meat mixture to bake paté.
11. Remove from oven and chill well. During baking the meat will shrink leaving a cavity under the crust, although the crust will hold its shape. When paté en croute is fully chilled, pour full-flavored meat aspic, to which port wine or sherry has been added, into the crust. Use a ladle or sauceboat to completely fill cavity with aspic.
12. Open hinges of mold to remove paté en croute. Excess juices and fat can be used for aspic making. Trim edges if necessary. Decorate paté en croute further, using one of the ham or poultry decorating ideas in Chapter XIV. Serve with Cumberland Sauce. (Recipe below).

To Carve

The crust of the paté en croute will be quite firm and slices most easily if an electric knife is used. A good bread knife with a scalloped or serrated edge will also slice through the crust satisfactorily.

CUMBERLAND SAUCE

Ingredients

Oranges, skin sliced into fine julienne and juice	6
Lemon, skin sliced into fine julienne and juice	1
Port or Red Wine or Mixture of Two	2 pt.
Red Currant Jelly	1 lb.
English Mustard	optional
Cayenne Pepper	optional

Method

Poach orange and lemon skins which have been cut into julienne strips for 10 minutes in wine. Add orange and lemon juice, currant jelly; if dry mustard is to be used, mix first in a little red wine. Heat until jelly dissolves. Cool and chill sauce, then store in covered glass jar. This sauce can also be served hot. It can be served with any paté.

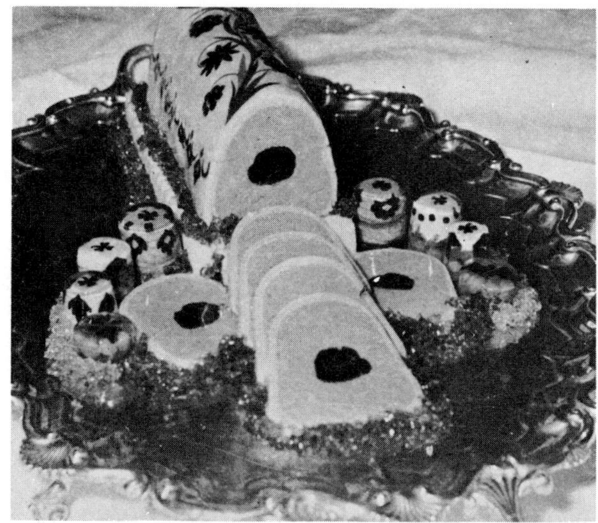

Pate Maison is sliced here to display truffle center and white frame of chaud froid. Slices are arranged on bed of chopped aspic; unsliced portion has easy-to duplicate floral design.

Perfectly round slices of Pate Maison have random garnish design. Interest is added to platter with vegetable timbales that repeat color of design on unsliced portion of pate. Timbales are trimmed with white chaud froid sheet flowers. Frame for platter is made of lemon half slices, ripe olive bits.

Above, galantine of turkey half slices line outer edges of tray with uncut decorated portion in center and individual pate molds with truffle design filling out row.

To Make 2-Lb. Loaf of Pate Maison

A pate of this size is enough to arrange attractively on a small round or square silver tray.

Ingredients	
Onion, medium sized	1
Butter to saute	
Allspice	1 tsp.
Pork Liver	1 lb.
Chicken Liver	½ lb.
Pork Fat	½ lb.
Eggs	2
Poultry Seasoning	1 tsp.
Anchovy Fillets	6
Salt and Pepper	to taste

Method

Slice onion and saute. Cool.

Cut pork liver and put through fine blade of meat grinder with onion, chicken livers and anchovy fillets.

Strain mixture through a fine sieve. Add eggs, mixing in thoroughly.

Line baking dish with salt pork slices. Pack mixture into baking dish tightly. Put baking dish in pan of water and bake slowly in 250° to 300° oven for 1¼ hours or until liquid on top is clear.

Cool pate and arrange on platter. (See pictures on facing page for suggested pate platters.)

Slices cut from pate should be coated with a wine-flavored aspic after they are put on platter.

Below, uncut portion of Galantine of Chicken is flanked by aspic squares. Outer V of half slices of galantine is lined with individual pate molds.

To Make Galantine of Capon

A galantine can be prepared using any poultry—turkey, duck, goose, or chicken. These directions are for the preparation of a galantine of capon. To prepare it, a completely boned capon is filled with force meat or the meat mixture used in paté maison. The capon is then wrapped in cheese cloth and poached in chicken stock.

In preparing the force meat for a capon, using the paté maison recipe, substitute dark capon meat for the veal called for in the recipe. The paté spice blend should not be used; instead use salt, white pepper, nutmeg and some garlic, if desired.

It will take an amount of force meat or paté meat mixture equal to one-half the weight of the capon to fill the boned bird; an 8-lb. capon will hold 4 lb. of force meat. Illustrated directions for preparing Galantine of Capon appear on following pages.

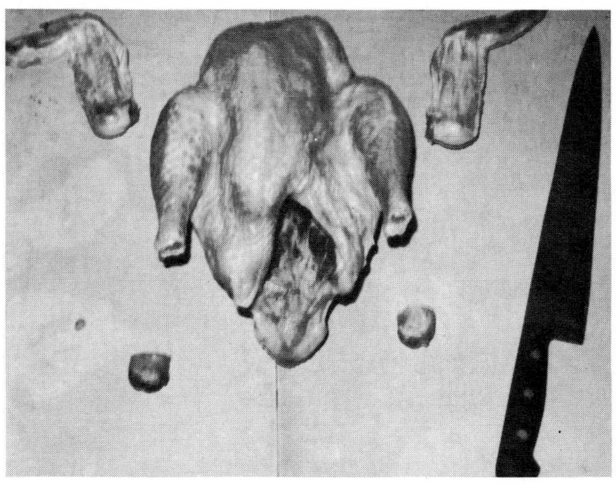

First step in boning chicken to be used in galantine requires large french knife. Remove wings at first joint and chop knuckles off drumsticks.

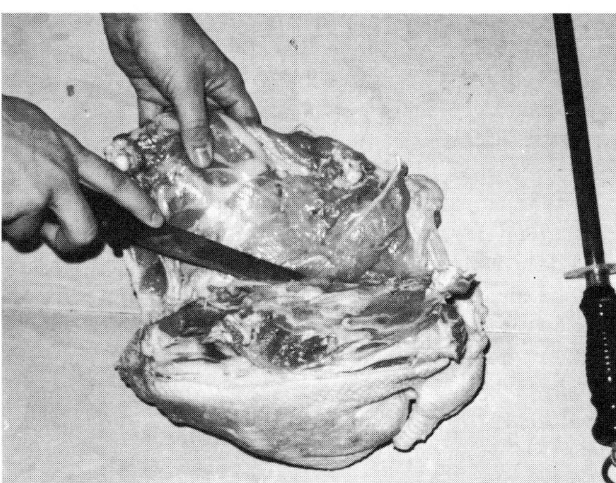

Next cut skin of chicken along center back from neck to tail.

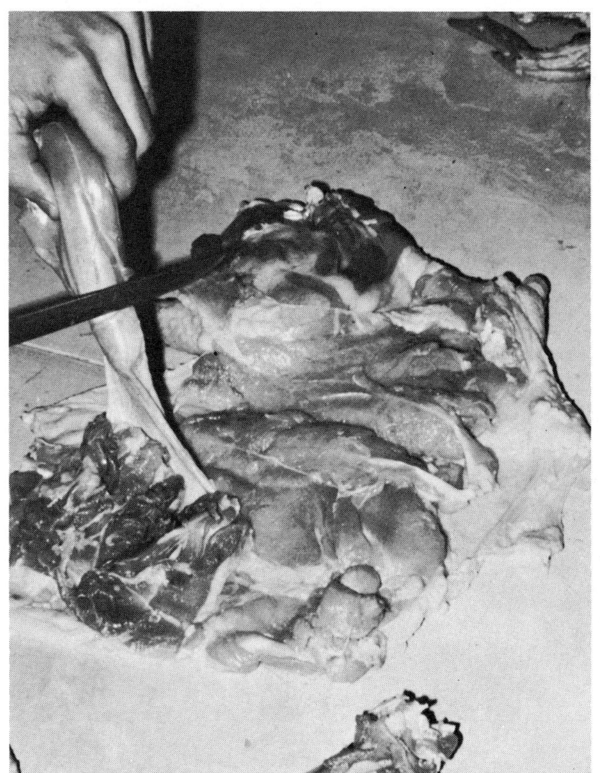

Left, after cutting skin around tail, lift out main carcass containing the viscera. Discard viscera reserving liver and heart.

TO MAKE GALANTINE OF CHICKEN

Chicken, duck and turkey can all be used to make galantines. This cylinder of delicately blended poultry and finely ground force meat filling is one of the less expensive haute cuisine items for a buffet.

GALANTINE OF CHICKEN

Ingredients

Roasting Chicken, 4 lb.	1
Onion, sliced	1
Carrot, sliced	1
Peppercorns	8
Salt	1 tsp.
Parsley, Celery, Bay Leaf	to season
White Veal or Pork	2 lb.
Medium Onion	½
Shallots	4
Poultry Seasoning	2 tsp.
Special Spice (see Pate Maison)	1 tsp.
Egg Whites	6
Light Cream	1 pt.
Beef Tongue Bars	3
Pate Maison Bars	3
Thin Strips Salt Pork	to wrap bars
Diced Cooked Mushrooms	1 cup
Truffle or Ripe Olives, diced	1 cup
Pistachio Nuts	1 cup
Sherry Wine	1 cup
Salt and Pepper	

Method

Bone chicken by removing wings at first joint. Cut skin of chicken along center back from neck to tail. Carefully cut away fibre that holds the flesh to the skin being careful not to cut skin.

Cut through wing and leg joints which attach wings and legs to body. Cut skin around tail and lift out main carcass containing viscera.

Scrape flesh from wing and leg bones and do not cut skin. Pull out bones.

Discard viscera from carcass, reserving liver and heart. Put carcass, bones and heart in kettle with sliced onion and carrot, peppercorns, salt, parsley, celery, bay leaf. Cover ingredients with water and bring to a boil, then simmer for two hours. Reserve broth.

Remove tendons from remaining chicken flesh and cut meat finely, then run through fine blade of meat chopper. Combine finely ground chicken meat with onions, shallots, ground veal and pork and stir in egg whites, salt, pepper and cream.

Spread chicken skin, skin side down on linen cloth. Spread half of ground meat evenly on skin and arrange salt pork wrapped bars of tongue and pate on filling. Sprinkle generously with chopped nuts and truffles, then spread remaining filling over it.

Bring skin around filling to make neat roll. Skin should overlap slightly. Wrap roll firmly in linen cloth and tie at each end. Also tie two or three times along length of roll.

Put the galantine in a kettle and cover with broth made above. Cover and simmer gently for two hours. Remove galantine to a board to cool. When cool, unwrap and chill.

Galantines can be coated with white chaud froid sauce and decorated with flowers for display.

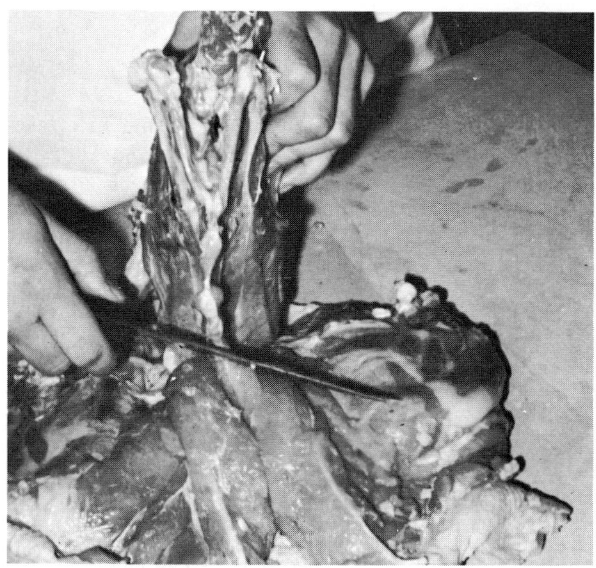

Above, scrape flesh from wing and leg bones. Pull out bones. These bones and the carcass are simmered with spices and vegetables to make broth that galantine is cooked in.

Beef tongue bars are wrapped in thin strips of salt pork for placement on the filling prepared for galantine of chicken. Filling should be prepared separately and chilled thoroughly before use.

Boned chicken is spread out skin side down on linen cloth. Filling is spread over skin and bars are added. Skin is brought up around completed filling and overlapped slightly.

Pates, Galantines

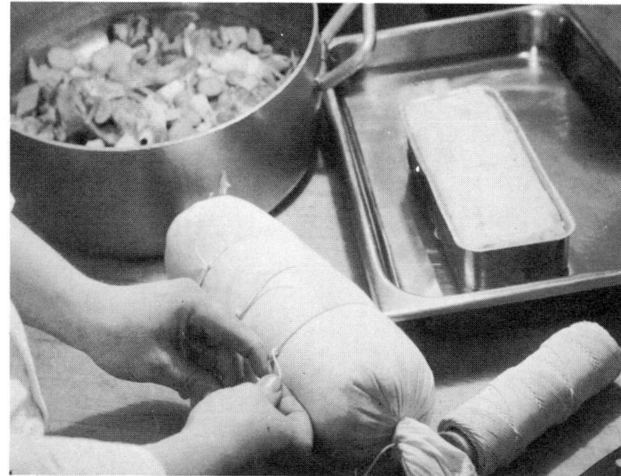

Next, linen cloth is wrapped tightly around chicken roll and tied at each end and at intervals along the roll. Galantine is ready to simmer in broth. Below, cooked and cooled galantine ready for service.

Galantine of Roast Suckling Pig is made of central portion of whole pig. Head and tail sections are cut away and roasted separately. Center section is boned, stuffed with forcemeat.

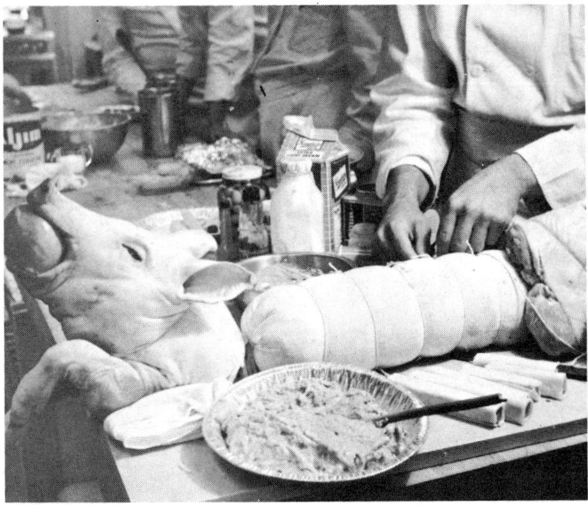

Skin is rolled around filling on linen cloth. Cloth, in turn, is rolled around filled skin and tied at each end and two or three times along roll. Roll is kept uniform in shape.

Galantine is simmered in broth until cooked, then cooled overnight in broth. Chilled galantine is unwrapped, placed on wire rack and covered with white chaud froid sauce and decorated. Galantine is cut in half lengthwise. One half is reserved for body of reassembled pig; other half is sliced.

TO MAKE SUCKLING PIG GALANTINE

A succulent sample of polynesian cooking here fashioned to preside over all accompaniments, Suckling Pig Galantine is presented with slices of roast pig completing the platter.

Head and shoulders of pig and rump and hind legs are cut away from center part. Center is completely boned. Skin is spread on linen cloth and is spread with layer of well seasoned forcemeat filling (see recipe, preceding page for galantine of chicken). Tongue and pate bars wrapped in thin layers of fresh salt pork are positioned on layer of forcemeat. A second layer of force meat covers the bars.

Pig skin is rolled tightly around filling with skin overlapping. Next, cloth is brought up around roll and tied at each end and along roll two or three times with stout twine. Roll is wrapped and tied to achieve a galantine of uniform shape.

The galantine is next simmered in a large stock pot containing water to cover, four cups of mixed cut vegetables, bay leaves, peppercorns and salt. Galantine should simmer for 2½ hours, then be cooled in stock til next day. When removed from stock, cloth around galantine should be cut away.

The remaining parts of the pig should be roasted on a wire rack for 3½ hours at 350°F. Cover ears, nose, feet and tail with aluminum foil. Baste occasionally during roasting.

Cover galantine with white chaud froid sauce and decorate as desired. Assemble head and tail with half of galantine in between. Slice other half of galantine and arrange slices on platter.

Garnitures for the platter can be added next, using small apple slices, orange segments and bits of maraschino cherries. Chopped aspic provides sparkling filler for the platter.

Slices of roast pig can be cut from the head and tail sections before they are positioned with the galantine. These slices of meat can be arranged with the sliced galantine.

Roasted head and tail sections have slices removed and are then positioned at either end of galantine. Reassembled pig is flanked on either side by slices of galantine and roast pig. Head and tail of pig are coated with aspic. Apple is inserted in pig's mouth, eyes outlined in hard cooked egg white.

NOTES

CHAPTER XIV DECORATING

This selection of decorating ideas for displays of salmon, poultry, ham and other meat is offered only as a foundation to be augmented with the unlimited number of ideas that can be developed by an imaginative chef or food worker.

Preliminary steps in preparation of salmon, poultry and ham for final decoration are outlined in the breakdown methods given in the subject chapters. The decorating ideas that follow are cross-referenced to the appropriate method. If pieces are to be elevated, fried bread socle or wedges can be used under them.

In selecting a decorating idea, the chef should always be sure to determine whether the breakdown method requires a chaud froid or an aspic coating. The proper coating will be indicated with each idea. Appropriate accompaniments for the decorated food item will also be noted.

Each buffet display (grosse piece) is divided into three sections for decorating reference. Directions will be given for:

(a) Decorations to be applied to the whole piece.
(b) Decorations to be applied to slices (if any).
(c) Decorations and garnishes for platter.

Some decorating ideas apply equally well to all three basic foods—salmon, poultry, ham or other meat; however, in some cases, the ideas are not interchangeable. For example, a fruit coating cannot be used with fish though it is excellent for a ham.

Aspic and chaud froid techniques must be thoroughly mastered before these decorating ideas can be carried out. When aspic and chaud froid work is understood, the chef's entire attention can be given to the development of the kind of comment-provoking decorating ideas that give a buffet the requisite dramatic flair.

To Decorate Fresh Salmon

Idea No. 1 for Method I—Classical

Whole Fish—Reshape salmon with russian salad or fish mousse. Place strips of aluminum foil along each side of salmon. Apply chaud froid. When chaud froid coat has set, pull foil off removing excess chaud froid at the same time, so pink salmon fillets will show on both sides.

With thinly sliced whole truffles and truffle sheet, create a seascape or a fishing scene. Since there are two sides to be decorated, two different scenes may be worked out. A sailboat decoration made from truffles could also be used; however, be sure to assemble sailboat on a plate first.

Arrange butterfly-cut shrimp down the spine of the salmon. If whole shrimps are used, push head into fish to hold shrimp firmly in place. Make eyes for salmon with a half cherry tomato and circle with egg white. Coat head with aspic.

Platter—Since there are no slices in this arrangement, fill space around salmon with more shrimp, lemon baskets filled with cocktail sauce and wedges of lemon.

Idea No. 2 for Method IV—Artificial

Whole Fish—Use a seafood mousse, russian salad with gelatin added, or fine diced potato salad to create the artificial salmon. Coat with aspic. Slice radishes thin in slicing machine and overlap over fish to give effect of scales. Head can be coated with chaud froid, or left uncoated. Put a piece of tomato in mouth.

Slices—Put a single vegetable flower on each slice. Use parsley stalks for stems, leeks for leaves and arrange radish slices as petals.

Platter—Hard cooked egg figures and eggs with caviar, stuffed cherry tomatoes, lemon slices to garnish.

Idea No. 3 for Method V—Scandinavian

Whole Fish—Coat fish with clear aspic, then arrange slices of hard cooked eggs, onion rings, sprigs of fresh dill and julienne lemon slices.

Slices—Arrange pimiento circles with ripe olive in center.

Platter—Dip tips of yellow asparagus spears in chopped parsley and arrange as bouquets; use strip of red pimiento for ribbon. Alternate bouquets with lemon baskets filled with capers. Add small clear aspic cubes and fresh cucumber slices.

Idea No. 4 for Method IV—Artificial

Whole Fish—Coat with white chaud froid. Make a delicate design for each side using leek strings, carrot stars and tear-drop shaped truffles. Leave head uncoated but play up eyes by arranging circles of red pimiento, egg white and truffles around them. Ripe olives can be substituted for truffles.

Slices—Make design with sliced ripe olives and leek and tarragon leaves.

Platter—Chopped aspic bed; use either clear fish aspic or chicken aspic with chopped parsley and chopped hard cooked egg whites sprinkled in a design. Add lemon wedges to platter.

Decorating Idea No. 5 for Method V

Whole Fish—Arrange spanish shrimp or scampis, cut butterfly style, down spine. Coat fish with clear aspic. Make eyes as in Idea 1 or 3.

Platter—Arrange empty scampi shells around fish, alternating with hard cooked eggs made into mushrooms and half lemon shells filled with russian dressing. Garnish with fresh dill sprigs or parsley.

Decorating Idea No. 6 for Method VI—Classical Not Boned

Whole Fish—Coat tail section with white chaud froid. Make large flowers from red pimiento sheet with leaves and stems made from leeks and arrange on tail section.

Slices—Make same flower in smaller size for each slice.

Platter—Timbale of salmon mousse or russian salad at side. Garnish with scored unpeeled cucumber and lemon slices.

Decorating Idea No. 7 for Method I—Classical

Whole Fish—Coat with white chaud froid. Arrange a

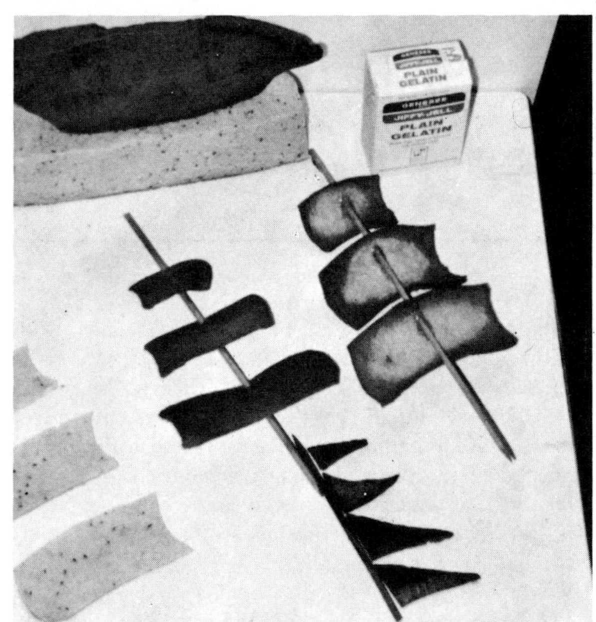

Parts assembled in preparation of bread sailboat. Hull hollowed out from pullman loaf of bread, toasted crusts for sails glued to wooden mast with gelatin. Whole assembled as in picture at right below.

large carrot flower on each side.

Platter—Use empty escargot shells as border. Make cucumber boats and fill with russian salad or remoulade sauce; surround with finely chopped pink aspic. Garnish with lemon wedges.

Decorating Idea No. 8 for Methods I and IV

Whole Fish—Poached squid heads arranged on back of fish. On sides arrange tiny fish made with small cutters from carrots, pimiento sheet, truffles, and lemon rind. Make fish in several shapes and place at random. Make border around base with lemon slices.

Slices—Put one hard cooked egg slice topped with black olive or pimiento strip on each slice. Add lemon twists and sprigs of parsley to garnish.

Platter—Tomatoes filled with mayonnaise; cherry stone clams on the half shell, lemon slices; lemon baskets filled with cocktail sauce, arranged alternately.

Decorating Idea No. 9 for Method IV—Artificial

Whole Fish—Coat with chaud froid; arrange medium shrimp split in half lengthwise on chaud froid at base of fish. Place circles of tomato skin between shrimp. Arrange whole ripe olives down back of fish, attaching them with piped egg yolk cream.

Slices—Place one shrimp split lengthwise on each slice. Garnish with sprig of parsley.

Platter—Alternate deviled eggs, hard cooked eggs stuffed with smoked oysters and lemon baskets filled with cocktail sauce. Garnish with lemon slices.

Decorating Idea No. 10 for Method I—Classical

Whole Fish—Make small broccoli flowers and combine with ornamental design made with carrot or truffle slices. Make border around base with half slices of lemon.

Platter—Arrange egg figures, egg heads or eggs made into drums, lemons cut into crowns and filled with capers on base of pink chaud froid combined with chopped chives or parsley. Mushroom caps coated with chaud froid may also be added.

Decorating Idea No. 11 for Method V—Scandinavian

Whole Fish—Use half of skinned salmon fillet. Use mousse to give top of fillet smooth surface and cover with reddish chaud froid sauce. Make set of bowling pins using hard cooked eggs and ripe olives; arrange on fillet and add ripe olive for bowling ball. Use a long pimiento strip to indicate bowling path.

Slices—Arrange around bowling decoration. Garnish with lemon twists, dill sprigs and onion rings.

Platter—Coat with clear aspic, using aspic cubes as border.

Decorating Idea No. 12 for Method VII—Any Whole Salmon

Whole Fish—(1) Remove piece of skin from center section of fish by making two parallel incisions with a paring knife. Space incisions about 8 or 10 in. apart. This can be done on both sides or only on one, if only one side will be visible. Either coat skinless area with white chaud froid or leave it natural. (2) Remove skin from entire salmon and coat with chaud froid. To decorate, make yellow buttercups from egg yolk sheet and arctic bluebells from light blue chaud froid, using green leeks for stems and leaves. If only part of fish has had skin removed, use truffle strips for border separating decorated panel from skin. Leave head natural, but build up eyes and place tomato strip in open mouth.

Slices—Put a buttercup blossom with stem and leaf made from dill sprig on each slice. Coat with clear aspic. Dill will add special flavor.

Platter—Eggs made into frogs; lemon crowns; light pink aspic around base of salmon and on border.

Notes:

1. A chilled mayonnaise-based sauce (tartar, remoulade, ravigote, verte, mousseline or russian dressing) should always accompany a salmon grosse piece on the buffet.
2. Do not use lettuce as it will wilt within a few hours. Aspic is equally colorful and lasts longer.
3. Ripe olives can be substituted for truffles in the above decorating ideas.

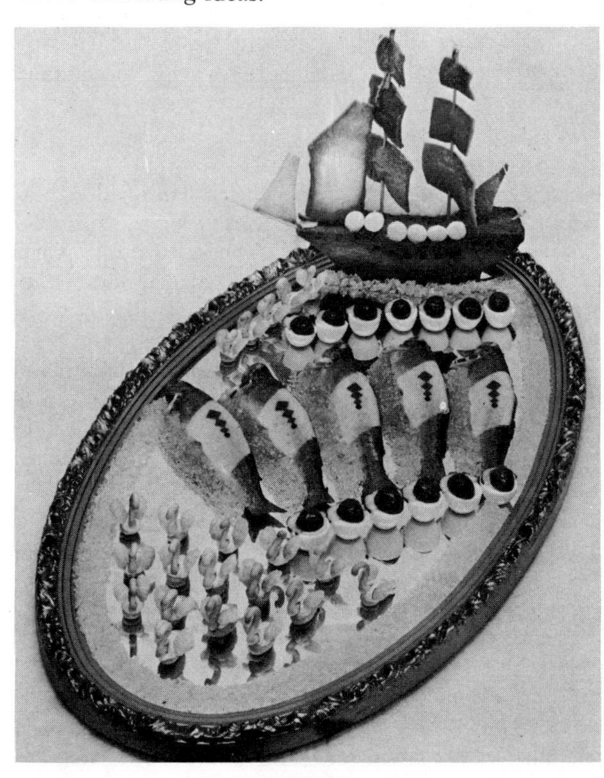

To Decorate Poultry

Decorating Idea No. 1 for Methods IV, V, VI

Centerpiece—Make flowers using radishes, cooked carrots and hard cooked egg whites with leeks for stems and leaves and arrange on breast.

Slices—Put a single flower on each slice using same design on all.

Platter—Tomatoes stuffed with russian salad or corn relish with a ripe olive on top of each tomato for garnish.

Decorating Idea No. 2 for Methods V and VI

Centerpiece—Make design of pieces of smoked beef tongue. Run line of fluted mushrooms down center, attaching them with picks or egg paste. Top mushrooms with truffle star or dot.

Slices—Use a diamond or half moon cut from tongue and leek leaves on each slice. Use same design on all slices.

Platter—Alternate artichoke bottoms filled with green peas and topped with cherry tomato halves with bundles of asparagus spears tied with strips of red pimiento around edge of platter. Coat with aspic.

Decorating Idea No. 3 for Methods III and IV

Centerpiece—Make ornamental design of black truffles on white chaud froid.

Slices—Repeat single motif of design of centerpiece.

Platter—Make a bed of diced light yellow aspic and arrange on it eggs made into mushrooms with tomatoes, other egg figures and egg white designs.

Decorating Idea No. 4 for Methods I and II

Centerpiece—Alternate green and purple grape halves with red cocktail cherries down the center of breast.

Slices—Pattern of tiny slices of truffles or ripe olives for each slice.

Platter—Pineapple cart filled with bunches of grapes; orange sections filled with fruit gelatin for garnish and chopped aspic piped in between decorative items on platter.

Decorating Idea No. 5 for Methods IV, V, VI

Centerpiece—Use tomato skin and leeks to make poppies. Add red dots of pimiento to design.

Slices—Miniature poppies or arrangement of small circles of pimiento for each slice.

Platter—Bouquets of brussels sprouts, cauliflower and broccoli on clear pink aspic base.

Decorating Idea No. 6 for Method VI

Centerpiece—Use ½-in. diamond-shaped cutter to make 3 dimensional design from pimiento sheet, truffle sheet and egg yolk sheet. Assemble design on plate first, then transfer onto capon breast. Make border of bits of same material to go around design.

Slices—Diamonds cut from yellow, red and black sheets (above) for each slice.

Platter—Cubes of imitation pate made from chicken, home made chicken liver pate, liver or ham mousse, coated with aspic and decorated with yellow, red and black diamonds like those used in centerpiece.

Decorating Idea No. 7 for Methods III to VI

Centerpiece—Make lilies of the valley from hard cooked egg whites, leeks and lemon skin.

Slices—Leek leaves shaped to match those on centerpiece for each slice.

Platter—Mounds of green peas alternated with radish roses with border of half circles of light pink aspic and four to six small vegetable timbales.

Decorating Idea No. 8 for Methods V and VI

Centerpiece—Arrangement of thin slices of pineapple, halves of red cherries with green mint leaves.

Slices—Thin slices of orange, halved or quartered, with bits of red cherries. Dry cherries before cutting them.

Platter—Orange baskets filled with chunks of pineapple, cantaloupe cart filled with fruits and oranges filled with fruit gelatin and sectioned.

Decorating Idea No. 9 for Methods I and II

Centerpiece—Bee with white flowers cut from chaud froid sheet made extra stiff with added gelatin.

Slices—Bee on each, wings made from leeks, body from red pimiento sheet, head and feelers from truffle bits or sheet.

Platter—Barquettes filled with belgium carrots and green peas set alternately in chopped aspic.

Decorating Idea No. 10 for Method VI

Centerpiece—Coat capon, which has been reshaped with mousse. Cover reshaped breast with small overlapping circles of smoked beef tongue. Coat drumsticks with brown chaud froid.

Slices—Make lines of music score with truffles on each supreme. Make notes from dots cut from truffle sheet.

Platter—Line with light pink or yellow clear aspic base, circle with aspic cube border.

Decorating Idea No. 11 for Method I

Centerpiece—Place white daisies, made from extra stiff white chaud froid, on roast poultry skin.

Slices—Arrange simple flowers made from radishes on each.

Platter—Place egg heads made from hard cooked eggs on potato nests and alternate with bunches of grapes.

Decorating Idea No. 12 for Method IV

Centerpiece—Reconstitute breast with russian salad. Place large sunflower, made from egg yolk sheet and egg plant skin, in center of breast. Frame with border made of black olive wedges and small circles of radish skins.

Slices—Alternate with slices of virginia ham.

Platter—Feature several small or one large timbale made from ham mousse or with asparagus; if chaud froid lining is used in timbale, arrange a sunflower inside mold or decorate with tulips made from radishes.

Decorating Idea for Roast Duck

Centerpiece—Arrange fluted mushrooms across breast with mandarin orange sections and ripe olive strips running down the sides.

Slices—Place back on carcass, before it is decorated.

Platter—Alternate orange baskets filled with cranberry relish with orange slices, port wine aspic croutons and potato nests filled with croutons.

Many of the decorating ideas described here are pictured in the sections on poultry, ham and salmon. Readers planning to create decorated pieces according to the directions given here should turn to the appropriate chapter, then to the method, where the picture illustrating the method will show the suggested decoration.

Many of the decorating ideas described here specifically for ham, poultry or salmon can be applied as well to other display pieces. The space available for decoration on the item selected is the limiting factor in choosing a decorating idea.

To Decorate Hams, Other Meat

Decorating Idea No. 1 for Whole Ham

Whole Ham—Use ready-to eat or sugar-cured ham which has had skin and excess fat trimmed off, aitchbone removed and chunk cut out as shown on diagram. Slice chunk into thin slices, roll the slices to be put back on ham later. Refrigerate ham rolls until time to use. Coat ham with chaud froid and chill.

To make design, prepare materials as follows: Cut truffles into paper thin slices; use cutters to make into desired shapes. Ripe olive skins may be substituted and prepared the same way. Thin slices of radishes, carrot balls cut out with ¼-in. french cutter and long strips of chives should also be prepared. Leeks may be substituted for chives but should first be dropped in boiling water for a few seconds, then cut into long thin strips. All of these design elements should be dipped in clear liquid aspic before being placed on chaud froid coated ham.

Tie string around ham as shown in diagram. On area of ham from which chunk was removed, use liver mousse as a base for the ham rolls prepared earlier. Position them as shown on diagram, using string as guide to arrange truffle scallops and diamonds as shown. Remove string.

Arrange leek or chive stems and leaves, placing flowers as shown. Make flower petals of pimiento or radish slices with carrot balls for centers.

When design is completed, coat whole ham with clear aspic and refrigerate.

Decorating Idea No. 2 for Whole Ham (Slices from Second Ham)—Moderne

Whole Ham—Trim fat from ready-to-eat ham and coat with liver mousse. Make oval paper pattern that will cover top of ham. Use pattern to make chaud froid shape on plate.

Use thin slices from second ham to cover whole ham. Arrange slices so they overlap, starting slices about 3 in. from bone end at side and working around ham back to bone end. Ham will be completely covered with overlapping slices that meet at the center of the top of the ham. Slide oval of chaud froid from plate to top of ham. Prepare squares of green pepper, truffle and pimiento to arrange in a block design in the center of chaud froid oval on top of ham. Alternate blocks to create colorful effect. Arrange bits of truffle or ripe olive around edge on the chaud froid, then circle outside edge of chaud froid with carrot balls. Coat bone end with dark brown chaud froid and decorate with rosettes of liver mousse.

Platter—Mound artichoke hearts with liver mousse and top rounds with a truffle or pimiento diamond. Edge platter with aspic triangles standing upright.

Decorating Idea No. 3 for Two Hams—Renaissance

Whole Ham—Remove shallow wedge from one side of one ham. Start wedge about one-third of the way down from the bone end, cutting a 2-in. slice from half of the ham. Coat ham with chaud froid and chill. Place ham on platter, elevating bone end with bread socle. Start arranging ham slices from second ham along wedge, fanning slices around ham and onto platter, completely circling whole ham.

On unsliced half of whole ham place basket made of crisscrossed leek or chive strips. In basket, position roses made by rolling thin slices of red pimiento. Make

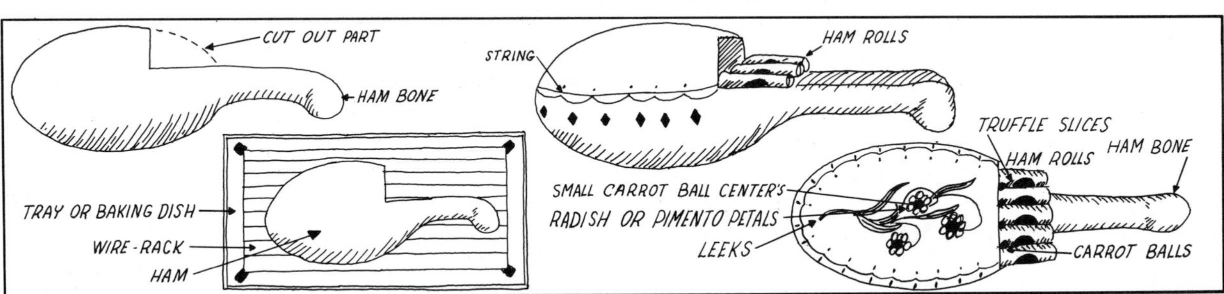

To prepare a cooked ready-to-eat whole ham for decoration, first trim skin and all excess fat from ham. At bone end of ham cut out chunk of meat as shown and also remove aitchbone. Place ham on wire rack which has been set in a tray or sheet pan.

To cover ham with chaud froid coating, keep chaud froid at room temperature until it is the consistency of heavy cream. Using a large ladle, pour chaud froid over ham, completely covering it. Place coated ham in refrigerator until chaud froid has congealed. Cover ham with a second coat following the same procedure. If ham is not completely covered, more chaud froid can be added; however, use only the amount of chaud froid needed to cover.

A clean piece of string can be tied around ham to provide guide for decorated border. Border may be made of pieces of truffle, eggplant skin or ripe olive skin, each cut paper thin and dipped in liquid aspic before being placed on ham. When border is completed remove string.

Line area of ham from which chunk was removed with pate. Chunk should be sliced into thin pieces that can be rolled and re-positioned as shown. The pate will hold them in place. A black circle is effective decoration for ham rolls. Floral decoration on ham is made of leek leaves and vegetable daisies. Centers of the daisies are carrot balls cut with a ¼-in. diam. french cutter and dipped in aspic before being put on the chaud froid coating. Radish slices dipped in aspic or petals from a pimiento sheet are placed around the carrot balls. Leek or chives used in the design should be dipped in boiling water first. When design is complete, cover whole ham with clear aspic and refrigerate.

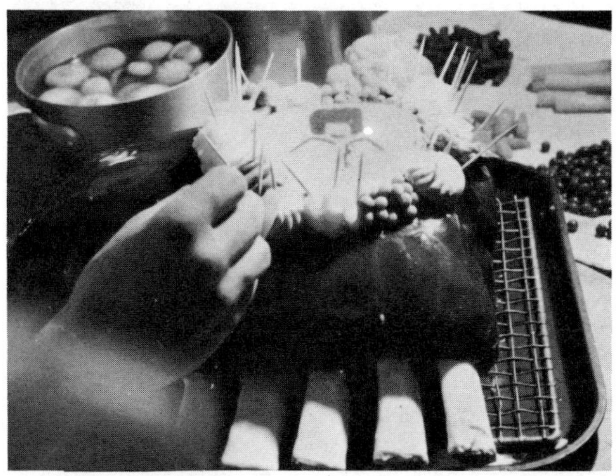

Toothpicks hold vegetables in place during decoration of Roast Prime Rib of Beef Bouquetiere. Prime ribs have been covered with brown chaud froid sauce. See pictures below.

leaves by shaping pieces of green pepper. Outline edge of uncut section of whole ham with truffle diamonds and designs. Coat with clear aspic and chill until time to serve.

Platter—Whole ham with the circle of slices will fill most of platter. Edge platter with aspic triangles, pointed ends up.

Decorating Idea No. 4 for Ham Rolls—Rose de Mai

Ham Rolls—For a small platter, cut off 18 to 20 thin slices from ham and trim neatly. Or use sliced cooked ham. Roll each slice of ham and use pastry bag with large fluted tube to fill ham rolls with ham mousse. Rolls can be filled from both ends. Chill filled rolls thoroughly.

Place filled rolls on wire rack over baking sheet. Garnish each ham roll with a truffle or ripe olive cut-out, topped by a design cut from hard-cooked egg white. Coat decorated ham rolls with three coats of aspic flavored with white wine. Chill ham rolls after each coat of aspic is added.

Platter—Coat round platter with thin layer of white wine aspic. Arrange rolls on aspic in circle around platter. Fill center of circle with watercress and radish roses. Pipe a ribbon of aspic between the rolls or garnish with additional watercress. Refrigerate until time to serve.

Decorating Idea No. 5 for Roast Prime Rib of Beef—Bouquetiere

Whole 6-Rib Roast of Beef—Roast 28 to 30 lb. rib of beef on day preceding service. Roast at 400° to 450°F. for 2 hours and 1 more hour in 400°F. oven. Cool and refrigerate overnight. On morning of service, trim fat off and coat roast with clear brown chaud froid. Clean end 2-in. of rib bones thoroughly and coat them with white chaud froid. Cut small oval of white chaud froid and place near end on top of roast. Center mosaic design made of squares of truffle or black olive, green pepper and hard cooked egg white on chaud froid oval. Use small slices of same ingredients to make border around chaud froid oval. Circle oval with small mounds of vegetables. Separate mounds of each of the following can be arranged for maximum color contrast: asparagus tips, white turnip balls, carrot balls, peas, cut green beans, whole mushrooms, cauliflower buds and brussels sprouts.

Platter—Slice 10 to 12 slices from undecorated end of roast. Place unsliced ribs on oblong platter with slices fanned along end of roast. End beef slices at corner of oblong platter and punctuate with five or six asparagus tips, crisscrossed with 2 pimiento strips. Place more vegetables in individual mounds or rows running out from rib ends to edge of platter. Keep rows about 2 in. wide, again alternating colors. Cover with aspic.

After vegetables are positioned, they are covered with a clear aspic and toothpicks are removed. Any of these vegetables may be used: broccoli, carrots, asparagus, mushrooms, stringbeans, cauliflower and peas. The white chaud froid circle has a truffle design. Before beginning work on the design, cut half of rib meat off, slice it into uniform slices to be arranged later starting as shown above right. When beef slices are all in place, add rows of vegetables as illustrated at left, with a vegetable timbale as a focal point. Chopped aspic can be used to fill out platter.

DECORATING

Decorating Idea No. 6 for Roast Sirloin of Beef—Jardiniere

Beef—Roast boneless shell strip of sirloin to medium rare. Cool. Cover with brown chaud froid and chill. Slice half of beef, leaving rest in one piece.

Platter—Fan beef slices in front of uncut piece. In front of meat on platter, make a circle of vegetable mounds, each mound made up of a different vegetable (see Idea No. 5 above for vegetables to use). In center of uncut half of sirloin, place a circle of chaud froid, decorated with a mosaic made from squares of ripe olive, carrots and green pepper. Fill in platter as needed with vegetable timbales, asparagus spears and chopped aspic. Coat entire arrangement with a clear wine-flavored aspic.

Decorating Idea No. 7 for Beef Tongue—Strassbourgoise Served with Remoulade Sauce

Tongues—Start with two large cooked beef tongues. Slice one of the tongues carefully into uniform slices. Coat unsliced tongue with brown chaud froid. Decorate uncut tongue with daisies made of hard-cooked egg white petals and carrot ball centers. White chaud froid could be substituted for the daisy petals.

Slices—Spread tongue slice with liver mousse, then fold slice over. Decorate each slice with design made of truffle or ripe olive bits and slices of hard-cooked egg white.

Sirloin of Beef Jardiniere is quickly assembled when central decoration is made in advance to be taken from the freezer. See directions below left.

Platter—Place whole tongue on platter with a row of overlapping slices of tongue alongside a row of whole tomatoes stuffed with vegetable salad and a row of artichoke bottoms topped with goose liver mousse and mushroom caps.

Decorating Idea No. 8 for London House Double Beef Tongue

Tongues—Boil 3 smoked beef tongues. Cool, skin but do not trim. Place two tongues together in upright position on a tray; fasten together with two skewers. Place another tray on top of the tongues and weight down by placing a heavy object on top of tray. Keep overnight in refrigerator. Next day place tongues on a wire rack, cover with brown chaud froid sauce.

After the chaud froid sets make a flower decoration out of white hard cooked eggs, or from a white chaud froid sheet. Also place red pimientos and green leeks on the tongues.

Slices—From the third beef tongue cut slices, fold slices over and fill with imported goose liver paté, set on wire rack and decorate with ripe olives and cut-outs of white of eggs.

Platter—Liver paté medallions (see Chapter XIII) can be placed in front of tongues with additional square cut aspic croutons and 2 in. pieces of cucumber stuffed with vegetable salad. The tongues and the garnishes are covered as usual with a clear wine-flavored aspic.

Pictured here and, right on facing page, is coating and decorating of London House Double Beef Tonque shown in final assembly on platter at right. Directions are outlined above.

The final display is covered with a wine-flavored aspic. It is a piece that adds height to a buffet arrangement. Individual folded slices are easy to handle portions.

What Garnishes Can Add

Presentations of both hot and cold buffet foods gain special dimensions when properly garnished. Garnishes range from the simple sprigs of parsley, watercress, to the more time-consuming fluted mushroom caps and medallions of paté.

Although more time-consuming, elaborate garnishes can do double duty, thus keeping costs in line. They may be prepared to be used as first course appetizers in addition to taking their place as platter garnishes or in special arrangements flanking the grosse piece or large buffet display.

The first rule of good garnishing is: all garnishes should be appetizing, eye appealing and suitable in character, flavor and size to the food they are to be displayed with.

The three garnishes described here are in the double duty category.

Stuffed Tomato—Remove top slice from small, ripe, peeled tomato. Scoop pulp from center of tomato and turn tomato upside down on rack for a few minutes to drain out excess moisture. Fill with shrimp, salmon or crabmeat salad and top with sliced cooked shrimp. Put top slice of tomato back on over salad and garnish with cutouts of hard cooked egg white and truffle or ripe olive. Little rosettes of mayonnaise can be pressed out between the shrimp, using a small fluted tube. Center a bright green cooked pea in each rosette. This filling is also used the same way with artichoke bottoms.

Garniture Princesse—Arrange three or more strips of asparagus in bunch. Crisscross strips of pimiento over asparagus. Chill thoroughly and glaze with aspic. If desired, asparagus may be marinated in french dressing and drained thoroughly before it is arranged for this garniture. For a base, place asparagus on slice of tomato.

Stuffed Cucumber a la Russe—Score straight, medium size cucumber from one end to other with a paring knife. Keep scoring lines uniformly spaced. Cut cucumber in 2 in. pieces. With a large melon scoop, make depression and remove seeds from each piece. Season inside of cucumber with salt and pepper. Fill hollow with a delicate vegetable Salad a la Russe. Decorate with sliced hard cooked egg, deviled egg cream, pimiento cut-out, mushroom cap, ripe or stuffed green olive, half small shrimp, circle of king crab. Cover with wine flavored aspic and keep in refrigerator.

Setting the stage for a polynesian or hawaiian buffet, these palm trees are made by inserting a carrot trunk into a melon. Pineapple leaves become palm leaves; chick peas, coconuts. Tomato garnishes: from top, row 1, tomato quarters topped with cream cheese, salami cones, asparagus tips; row 2, tomato quarters with egg yolk cream, salmon rollatini; row 3, tomato quarters with egg yolk cream, broccoli flowers; row 4, whole tomato stuffed with egg yolk cream topped with avocado ring, standing asparagus tip; row 5, cherry tomato filled with egg yolk cream on cucumber slice; row 6, tomato quarter with egg yolk cream, wedge of hard cooked egg; row 7, tomato quarter with egg yolk cream, cherry tomato and parsley added; row 8, tomato quarter with cream cheese, ripe olives; row 9, whole tomato filled with russian salad, lid topped with flower of hard cooked egg whites; row 10, tomato quarter, egg yolk cream, asparagus spears; row 11, tomato quarter, pulp removed, cut to shape. Below right.

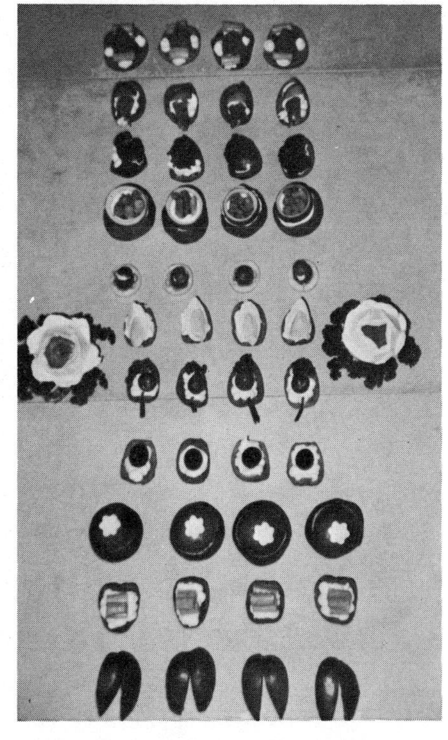

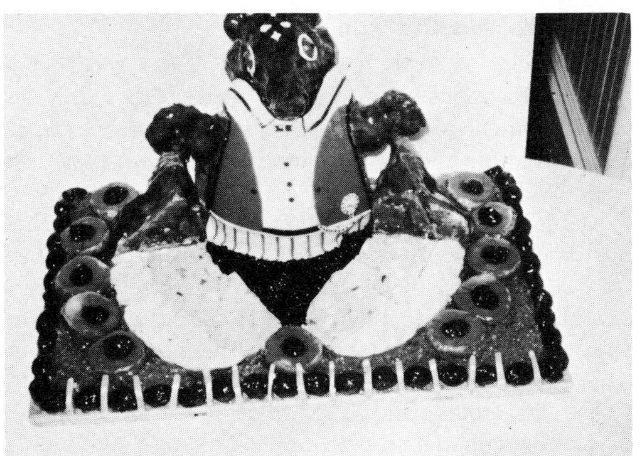

Red-coated pig presides over succulent slices in this display presenting seated Roast Suckling Pig.

To Prepare Roast Suckling Pig

One of the most intriguing items on any buffet table is a whole roast suckling pig. A note of special gaiety is contributed when pig is presented as a recoated figure presiding over a platter of succulent slices of pork filled with ham mousse.

Basic Preparation of Roast Suckling Pig—Excess hair on face should be shaved or burned off. Making insert under head, remove rib cage and remove all bones to hip. Also remove thigh bones.

Open pig up, spreading flesh flat. Salt lightly.

Place wax paper on sheet pan and place pig on it. Cover pig with wax paper and refrigerate. Do not stuff pig until just before time to roast.

When ready to stuff, wash inside of pig thoroughly with cold water and dry with clean towel. After putting stuffing in pig, sew opening, being careful not to draw it too tightly as stuffing will expand during roasting.

Place stuffed pig in roasting pan. Oil lightly. Cover ears, nose, feet and tail with aluminum foil. Start roasting in 300°F. oven. Moisten or baste with beer and pale dry gingerale that has been heated together. It will take approx. 15 minutes to the lb. for roasting a 15 to 16 lb. pig.

Note: It will take stuffing weighing approximately ⅓ of the drawn weight of the pig to stuff it properly.

To Make Sitting Pig: When roasted pig has cooled, cut into three parts: the head, middle two-thirds and tail third. Build up lower part of middle section with ham mousse. Make red tuxedo jacket from pimiento chaud froid sheets and arrange on middle section; make shirt front of white chaud froid. Coat head and feet with brown aspic.

Set middle section in vertical position on platter. Position head in mousse. Place white chaud froid around eyes and decorate top of head between ears.

Slice remaining portion of pig and arrange slices on either side of platter. Finish platter with arrangement of baked apple halves, prunes, cubes of brown aspic, and cherry tomatoes.

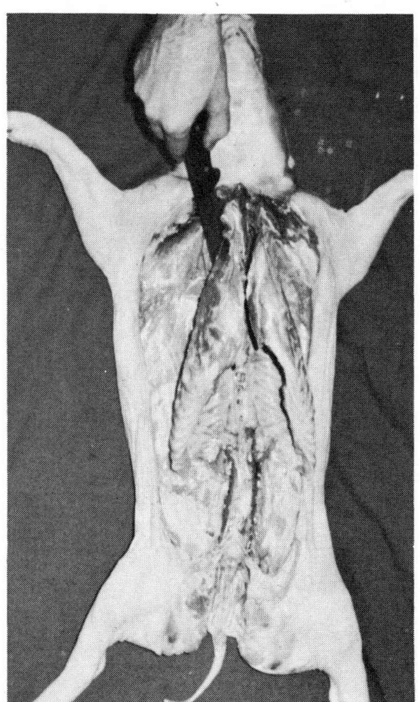

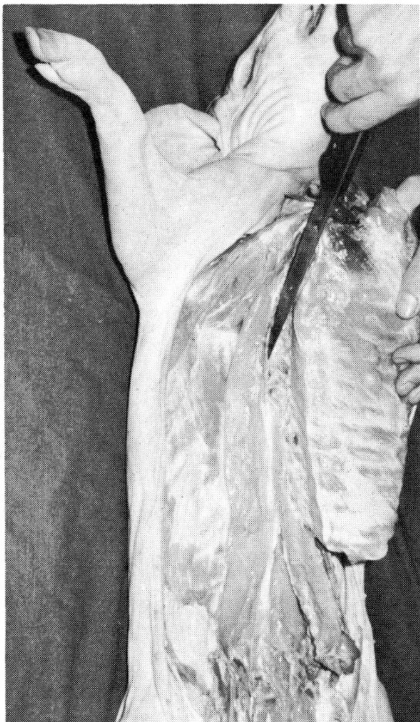

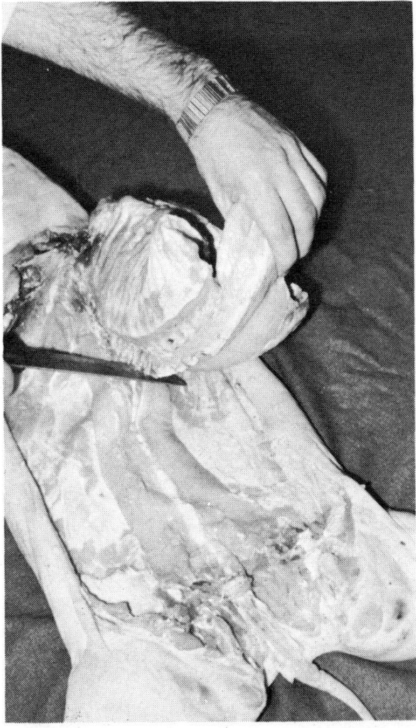

Above, in preparation for roasting, pig is spread out flat while bones are removed.

Center and right, two steps in boning to remove rib cage. Maximum area is left for stuffing.

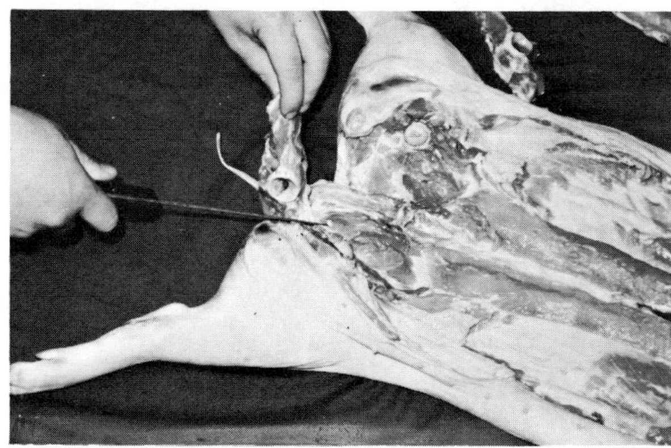

In final boning step, thigh bone is removed. Flesh is lightly salted and carcass refrigerated.

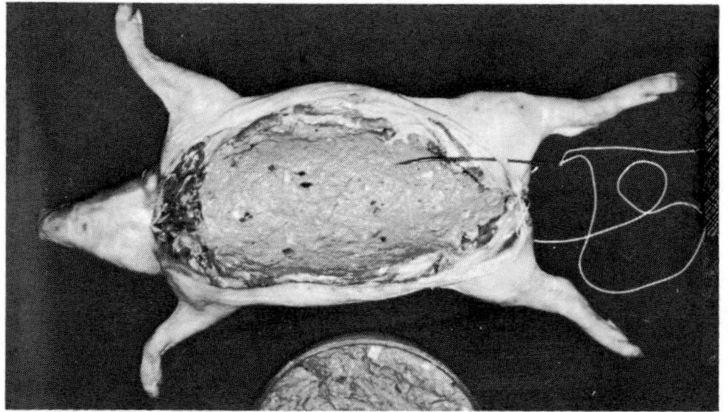

Inside of pig is thoroughly washed with cold water and then dried with towel before stuffing is put in. Pig is stuffed just before roasting.

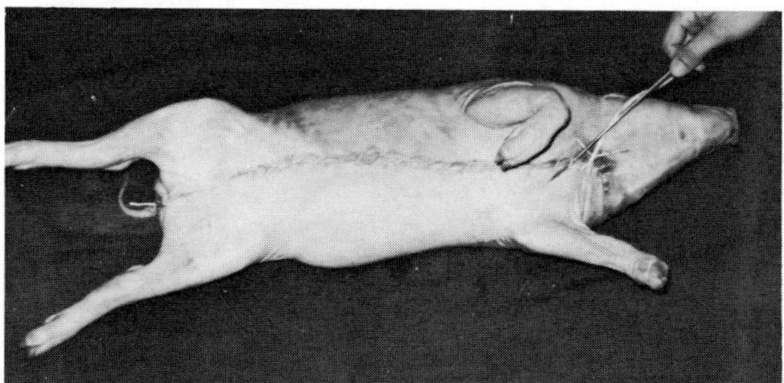

When stuffing is all in, sew up opening from tail to head, being careful not to sew too tightly as stuffing will expand during roasting. Place pig, stomach down, in roasting pan and oil lightly.

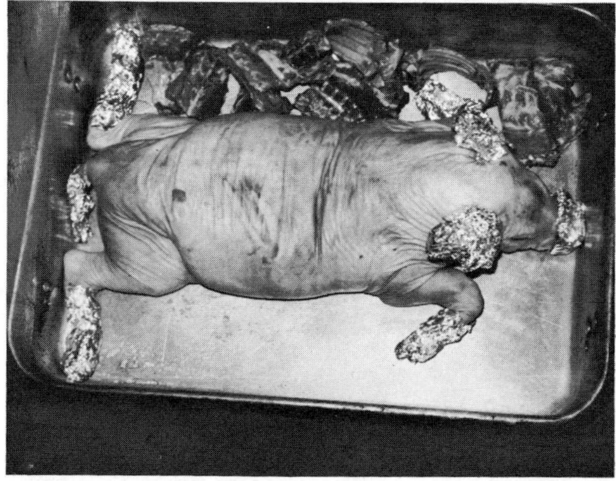

Next cover ears, nose, feet and tail of pig with aluminum foil. Start roasting in 300°F. oven. Heat beer and pale dry gingerale together and use to baste pig during roasting.

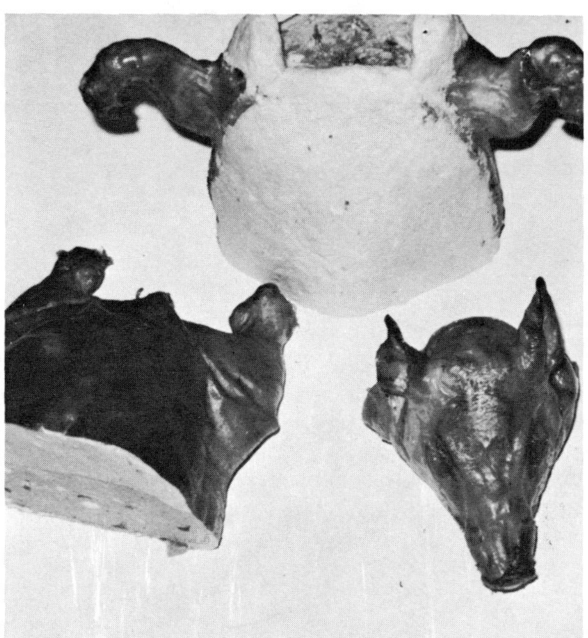

Roasted pig is cut into three parts as shown. Middle section with legs extended has been built up with ham mousse. This section becomes the body of the sitting pig and is decorated with red coat. Bottom third is sliced and slices are arranged on platter around seated pig.

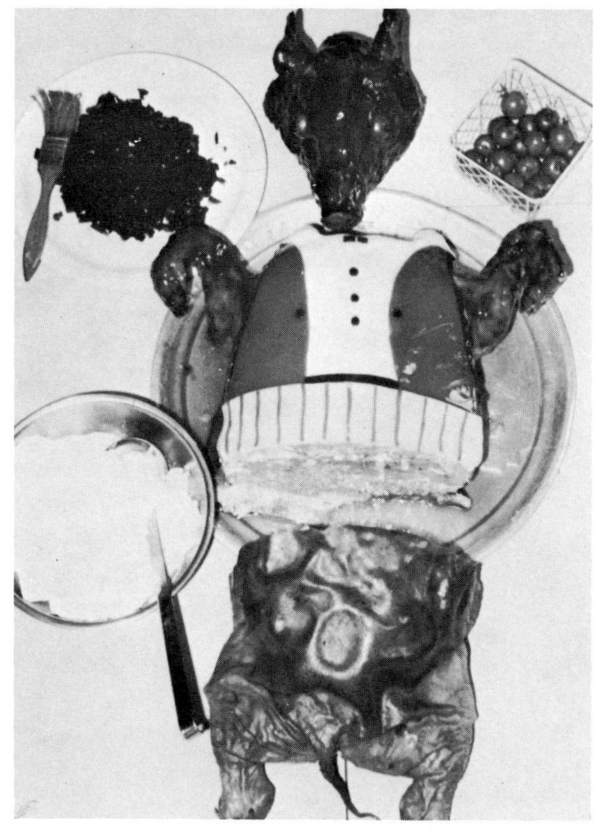

The pig's red coat is cut around pattern on red pimiento sheet; vest is white chaud froid; buttons and other black decor are truffles or ripe olive skin; head and legs are coated with shiny brown aspic. Directions for assembling and garnishing sitting figure on facing page.

NOTES

CHAPTER XV

Jellied Molds

Aspic molds, also known as piece montee or classical aspic timbales, can be created in any size from 3 to 10 in. in diameter. The piece montee is made up with pieces of meat or seafood positioned in a large mold with aspic. The aspic timbale is usually smaller and requires less precision in its assembly.

Large molds, usually called piece montee, when built up to impressive heights with shrimp, lobster chunks or pheasant supremes around a mousse, are certain to attract maximum attention. Small vegetable-filled aspic timbales will heighten the effectiveness of large molds or other food displays (grosse piece) on the buffet.

While the outer layer of all molds is aspic, the fillings for the molds may vary. However, the aspic selected will always govern the choice of mousse to be used as filling. Poultry aspic would go with poultry or meat filling; seafood aspic with salmon and fruit gelatin with fruit fillings. Instant aspic can be used with any filling material as it is neutral in flavor. Russian salad or other jellied salads are also often used as fillings for molds.

All of these molds require basic knowledge of aspic preparation. It is also important to remember that aspic molds and timbales must always be assembled in containers made of metal. The shapes can vary from ring molds to concave stainless bowls, silver dishes, fancily shaped copper or aluminum molds (fish, crowns and similar shapes are available). Metal is preferred because it is easier to remove jellied contents from metal.

Two additional factors increase the usefulness of these creations. A properly filled and decorated mold can be stored in a refrigerator safely for a week if tightly covered with transparent wrap. This makes it possible to schedule production during slow periods, thus reducing labor costs.

Since leftover ingredients are usually available for use with aspic in a piece montee or timbale, these items can be prepared for the buffet with a low food cost; yet properly executed the piece montee can be the most eye catching dish on the table.

To Prepare Aspic Mold Without Chaud Froid Lining

1. Cool metal mold in freezer or in crushed ice; use both for maximum speed in cooling.

2. Cool aspic or gelatin by placing it in metal container, itself placed in crushed ice. Stir liquid slowly to chill but do not let it congeal.

3. Pour liquid aspic into chilled mold, filling mold up to the rim. Let set a few minutes, checking with spoon every 20 seconds to see whether a ⅛-in. layer has formed on mold. Keep mold in crushed ice while layer is forming. As soon as layer has formed, pour excess aspic out immediately, using circular motion.

If bulk of aspic becomes congealed in the mold, all aspic must be dumped, the mold washed and the procedure started over again. This happens when aspic is

Above, bowl mold in ice holds aspic lining with center decoration cut from chaud froid sheet. Slices from capon breast are positioned in jellied aspic. Below, after capon slices are set in place, a second coat of aspic is added; bowl is rolled around gently so new coat of aspic covers completely.

A sample of the variety of molds used in aspic work. Ring, silver bowl, pimento can (sterilized), small aluminum mold, fish. Keep molds in second ice-filled container while they are being built up with aspic.

When aspic mold is to be lined with chaud froid coating, a mayonnaise chaud froid must be used. Chaud froid layer is applied to mold placed in ice-filled bowl to speed cooling of chaud froid layer.

After chaud froid layer has set so it will adhere firmly to aspic, center of mold can be filled with diced poultry meat and russian salad as shown here. These ingredients should be sealed with a final coating of aspic to complete mold.

When putting the first layer of ingredients into an aspic lined mold, keep in mind that they will be the outer layer when mold is turned out on platter. Plan these ingredients for maximum contrast.

cooled too much before it is poured. It is also true that if there is not enough gelatin in the aspic, the lining will not hold up.

4. Turn aspic-lined mold upside down and chill in freezer or refrigerator for a few minutes to be sure lining is firmly set on the sides of the container.

Note: Repair an uneven or lumpy aspic lining, (1) by holding a heated metal ladle over uneven area; (2) by pouring boiling hot aspic into mold, swishing it around and pouring it out immediately.

5. Plan the food and garnish items to be used in the mold to go with the color scheme of the buffet or to complement the items selected to go with it. The colors of the food and aspic in the mold itself should always be selected to make an attractive and colorful mold.

The food and garnish items placed on the first layer of aspic will be the most clearly seen when the mold is turned out. If it is a deep mold, tweezers or skewers will make the positioning of items easier and more accurate. Bits of truffle or leek should be dipped in liquid aspic before they are positioned as this will help to keep them in the desired place.

6. As soon as the decorative pieces for the outer aspic layer are in place, pour a few ladles of cool liquid aspic into the mold, turning the mold in crushed ice while layer forms evenly over decorations. Let aspic set. This second layer of aspic will hold the solid decorative items in place, such as vegetables, slices of tongue, lobster medallions and similar foods.

7. When second layer has set firmly, fill center of mold with a mousse or a jellied salad. Let set until firm, then seal entire top of mold with aspic.

8. Mold should always be refrigerated for several hours before service. These molds can actually be prepared several days in advance of a scheduled buffet if they are properly sealed, covered with transparent wrap and refrigerated. Never freeze a mold.

9. To remove contents of mold, dip container into boiling hot water for 1 to 3 seconds; then loosen edges with paring knife or long narrow spatula; place platter over mold and turn over and out.

When dipping mold in hot water, be sure not to let hot water get into the mold as it will damage the decorative appearance of the contents irreparably.

To Prepare Aspic Mold with Chaud Froid Lining

This more classical technique is especially appropriate when the mold is to be filled with a mousse. The objective is to prepare a smooth white or pink chaud froid background for the contents of the mold.

Follow steps 1 through 7 for preparation of aspic mold without lining. After the second aspic layer, apply a layer of mayonnaise colle chaud froid.

Ladle this mayonnaise chaud froid carefully into the finished decorated mold. Roll mold around in crushed ice until chaud froid layer sets and has adhered to the aspic layer. When chaud froid has set firmly in mold, fill center space with a mousse.

Note: Only the mayonnaise colle chaud froid is certain to adhere to aspic layers, so no other chaud froid should be substituted for it. There is always danger that the aspic layers will separate from the chaud froid layer in a deep mold so directions should be carefully followed. When properly executed, this is a most effective method of preparation.

Creating an effective molded dish is easiest when the copper mold is as unusual as the one pictured here. At far right, a glistening lining of aspic highlights the simply-decorated chaud froid layer which coats a center of salmon mousse. More elaborate decoration is used on plain round mold.

To Prepare Small Vegetable Timbales

These small timbales should be designed to add interest to whatever large piece will be displayed with them.

A crystal clear aspic should be used to make small timbales and any of the following may be arranged in the aspic to make a colorful and pleasing pattern:

Blanched frozen green peas, cut green beans, cauliflower flowerets, whole brussels sprouts, cooked carrot balls or uniform carrot cut-outs; slices or slivers of radishes, red pimientos, ripe or green olives and hard cooked egg whites.

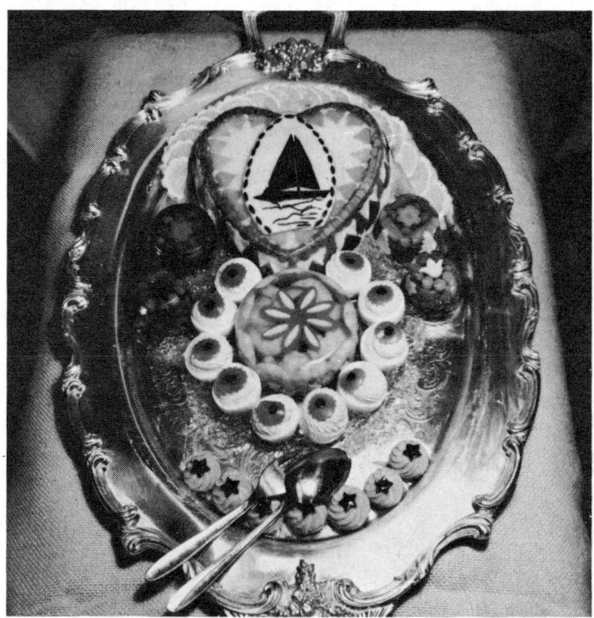

Timbales of all sizes start with a decorative layer; a variety of possible patterns is pictured at right. Above right, aspic is ready to coat pattern layer, rest of timbales will be filled with assorted cooked vegetables, mousse or salad. Right, rows of empty molds and unmolded timbales. Above, platter holds heart-shaped timbale with truffle sailboat, round timbale with shrimp surrounded by stuffed eggs; fluted mushrooms line up at front of platter.

Jellied Molds

The three piece montee pictured on this page can be prepared with a variety of ingredients. Piece montee, above, is designed to fit buffet planned around musical theme. Immediately below, is round mold with eye catching pattern surrounded by alternating olive-topped stuffed egg halves and avocado halves, then circle of aspic squares with border of half lemon slices and bits of ripe olive. Below right, three-level piece montee circled by individual timbales variously decorated.

To Make the Large Piece Montee

With Shrimp—Line mold with dill aspic, combine medium size cooked and deveined shrimp with bits of truffle and/or red pepper to make design. Add second layer of aspic and fill mold with mousse. Place layer of aspic over mold.

With Medallions of Liver Pate—Slice either homemade or canned commercial paté into small circles and arrange in pattern with one or more of the following: fluted mushrooms, white asparagus tips, truffle slices made into chain or other design, rosettes made from hard cooked egg whites. Cover with second layer of aspic and a coating of mayonnaise chaud froid, if desired. Fill center with liver mousse.

With Supremes of Poultry—Line mold with aspic. Make design of uniform very thin slices of capon, turkey, breast of pheasant, smoked beef tongue, halves of ripe olives, red cut-outs from pimiento sheet and leek leaves. Add second layer of aspic and fill mold with diced poultry meat, either white or dark, or diced smoked tongue or ham held in place with more aspic.

With Virginia Ham and Asparagus—Line mold with aspic and make star of whole white canned asparagus spears. Thin slices of virginia ham can be positioned around star or around sides of mold. Add second layer of aspic and let design set. Fill center of mold with asparagus and ham layers alternated with aspic.

With Smoked Tongue—Use fancy brochette for mold. Line mold with aspic layer. Make design of rounds cut from cooked smoked beef tongue, pieces of truffle and hard cooked egg whites combined with peas or cut green beans. Add second layer of aspic, then fill center with chopped pickles and tongue in more aspic.

With Lobster—Line mold with aspic. To make design, combine meat from split lobster claws; slices from lobster tails; leeks and pimientos; half brussel sprouts; bits of truffle or ripe olives. Add second layer of aspic, then use russian salad, to which pieces of lobster have been added, for filling.

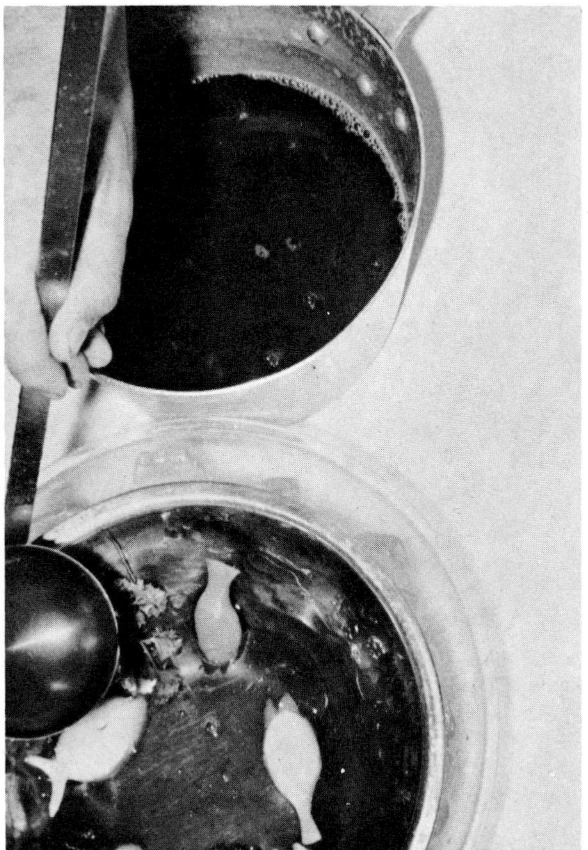

Left above, ingredients assembled to create Submarine Scene; see directions below. Above, gelatin-lined mold with vegetable fish in place gets more gelatin. Left, finished mold is circled by pear halves topped with maraschino cherries to make edible frame for mold.

To Make Fish Molds

Line fish molds with fish aspic, chicken aspic or instant aspic. Add white wine to any aspic prepared for use with fish.

Any leftover cooked fish pieces can be arranged in the mold. Canned fish is also suitable. Tuna, salmon, cod, sole and similar fish are excellent. Cut fish into bite-size pieces before placing in mold. Arrange fish on aspic layer, add second layer of aspic, then coat with mayonnaise chaud froid, and fill with green peas in more aspic.

Either a ring mold or a fish mold would be effective for this arrangement. If another type of mold is used, a design in the bottom of the mold would be enough and would simplify preparation.

To Make Submarine Scene: A stiffer than usual lime gelatin is required for this mold. Reduce liquid called for to ⅗ of the amount specified; if one gallon of water is suggested, use only 2½ qt.

Line mold with layer of lime gelatin. This light green layer provides the underwater effect. With paring knife or small fish cutters, cut out a variety of fish shapes from cooked carrots (to make gold fish), white or yellow turnips, lemon rind. Use sprigs of parsley, watercress and fresh dill to create seaweed. Ripe olives can become oysters, an octopus can be devised from thin pieces of eggplant skin, a seahorse or a star fish from sliced turnips.

Use several of the fish shapes, pieces of seaweed, etc., on the first layer of lime gelatin. Cover with a second layer of lime gelatin, then add more fish shapes. Continue building up mold, adding seascape figures after each layer of gelatin. Refrigerate mold for several hours. When turned out, fish shapes in the light green gelatin will resemble those seen in an aquarium.

To Serve—Accompany with sour cream or a sauce that is half mayonnaise and half sour cream.

To Make Fruit Gelatin Molds

Fruit gelatin molds can range from the very simple to elaborate jewel-colored towers of fruit and sparkling gelatins. The easiest arrangements are made in large square pans and often combine canned fruits with gelatins of complimentary colors.

To make the fancy molds that get "oh and ah" reactions, a method similar to the assembly of the piece montee must be used. If a mold 8 to 10 in. deep is to be used, the gelatin or gelatins selected to fill it must be made stiffer than usual. Reduce liquid called for to ⅗ of the amount specified; if 1 gal. of water is suggested, use only 2½ qt.

Canned fruits can be used in the most glamorous molds. The impressiveness of the mold will depend on the arrangement of the fruit and the color combinations worked out. Some suggested combinations follow; however, these are only a few of the numerous arrangements that can be put together:

Cherry gelatin, peaches, mandarin orange sections, green cherries.

Lime gelatin, pears, green cherries, mint leaves.

Above, finishing touches for fruit gelatin platter include pear halves filled with cottage cheese. Fruit-filled ring mold would be centered on tray first, then outer circle of pears put in position and filled. Completed platter, above, shows colorful jam topping in place on cottage cheese with dark green parsley adding contrast to the border.

Orange gelatin, orange sections, pineapple segments, banana slices, red cherries.

To Make a Rainbow Mold: A rainbow mold must be at least 4 in. high and is made of layers of orange, lime and raspberry or cherry gelatin. Fill bottom third of selected mold with orange gelatin and refrigerate to set. When layer is firm, add enough gelatin to fill mold two-thirds full, set in refrigerator again. When second layer is firm, fill mold to the brim with red gelatin.

Note: Gelatin molds with or without fruit are very effective accompaniments for ham platters. Guests often prefer them for dessert also.

To Make Shrimp Pyramid

This unusual pyramid or cone-shaped mold is arranged for heightened effectiveness on a ring mold. It is easily the highlight of the buffet section where it is placed.

1. Line 8 or 10-in. ring mold with aspic, decorate with vegetables, add layer of aspic and fill rest of mold with shrimp or crabmeat salad. Refrigerate.
2. Turn ring mold out on round platter and chill.
3. Prepare a seafood mousse of crabmeat, salmon or other compatible fish or use more crabmeat salad.
4. Shape mousse or salad into cone inside ring mold. Make cone or pyramid about 8 in. high, shaping with hot spatula, until solid. Chill.
5. Take chilled mold from refrigerator and arrange spiralling row of cooked shrimp around it all the way to the top of cone. Dip shrimp in fish, chicken or neutral liquid aspic before placing them on cone. If whole shrimp are used, push heads into mousse to keep them firmly in place. If medium or small shrimp are used, position them with toothpicks. Top with a rose made from a tomato or turnip.

Note: This mousse may also be covered with egg yolk cream colored green, with dill added.

To Serve: Offer cocktail sauce.

Above, the initial steps in preparation of Shrimp Pyramid show vegetable ring mold in place with cone of mousse filling center. Shrimp are dipped in aspic, then positioned on mousse with toothpicks. If shrimp with heads are used, the head can be pushed into the mousse to hold shrimp in place. Right, when mousse is covered with rows of shrimp, a decorated timbale is placed on top and small timbales and sparkling aspic arranged around outer edge.

☐ Building a buffet around a theme more than makes up in acceptance what it takes in extra effort. The menus suggested for the theme buffets which follow do not have to be reproduced in their entirety. Just select the number of dishes needed to meet the patron or price requirements of a specific buffet, but present them against a background that will help to set the theme.

The main decorative scheme may be carried out in flowers, fruit, leaves, carved ice pieces, figures of china or tallow or any combination of these, with or without attractive candelabra. Garden-fresh vegetables, silvery driftwood, gilded magnolia, garlands of smilax and other inexpensive items may be used with great effectiveness.

The buffet planner in one operation reports: "We turn to nature for many of our decorative ideas and use wild flowers, grasses, flowering shrubs and fruits that grow in this area. With a little daring and imagination, we bring into our color scheme patterns found in the great out-of-doors. For instance, what could better accent a spring decor than trailing blackberry vines laden with green and early ripening berries? In summertime, our emphasis is on flowers, gay fruits and vegetables.

"In the fall, autumn leaves, grapes, small pumpkins and dried grasses add to our color effects."

Be sure to plan foods that will repeat, blend with or, in some instances, intensify theme colors.

The buffets listed in this chapter have all been prepared at the Culinary Institute of America. The settings have been worked out to take advantage of appropriate "props" that would increase the effectiveness of the selected theme. At the Institute, posters are often used to announce the theme of the buffet presentation.

Travel posters or lengths of appropriate fabrics are easily obtained and can be used to create backdrops that focus attention immediately on the central theme. Party goods departments, theatrical supply houses and antique shops can often provide inexpensive items to underscore a theme. In many places, these props can be rented for short periods of time for a minimum cost. Oriental accessories and foods are available from Paradise Products, Inc., P. O. Box 415, El Cerrito, Calif. 94532.

Two popular buffet themes—the luau and the smorgasbord, are described separately. Preparation of appropriate food and decorating ideas for a luau on pp. 58-59; for a smorgasbord, on pp. 189-198.

The theme buffet menus, each accompanied by sug-

FRENCH CLASSICAL BUFFET

Inedible Centerpieces:

Arc d' Triomphe or Eiffel Tower, either in ice carving or made of gum paste
Cafe De Paris, a miniature replica of a Boulevarde cafe in wax and tallow
French Wine Bottles with Red Candles, candle drippings on bottles

Hore D'Oeuvres Varies Froid:

Poireau Vinaigrette Avec Jambon
Coeur De Celery Marinet
Oeufs Farci Saumon Fumé
Pate De Fois Gras Strassbourgoise Truffes
Crevettes Sauce Vert
Huitres Fume Garni Avec Salade Russe
Anchois En Tomate
Cornet De Salami Farci

Grosse Piece Froid:

Homard A La Parisienne
Saumon A La Bellevue
Galantine De Capon
Chaud Froid De Jambon Classique
Mousse Fois En Gelee (Piece Monte)
Assortement Ouefs Froid
Pate En Croute

Entree:

Fillet De Boeuf A La Wellington
Canneton Roti Bigarrade
Coque Au Vin
Truit A La Riche

Salades:

Salad Nicoise
Salad Russe
Salade Endive
Salade De Cepes
Salad Mignon

Desserts:

Gateau St. Monroe, Gateau Des Pommes
Pattisserie Francais
Brioche
Camembert, Brie, Boursault, Gervais
Pain Francaise

gestions for appropriate accessories, include:

1. International Buffet
2. French Classical Buffet
3. Scandinavian Smorgasbord
4. German Buffet
5. St. Patrick's Day Buffet
6. Feast of the Forest Buffet
7. Appalachian (Hillbilly) Buffet
8. Mexican Buffet
9. Roman Buffet
10. New England Buffet
11. All-American Buffet
12. Pirate Buffet
13. Hawaiian Buffet
14. Austrian Buffet
15. Russian Buffet (Zakuski)
16. Chinese Buffet
17. Old English Buffet
18. Pool Party Buffet
19. Oriental Buffet
20. Springtime Buffet
21. Neptune Buffet

Buffets can be tied into a wide variety of special events and days. The themes presented here cover about every category that might be suggested. Additional themes can easily be treated buffet-style however. Just adapt one of the patterns presented in the following pages.

SCANDINAVIAN SMORGASBORD

Inedible Centerpieces:
Vikng Ship Ice Carving, floral sail
Deep Sea Grotto, carved from tallow
Swan Ice Carving

Sill Board—Herring Specialties: (cold)
Inlagged Sill
Bismarck Herring in Aspic
Herring in Mustard Sauce
Matjes Herring with Sour Cream Sauce
Marinated Herring with Swedish Horseradish Sauce

Cold Sea Food Platters:
Inkokt Laks (Poached Spiced Salmon Pieces)
Smoked Eel
Norwegian Smoked Salmon, with Garnish
Shrimp on Ice Block, with Two Accompanying Sauces
Cold Lake Trout (10-15 lbs.) made into Viking ship
Eggs a la Riga (Anchovies)
Lump Fish Caviar in Clam shells, garnished with Chopped Onion and Hard Cooked Eggs

Cold Meat Platters:
Pressed Veal
Oestarp's Liver Pate
Mustard Baked Ham
Smoked Reindeer Meat

Salads:
Viking Salad
Herring Salad
Danish Cucumber Salad
Swedish Potato Salad
Kidney Bean Salad
Pickled Red Beets

Small Hot Dishes:
Prune Stuffed Pork Loin
Meat Balls
Pytt I Pana
Sillgratin

Desserts:
Franchipan Tartlettes
Princess Torta
Marzipan Figures
Assortment of Rye Wafers, Swedish Cheese

CHINESE BUFFET

Inedible Centerpieces:
Chinese Pagoda, made from tallow, styrofoam or gum paste
Rikshas, in miniature made from wire, tallow
Potato Chain, around table on sticks
Dummy Ham Chaud Froid, decorated with chinese face or pagoda

Cold Dishes:
Chinese Radish Salad
Chinese Cucumber Salad
Chinese Chicken Salad
Pickled Watermelon Rind
Asparagus Mold, Asparagus arranged in Chicken Aspic
Chinese Junk, carved from Watermelon
Hard-Cooked Eggs made into Kuli Heads

Hot Dishes:
Egg Rolls with Sweet Sour Sauce
Chinese Barbecued Spareribs
Fried Rice and Fried Noodles
Jetsu Yaki, Halibut with Saki
Honeydew Melon Stuffed with Pork
Beef with Oyster Sauce
Beef with Green Peas and Mushrooms
Snails with Black Beans
Chicken Chow Mein
Soy Sauce, Mustard Sauce

Desserts:
Green Tea
Chinese Fried Cream
Oranges Filled with Custard Cream, placed on orange tree ice carving

GERMAN BUFFET

Inedible Centerpieces:
German Map, carved from tallow
Brandenburg Gate, ice carving

Vorspeisen: (cold)
Rheinlachs (smoked salmon) with Cream Cheese (Gervais)
Smoked Trout in Aspic
Bismarck Herring—Rollmops
Fresh Cold Salmon with Remoulade Sauce
Westphalian Ham with Cucumbers

Cold Sea Food Platters:
Poached Halibut with chaud froid coating
Cold Trout in Aspic

Cold Meat Platters:
Knockwurst in Vinegar and Oil with Onions
Stuffed Capon in Aspic (Galantine)
Beef Salad
Blood Sausage with Dark Bread, Pumpernickel
Assorted German Cold Cuts
Smoked Ham Rouladen with Asparagus

Salads:
Cucumber Salad with Sour Cream
Sauerkraut Salad
Cabbage Salad with Caraway Seeds
Potato Salad with Bacon
Braunschweiger Schloss Salad

Hot Foods: (Chafing Dishes)
Boiled Brisket of Beef, Horseradish Sauce
Bear Fillet in Burgundy Wine
Roast Leg of Venison
Hausenpfeffer
Bratwurst

Desserts:
Apfelschnitten
Milchrahmstrudel
German Cheese Cake

FEAST OF THE FOREST BUFFET

Inedible Centerpieces:
Tallow Carvings: Squirrel
Deer
Snow White and the Seven Dwarfs
Dummy Hams with Forest Scenes arranged on chaud froid coating

Cold Dishes:
Feast of the Forest Display (Plumage of pheasant, roasted quail in potato nests, eggs made into frogs and mushrooms)
Boar's Head in Aspic
Roast Wild Goose
Brook Trout Up the Creek
Smoked Ham Mousse
Cranberry Relish with Chestnuts

Salads:
Bohemian Salad
Augusta Salad
Salad Christoph

Hot Foods:
Roast Saddle of Venison Garni, presented on plank
Roast Cornish Game Hen Forestiere
Hasenpfeffer with Bread Dumplings
Roast Duckling with Apples (baked)

Desserts:
Black Forest Cherry Cake
Croque En Bouche
Logs
Fresh Cherries (with Stems)

NEPTUNE FEAST BUFFET (Cold Food)

Inedible Centerpiece:
Seahorse, ice carving

Cold Appetizers:
Smoked Salmon with Cream Cheese
Green and Ripe Olives
Pearl Onions
Liver Pate en Aspic
Hearts of Celery
Carrot Sticks
Indian Relish
Sardines
Cottage Cheese
Antipasto American

Cold Platters Main Dishes:
Poached Stuffed Brook Trout "Lucullus"
Sliced Maine Lobster "Portland"
Stuffed Tomato Alaskan King Crabmeat & Aspic Timbale
Galantine of Chicken "New Hampton"
Baked Sliced Ham, "American Beauty"
2 Watermelons Filled with Bite-size Fruit "Florida"
Salmon Slices with Fresh Asparagus "Argentuil"

Desserts:
Rum Cream Pie
Fresh Strawberry Tart
Cinnamon Sugar Doughnuts

ALL-AMERICAN BUFFET

(See pictures, pp. 10 and 11)

Inedible Centerpieces:
American Eagle, ice carving — American Flag, gum paste — Fife, Drum, Other Americana

Appetizers:
Relish Tray; Fresh Vegetables; Home Made Relishes
Corn Relish Cranberry Relish Cottage Cheese Lobster Salad Rhode Island
Shrimp Bowl or Shrimps Arranged with Picks around Watermelon, Cocktail Sauce

Cold Meat Platters:
Fruit Glazed Ham, Canned Fruit in Gelatin
Roast Long Island Duckling with Oranges
Sliced Smithfield Ham with Mustard Relish
Roast Turkey with Indian Head

Salads:
Potato Salad
Garden Salad
Jellied Vegetable Salad
Cole Slaw
Tomato Molds
Waldorf Salad

Piece De Resistance:
Whole Alaskan King Crab, Meat Removed and Decorated

Hot Foods:
Roast Buffalo Rib (carved on table)
Steamship Round
Baked Beans
Grizzly Bear Stew
Corned Beef and Cabbage
Barbecued Spare Ribs
Oven Baked Haddock, Marblehead

Desserts:
Fruit Salad Presented in Carved Watermelons Pineapple Carvings Canteloup Pies Bird of Paradise

ENGLISH BUFFET

Inedible Centerpiece:
Big Ben, ice carving
British Flags
Coats of Arms

Cold Appetizers:
Pickled Mushrooms
Stuffed Cucumbers, Stuffed Deviled Eggs
Smoked Salmon with Cream Cheese, Pumpernickel
Sweet Gherkins, Celery, Carrot Sticks
Ripe and Green Olives

Cold Platters:
Roast Prime Rib of Beef "Bouquetiere", on mirror
Baked Sliced York Ham
Browned Chaud Froid of Beef Tongue, Buckingham
Home Made Pate with Wine Aspic
Stuffed North Sea Salmon Trout with Smoked Pink Salmon, Dill Sauce
Stuffed Eggs "Jockey Club" with Vegetable Timbale

Salads:
Green Bean Salad
Macaroni Salad
Potato Salad
Melon with Fresh Fruits
Fresh Pear in Lime Gelatin
Grapefruit Baskets with Fresh Fruits

Hot Dishes:
Beef & Kidney Pie
Roast Leg of Lamb, Mint Jelly
White Beans, Bretonne

Desserts:
Apple Turnover
Stilton Cheese
Ginger Cream Cookies
Cubed Cheddar Cheese, Old English
Black Walnut Cake

ORIENTAL BUFFET

Inedible Centerpieces:
Oriental Buddha, ice carving Chaud Froid Coated Ham, decorated with mosque made from truffle sheet

Cold Dishes:
Javanaise Rice Salad
Chicken Salad Indienne
Shrimp Cocktail on Ice Fuji (make volcano with well for shrimp; use dry ice for smoke effect inside volcano)

Hot Dishes:
Chicken Yakitori
Beef Teriyaki
Pork Adobo
Fried Lumpia, Sweet Sour Sauce
Pansit
Halibut Steak Nippon Style
Steamed Long Grain Rice
Atsara
Barbecued Pork Riblettes

Piece de Resistance:
Roasted Suckling Piglette Oriental Style, carved at table on wooden plank

Desserts:
Bananas, Mango Fruits with custard
Mandarin Oranges

SPRINGTIME EASTER BUFFET

Inedible Centerpiece:

Flower Basket, ice carving — Assorted Bonnets; decorated Petit Fours or Paper — Flowers; real or artificial

Cold Appetizers:

Carrot Sticks, Scallions, Dill Pickles, Pearl Onions — Pickled Mushrooms, Cranberry Sauce, Artichoke Vinaigrette
Liver Pate with Aspic Coating — Stuffed Celery Hearts Roquefort — Stuffed Deviled Eggs

Cold Platters:

Poached Brook Trout in Aspic "Princesse"
Baked Ham "Easter Time"
Galantine of Spring Chicken "Spring Delight"
Sliced Maine Lobster on Vegetable Salad "Spring Style"
Jellied Stuffed Salmon Trout, Dill Sauce
Supremes of Capon with Medallion of Foie Gras "Jeanette"

Salads:

Mixed Green Garden Salad, French Dressing
Potato Salad with Diced Bacon
Macaroni Salad "Printaniere"
Cole Slaw
Assorted Vegetable Timbales "Jardiniere"
Bartlett Pear Halves with Cottage Cheese in Raspberry Gelatin
Cucumber Salad with Dill and Sour Cream

Hot Dishes:

Roast Baby Lamb, Mint Jelly

Desserts:

Springtime Almond Petit Fours — Raspberry Bavarian Cream Pudding — Open Early Fruit Pie

RUSSIAN BUFFET

Inedible Centerpieces:

Polar Bear, ice carving — Vodka Bottles on table

Zakuski—Russian Hors D'Oeuvres (cold):

Coquille A La Russe
Smoked Sturgeon Herring Salmon Chubs Eel
Caviar on Ice with Condiments
Eggs A La Russe
Pickled Mushrooms
Luchow Canape

Grosse Piece:

Standing Ham with Butter Sculpture or Turnip Carving
Chaud Froid of Salmon with Ballerina Truffle Design
Galantine of Suckling Pig with Apples and Prunes
Roast Wild Duck with Baked Apples, Prunes
Roast Turkey Made into Old Russian
Paté En Croute with Cranberry Relish

Salads:

Cucumber Salad with Sour Cream — Russian Salad — Placky (White Bean Salad) — Apple and Red Beet Salad
Herring Salad — Sauerkraut Salad with Apples — Pickled Beet Salad

Hot Foods:

Veal Stroganoff — Roast Whole Fresh Ham with Boiled Potatoes — Pirojki

Desserts:

Bread Pudding with Custard Sauce — Russian Cheese Cake — Carrot Cake

INTERNATIONAL BUFFET

Inedible Centerpieces:

"U. N." Letters Carved from Ice
Globe of Tallow, with continents painted on with oil paint, placed on top of a Crown Roast of Pork
Peace Doves Carved of White Tallow — Dummy Hams Chaud Froid, holding flags from various countries.

One Cold Food Display from Each Country:

U.S.A.—Lobster Cocktail on Ice
AUSTRIA—Head Cheese Vinaigrette
ITALY—Italian Antipasto Tray
EGYPT—Sayadia (Poached Salmon Fillets with Saffron, Capers, Onion)
NORWAY—Homemade Pickled Herring
RUSSIA—Beluga Caviar on Ice
POLAND—Kilbassy with Plaky, Dark Bread
BELGIUM—Belgium Endive with Roquefort Dressing
FRANCE—Caneton Roti Froid Strassbourgoise
DENMARK—Half Eggs with Smoked Salmon and Dill
ENGLAND—Crown Roast of Pork
HUNGARY—Hungarian Salami with Paprika Salad or Hungarian Cheese
SWITZERLAND—Yellow Asparagus with Virginia Ham
SWEDEN—Languste Moderne
GERMANY—Assorted Cold Cuts with Stuffed Tomatoes

Desserts:

French Pastry, Viennese Apple Tarts, Backlava
French and Italian Bread in Cornucopia, Grapes on Ice
International Cheese Board with Assorted Rye Wafers

Inedible Centerpieces

Irish Flag · *Ice Carving Centerpiece: Shamrock* · *Green Paper Tablecloth*

Cold Appetizers

Various Herrings: Rolled, Creamed · *Mustard Dill Tidbits*

Pearl Onions · *Dill Pickles* · *Stuffed Eggs*

Smoked Salmon Rolled in Asparagus · *Pumpernickel and Cream Cheese*

Sliced Beef Salad · *Onions* · *Green Peppers* · *Barm Breck Bread*

Cold Platters

Baked York Ham "St. Patrick" · *Roast Leg of Lamb, Mint Jelly*

Tongue Display, sliced, "Leprechaun" · *Chicken and Meat Loaf*

Emerald Chicken Salad in Avocado Pears

Salads and Dressings

Stringbean Salad, Dublin Style · *Cubed Potato Salad*

Lime Gelatin with Pears and Cottage Cheese · *Mixed Green Salad Bowl, French Dressing*

Sliced Cucumbers in Sour Cream and Dill

Hot Dishes

Corned Beef and Cabbage, Irish Potatoes · *Irish Spring Lamb Stew with Vegetables*

Desserts

Irish Almond Cake · *Lime Chiffon Pie* · *Shamrock Cookies*

Inedible Centerpieces

Large 15 lb. Lobster Made into Hillbilly

Whole Buffet Table Covered with Hay

Large Bear, ice carving

Stone Crocks, Pipes, Old Guns and Rifles

Entymological Specialties

Diamond Back Rattlesnake Meat in Supreme Sauce

Fried Baby Bees

Fried Grasshoppers

Fried Agave Worms (from Mexico)

Chocolate Covered Ants

Cold Platters

Roast Turkey Made into a Chef

Pickled Pig's Feet

Roast Suckling Pig, Baked Apples, Spiced Pears

Pickled Crow Gizzards

Cold Roast Pheasant, Plumage, Cranberry Sauce

Virginia Ham sliced with Relishes

Salads

Mountain Grown Vegetable Salad

Dandelion Salad

Kidney Bean Salad

Potato Salad

Mustard Greens

Hot Foods

Brunswick Stew (Opossum or Rabbit)

Black Eyed Peas

Stuffed Baked Porgies with Hush Puppies

Meat Pudding

Roast Leg of Venison, carved on plank

Corn Basket, Corn Bread

Desserts

Chestnut Rice Pudding

Cherry Pie

Cheddar Cheese

Inedible Centerpieces

Roman Chariots made from Lobster Shells

Chianti Wine Bottles

Gladiator ice carving or painted tallow relief in frame

Green Leaves Around Table

Antipasto

Tuna with Antipasto Relish

Marinated Mixed Vegetables

Clams on Ice

Genoa Salami

Sardines in Tomato Sauce

Pickled Melon Rind

Assorted Olives

Marinated Mushrooms A La Greque

Cold Platters

Whole Prosciutto Ham, Fresh Figs and Melon

Tuna Mold in Chicken Aspic

Whole Salmon Chaud Froid with Squid

Sliced Mortadella Sausage with Pickles

Roast Suckling Pig with Grapes and Other Fruits

Roast Turkey with Melon Carts

Salads

Italian Tomato Salad with Julienne of Green Peppers

Spaghetti Salad

Caesar Salad

Calarami Salad

Hot Foods

Osso Buco with Rice

Lazagna

Manicotti

Polenta

Spaghetti Neapolitain or Marinara

Desserts

Grapes on Ice Block

Zupa Inglese

Spumoni

Roman Fruit Tarts

Marone Glace

Provolone, Gorgonzola, Ricotta, Italian Bread

Inedible Centerpieces

Antique Naval Cannon *Wooden Keg with Fishing Net* *Shipwreck, carved tallow*

Driftwood, Sea Shells *Chocolate Gold Coins* *Rum Bottles*

Two Hams, coated with chaud froid and decorated with Captain Kidd, Frigate, Pirate Hat

Appetizers

Ice Barrel filled with Shrimp and Clams *Herring Assortment*

Whole Salmon made into Schooner, sails made of watermelon rind *Crabmeat Salad*

Cold Platters

Languste or Lobster Display, arranged around ice carving of pirate ship

Decorated Roast Turkey *Watermelons carved into ships*

Roast Whole Game Hens on Spit

Salads

Fish Salad, on potato salad base *Red Beet Salad* *Pirate Salad* *Mixed Vegetable Salad*

Hot Foods

Sauteed Softshell Crabs *Curried Shrimp* *Fried Smelts*

Fried Salt Herring with Onion Sauce *Standing Rib Roast*

Desserts

Half Coconuts Filled with Fruit Salad *Rum Cake* *Rum Balls* *Bananas* *Rye Wafers*

Inedible Centerpieces

Totem Pole of tallow, about 4 ft. high

Outrigger, ice carving

Hawaiian Islands, replica in wax and tallow

Flower Kahilis, substitute other flowers if unobtainable

Tiki Head, wood

Ti Leaves on Table or Banana Leaves

Appetizers

Lomi Lomi Salmon

Pineapple Carrot Salad

Rumakis

Smoked Salmon in Coconut Shells with Cream Cheese and Pineapple Chunks

Raw Shrimp with Poi

Cold Platters

Ham with Chaud Froid Coating and Hula Girl, Hawaiian Seal or Tropical Seascape, modeled from Sweet Potatoes

Pineapple Carvings: Bird Houses, Stands, Carts filled with Fruit Salad

Watermelon made into Outrigger, sliced smoked ham inside

Turkey made into a Tiki Head, modeled from Sweet Potato

Pineapple Sticks with Maraschino Cherries

Roast Suckling Pig with Pineapple Stuffing, on plank, carved at table

Hot Foods

Polynesian Chicken (cooked in coconut milk)

Sweet and Sour Spareribs

Crabmeat Papeete

Hawaiian Sticks

Poi or Fried Rice

Beef with Black Beans

Desserts

Coconut Pudding

Banana Muffins

Pineapple Upside Down Cake

Polynesian Specialties for Table of Hot and Cold Appetizers Especially Suitable for Cocktail Buffet

Barbecued Spareribs

Pineapple Chunks with Cubed Ham

Curried Chicken Croquettes with Shredded Coconut

Stuffed Mushrooms with Rice and Orange Segments

Barbecued Fried Shrimp

Meat filled Cabbage or Grape Leaves

Deep-Fried Bananas, Cut in Fourths

Duckling Tidbits to Dip in Orange Sauce

Marinated Lamb Shaslik with Pineapple Chunks

Chicken Livers and Kumquat Rolled in Bacon, Sweet Sour Sauce

Curried King Crabmeat Rolled in Pancake

Barbecued Meat Balls, Sweet Sour Sauce

Foo Yong Egg Fritters

Waldorf Salad in Coconut Shells

Bananas Stuffed with Fruit-Nut Mixture

Half Pineapples Filled with Fresh Fruit and Topped with Shredded Coconut

Pool Party Buffet

(Cold Food Only)

Inedible Centerpiece

Swimming Pool carved from tallow, tallow figures in bikinis

Floral Arrangements

Cold Seafood Platters

Whole Salmon Display with Fishing Scene, made from truffles

Lobster Salad Rhode Island

Shrimp Mold (Piece Montee)

Nymphen Tights at Dawn (chaud froid dipped froglegs around ice pyramid)

Tuna Salad with Stuffed Eggs

Cold Meat Platters

Virginia Ham Chaud Froid, with floral design

Cold Roast Duckling A l' Orange

Cold Roast Beef with Chopped Aspic, Radishes

Cold Roast Fresh Ham with Gherkins

Chicken Liver Pate in Aspic

Cold Roast Capon Moderne

Salads

German Potato Salad

Chicory Salad

Austrian Cucumber Salad

Russian Salad

Macaroni Salad with Green Peppers

Egg Salad with Smoked Salmon and Asparagus

Tomato Salad

Desserts

Fresh Fruit

Strawberry Short Cake

Assorted Breads

Pheasant Gastronomy Style

Liver Pate Aspic Mold

Saddle of Venison

Pate Maison

Inedible Centerpieces

Replica of Schoenbrunn Castle made of tallow or gum paste

Alpine Flowers in Basket of pulled sugar

Renaissance Statue, ice carving

Vorspeisen

(*See Classical French Hors D'Oeuvres*)

Cold Sea Food Platters

Home-Made Pickled Salmon

Barquettes with Ham Mousse

Cold Carp Fines Herbes Sauce

Cold Meat Platters

Galantine of Poularde Viennese Style, decorated with truffle scenes from Vienna

Pate Maison

Pheasant Gastronomy Style

Westphalian Ham Rolladen Garni

Boned Stuffed Rainbow Trout in Aspic

Calves Brains Vinaigrette

Salads

Austrian Cucumber Salad

Root Celery Salad

Kraut Salad

Kipfler Potato Salad

Steinpilzsalat

Haeuptelsalat

Salad Stephanie

Desserts

Sacher Torte

Indianer Krapfen

Topfen Strudel

Mit Schlagsahne

Westphalian Ham Rouladen Garni

Pastry

MEXICAN BUFFET

Inedible Centerpieces:
Mexican Under Blanket Sleeping Against Potato Bag
Mexican Dancer carved from Tallow
Aligator carved from Carrots or Tallow
Dummy Hams coated with Chaud Froid and decorated with Fighting Roosters, Drummer, Bull

Appetizers:
Tortillas
Tacos
Tostadas
Scampi or Mexican Shrimp on Ice
Mexican Relish Tray

Cold Platters:
Whole Salmon with Pimiento Decor
Lobsters standing around pot of Bean Salad
Roast Capon with Cantaloup Carts
Sliced Roast Beef
Pig's Head Made into Bull's Head, Brown Chaud Froid coating

Salads:
Guacamole Salad
Sliced Tomato Salad
Rice Salad
Green Pepper Salad
Watermelons filled with Fruit Salad
Kidney Bean Salad

Hot Foods:
Oysters Casino, Rinones De Carnero A La Senorita
Beef Camponesa with Cold Piquant Sauce
Stuffed Green Peppers, Biftek A La Andaluza
Farinna De Manioca, Politos Salteados

Desserts:
Caramel Pudding
Bread Cornucopia Filled with Tropical Fruits

NEW ENGLAND BUFFET

Inedible Centerpieces:
Dolphin, Fishing Boat, Whale, ice carvings
Indian Made from Lobster Shells with Turnip
Fishing Net Clam Shells Empty Lobster Shells Sponges Starfish

New England Relish Tray:
Corn Relish Cranberry Orange Relish Prunes Stuffed with Cream Cheese
Cottage Cheese Celery Sticks Carrot Sticks Pickled Mushrooms Olives

Cold Sea Food Platters:
Cherry Stone Clams on Ice (use ice carving for presentation)
Shrimp Boat with Cocktail Sauce
Half Small Lobsters served in Shell
Molded Salmon Salad in Aspic
Smoked Salmon with Garnishes Arranged with Bread Sail Boats
Eggs Stuffed with Crabmeat Salad
Whole Salmon Masterpiece, coated with Chaud Froid and Decorated

Cold Meat Platters:
Roast Turkey Made into Indian Head
Sliced Roast Beef with Pickles
Fruit Glazed Baked Ham
Roast Pig's head with Baked Apples
Crown Roast of Pork, stuffed with cauliflower vinaigrette

Hot Foods:
New England Clam Bake, simulated in large square pans with heated rocks
New England Boiled Dinner
New England Baked Clams

Salads:
Tossed Green Salad, assorted dressings
Potato Salad
Macaroni Salad
Red Beet Salad

Desserts:
Indian Pudding
Corn Bread
Blueberry Pie, Other Pies

CHAPTER XVII Smorgasbord

There's an established pattern for the Scandinavian smorgasbord. It's been perfected during 500 years of historic eating and tradition requires that it be followed precisely.

To present a traditional smorgasbord, the table must contain the required 60 items to be divided between four courses. Guests are advised to select fish first, choosing a few items at a time so each can be savored for its special flavor. Second, salads, meats and pickles should be eaten. Third, hot dishes and, last, cheeses.

One traditional East Coast hotel smorgasbord has displayed from 75 to 100 Scandinavian specialties on a table 15 ft. long and 5 ft. wide. This list of authentic specialties includes:

TRADITIONAL SMORGASBORD

Matjes Herring
Glassmaster Herring
Homemade Pickled Herring
Marinated Herring in Cream Sauce
Marinated Herring in Mustard Dill Sauce
Norwegian Anchovies, whole
Domestic Caviar
Spanish Filet Anchovies
Smoked Nova Scotia Salmon
Smoked Eel
Smoked Whitefish
Baked Mackerel in Tomato Sauce
Marinated Fried Fish
Fish Pudding
Fresh Eel Roulade
Jumbo Shrimps
Maine Lobster
King Crab
Danish Blue Cheese
American Cheese
Swiss Cheese
Norwegian Rindless Cheese
Cottage Cheese
Goet Cheese (made from goat's milk)
Nokkel Ost (pickled cheese with caraway and cloves)
Tilsiter Ost Cheese
Celery Stuffed with Cheese
Deviled Eggs
Fruit Gelatin, Fruit Salad
Tomato and Macaroni in Aspic
Cooked Vegetable and Mushroom in Aspic
Roast Turkey, Chicken and Duckling
Prime Top Sirloin Roast Beef
Corned Beef
Danish Imported Ham
Smoked Beef Tongue
Norwegian Salami
Liver Paste
Sylta (head cheese)
Veal Roulade

SALADS

Spiced Beets
Swedish Style Cucumber Salad
Cole Slaw
Egg Plant
Cooked Vegetable Salad
Potato Salad
German Potato Salad
Tossed Salad
Celery, Radishes, Olives
Pickles (several kinds)
Sweet Cauliflower
Sweet Red Peppers
Sour Tomatoes
Marinated Pigs' Feet
Mushrooms Cooked in Wine
Curried Salad
Chicken Salad
Italian Salad
Tuna Salad
Seafood Salad
Bologna Salad
Fresh Vegetable Salad
Nova Scotia and Potato Salad

DRESSINGS

Sour Cream, Lingonberries, Cocktail Sauce, Remoulade Sauce, Mayonnaise, Russian Dressing, French Dressing

HOT DISHES

Swedish Meat Balls
Red Kidney Beans
Boiled Potato in Dill
Curry of Shrimp
Shrimp Creole
Chicken Chow Mein
Shrimp Chow Mein
Beef a la Deutsch
Ragout of Lamb
Boiled Swedish Sausage
Breaded Fried Swedish Sausage
Turkey Goulash
Swedish Beef Stew
Norwegian Fish Balls
Barbecued Baby Spareribs
Herring-Potato and Onion Au Gratin
Rice Pilaf
Southern Fried Chicken Tidbits
Turkey Wings a la Creole
Curry of Chicken and Curry of Lamb
Chicken Livers with Mushrooms
Petytt Panna (cubed beef with saute onions and potatoes)
Elbow Macaroni with Meat Sauce
Boiled Miniature Frankfurters
Crayfish (in season only)
Reindeer Meat Balls

Iran—Caviar

Poland—Kielbasa with Plaky, Dark Bread

Hungary—Salami and Paprika Salad

Drama With Ice
Switzerland—Yellow Asparagus with Virginia Ham
Japan—Shrimp
Java—Rice Salad

However, like all other customs that have come to American shores, the smorgasbord has been adapted. To be sure, in celebrated smorgasbord dining rooms, the food ways of the old country continue to be followed faithfully and eating at the smorgasbord is an out-of-this-country experience to be enjoyed to the fullest.

Many American smorgasbords today offer a few of the traditional dishes, but surround them with easy to prepare American favorites with dependable appeal to all comers.

With this lavish display of food, little is needed in the way of additional decor. Lemon leaves add a needed touch of glossy green, but other touches of color are achieved with such edible decorations as orange and grapefruit wedges, wheels, twists and baskets; carved and colored turnips or radish roses and spun sugar baskets.

A more selective menu and one more easily assembled has been culled from traditional dishes. This is a menu that could be reduced even further, yet it would retain the true smorgasbord flavor:

SCANDINAVIAN SMORGASBORD

Inedible Centerpiece
Mermaid on Rock
Ski Jump
Fisherman

Sill Board and Swedish Hors D'Oeuvres
Smoked Herring with Apple Cream
Sardines in Tomato Sauce
Shrimp Salad
Eggs with Smoked Salmon Rolls
Yellow Asparagus Vinaigrette with Radishes
Swedish Anchovies with Sour Cream, Chives
Leeks Vinaigrette

Cold Seafood Platters
Bird's Nest
Striped Sea Bass or Large Fresh Salmon, Norwegian Style
Salmon Mousse, decorated with clock design made with hard cooked eggs
Lobster Display
Crawfish in Dill

Cold Meat Platters
Sylta, veal and pork strips molded in aspic
Roast Turkey
Ham Rouladen with Egg Quarters and Pickles
Cold Prune-Stuffed Pork Loin
Cold Fresh Roasted Ham with Spiced Fruits

Salads
Green Bean Salad
Curried Rice Salad
Russian Salad

Small Hot Dishes
Cropcakor (Potato Dumplings Filled with Smoked Meats)
Spinach Pancakes with Meat Balls
Flaesk Korv (Boiled Pork Sausage)
Fried Baltic Herring
Smoked Beef Tongue in Cumberland Sauce

Desserts
Rice Pudding
Mixed Swedish Berries, Marinated in Liqueur and Sugar

Foods for the kind of simple smorgasbord-type buffet that is especially popular with business men and shoppers at lunch, and patrons generally at dinner, are usually fewer in number and less traditional. If a few well known scandinavian specialties are featured, the remaining dishes for this adaptation of the smorgasbord can be more familiar and easier to prepare.

A list from which smorgasbord foods might be scheduled contains 20 hot and 20 cold foods, only a sprinkling of which are traditional, but all of them popular with American patrons.

Cold Foods
Variety of marinated herring, sardines, eels and anchovies
Smoked Salmon
Assorted Liver Pates
Assorted Sliced Sausages
Marinated Mushrooms
Marinated Baby Artichokes
Head Cheese Vinaigrette
Pickled Beets
Shrimp Salad with Asparagus
Macaroni Salad with Ham
German Potato Salad
Stuffed Eggs
Calves Brains Vinaigrette
Sliced Pickled Apple or Whole Crabapple
Gefilte Fish or Fish Dumplings
Smoked White Fish
Smoked Beef Tongue
Meat Salad with Mayonnaise
Assorted Cheese Tray
Fruit Platters

Hot Foods
Corned Beef Hash
Swedish Meat Balls in Dill Sauce
Bratwurst and Sauerkraut
Individual Beef Roulades
Potato Pancakes
Pork Spareribs, Barbecued
Beef and Kidney Stew
Chicken Croquettes
Stuffed Cabbage
Boiled Lamb with Caper Sauce
Chicken Livers with Rice
Spaghetti with Meat Balls
Baked Clams Casino
Creamed Finnan Haddie
Smoked Pork Butts with Sauerkraut
Stuffed Clams
Sauerbraten with Red Cabbage
Marinated Mussels
Boston Baked Beans and Bacon
Italian Lasagna

The focus is on the food on smorgasbord tables. Eye appealing displays like these capitalize on the red of rare roast beef and unusual high-molded salads. The effect should be lavish and enough dishes should be planned so that the table is unmistakably a "groaning board."

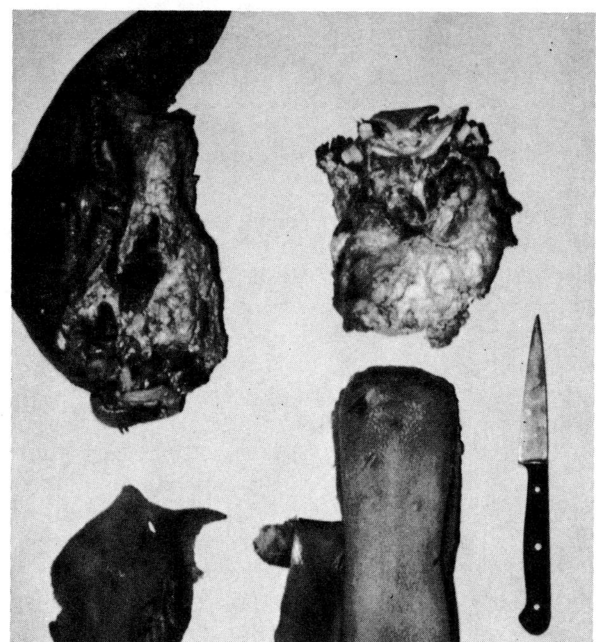

Beef tongues comes out of simmering water as in upper left, picture above. Chill in cold water, then peel off outer skin. Remove excess fat and bones from base of tongue.

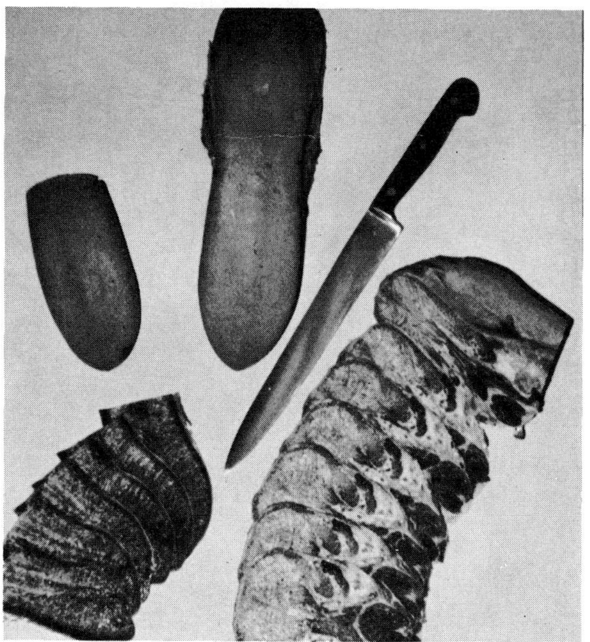

Above, slice peeled tongue in slicing machine or by hand. Slice tip lengthwise and thick section crosswise. Keep tongue slices in order for best arrangement.

Smoked beef tongue sliced and surrounded by salad is a favorite smorgasbord item. It offers the advantage of advance preparation. Two tongues can be combined for more dramatic display if that many portions can be utilized.

To Prepare Tongue

Bring beef tongue to boil in water with bouquet garni and mirepoix; simmer for about three hours. When tongue is tender, chill in cold water and peel immediately. Remove fat and bones at base of tongue.

Slice peeled tongue in slicing machine or by hand. Slice tip lengthwise and thick section crosswise. If platter to be produced requires two tongues, leave second tongue unsliced.

Use stock in which tongue was cooked to make aspic.

Tongue may be displayed on platters in many ways; here are five suggestions.

Platter Idea No. 1—Whole Tongue and Slices

Whole Tongue—Coat with white chaud froid sauce; add design made of cherry tomatoes and green pepper strips or cut-outs.

Slices—Top slices with halves of hard cooked eggs made into baseball hats.

Platter—Place round mold filled with tongue aspic, green peas, and diced egg yolk below tongue. Surround tongue with aspic cut in squares or chopped; brussels sprouts; fluted mushrooms; more stuffed hard cooked egg halves; pickles; tomato quarters.

Large heart-shaped vegetable timbale is decorated with white chaud froid display design picturing horse's head. (See p. 127.) Jockey caps created from stuffed eggs are covered with chaud froid, then decorated with colored stripes. Aspic covered tongue slices hold caps.

Platter Idea No. 2 (directions next page)

Whole Tongue, Platter Idea No. 3

One Tongue, Platter Idea No. 4

Platter Idea No. 2—Sliced Tongue
(See picture preceding page)
Centerpiece—Line ring mold with tongue slices, add chaud froid cut-outs for design and fill with tongue aspic. Chill until set.
Platter—Unmold aspic on platter, fill center with blue grapes. Surround mold with whole hard cooked eggs made into alpine hats with tongue circles, pimiento cut outs, white leek feathers; add to arrangement with aspic triangles, hard cooked egg halves filled with cherry tomatoes and sprigs of dill.
Platter Idea No. 3—Whole Tongue
Whole Tongue—Cover with white cream cheese chaud froid coat. Make face using truffles for features, outline face with pimento. Use pimento for hat.
Slices—On mound of liver mousse, place tongue aspic mold lined with chaud froid and decorations of yellow flowers with leek stems alternated with aspic cut-outs. Fill mold with tongue aspic and tongue salad.
Platter—Arrange tongue and mold, line remainder of platter with chopped tongue aspic on which hard cooked eggs with truffle faces and salami hats can be placed between medallions of liver pate.
Platter Idea No. 4—One Tongue
Platter—Slice part of tongue. Place unsliced part in ring mold.
Platter—Slice half of tongue, chop remainder. Put chopped tongue in aspic in ring mold, using fluted mushrooms to decorate. Chill. Unmold and fill center with russian salad. Surround ring mold with folded slices of tongue and chopped aspic. Garnish with pickles.
Platter Idea No. 5—Two Tongues
Make two tongues into clock by attaching each to piece of corned beef or ham placed between them. Use skewers to hold each tongue to centered corn beef or ham. Coat with chaud froid and make clock design.

To Accompany Smoked Tongue—Cumberland sauce, cranberry relish, waldorf salad, stuffed dill pickles, tomato relish, various potato salads, russian salad and pickled mixed vegetables combine well with tongue.

For the American Smorgasbord

Food service operators who have been successful in adapting the smorgasbord to their customer's tastes suggest a combination of scandinavian specialties and dishes popular with Americans. A few traditional dishes are highlighted but the majority of dishes are planned and seasoned to suit local palates. The combination has worked well at lunch and dinner and for a change in banquet fare.

The recipes which follow are easily prepared, yet hearty in the true tradition of smorgasbord fare. Spiced to be generally pleasing, they provide basic dishes which go well with special scandinavian fare.

MEAT BALLS IN SOUR CREAM GRAVY

Yield: 32 servings (3 medium-sized meat balls each)

Ingredients

Ground Beef	7 lb.
Fine Dry Bread Crumbs	3 cups
Whole Eggs, beaten slightly	1½ cups
Salt	1 tbsp.
Pepper	⅛ tsp.
Oregano	1 tbsp.
Marjoram	1 tsp.
Rosemary (about 20 small needles crushed)	
Milk	3 cups
Onions, sliced	1 lb.
Shortening	8 oz.
Beef Broth	1 qt.
Sour Cream	1½ qt.
Lemon Juice	⅓ cup

Method

Combine ground beef, crumbs, eggs, salt, pepper, herbs and milk. Mix well and shape into balls.

Brown the sliced onions in the hot fat. Remove the onions and set aside.

Brown the meat balls, turning until they are uniformly brown. Then add 1 qt. of beef broth. Cover and cook slowly for about 30 minutes or until the meat is thoroughly cooked.

Remove the meat balls and keep in a warm place.

Thicken the liquid remaining in the pan with a flour and water mixture until it becomes a fairly thick gravy.

Add the browned onion slices, sour cream and lemon juice. Heat thoroughly but do not boil. Pour over the hot meat balls and serve.

CREAMED TURKEY WITH PINEAPPLE AND ALMONDS

Yield: 30 servings

Ingredients

Margarine	8 oz.
Flour	5 oz.
Turkey Broth	1½ qt.
Milk or Thin Cream	1 qt.
Salt	2 tsp.
Pepper	¼ tsp.
Onion, grated	2 tbsp.
Turkey, cooked, diced	4 lb.
Pineapple, shredded, drained (canned or fresh)	3 cups
Almonds, toasted, sliced	6 oz.

Method

Melt the margarine, add the flour and stir until blended.

Add the broth and milk, stirring constantly over low heat until mixture is uniformly thickened. Then place over hot water.

Add the seasoning and turkey and heat thoroughly.

Just before serving stir in the pineapple and almonds.

Serve over noodles, rice, toast, baking powder biscuits or shredded wheat biscuits.

VEAL WITH MUSHROOMS ON BROWN RICE

Yield: 32 servings

Ingredients

Veal Stew Meat, cut into thin strips	8 lb.
Fat	8 oz.
Salt	2 tbsp.
Pepper	½ tsp.
Marjoram	1 tsp.
Monosodium Glutamate	1 tsp.
Water	1 qt.
Fresh Mushrooms, sliced	2 lb.
Onion, chopped fine	1 qt.
Butter or Margarine	8 oz.
Brown Rice	3 lb.

Method

Brown veal in hot fat. Add salt, pepper, monosodium glutamate and marjoram. Add 1 qt. of water. Cover and cook over low heat until meat is tender—about 30 minutes.

Saute the fresh mushrooms and onions in butter or margarine. Add to the meat.

Cook uncovered until the sauce is reduced to desired quantity or thicken if you prefer.

Cook brown rice, drain, serve with veal and mushrooms over it.

MACARONI-CORNED BEEF CASSEROLE

Yield: 32 servings

Ingredients

Elbow Macaroni	1½ lb.
Canned Corned Beef Pieces	4 lb.
Worcestershire Sauce	1 tbsp.
Cream of Chicken Soup	4 cans (10½ oz.)
Milk	1 qt.
Green Pepper, chopped	1 cup
Onion, chopped	1 pt.
Cheddar Cheese, grated	1 lb.

Method

Cook the macaroni in salted water. When tender drain well. Then add all other ingredients; combine thoroughly.

Put into greased baking pan or individual casseroles.

Top with buttered crumbs or more grated cheese if that is preferred. Bake at 350°F. for about 45 minutes.

DEEP SEA CASSEROLE

Yield: 32 servings

Ingredients

Crabmeat	6 cans (6½ oz.)
Shrimp, cooked and peeled	2 lb.
Macaroni Shells	2 lb.
Cream of Celery Soup	3 cans (10½ oz.)
Mushroom Soup	2 cans (10½ oz).
Water	1 pt.
Lemon Juice	¼ cup
Cheddar Cheese, grated	1 lb.
Soy Sauce	1½ tbsp.

Method

Remove the hard membrane from the crabmeat. Flake, saving some chunks for topping.

Cook macaroni shells and drain.

Heat soups and water

Add lemon juice, cheese and soy sauce.

Add crabmeat and shrimp. Heat thoroughly.

Combine with cooked macaroni shells saving some shells to border the tops of the casseroles.

Fill individual casseroles or baking pans. Top with chunks of crabmeat and border with shells. Bake at 375°F. for 15 minutes or until bubbly.

Garnish with parsley.

TUNA FISH MOLD

Yield: 3 large fish molds, or 36 individual 4 oz.

Ingredients

Tuna Fish	6 cans (6½ oz.)
Hard Cooked Eggs	9
Stuffed Olives, sliced	1½ cups
Capers	6 tbsp.
Onion, minced	3 tbsp.
Plain Gelatin	1½oz.
Cold Water	¾ cup
Mayonnaise	1½ qt.

Method

Combine flaked tuna, eggs, olives, capers and onion.

Soak gelatin in cold water for five minutes. Then dissolve over hot water. Add dissolved gelatin to mayonnaise, stirring constantly.

Add mayonnaise to fish mixture. Mix thoroughly.

Place in molds and chill.

When serving, unmold onto lettuce or endive. Garnish with deviled eggs, tomato or avocado wedges. If large fish molds are used, ripe olives can be cut in thin wedges and laid in a row along the back to simulate fins, stuffed olives can be sliced and used as eyes, and thin lengths of pimento can decorate one end of the mold to suggest a fish tail.

JELLIED VEGETABLE SALAD

Yield: 24 servings

Ingredients

Gelatin, lemon flavored	2 oz.
Hot Water	1 pt.
Sweet Pickle Vinegar	1 pt.
Cold Water	1 pt.
Lemon Juice	¼ cup
Sour Cream	1 pt.
Salt	2 tsp.
Onion, grated	2 tbsp.
Vegetables, chopped, raw (cabbage, carrots, green peppers)	2 qt.
Stuffed Olives, sliced for garnish	½ cup

Method

Dissolve gelatin in hot water. Add cold water, pickle juice, lemon juice, salt, onion and sour cream.

Blend well and chill until mixture begins to congeal. Then fold in vegetables and chill until firm.

Serve on crisp lettuce and garnish with sliced olives.

CHICKEN MOUSSE

Yield: 32 individual molds

Ingredients

Plain Gelatin	2 oz.
Water	½ cup
Chicken Stock	4¾ cups
Chicken Meat, cooked and finely diced (approx. 2 lb.)	6 cups
Salt	1 tsp.
Pepper	½ tsp.
Cream, whipped	1 qt.
Mayonnaise	1 qt.

Method

Soak gelatin in cold water for 5 minutes.

Then dissolve in hot chicken broth. Cool.

Add diced chicken, salt and pepper, and chill until mixture begins to set.

Fold in whipping cream and mayonnaise.

Cooking sherry may be added, too, if desired. Toasted sliced almonds may also be added.

Mold. Chill until firm. Serve on lettuce.

HAM MOUSSE

Yield: Four loaves, 7½ by 3½ by 2 in. (will make 8 to 10 slices each) or 32 individual 4-oz. molds.

Ingredients

Plain Gelatin	1½ oz.
Cold Water	1 cup
Boiling Water	2½ cups
Ham, cooked, chopped or ground	5 lb.
Onion, minced	2 tbsp.
Cream, whipped	1 pt.
Mayonnaise	1 cup

Method

Combine ham, mustard, pepper and onion. Soak gelatin in cold water for five minutes. Then dissolve with boiling water. Add to ham mixture.

Fold mayonnaise and whipped cream into mixture.

Place in molds and chill.

SALMON SALAD

Yield: 32 servings

Ingredients

Mayonnaise	1 qt.
Chili Sauce	1 pt.
Green Pepper, chopped	½ cup
Anchovies, chopped	½ cup
Stuffed Olives, chopped	½ cup
Hard Cooked Eggs, chopped	1½ doz.
Red Salmon, flaked	8 1-lb. cans

Method

Combine the mayonnaise, chili sauce, green pepper, anchovies, olives and eggs to make salad dressing.

Chill dressing thoroughly before tossing with cold flaked salmon. Pile high in lettuce cups on serving plates.

Surround with whole or half slices of cucumber. Leave the peeling on the cucumber and score lengthwise with a fork before slicing.

SHRIMP MOLDED IN LIME GELATIN

Yield: 30 servings

Ingredients

Lime-Flavored Gelatin	2 oz.
Hot Water	1½ qt.
Mayonnaise (or mayonnaise and salad dressing combined)	1½ qt.
Shrimp, cooked and peeled	3 lb.

Method

Dissolve gelatin in hot water. Cool.

When it begins to congeal, fold in the mayonnaise and shrimp.

Place in molds. Chill until firm.

Serve on crisp salad greens.

TOMATO CHEESE SALAD WITH SEAFOOD

Yield: 30 4-oz. molds

Ingredients

Lemon Favored Gelatin	3 oz.
Hot Water	1½ qt.
Condensed Tomato Soup	2 qt.
Cream Cheese	1½ lb.
Salt	1 tbsp.
Onion, finely chopped	3 tbsp.
Celery, finely diced	1 qt.
Mayonnaise	¾ qt.
Shrimp, cooked, peeled and chopped (other seafoods may be used)	1½ lb.

Method

Dissolve gelatin in hot water. Warm the soup and blend in the cream cheese, stirring until thoroughly mixed.

Add mayonnaise and salt. Mix.

Add to the gelatin and chill until it begins to congeal.

Then fold in celery, onion and seafood.

Pour into molds and chill until firm.

If individual molds are used, a whole shrimp can be reserved for each mold and placed in the bottom before filling.

Serve on crisp greens.

CABBAGE SLAW

Yield: 30 servings

Ingredients

Cabbage, chopped or shredded	5 lb., a.p.
Parsley, chopped	½ cup
Onion, chopped	2 med.
or	
Instant Minced Onion	2 oz.
Celery, chopped	2 cups
Green Pepper, chopped	2 cups
Pimiento, chopped	4 oz. jar
Granulated Sugar	½ cup
Vinegar	1½ cups
Salt	2 tbsp.
Pepper	¼ tsp.

Method

Combine cabbage, parsley, onion, celery, green pepper and pimiento.

Dissolve sugar in vinegar. Add salt and pepper.

Add vinegar mixture to chopped vegetables and mix well.

Keep in cool place.

This slaw may be prepared hours in advance of serving time.

The smorgasbord at Scandia Restaurant, Hotel Piccadilly, New York City is lavish yet inviting. Platters of food are arranged for easy self service.

SHRIMP MACARONI SALAD

Yield: 30 servings

Ingredients

Macaroni, cooked	1½ lb.
Celery, chopped	1 qt.
Green Pepper, chopped	1 cup
Pimiento, chopped	1 cup
Onion, ground or grated	1 cup
Salt	1½ tbsp.
Paprika	1 tsp.
French Dressing	1 cup
Shrimp, cooked and peeled	1½ lb., a.p.
Mayonnaise	1 qt.

Method

Marinate the cooked macaroni with the french dressing, salt and paprika while the macaroni is still warm.

When cold combine with all other ingredients.

Serve in lettuce cups and garnish with parsley and hard cooked egg.

MOLDED CHEESE RINGS

Yield: 34 individual ring molds

Ingredients

Gelatin, unflavored	1 oz.
Cold Water	1½ cups
Cream Cheese	1½ lb.
Roquefort Cheese	½ lb.
Salt	1½ tsp.
Cream, whipped	1½ pt.

Method

Soak gelatin in cold water for 5 minutes. Then heat over boiling water until it is completely dissolved.

Have the cheeses at room temperature. Cream and mix them well.

Add the gelatin (which has been slightly cooled) gradually and stir until well combined.

Fold in the whipped cream last.

Fill individual ring molds. Chill until firm.

Serve on lettuce or other greens and fill the center with fresh fruit.

JELLIED VEAL LOAF

Yield: 24 slices, ¾ by 3 by 2 in.

Ingredients

Boneless Veal Shoulder, cooked, diced finely (approx. 1½ qt. diced)	4 lb.
Veal Stock	1½ qt.
Onion Juice	3 tbsp.
Vinegar	⅓ cup
Salt	1½ tbsp.
Pepper	¼ tsp.
Plain Gelatin	1¼ oz.
Cold Water	1 cup
Stuffed Olives, sliced	½ cup
Eggs, hard cooked, sliced,	6
Pimiento, diced	½ cup
Parsley, chopped	¼ cup

Method

Cook veal in salted water for about 2 hours or until well done. While cooking add an onion, a stalk of celery and a tsp. of pickling spices. When the veal is tender, remove it, cook and dice finely.

Cook the broth down until only 1½ qt. remains. Strain it and while still hot add to it soaked gelatin.

Add the onion juice, vinegar, salt and pepper. Allow to cool but not to set.

In the bottoms of the loaf pans arrange slices of egg and olives. Cover with the gelatin mixture. Chill until congealed before filling further.

Mix the parsley with the veal. Place a layer of this over the congealed layer, then a layer of chopped eggs and pimiento. Top with another layer of veal and cover all with the gelatin mixture. Chill until firm.

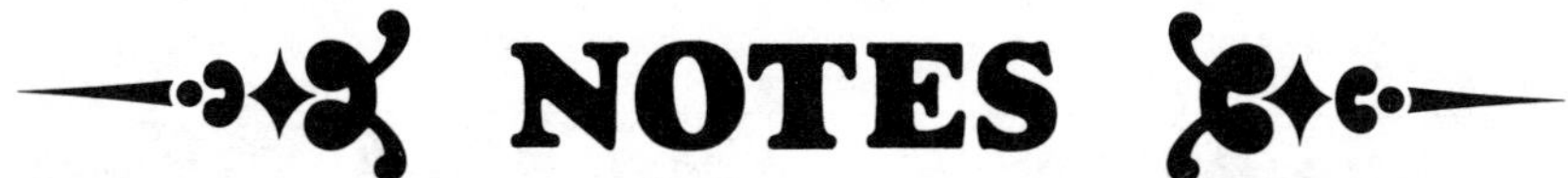

NOTES

CHAPTER XVIII
ICE CARVING

Elegant swan ice carvings lighted to maximum advantage are one of the hallmarks of buffets scheduled at the Century Plaza Hotel in Century City, Calif. Proper lighting will heighten the effectiveness of the simpler ice carvings made by beginners.

As an effective focal point for the buffet table, a well conceived and executed ice carving can set the theme, while capturing extra attention as an item never encountered away from professional circles.

The mastery of ice carving has classically been the mark of established culinarians. Not too long ago, many chefs feared that ice carving might be a vanishing art, but recently ice carving was given new impetus with the introduction of ice cream bombes which were best preserved if given an ice base.

The standard block of ice selected for carving weighs 300 lb. and measures 11 in. deep, 22 in. wide and 42 in. high. It takes an ice block of this size some 50 hours to freeze and about 48 hours to melt at room temperature. Almost any ice carving will last for 5 to 6 hours; the length of time it survives will depend on the melting rate of the thinnest part of the carving.

Ice carvings can be done outdoors at temperatures in the 70's or below, or indoors in a well ventilated walk-in refrigerator.

Even a relatively unskilled ice carver can turn out a satisfactory design in an hour or two, if given the right tools.

Ice carvings that can help to develop themes include:

Valentine's Day or Wedding ...... Love Birds on a Heart
Easter .... Rabbit or Flower Basket
Anniversary .... Letters or Numbers
Sporting Events .... Sail Boat or Automobile
Thanksgiving .... Turkey or Horn of Plenty
Christmas .... Santa Claus or Christmas Tree
New Year .... Numerals of New Year

In addition to establishing themes, ice carvings hold temperatures at satisfactory levels for bowls of caviar, other seafood or chicken.

The tools needed for various ice carving steps are:

Ice tongs—to move block of ice from place to place.

Ice pick—for splitting block into smaller pieces and removing large parts not needed in the design.

Six-pronged ice shaver—to carve and cut around small areas, for example, between the head and wings of an eagle, the handle of a fruit or flower basket, or around rabbits' ears.

Wood and V-shaped chisel—for heavy duty carving, fine grooving and channeling.

Single handed tree saw with coarse teeth—teeth set at proper angles make it possible to remove large chunks from block of ice without danger of cutting into the design.

Yardstick—to help in laying out design.

Before starting to carve, prepare a small model of the design or trace the design, full size, on tissue paper, place tissue paper on block and trace outline in the ice.

Ice carvings must be handled with special care when in transit from preparation point to point of display. These carvings are actually more fragile and brittle than glass; sudden jarring may cause piece to break.

The illumination of ice carvings adds much to their effectiveness. Colored lights can be placed in the back or in a hole on the bottom of the carving. If lights are used, be sure the light bulb and the wiring are well-insulated so that the water from melting ice does not cause a short circuit. Drip pans with wooden blocks and rubber hose to take care of melting are required.

Other Decorative Figures

Styrofoam, tallow and butter can all be sculptured for use as centerpieces. Styrofoam and tallow will provide centerpieces that can be held over for future use. However, tallow sculptures are quite time-consuming and their use should be carefully scheduled, with the time required to produce them set off against the number of times they can be used.

Tallow carvings can be stored indefinitely at temperatures that do not go over 90°F. To keep them from becoming dusty, cover with plastic.

Tallow carvings can never be permitted to touch food that is to be eaten. On a buffet table, small tallow figures can be placed on platter which contains no food and larger sculptures can be arranged on pedestals or tiers at the back of the table, removed from the food. Because of the mutton fat in the tallow, any food displayed on a tallow base, would become inedible very soon. These bases are sometimes used in food exhibitions where it has been clearly established that the food will be discarded at the end of the exhibition.

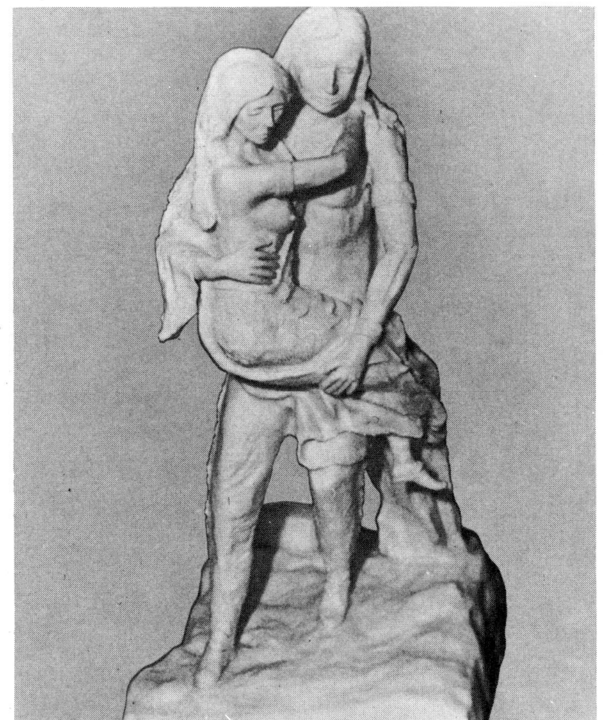

Figures shown at the top are made by process similar to that pictured here. Klaus Mitterhauser shown at work on tallow figure prepares figures to highlight food displays.

There are three basic formulas for making tallow:

Very firm	⅓ rendered beef or mutton fat ⅓ paraffin ⅓ bees wax (white)	for fragile figurines, animals, etc., made in molds
Medium	½ rendered beef or mutton fat ¼ paraffin wax ¼ bees wax	for carving from block, for busts, relief work
Soft	⅔ rendered beef or mutton fat ⅓ bees wax	for coating over styrofoam base, used for letters, numbers, etc.

Note: White candles can be used as a substitute for bees wax and paraffin.

Rendered beef fat can be purchased in 50 lb. cans or fat can be saved and rendered on the premises.

To render fat, give fat trimmings a coarse grind or cut in 2 in. pieces. Soak fat overnight in cold water to rinse out blood and to bleach. Place trimmings in steamer or in 250°F. oven. Do not let fat overheat as it will turn yellow.

Base choice of wax for tallow on these facts: white candles will give tallow a marble like appearance; paraffin will make tallow more stable; bees' wax will make tallow more malleable and easier to shape.

Whatever is selected as the wax ingredient should be melted in a bain marie. Avoid overheating wax as well as tallow. Mix wax thoroughly with rendered fat.

Pour fat-wax mixture into empty milk cartons to harden, using sizes up to 1 gal. Do not try to harden tallow in metal containers as it is too hard to remove blocks of tallow from them, except for containers that can be opened, after tallow hardens, from the bottom. Tallow could then be pushed out.

Coloring materials for tallow should also be added during the melting process. To color tallow, use: oil paint diluted with linseed oil, coloring powder like that used in colored candles, brown artificial bees' wax, or colored candles. Tallow in its natural white is very effective in carvings or molds.

Anyone attempting to create tallow carvings or sculptures should have artistic ability. He should also have the proper tools. Wooden carving tools like those used on clay or inexpensive Japanese metal carving tools and a french paring knife are essential.

Tallow may be used in various ways: ground tallow can be modeled like clay; when hardened into blocks, tallow can be carved; as a liquid, tallow can be poured into molds similar to those used for clay and china figures.

Tallow Modeling of Human Figures, Statues or Animals—

1. Cut up tallow blocks and put pieces through heavy duty meat grinder, using ⅛ or 3⁄16 in. plate.
2. Select a wooden base that will properly support the proposed figure. Build a skeleton of wire, varying the size of the wire to match the weight of the tallow that it will have to support. You must have a sketch or photograph of the figure being modeled, shown in exact size, so you can determine what the size and weight of the wire skeleton should be.
3. In figures, such as horses, use styrofoam, fine chicken wire or similar filler in the body so figure will weigh less and there will not be so much strain on the legs. Wires supporting the skeleton figure should be nailed to the wooden base.
4. Apply tallow to the wire skeleton with your hands to build up the rough shape of the figure you want to make. Heat from your hands will soften the tallow and make it easier to apply.
5. With wooden sculpturing tools (like those used in clay modeling) work out details of the figure. Work slowly over a period of several days to make sure that proportions and features are correct and the position of the figure is as you want it.
6. The tallow model can be at room temperature while you are working on it but between work periods put figure in freezer or refrigerator to keep parts like fingers, folded gowns, etc., hard. This makes the finishing of these detailed parts easier.
7. When all detail has been completed, smooth figure with palms of hands and finger tips. (Do not use water.) Refrigerate figure for 20 to 30 min., or put in freezer for approx. 5 min. Then to get the final glossy finish, remove figure from refrigerator and blow hot air from an electric blower (a hair dryer can be used) over the entire figure. The hot air melts a thin layer on the outer surface which, as soon as the stream of hot air is turned off, hardens instantly and very smoothly. This treatment gives the figure a dust repellent surface resembling white marble.
8. The finished figure can be stored at regular room temperature for many years. However, to protect figures keep them covered with plastic when not in use. Note: Do not attempt to paint the outer surface of any tallow figure since paint reduces the effectiveness of the detail. In addition, oil paint will not dry when applied to tallow and this makes figures difficult to handle.

Carving Figures from Solid Blocks of Medium Formula Tallow—The size of the figure to be carved will be determined by the size of the available block. Tallow in blocks is harder to handle as it is more brittle and may break. Shaved tallow can be used to repair some breaks.

Carving is easiest when a pattern of the desired figure is cut from cardboard or heaving paper and carving is done around it.

Tallow Molding and Relief Carving—Instant tallow sculptures can be created using the same kind of plaster of paris molds used for clay and china figures. This method requires no special artistry, yet provides permanent decorative figures appropriate for a wide variety of buffet themes. Use Very Firm formula for tallow when it is to be used in the molds as it will make the finished figure harder and, therefore, easier to unmold. Use Medium formula when making tallow to be used in relief carving.

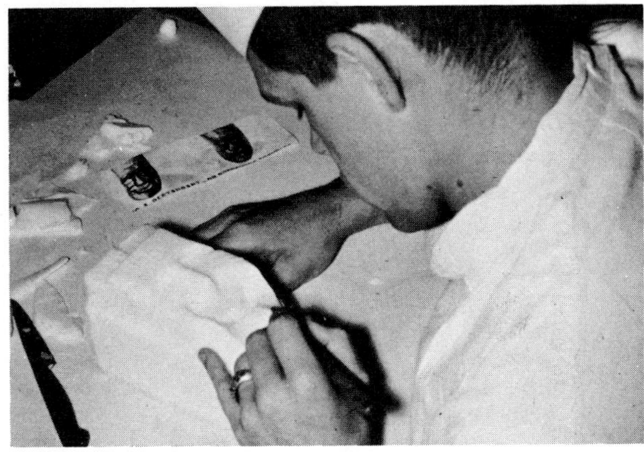

Set-up and tools for carving tiki head from block of tallow. Blocks are most easily carved when a pattern is made and carved around. A styrofoam support can be used to elevate tallow figures. Suitable tallow carvings can be displayed in "pools" made of green gelatin. The white figures gain dimension when displayed against the green background.

The molds come in sections that are normally held together with rubber bands after molds are filled. To use these molds with tallow, they must first be completely taped together at all seams. The insides of the molds must also be greased well with oil.

Pour liquid tallow into mold and set aside for several hours to harden. It is not necessary to put mold in refrigerator. When tallow is completely hardened, remove figure from mold by taking sections apart. Figure should come out easily if the molds have been properly greased.

Relief carvings are made by sealing picture frame to plywood backing, then filling frame with liquid tallow. When tallow has hardened, a scene or motif can be carved into the tallow. This method is not too difficult. Some cracks will occur in the tallow base as it contracts but they can be repaired with shaved tallow.

Models for Tallow Sculptures—Pictures from magazines, figures made of china, wood or clay may be reproduced in tallow. These can be used as tallow sculpture patterns or templates by taking a colored slide of the piece to be duplicated and projecting it on a piece of white cardboard, 3 by 4 ft. Use a marking pen or a regular pen to outline figure. Slide can be projected at a height that makes it easy for the worker to draw the outline. Mark all important features on the sketch.

With a slide projection obtained in this manner, the dimensions of the projected piece can be reduced easily in perfect proportions. The template or pattern resulting from this reduction can be used as a guide in building up the desired shape and form, with shaved tallow going right on the template.

These sculptures are most suitable for canape or hors d'oeuvres centerpieces or for cheese displays. Roses piped from butter can also be used as decorations.

Butter Sculptures—Butter sculptures must be done in a large walk-in refrigerator or outside in winter. Well-chilled blocks of butter or margarine are needed and the carving is done with wooden carving tools. Figures are made in much the same way as tallow figures except that butter is a much lighter material and figures made of it are limited to about 8 or 10 in. in height. Hot water will smooth the surfaces.

The glamour of presentation, associated in the guest's mind with haute cuisine, plus the mechanism needed for speedy service of patrons in large numbers: This effective combination is assured with a well planned, smooth running buffet, featuring elaborate displays created from gourmet ingredients.

Theme setting displays capture immediate attention and elaborate arrangements of food establish the elegant tone of the affair. To create this type of buffet takes organization and planning, essential characteristics of the buffet catering expert.

Less elaborate buffets must be planned with equal care, although the preparation required is considerably lessened. Diagrammed at the end of this chapter are table arrangements varying from simple to most elaborate. The buffet organizing procedures which follow can be adapted as dictated by the size and complexity of the buffet that is being planned.

Basics of Buffet Set-ups

1. When buffet arrangements are worked out with the host, these points should be settled: price per person; number of people guaranteed; special theme; menu, and date and time of buffet.

2. If extra carpenter work is to be required, for tiers or other necessary additions to set-up, schedule it well ahead of time. Also arrange for a sufficient supply of large banquet table cloths to use on the buffet tables.

3. Work out buffet menu that will be profitable or possible in the price range that has been set. List all items to be served and make plans to utilize leftovers. Do not permit last minute changes of the buffet menu. These will destroy the coordinated effect produced by a good master plan. Make a detailed plan and stick to it.

4. Foods should be arranged on the buffet in the order they are served from a menu: Cold hors d'oeuvres, cold seafood platters, cold meat platters, salads, hot foods, dessert and coffee.

(Foods presented buffet style for cocktail party guests do not have to follow this sequence.)

5. Plan to place any inedible displays—flowers, ice carvings, etc., toward the back of the buffet table so they do not interfere with the guest as he serves himself from buffet platters.

6. Do not use complicated or time-consuming methods of food presentation. The advantage of buffet service is the speed with which the guest can serve himself. Arrange all platters so that the guest may easily serve his own portion.

7. In planning grosse pieces (sizable displays of salmon, meat or poultry), specify small slices with garnishes in sufficient number for each serving.

Setting Up a Zoning System for Large Buffets

The larger the buffet, the more important it is that patron traffic be planned to move smoothly and speedily. Buffet foods, when properly placed, will provide this essential traffic control.

On small buffets (for 20 to 30 guests), foods may be arranged without concern for traffic as there will be no problems with this number.

There are also few traffic problems in establishments where the guest indicates to a waiter what he wants from the buffet and has his plate filled and served by the waiter. This kind of service is quite rare and is expensive as well.

When a buffet is planned for 50 to 80 persons or more, the tables should be divided into zones. Each of these zones should offer enough food for 50 of the guests; i. e., a buffet for 200 would require four zones set up to serve 50 guests each. Zones may also be established to serve 100 people, if there is not enough equipment to supply smaller zones.

The zone set-up requires a separate set of all of the chafing dishes, serving dishes, carving boards and platters needed for each zone. The foods offered in each zone should be identical, with the exception that the main display pieces (grosse pieces) might be decorated slightly differently so that each zone adds a separate note to the overall presentation.

Each zone should also be staffed with a waiter, waitress or cook to answer questions about the contents of the various bowls and platters of food and, if necessary, to help serve. This worker will also keep platters, bowls, chafing dishes properly filled, see that empty plates are speedily removed, that serving utensils are available and that the table stays at its most attractive throughout the serving period.

To Schedule Buffet Food Preparation

To provide food for a buffet that will be at its most eye capturing, a time schedule for food production must be set up and followed. The sequence suggested here can easily be adapted to meet varying buffet requirements:

1. *Well in Advance*—Prepare non-perishable, inedible items such as blown sugar work, gum paste items, dummy hams made of plastic or plaster of paris, ice carvings to store in freezer.

2. *3-4 Days in Advance*—Prepare foods that stand up well for this long in the refrigerator. These would include pateś and galantines which should be cooked but not given final decoration; basic aspic and chaud froid for coatings; molds for piece montee; gelatin molds, with or without fruit; boiled lobsters; poached salmon; basic preparation for hors d'oeuvres.

3. *1-2 Days in Advance*—Assemble and decorate all pieces requiring aspic or chaud froid, especially the large pieces. Do all basic work on platters the day before the buffet.

4. *Day of Buffet*—Prepare perishable foods such as

green salads, combination salads, fruit carvings; finish arrangements on large platters; set up trays of cold hors d'oeuvres; do final preparation on hard cooked eggs; finish off hot foods to be served in chafing dishes.

Note: Schedule work so that all foods can be produced easily by time guests arrive. Do not let work pile up in the last few hours as food items suffer if they must be prepared too hurriedly. Make realistic food production plans, keeping in mind how many people can be assigned and how many units they can be expected to turn out.

The Buffet of the Future

As more and more people want to be fed at an ever faster rate, the permanent buffet set-up becomes more feasible for many food service operations. It offers increased efficiency and sanitation as well as speedy service.

The buffet unit can be built in with heated food displays or stainless refrigerated tables with wells or crushed ice as backgrounds for food presentation. Foods can be kept glass covered. The system can be flexible since carts can be used for displays of additional items such as hors d'oeuvres.

The cost of such equipment will be considerably offset by the savings in food as items will be kept at optimum temperatures at all times.

The permanent buffet has already won acceptance overseas. In Switzerland, this type of service is common wherever food in a hurry is needed. It has proved especially satisfactory in airports, railroad stations, steamships and dining cars.

The supersonic airplanes of the future may well find this the answer to food service for the hundreds of passengers they will be carrying.

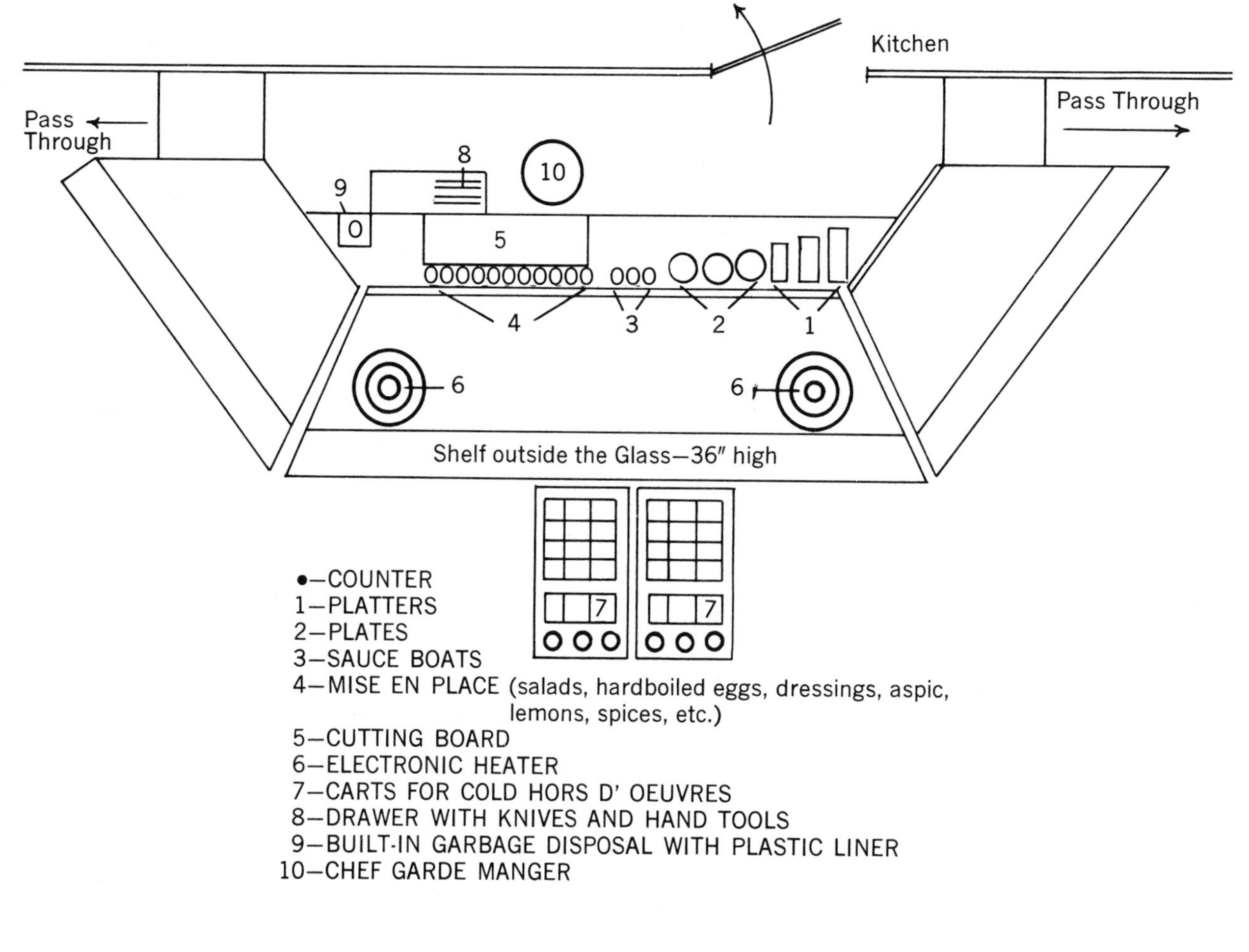

VARIOUS TABLE SHAPES FOR BUFFETS

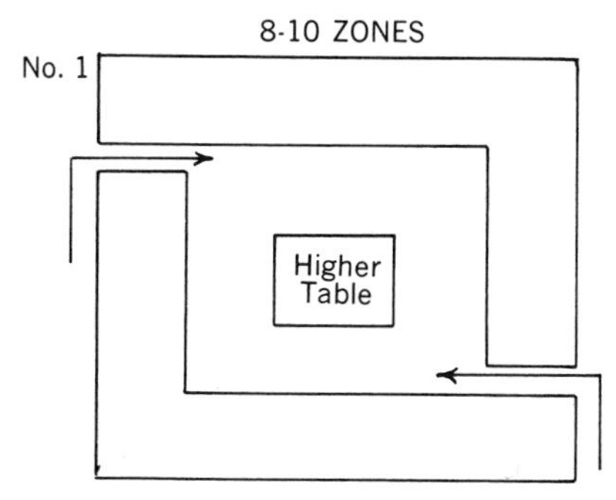

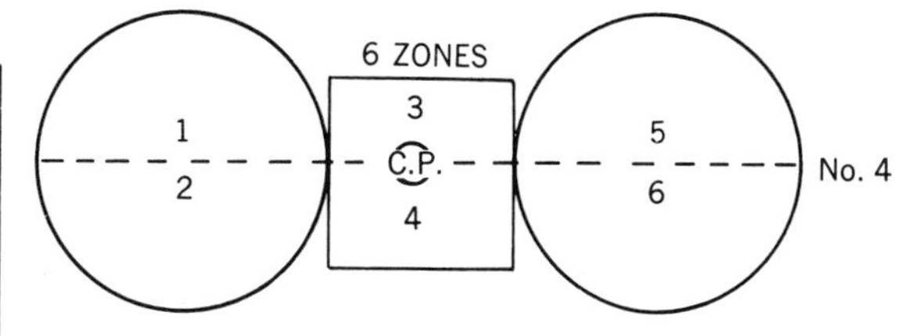

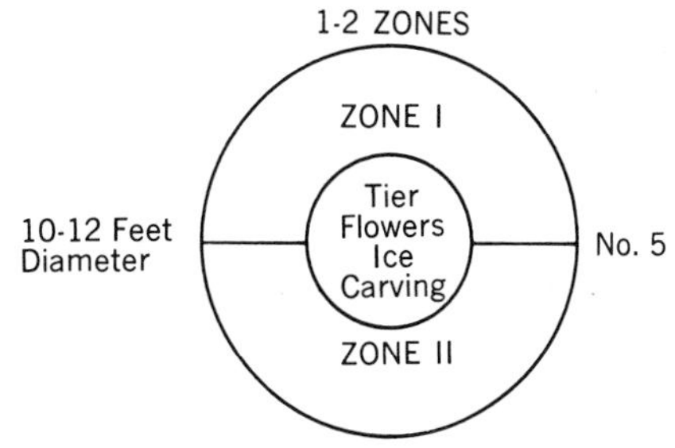

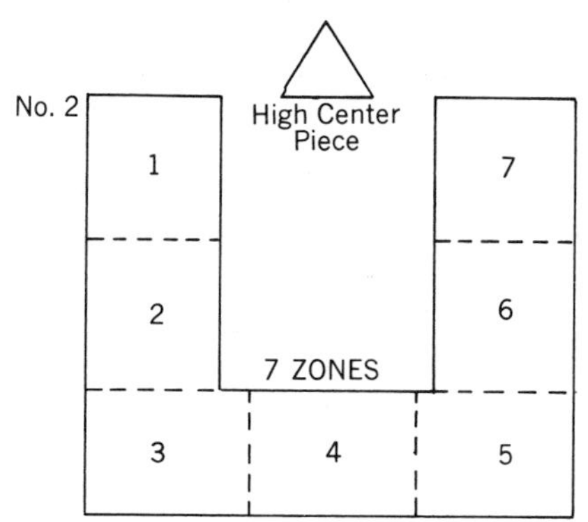

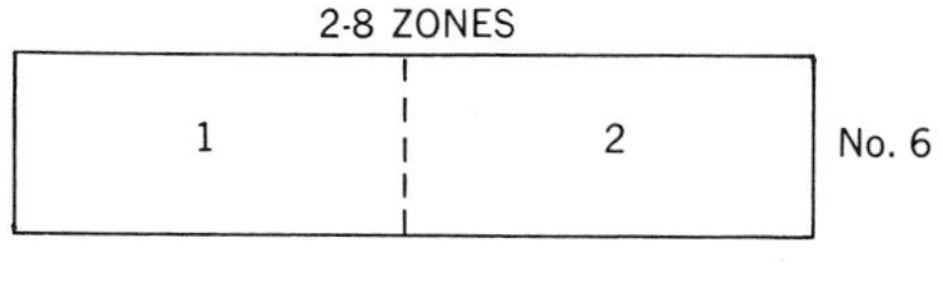

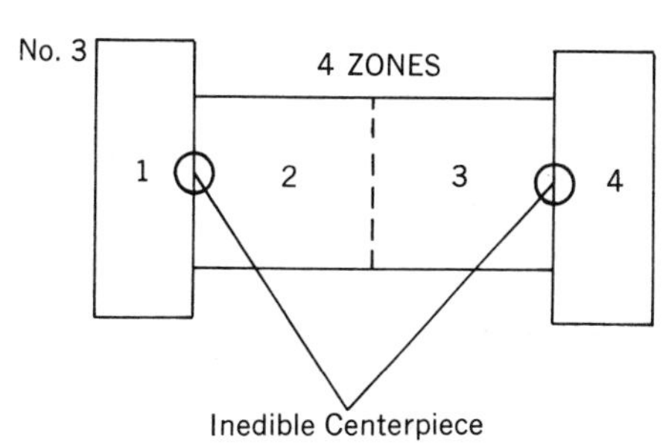

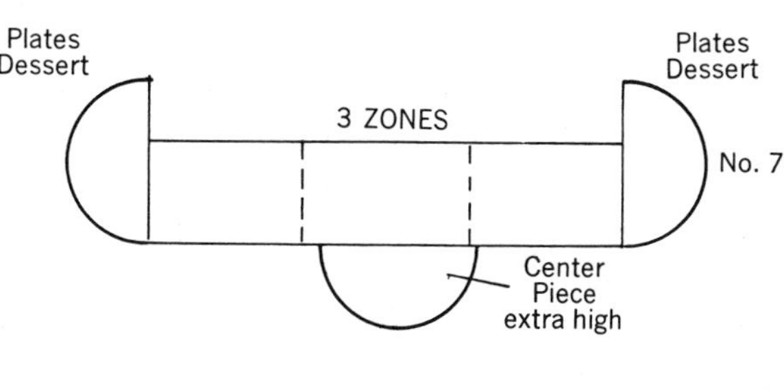

12 ZONES
600 Persons
No. 8

150 Plates | 1 | 2 | 3 | 150 Plates
12 | 11 | 10
Tier high Sculpture
4 | 5 | 6
150 Plates | 9 | 8 | 7 | 150 Plates

NOTE:

Each table shape is appropriate for a particular location. Center squares (No. 1 and No. 8) always set up in the center of a large hall or ballroom. Circular shapes are also placed so that access is possible from all sides, while straight tables are more appropriate against walls with an aisle between wall and buffet table. Horse shoe shape or L-shaped tables are practical in corners or at one end of the hall. Always keep in mind the access from behind the buffet to the kitchen in order to ensure smooth traffic.

Ice carvings and other uneatable center pieces should always be placed on a higher platform with spotlight illumination as a scenic background.

Due to the ZONING SYSTEM, guests will automatically spread out around the entire buffet table and select their food from one particular zone.

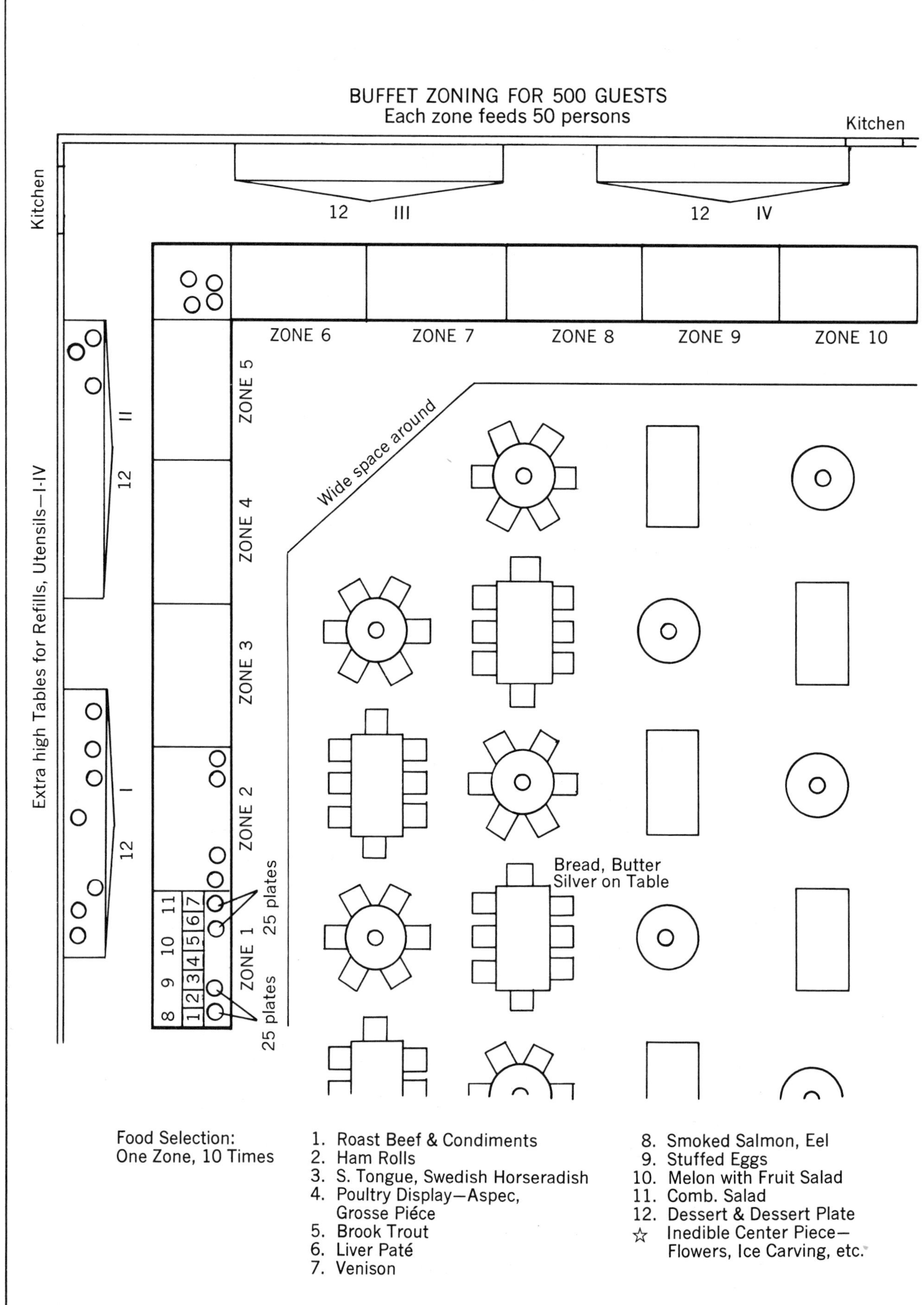
BUFFET ZONING FOR 500 GUESTS
Each zone feeds 50 persons
Kitchen
Kitchen
12 III
12 IV
ZONE 6
ZONE 7
ZONE 8
ZONE 9
ZONE 10
ZONE 5
ZONE 4
ZONE 3
ZONE 2
ZONE 1
12 II
12 I
Extra high Tables for Refills, Utensils—I-IV
Wide space around
25 plates
25 plates
8 9 10 11
1 2 3 4 5 6 7
Bread, Butter
Silver on Table
Food Selection:
One Zone, 10 Times
1. Roast Beef & Condiments
2. Ham Rolls
3. S. Tongue, Swedish Horseradish
4. Poultry Display—Aspec, Grosse Piéce
5. Brook Trout
6. Liver Paté
7. Venison
8. Smoked Salmon, Eel
9. Stuffed Eggs
10. Melon with Fruit Salad
11. Comb. Salad
12. Dessert & Dessert Plate
☆ Inedible Center Piece—Flowers, Ice Carving, etc.

BIRD'S NEST (Swedish Hors d'oeuvre)

Yield 20

Ingredients

Pickled Red Beets, chopped (see Beet Salad)	2 cups
Yellow Onions, chopped	2 cups
Capers, whole	1 cup
Swedish Anchovy Fillets in Red Wine Oyster Sauce (imported)	20
Lettuce, julienned, mixed with parsley	1 head
Egg Yolks, raw in half shell	20

Method

All chopped ingredients are arranged in circles like a bird's nest on a ceramic or glass (round) platter. Lettuce base, beets on outside, onions, capers inside nest with half egg shells containing yolks placed inside nest.

For serving: One anchovy is mixed with chopped ingredients, plus egg yolk.

MUSHROOMS A LA GREQUE

Yield 20

Ingredients

Fresh Mushrooms, quartered if large	3 lb.
Marinade	
Water	4 cups
Olive Oil	2 cups
Lemons	Juice of 2
White Vinegar	2 tbsp.
Celery, diced	2 stalks
Garlic Cloves, peeled	2
Sage	1 tsp.
Rosemary	1 tsp.
Thyme	1 tsp.
Ground Coriander	1 tsp.
Peppercorns	1 tsp.
Fennel	1 tsp.
Bay Leaves	3
Salt	1½ tsp.

Method

Mix ingredients for marinade, add mushrooms and bring to boil. Cool and pour into jar or crock for storage. Refrigerate.

MIXED PICKLES

Yield 20

Ingredients

Carrots, unpeeled	4
Cauliflower, in flowerets	1 lb.
Celery Stalks	2
Small White Onions, blanched	20
Marinade	
White Vinegar	3 pt.
Sugar	2 cups
Water	1 cup
Pickling Spice (in bag)	6 tbsp.

Method

Boil carrots until barely tender. Remove skin and cut into chunks. Boil marinade with spice bag for 5 minutes. Put all vegetables in jar and pour hot marinade over them.

TOMATO PEPPER RELISH

Yield 20

Ingredients

Ripe Tomatoes	12 large
Green Peppers	4
Red Peppers	4
Onions	2
Sugar	½ cup
Vinegar	2 cups
Cinnamon	½ tsp.
Salt	2 tsp.

Method

Peel tomatoes, chop peppers and onions fine. Combine with liquids, etc., and simmer for 1½ hours.

MINNESOTA PICKLES

Yield 20

Ingredients

Cucumbers, sliced thin, not peeled (Use fresh slim cucumbers)	4 qt.
Onions, sliced	1 pt.
Sugar	2 cups
Vinegar (cider)	2 cups
Celery Seeds	2 tsp.
Tumeric	2 tsp.

Method

Mix sliced cucumbers and onions with plenty of salt and let stand for half an hour. Wash and drain.

Boil sugar, vinegar, tumeric and celery seed, add cucumbers, simmer for 10 minutes, put in jar and seal air tight.

Note: Opened jar will keep under refrigeration several weeks. For immediate use, keep pickles in glass jar without seal.

LIPTAUER CHEESE (Homemade Austrian Cheese)

Yield 20

Ingredients

Cottage Cheese, salted	4 cups
Butter	2 cups
Onion, chopped	1
Chives, chopped	Some
Caraway Seeds	2 tbsp.
Capers, minced	2 tbsp.
Anchovies, minced	2
Hungarian Paprika	2 tbsp.

Method

Put cottage cheese through sieve or meat grinder.

Cream butter until fluffy; add all condiments and spices plus cottage cheese. Mix well. Sprinkle with paprika when serving.

SAUCES

SWEDISH HORSE RADISH SAUCE

Yield 20

Ingredients

Mayonnaise	1 cup
Apple, peeled, grated	1
Cream, whipped	1 cup
Fresh Horse Radish, grated or preserved horse radish (without liquid)	½ cup

Method

Combine all ingredients.

Serve with Matjes herring and other herring varieties, corned beef, roast beef, smoked salmon.

MEAT

STEAMSHIP ROUND ROAST

Yield Servings for 70 to 80 people

Ingredients

Steamship Round of Beef, with bone in	40-50 lb.

Method

Round may be roasted in oven or on spit. It will take 7 to 8 hours of roasting time at a temperature of 250° to 300°F. When round is done, it should be held 90 minutes before carving is started.

To Serve

Round should be sliced thin and served with pan gravy or natural juices.

BEEF IN OYSTER SAUCE

Yield 20

Ingredients

Black Beans (soaked in water over night)	1½ lb.
Lean Beef, sliced thin	4 lb.
Oysters (frozen or canned) with juice	1 lb.
Bacon, julienne	½ lb.
Bay Leaves	4
Black Pepper	1 tbsp.
Onions, chopped	2
Scallions	4
Soy Sauce	½ cup

Method

Cook beans with spices till half tender.

Saute bacon with beef and onions, add to beans and simmer till everything is tender.

Add oysters, scallions and soy sauce (keep on thick side). Serve with plain steamed rice.

CHINESE BARBECUED SPARERIBS, SWEET SOUR

Yield 20 to 25 portions

Ingredients

Fresh Spare Ribs, cut into 4-in. pieces	8-10 lb.
Peppercorns	12
Bay Leaves	2
Salt	2 tbsp.
Barbecue Sauce	
Oil or butter	½ cup
Onions, diced fine	2 medium
Prepared or English Mustard	2 tbsp.
Apricot Jam	1 cup
Tomato Sauce	1 cup
Brown Meat Sauce	1 cup
Cider Vinegar	½ cup
Soy Sauce	3 tbsp.
Worcestershire Sauce	2 tbsp.

Method

Cover spareribs with water, add peppercorns, bay leaves and salt. Bring to boil, turn heat down and simmer until meat is done. Do not overcook.

Saute onions in oil or butter in large frying pan until golden brown. Add mustard, jam, tomato sauce, brown meat sauce, vinegar, soy sauce and worcestershire sauce, bring to boil and simmer for 30 minutes.

Drain liquid from spareribs. Brown spareribs under broiler or in frying pan, then combine with barbecue sauce. Season to taste.

MUSTARD BAKED HAM

Yield 20 to 25 servings

Ingredients

Ham, bone in, ready to eat	10-12 lb.
Dry Mustard	3 oz.
Brown Sugar	1 cup
Whole Cloves	24
Apricot Jam	1 cup
Pineapple Slices	8
Maraschino Cherries	12

Method

Remove short bone from ham, trim off excess fat and rind. Rub ham with dry mustard and apricot jam; sprinkle brown sugar over it. Insert whole cloves about 1 in. apart over top of ham. Bake in 300° to 350°F. oven for 1½ to 2 hours. At the end of first hour take ham from oven and arrange pineapple slices and maraschino cherries over the top of the ham. Return to oven until nicely browned.

BARBECUED CORNED BEEF

Yield 20 to 25 buffet size portions

Ingredients

Fresh Brisket of Corned Beef	10-12 lb.
Pickling Spices	2 tbsp.
Barbecue Sauce	
Apricot Jam	1 pt.
Strong Veal or Beef Stock	2 cups
Lemons	Juice of 4
or	
Pineapple Juice	4 oz.
Dry Mustard	2 tbsp.
Worcestershire Sauce	2 tbsp.

Method

Cover corned beef with water and pickling spices; cook slowly until tender. Cool meat, trim fat. Cover with barbecue sauce and bake in 350°F. oven for 1 hour until corned beef is nicely glazed.

To Serve

Cut in 1-in. squares, serve with toothpicks as hot appetizers or on small plates.

ROAST SUCKLING PIG WITH BAKED APPLES

Yield 20 to 25 servings

Ingredients

Whole Suckling Pig	10-12 lb.
Stuffing	
Apples, sliced	4 lb.
Raisins	½ lb.
White Bread	3 lb.
Milk	2 cups
Salt	to taste
Pepper	to taste
Sugar	to taste

Method
Trim bread, removing crusts, cube. Soak bread in milk, squeeze liquid out of bread and mix with other stuffing ingredients.

Clean pig, place in roasting pan, stuff. Rub outside of pig with garlic, salt and freshly ground pepper, oil or shortening.

Cover with foil and roast for 4½ to 5 hours. in 350°F. oven. Baste or brush pig with oil or butter during roasting time. While pig is roasting, bake 15 to 20 small apples to serve with portions of roast suckling pig.

Note: Pig can also be roasted without stuffing. This will take only 3½ to 4 hours in a 350°F. oven.

ROAST SPRING LAMB EN CROUTE

Yield 20 to 25 servings

Ingredients

Leg of Lamb, 5 to 6 lb. ea.	2
Pie Dough, for crust	2 lb.
Soubise	
Onion Puree	1 cup
White Bread Crumbs	1 cup
Cream Sauce	½ cup
Salt	to taste
Pepper	to taste
Garlic Powder	to taste

Method
Bone and roast legs of lamb in 350°F. oven for 35 minutes per lb. or until medium rare. Remove from oven. Make clear gravy from drippings.

Roll out pie dough ½ in. thick. Coat lamb with soubise (onion puree with cream sauce and bread crumbs) then wrap tightly in pie dough, being sure there are no openings in dough through which steam can escape.

Put wrapped roast back in 275°F. oven for another hour. Remove from oven and cool for ½ hour. Slice carefully through pie dough.

To Serve
Accompany lamb with (1) clear gravy made from the drippings; (2) plain lamb juices or (3) mint jelly or sauce.

SHREDDED BEEF WITH GREEN PEAS AND MUSHROOMS

Yield 20 to 25 buffet size portions

Ingredients

Bottom Round or Chuck of Beef	10 lb.
Onions, diced fine	3 lb.
Paprika	2 tbsp.
Mushrooms, quartered	3 lb.
Butter or Oil	1 cup
Flour	½ cup
Tomato Puree	2 cups
Beef Stock or Water	to cover
Green Peas, frozen	2½ lb.
Red Wine	2 cups

Method
Cut beef on bias into small pieces. Season beef with salt, pepper and paprika and brown in hot oil or shortening.

In a separate pot, saute diced onions in butter until they are light brown. Add mushrooms and dust mixture with flour. Mix flour in well then add 2 cups tomato puree. Cover mixture with hot beef stock or water and bring to a boil. Add beef chunks and simmer for 1½ hours or until meat is tender.

To Serve
Add fresh peas and cook for 15 minutes more, check seasonings and stir in wine. Seve in large chafing dish with noodles or rice to accompany.

CROPCAKOR—SWEDISH MEAT POTATO DUMPLINGS

Yield 40 dumplings, split, 20 portions

Ingredients

Potato Dough	
Potatoes	6 lb.
Eggs	4 whole
Flour	2 cups
Corn Starch	2 cups
Butter or Margarine, melted	5 oz.
Salt	1 tsp.
Filling	
Smoked Ham, Shoulder or other smoked meats (diced or through large blade in grinder)	3 lb.
Onions	2 large
Crushed Black Pepper	Plenty
Chives or Scallions, chopped	3 tbsp.

Method
Prepare potato dough with *hot* cooked, peeled and drained potatoes by pressing them through a potato ricer. (For larger quantity dough, use mixing machine with wire whip.)

Add all other ingredients and blend.

Form patties, fill them with meat filling and poach dumplings in boiling salt water until they float.

Place cooked dumplings on oiled sheet pan and cool.

Slice each cold dumpling horizontally and pan fry until golden brown; sprinkle remaining meat filling over dumplings when served. Use chafing dish to serve.

Filling: All ingredients are sauteed with black pepper until crisp; chives are added later.

PRUNE STUFFED PORK LOIN

Yield 20

Ingredients

Pork Loin, whole, oven ready (can be either boned or boneless)	1
Prunes, pitted	1 lb.
Prune Sauce	1 pt.
Salt	1 tsp.
Pepper	1 tsp.

Method
With a sharpening steel make a slit at the rib eye running all the way through the loin; cut whole loin into two sections, if desired.

Push dry, pitted prunes through slit all the way through loin.

Roast as usual for about two hours; add salt, pepper.

Serve with prune sauce and garnish with prunes. Can be served cold also.

MEAT

ROAST CROWN OF PORK

Yield 20

Ingredients

Loins (only part of loin with long ribs can be used to make a crown roast)	2

Method

With meat saw, remove strip of back bone on the inside of loin.

Make incision from outside through the back bone between each rib with meat saw.

Shave meat from all ribs for one inch from the top.

Bend two loins into a circle and tie, wrapping string around loins several times.

Cover rib bone ends with foil. Roast at 325°F. for approximately 2 hours.

Note: If bread stuffing is used inside the crown roast, serve hot. If served cold, fill inside of crown with pickled vegetable or cauliflower vinaigrette, after it is chilled.

BRUNSWICK STEW

Yield 20

Ingredients

Chickens, disjointed, small pieces	3 2-lb.
Rabbit or Opposum (cut in 2 in. pieces)	2 lb.
Tomatoes, canned with juice	1 qt.
Onions, sliced	6
Green Peppers, diced	4
Kernel Corn (frozen, vacuum pack)	2 lb.
Lima Beans (frozen, vacuum pack)	2 lb.
Paprika	2 tbsp.
Butter	½ lb.
Liquid Pepper Sauce	few drops
Worcestershire Sauce	few drops
Flour	3 cups
Parsley, chopped	2 tbsp.
Black Pepper	2 tsp.

Method

Dredge chicken and opposum pieces in flour, paprika and salt. Saute in butter till brown.

Saute onions and peppers in a separate sauce pan till transparent, add chicken plus all other ingredients and seasonings and some water or chicken stock.

Braise the stew for 15 minutes; add lima beans and corn, cook another 20 minutes until tender.

Thicken with flour and water, garnish with chopped parsley.

POLENTA

Yield 20 to 25 portions

Ingredients

Water	3 qt.
Corn Meal, yellow, coarse	3 cups
Salt	2 tsp.

Method

Bring 2 qt. water to boil; salt.

Add corn meal and stir with wire whip.

Cook over double boiler 45 minutes (stir constantly).

Pour thickened mixture in ½-in. layer into greased hotel pan.

Let polenta cool well and turn out of pan.

Cut into small squares and broil with melted butter for few minutes.

PIROJKI (Russian Meat Pie)

Yield 20

Ingredients

Dough

Flour	6 cups
Butter	½ lb.
Egg Yolks	4
Cream	4 tbsp.
Salt	1 tsp.

Method

Mix eggs and cream and blend with rest of ingredients into firm dough. Chill dough for an hour.

Meat Filling

Cooked Veal and Chicken Leftovers, ground finely	6 cups
Onions	3
Hard Cooked Eggs	4
Ground Black Pepper	1 tbsp.
Dill, chopped	1 tbsp.
Nutmeg	1 tsp.
Parsley, chopped	2 tbsp.
Salt	2 tbsp.
Bouillon	to make paste

Method

Put all ingredients through meat grinder, season well.

Line a buttered hotel pan on bottom and sides with half the dough.

Apply meat filling (one inch thick) over dough.

Cover with rest of dough. Brush on eggwash, punch holes in top with fork. Bake in moderate oven for 45 minutes. Serve with hot melted butter, sour cream.

BEEF TERIYAKI (Hawaiian)

Yield 20

Ingredients

Beef Tenderloin or other tender beef parts, sliced thin	5 lb.
Fresh Mushrooms, sliced	1 lb.
Green Peppers, julienne	4
Onions, sliced	2 or 3 large
Teriyaki Sauce	6 oz.
Corn Starch or Sherry	⅓ cup
Water	½ cup

(Teriyaki sauce is available in super markets, however it is easy to prepare your own.)

Teriyaki Sauce

Soy Sauce	3 cups
Onion, chopped	3
Ginger, powdered	4 tsp.
Sugar	6 tbsp.
Sherry Wine	1½ cups
Whole Garlic Cloves, mashed	5
Sesame Seed Oil or regular Salad Oil	1 cup

Blend sauce ingredients, pour over beef and let stand for a day before using.

Method

Saute sliced beef in hot skillet with sesame seed oil until brown. Add mushrooms, peppers, onions and braise for 10 minutes.

Add Teriyaki Sauce to which enough blended corn starch and water or sherry has been added to thicken sauce to medium consistency. Add water or stock if more sauce is desirable.

Note: Similar Teriyaki dishes can be prepared with chicken, spareribs, hamburger, pork chops, steaks, etc.

CHICKEN

POLYNESIAN CHICKEN

Yield 20

Ingredients

3-lb. Chickens, disjointed, breasts, split in two	5
Onions, sliced	3 large
Bean Sprouts	3 cups
Bamboo Shoots	2 cups
Crushed Pineapple	2 cups
Soy Sauce	to taste
Sherry	1 cup
Corn Starch	½ cup
Sesame Seed Oil or other oil for sauteeing	

Method

Fry disjointed chickens in oil till brown.

Saute onions in same pan, add sherry and stir, scraping brown bits loose and blending into liquid to combine with chicken in sauce pan. Add crushed pineapple, water or stock, and braise 25 minutes.

Add bean sprouts and bamboo shoots; thicken with corn starch.

To Serve

Add glacéd pineapple slices as garnish. Serve rice as accompaniment.

CANTALOUPES BAKED WITH CORNISH GAME HENS

Yield 20

Ingredients

Cornish Game Hens (split and boned, 6 rib cage only)	10 small
Cantaloupes, split in half, seeds removed	10
Fried Rice	20 cups
Sherry Wine } Soy Sauce } Mixture for basting	½ cup
Sweet and Sour Sauce	1 cup

Method

Oven broil split game hens, basting frequently with soy sauce and sherry until done.

Prepare fried rice. (See recipe, page 219.)

Slice bottom off cantaloupes, place on sheet pan; half fill with fried rice. Place half a broiled game hen on top of each cantaloupe. Baste with peanut oil. Wrap in foil and bake in moderate oven for half an hour.

Pour sweet and sour sauce over game hen before serving.

FISH

LOMI LOMI SALMON
(Hawaiian Salmon Appetizer—Raw)

Yield 20

Ingredients

Pickled Salmon Fillet or Raw Salmon	5-6 lb. slab
Tomatoes, diced, peeled, and seeds removed	6
Scallions	6
Onions, chopped	1
Soy Sauce	3 tbsp.
Black Pepper	2 tbsp.

Method

Cut pickled salmon in small pieces and mix with equal amount of diced, peeled and seeded tomatoes, scallions, chopped onions, soy sauce and black pepper.

Note: If fresh raw salmon is used for this appetizer, salt will have to be added.

COLD SALMON TROUT, FINES HERBES

Yield 20 to 25 buffet size portions

Ingredients

Salmon Trout, 4 to 5 lb.	2
Water	2 cups
White Wine	2 cups
Lemons, juice of	4
Onions, sliced thin	3
or	
Shallots, chopped fine	5
Celery, cut fine	3 pieces
Dill, chopped	few sprigs
Chopped Parsley	small bunch
Chervil, optional	few sprigs
Tarragon, optional	one bunch
Salt	1 tbsp.
Pepper	½ tsp.
Gelatin, unflavored	2 oz.
Cold Water	1 cup
Mayonnaise	1 pt.
Tarragon Vinegar	½ cup

Method

Scale and wash trout. Fillet fish, remove all bones from fillets and cut in 1-in. pieces. Place in buttered baking pan. Cover with water, white wine, lemon juice; add onions or shallots, celery, dill, parsley, chervil, tarragon, salt and pepper.

Dilute gelatin in cold water and pour over trout. Cover trout with buttered waxed paper or aluminum foil. Place in 350°F. oven and bake for 15 to 20 minutes. Cool in refrigerator. Serve chilled with jellied liquid. Tarragon-flavored mayonnaise may be served on the plate with the salmon or offered in a sauce boat.

Note: Salmon trout may also be completely boned, stuffed with raw smoked salmon or whitefish mousse, wrapped in cheesecloth and cooked in a fish poacher.

OVEN BAKED HADDOCK, MARBLEHEAD

Yield 20 to 25 portions

Ingredients

Fresh Haddock	8 to 10 lb.
Oil	½ cup
Lemons, juice of	4
Thyme	2 tbsp.
Carrots	4 medium
Onions	4 medium
Celery	4 stalks
Mushrooms	16 oz.

Method

Scale and wash haddock. Season with salt and pepper and place in baking pan on sheet of aluminum foil large enough to wrap around fish. Add oil, lemon juice and thyme and wrap foil around fish. Place fine sliced carrots, onions, celery and mushrooms in same pan alongside foil-wrapped fish, closing foil tightly so no flavor can escape. Bake for about 45 minutes in a 350°F. oven.

When done, remove foil and serve at once with buttered parsley potatoes. Accompany haddock with plain melted butter and lemon juice, a delicate mustard sauce or a light horseradish sauce.

FISH

FRESH COLD SALMON WITH RUSSIAN DRESSING

Yield 20 to 25 portions

Ingredients

Salmon	8 to 10 lb.
Large Shrimp	12
Hard Cooked Eggs, sliced	8
Asparagus, fresh, frozen or canned	4 lb. or 3 cans
Leeks	to decorate
Pimientos	1 small can
Court Bouillon	
Water	6 cups
Vinegar	2 cups
White Wine, optional	2 cups
Salt	½ cup
Onions, cut	3 cups
Celery, cut	2 pcs.
Carrots, cut	3 medium
Mixed Pickling Spices	1 tbsp.
Russian Dressing	
Mayonnaise	1 pt.
Chili Sauce	¾ cup
Catsup	¾ cup
Green Peppers, chopped	2
Pimientos, chopped	2

Method

The day before planning to serve this dish, scale salmon clean and wash well. Place in fish poacher, large pot or in deep baking pan. Cover with court bouillon and boil slowly for 20 minutes, then simmer for another 15 minutes. Let salmon cool in broth in refrigerator overnight.

Next day place chilled salmon on wire rack and carefully remove skin. Decorate with sliced hard cooked egg slices, asparagus tips, strips of leek, pimiento, green or ripe olives and 12 large shrimp.

Serve with Russian Dressing made by combining ingredients listed above.

Note: The Russian Dressing may be made with a sweet sour chopped India relish instead of green peppers and chopped pimientos.

The salmon can be sliced, poached and decorated in 20 to 25 portions.

ORIENTAL COLD SALMON

Yield 20

Ingredients

Whole Salmon Fillet (half a fresh salmon) completely boned, with skin on	1
White Wine	2 cups
Water	to cover
Saffron	½ tsp.
Onion, sliced	1
Lemon	1
Salt	3 tsp.
Hard Cooked Eggs	6 to 8
Russian Dressing	1 pt.
Capers	½ cup

Method

Place whole fillet, skin side up in oiled hotel pan, add 2 cups white wine, water to cover, pinch of saffron, sliced onions, salt and lemon slices.

Poach salmon for 20 minutes and let cool in broth.

Arrange on platter with capers, chopped eggs mixed with parsley, fresh lemon wedge; serve with Russian Dressing.

NEW ENGLAND BAKED CLAMS (Hot)

Yield 20

Ingredients

Cohaug Clams	20
White Bread, diced	4 to 5 cups
Butter, melted	1 cup
Milk	to moisten bread
Canned Water Chestnuts, diced	½ cup
Soy Sauce	4 tbsp.
Bacon, smoked diced	6 slices
Ginger	½ tsp.
Scallions	4
Parsley, chopped	4 tbsp.
Black Pepper	2 tsp.
Sesame Seed	2 tbsp.
Parmesan Cheese, grated	1 cup
Paprika	to sprinkle

Method

Chop clams and mix with moistened crumbs, butter, diced chestnuts, bacon crumbs and spices.

Fill shells with mixture, sprinkle with sesame seeds, paprika and parmesan cheese plus melted butter. Bake in hot oven for 10 minutes. Serve with cocktail sauce.

ROLLS

BRIOCHE

Yield 18 to 24 brioche

Ingredients

Yeast	1 pkg.
Sugar	2 tbsp.
Soft Butter	1 cup
Eggs	7
Lukewarm Water	⅓ cup
Flour	4 cups, approx.
Salt	1 tsp.
Milk, scalded and cooled	½ cup

Method

1. Soften yeast in ⅓ cup lukewarm water. Add 1 tsp. sugar and 1 cup flour. Mix and then knead until smooth. Place ball of dough in bowl and cover with lukewarm water. Let rise until ball of dough floats, about 1 hour.
2. Put remaining flour in a large bowl. Add ball of dough, half of butter, remaining sugar, salt and 2 eggs, slightly beaten. Mix well with fingers, adding enough milk to make a soft but not sticky dough. Turn out on a lightly floured board and knead until smooth.
3. Work in remaining butter and 2 more eggs. Knead again, lifting the dough and slapping it on the table until it is very smooth.
4. Add 2 more eggs and work them into the dough. Knead as in Step 3.
5. Shape dough into ball and place in greased bowl. Cover and let rise in a warm place until double in bulk.
6. Punch dough and stir down. Shape into a ball, place in a clean, greased bowl, cover tightly with foil and chill overnight.
7. To shape brioche, turn dough out onto floured board. Cut off about ⅙ of dough to use for small round topknot to finish off brioche. Divide remainder of dough into 18 to 24 portions and shape each into

a ball. Place in greased brioche pans or muffin tins (2¾ by 1¼ in. deep). Divide reserved dough into 18 to 24 small balls. Dampen finger slightly and poke depression in top of each large ball in the center. Place small ball in the resulting depression. Cover brioche and let rise in a warm place until double in bulk, about 1 hour.

8. Preheat oven to 450°F. and place rack near bottom.
9. Lightly beat remaining egg and brush top of brioches. Bake at 450°F. until well browned, about 15 minutes.

SALADS

PINEAPPLE CARROT SALAD

Yield 20 to 25 buffet size portions

Ingredients

Pineapple, fresh, julienne	2
or	
Pineapple, No. 2½ cans	2
Carrots, slivered	1 lb.
Blond Raisins	6 oz.
Oil	1 cup
Vinegar	½ cup
Salt	1 tbsp.
Pepper	dash
Mayonnaise Sour Cream Dressing	1 pt.

Method

Mix all ingredients except dressing.

To Serve

Place portion on lettuce leaf and top with mayonnaise sour cream dressing.

SHAMROCK SALAD

Yield 20 to 25 portions, buffet style

Ingredients

Lime Gelatin	16 oz.
Pears, No. 2½ can, small halves	3
Cottage Cheese	1 qt.
Creamed French Dressing	1 pt.

Method

Cover bottom of large angel food cake pan with thin layer of lime gelatin. Put in refrigerator to set. When gelatin has thickened, place layer of pear halves on top of it. Cover pears with another layer of gelatin. Return to refrigerator to set. When last layer of gelatin has thickened, place a second layer of pears around mold and fill rest of mold with lime gelatin. Let stand in refrigerator overnight. To unmold, place mold in hot water and turn over on a large round silver platter. Place cottage cheese in center of mold and arrange pear halves around mold. Decorate with fresh mint leaves. Strawberries, when in season, can also be used. Serve with creamy french dressing, ladled over top or in pitcher on the side.

SAUERKRAUT SALAD

Yield 20 to 25 buffet size portions

Ingredients

Sauerkraut	4 lb.
Onions, diced	2 medium
Carrots, shredded	1 bunch
Apples, diced	4
Vinegar	½ cup
Oil	½ cup
Pepper	½ tsp.
Bacon, crisp, diced	1 lb.
Parsley, chopped	2 oz.

Method

Wash sauerkraut thoroughly. Add all other ingredients except bacon and chopped parsley.

To Serve

Place portion on lettuce leaf. Sprinkle crisp cooked diced bacon and parsley on top of portion.

SHRIMP SALAD

Yield 20 to 25 portions

Ingredients

Shrimp, medium (20 to 25 to the lb.)	10 lbs.
Celery, diced	2 lb.
Court Bouillon	
Water	6 cups
Vinegar	2 cups
Onion, cut	1 medium
Celery Stalks	2
Bay Leaves	2
Peppercorns	6
Salt	2 tbsp.
Celery, diced	4 cups
Sauce Vert	
Mayonnaise	1 pt.
Capers or Dill Pickles, chopped	4 tbsp.
Dill, chopped	small bunch
Tarragon, chopped, optional	small bunch
Parsley, chopped	small bunch
Watercress, chopped	½ bunch
Worcestershire Sauce	2 tbsp.
Vinegar	½ cup
Liquid Hot Pepper Sauce	few drops

Method

Cover shrimp with court bouillon ingredients and bring to boil. Rinse shrimp with cold water, shell and clean. Drain shrimp, cut into good sized pieces.

Combine ingredients for Sauce Vert and mix shrimp and diced celery in sauce.

BRAUNSCHWIEGER SCHLOSS SALAD

Yield 20 to 25 buffet portions

Ingredients

Swiss Cheese	2 lb.
Frankfurters	2 lb.
Dill Pickles	2 lb.
Onions, sliced thin	1 lb.
Prepared Mustard	2 tbsp.
Oil	1 cup
Vinegar	1 cup
Salt	1 tbsp.
Pepper	½ tsp.
Worcestershire Sauce	2 tbsp.
Sugar	1 tbsp.

Method

Slice cheese, frankfurters, and dill pickles. Mix together with onions and remaining ingredients. Serve on lettuce leaves with tomato wedges.

SALADS

CUCUMBERS WITH SOUR CREAM AND DILL

Yield 20 to 25 portions, buffet size

Ingredients

Cucumbers	8
Salt	1 tbsp.
Sour Cream	1 pt.
Lemons, juice of	3
White Pepper	½ tsp.
Fine Cut Dill	small bunch

Method

Peel cucumbers, split in half, remove seeds and cut into fine slices. Place cucumbers in bowl and sprinkle salt over them. Let cucumbers stand for 1 hour. Squeeze liquid from cucumbers, pressing in towel or with back of spoon. Remove cucumbers from liquid and mix with sour cream, lemon juice, white pepper and dill.

NICOISE SALAD

Yield 20 to 25 buffet size portions

Ingredients

Green Beans, fresh or frozen, cut in 1 in. pcs., cooked	3 lb.
Potatoes, cooked and diced	3 lb.
Onions, diced	2 medium
Vinegar	¾ cup
Oil	1 cup
Salt	to taste
Freshly Ground Pepper	to taste

Method

Mix all ingredients thoroughly. Season to taste.

To Serve

Place individual portions on lettuce leaves and sprinkle with chopped parsley.

KNOB CELERY SALAD

Yield 20 to 25 buffet size portions

Ingredients

Knob Celery Roots, medium size	10 to 12
Vinaigrette	
Vinegar	¾ cup
Oil	1 cup
Salt	1 tsp.
Pepper	¼ tsp.
Onions, diced	2 medium
Water, optional	1 cup
Sugar	to taste
Hard Cooked Eggs, chopped	6
Chopped Parsley	to garnish

Method

Wash knob celery roots well and cover with water; cook with skins on. When done, cool celery, remove skins, slice and place in a shallow pan or bowl. Pour vinaigrette sauce over celery. If it does not cover, add water and sugar to taste. Let celery marinate for several hours.

To Serve

Remove celery from marinade and arrange on lettuce leaves. Sprinkle chopped eggs and parsley over salad.

ASSORTED COLD CUTS

Ingredients

a) Chicken Loaf
b) Luxury Loaf
c) Pepper Loaf
d) Pimiento Loaf
e) Veal Loaf
f) Blutwurst
g) Head Cheese
h) Jellied Veal and Tongue Loaf
i) Jellied Corned Beef Scraps
j) Liverwurst
k) German Salami
l) Mortadella Sausage

Method

The above listed cold cuts, plus others, are practical for cold buffet platters. Arrange them in attractive patterns and garnish.

ANTIPASTO TRAY

(An Italian cold assortment of hors d'oeuvres)

Yield 20

Ingredients

Genoa Salami, sliced
Anchovy Fillets with Capers
Tuna
Prosciutto Ham, thinly sliced
Mortadella, etc.
Sardines or other Mediterranean Fish
Pickled Mushrooms and Vegetables
Red and Green Peppers
Onion Rings

Method

Arrange everything neatly on Boston lettuce leaves.

Note: Antipasto relish is designed to be served also as part of an antipasto tray. In this case other vegetables can be eliminated. Pickled zucchini and eggplants (see Marinated Mixed vegetable) are also part of an Italian antipasto.

SALAD STEPHANIE

Yield 24 buffet size portions

Ingredients

Artichoke Bottoms	3 cans or 24 portions
Asparagus, green or white tips	3 to 4 per serving
Red Pimientos, cut in strips	1 small can
Mayonnaise, creamed	1 pt.
Walnuts, chopped fine	8 oz.

Method

Select artichoke bottoms that are uniform in size and arrange 3 to 4 asparagus tips on each one. Size of asparagus will determine number of strips to be used. Place a strip of pimiento across tips. Place 1 tsp. of creamed mayonnaise on salad and sprinkle with chopped walnuts.

SALAD LORETTE

Yield 20 to 25 buffet size portions

Ingredients

Beets, cooked, sliced	2 No. 2½ cans, or 3 lb. fresh
Knob Celery, cooked, sliced	2 No. 2½ cans, or 3 lb. fresh
Hard Cooked Eggs, chopped	6
Parsley	2 oz.

Method

Cook beets and celery separately. Remove skins, cool.

To Serve

Alternate slices of beets and celery on lettuce, romaine or chicory leaf. Sprinkle with chopped egg and parsley. Offer basic french dressing as an accompaniment.

AUGUSTINE SALAD

Yield 20 to 25 buffet size portions

Ingredients

Iceberg Lettuce, shredded	4
Green Beans, frenched, cooked	3 lb.
Tomatoes, peeled and quartered	3 lb.
Dressing	
Mayonnaise	1 pt.
Worcestershire Sauce	2 tbsp.

Method

Combine salad ingredients. Add dash of worcestershire sauce to mayonnaise and serve with salad. Serve either in large bowl or in individual portions.

BOILED BEEF SALAD

Yield 20 to 25 buffet size portions

Ingredients

Brisket of Beef	
Carrots	3 medium
Onions	3 medium
Celery	3 stalks
Pickling Spices	1 tbsp.
Onions, sliced thin	4 medium
Dill Pickles, sliced	6
Celery, julienne	6 pieces
Salt	2 tbsp.
Pepper	½ tsp.
Prepared Mustard	2 tbsp.
Oil	1 cup
Vinegar	1 cup
Worcestershire Sauce	2 tbsp.

Method

Simmer brisket of beef until tender in water to cover with carrots cut in pieces, onions, celery, salt and pickling spices. Cool. Trim all fat from meat and cut into 1-in. squares. Combine with all other ingredients and mix thoroughly.

Note: This salad can also be served as a main dish.

BRAISED LEEKS VINAIGRETTE WITH SLICED HAM

Yield 20 to 25 portions, buffet style

Ingredients

Leeks, large bunches	4
Chicken or Beef Broth	2 cups
Sliced Boiled Ham	2 lb.
Vinaigrette Sauce	
Onions, chopped fine	2
Dill Pickles, chopped	2
Parsley	1 oz.
Hard Cooked Eggs, chopped	6
Vinegar	1 cup
Olive Oil	1 cup
Salt	to taste
Pepper	to taste

Method

Cut off green ends of leeks, wash white stalks carefully and cut in 2½ to 3 in. pieces. Place white stalks in 2 cups of broth with half cup of vinegar and olive oil in saute pan. Cover tightly and simmer until done. Cool. Blend rest of ingredients for vinaigrette sauce.

To Serve

Place cooked leeks in center of china platter. Arrange slices of ham around leeks. Cover with vinaigrette sauce.

CABBAGE SALAD WITH CARAWAY SEEDS

Yield 20 to 25 buffet size portions

Ingredients

Cabbage, large white	2
Salt	2 tbsp.
Pepper	¼ tsp.
Vinegar	1 cup
Sugar	2 tbsp.
Caraway Seeds	3 tbsp.
Carrots, shredded	5 medium
Green Peppers, julienne	3 medium
Hard Cooked Eggs, sliced	6
Chopped Parsley	2 oz.
Mayonnaise	2 cups

Method

Mix all ingredients together and let stand for 2 hours.

To Serve

Drain liquid and place salad on lettuce leaves arranged on platter or in bowl. Garnish with sliced hard cooked eggs and chopped parsley. Individual portions may also be arranged on lettuce leaves with the same garnitures.

HUNGARIAN SALAMI WITH GREEN AND RED PEPPER SALAD

Yield 20 servings, buffet style

Ingredients

Red Peppers, cut in strips	2 lb.
Green Peppers, cut in strips	2 lb.
Onions, sliced	2 large
Garlic, chopped fine	2 cloves
Olive Oil	1 cup
Salt	to taste
Pepper	to taste
Small Spice Bag	1
Cider Vinegar	1 cup
Hungarian Salami	2 lb.

Method

Wash peppers, remove seeds carefully, slice and set aside. In saucepan, saute onions and garlic in olive oil until onion is golden. Add peppers, salt and pepper and spice bag. Set on low fire until pepper is tender. When pepper is cooked, add cider vinegar and cool. Remove spice bag.

To Serve

Place salad in center of deep china platter with thin slices of Hungarian salami arranged around it. Decorate top of salad with hard cooked eggs.

SPAGHETTI SALAD

Yield 20

Ingredients

Spaghetti, cooked and cut into 2-in. strings	1½ lb.
Smoked Ham, Other Smoked Meat, or Sausage, diced	2 cups
Celery, diced	2 stalks
Green Pepper or Pimiento, diced	2
Dressing	
Mayonnaise	2 pt.
Chilli Sauce	1 pt.

Method

Combine mayonnaise and chili sauce for dressing. Mix all ingredients thoroughly with dressing.

To Serve

Garnish with small tomato wedges.

SALADS

BRAISED HEARTS OF CELERY GOURMET

Yield 20 buffet size portions

Ingredients

Canned Celery Hearts, No. 2½ cans	3
Hard Cooked Eggs, sliced	6
Chives, cut fine	2 bunches
Sauce	
Ham or Tongue, cut in fine julienne	1 lb. of ea.
Carrots, sliced	3 medium
Onions, sliced	3 medium
Green Peppers, cut in julienne	4
Red Pimientos, sliced	1 small can
Radishes, sliced	12
Salt	to taste
Pepper	to taste
Oil	1 cup
Vinegar	1 cup

Method

Combine sauce ingredients and pour over canned celery.

To Serve

Place canned celery stalks on a deep china platter. Cover with sauce. Garnish with row of hard cooked egg slices alternated with thin slices of radish. Sprinkle cut chives over celery.

VIKING SALAD

Yield 20

Ingredients

Shrimp, tiny or medium, peeled and deveined	2 lb.
Lobster Meat, diced	1 lb.
Smoked Oysters	4 cans
Frozen Green Peas, cooked	1 lb.
Tomatoes, cut in wedges	5
Dressing	
Wine Vinegar	1 pt.
Oil	3 pt.
Egg Yolks	4
Medium Cream	½ cup
Dill, Chives or Scallions, chopped	1 tbsp.
Crushed Black Pepper	1 tbsp.

Method

Combine dressing ingredients and blend thoroughly with shrimp, lobster, smoked oysters and peas.

To Serve

Garnish with tomato wedges and fresh dill sprigs.

SWEDISH POTATO SALAD

Yield 20

Ingredients

Potatoes, cooked and diced	8 lb.
Celery, diced	4 stalks
Onions, medium, chopped	2
Pickled Beets, chopped	3 cups
Hard Cooked Eggs, chopped	6
Dressing	
Mayonnaise	4 cups
Pickled Beet Juice	½ cup

Method

Thin mayonnaise with beet juice and mix with potatoes, celery and onions. Top with wheel made of alternate sections of chopped pickled beets and chopped hard cooked eggs.

CALAMARI SALAD

Yield 20

Ingredients

Squid, cooked, julienned (white part only)	2 lb.
Onion, sliced	1 large
Red and Green Peppers, julienned	6
Dried Hot Peppers	½ tsp.
Dressing	
Italian Dressing	1 cup
Freshly Ground Black Pepper	1 tsp.

Method

Remove stomach and head of raw squid. Dip remainder into hot water for a few seconds, then peel off purple skin. Cook remainder of squid (it looks like a white bag) for 10 minutes in boiling water. Chill and slice into julienne strips. Add freshly ground pepper to italian dressing and blend thoroughly with squid, onion, and fresh dried peppers.

To Serve

For special display, purple squid heads can be blanched and used as a decorative accent for this salad.

CURRIED RICE SALAD

Yield 20

Ingredients

Rice, well cooked and drained	1½ lb.
Apples, peeled and diced	6
Cooked Turkey or Other Poultry, diced	½ lb.
Celery, diced	1 stalk
Dressing	
Mayonnaise	3 cups
Curry Powder	1 tsp.
Mango Chutney	2 tbsp.
Crushed Pineapple	1 cup
Heavy Cream	½ cup

Method

Make dressing by dissolving curry powder in ½ tsp. oil over moderate heat. Add to mayonnaise with chutney, crushed pineapple and heavy cream. Blend well.

Mix all ingredients thoroughly with dressing.

RUSSIAN CUCUMBER SALAD

Yield 20

Ingredients

Cucumbers, peeled and cubed	10-12
Sour Cream	3 cups
Onions	1 medium
Chives	2 tbsp.
Salt	1 tsp.
Pepper	½ tsp.

Method

Combine all ingredients. Garnish with parsley sprigs and radish roses.

PICKLED BEET SALAD

Yield 20

Ingredients

Beets, sliced	1 No. 10 can
Beet Juice, from can	3 cups
Sugar	3 cups
Cider Vinegar	3 cups
Bay Leaves	4
Whole Black Peppercorns	1 tbsp.

Method

Bring beet juice, sugar, vinegar and spices to boil, pour over beets, cool and serve.

SALAD MIGNON

Yield 20

Ingredients

Shrimp, medium or small, cooked	4 to 5 lb.
Artichoke Hearts, quartered	10
Truffles, julienned	1 whole
or	
Pitted Black Olives, sliced	6
Chicory, broken into bite size pieces	2 heads

Dressing

Mayonnaise	2 cups
Sour Cream	2 cups
Cayenne Pepper	dash

Method

Combine mayonnaise, sour cream and cayenne pepper. Blend thoroughly with chicory, shrimp, artichoke hearts, truffles or black olives.

Garnish with artichoke quarters, shrimp and ripe olives.

OXFORD SALAD

Yield 20

Ingredients

Crabmeat, frozen Alaskan or Japanese	3 lb.
Cucumbers, cut in julienne strips	6
Lemons	juice from 2
Hard Cooked Eggs, sliced	6

Dressing

Russian Dressing	3 cups
Scallions, chopped	2 tbsp.

Method

Mix chopped scallions with russian dressing and blend thoroughly with crabmeat, cucumbers and lemon juice.

To Serve

Garnish with hard cooked egg slices and cucumber twists.

SWEDISH CUCUMBER SALAD

Yield 20

Ingredients

Cucumbers, scored, medium slice	10-12

Dressing

White Vinegar	2 cups
Sugar	1 cup
Salt	1 tsp.
Parsley, chopped	2 tbsp.
Chives, chopped	2 tbsp.

Method

Combine dressing ingredients and add cucumbers. Cucumbers should float in dressing when served in deep wooden bowl.

GREEN SALAD OR GARDEN SALAD

Yield 20 servings

Ingredients

Iceberg Lettuce	4 heads
or	
Boston Lettuce	6 heads

Dressing

Lemons	juice from 3
Sugar	6 tsp.
Salt	½ tsp.
Garlic Powder	½ tsp.

Method

Break or tear greens into bite size pieces. Blend dressing ingredients and toss with greens.

RADISH SALAD

Yield 20

Ingredients

Radishes, washed, trimmed and sliced thin	10 bags
Cauliflower, cooked, broken into flowerets	1 lb.
Hard Cooked Eggs, chopped	5

Dressing

Oil	1 cup
Vinegar	½ cup
Pepper	½ tsp.
Chives	1 tsp.

Method

Combine ingredients for dressing and blend with radish slices. Cook cauliflower until barely tender, break into flowerets and use with chopped hard cooked eggs to garnish salad.

Mix dressing with sliced radishes. Circle with cauliflower buds and hard cooked egg slices.

BOHEMIAN SALAD

Yield 20

Ingredients

Red Peppers, julienned	8
Green Peppers, julienned	8
Apples, peeled, cored, diced	6
Boston Lettuce	2 heads

Dressing

Oil	1 cup
Vinegar	½ cup
Salt	1 tsp.
Pepper	½ tsp.
Sugar	2 tbsp.

Method

Separate lettuce into leaves. Blend dressing ingredients and mix with red and green peppers and apples. Serve on lettuce leaves.

DANISH CUCUMBER SALAD

Yield 20 portions

Ingredients

Cucumbers	4 lb.
Salt	1 tbsp.
Tumeric	1 tsp.
Water	½ pt.
Vinegar	½ pt.
Raisins	¼ lb.
Sour Cream	1 pt.
Onions, grated, with juice	2 tbsp.
Parsley, chopped fine	2 tbsp.
Mayonnaise	½ pt.
Lettuce	4 heads

Method

Peel cucumbers. Slice approximately ⅛ in. thick on bias.

Mix salt and tumeric until smooth in stainless steel bowl.

Add water and vinegar.

Add cucumbers and mix well. Refrigerate for 2 or 3 hours, turning over occasionally.

Plump raisins in hot water, cool, drain well.

Combine sour cream, onions and juice, parsley and mayonnaise.

On tray, arrange individual salads of 3 to 4 drained cucumber slices in lettuce cups.

Top with generous teaspoon dressing and sprinkle with raisins.

SALADS

AUSTRIAN CUCUMBER SALAD

Yield 20

Ingredients

Cucumbers, peeled, thin sliced	10-15
Dressing	
Salt	2 tbsp
Oil	1 cup
Vinegar	½ cup
Pepper	1 tsp.
Chives	2 tbsp.
Scallions	2 tbsp.

Method

Sprinkle sliced cucumbers with salt and marinate for 30 minutes. Drain off any liquid; rinse with cold water in sieve; then mix with other dressing ingredients. Combine dressing with cucumbers.

To Serve Sprinkle paprika over salad.

LENTIL SALAD

Yield 20

Ingredients

Lentils, cooked, drained	1½ lb.
Pimientos, diced	1 small can
Green Pepper Rings	3 peppers
Dressing	
Oil	1 cup
Vinegar	½ cup
Onion, chopped	1 medium

Method

Blend dressing ingredients and combine with lentils and diced pimiento.

To Serve Garnish salad with green pepper rings.

ANTIPASTO RELISH

Yield 20

Ingredients

Carrots, cut in sticks	3
Celery Stalks	3
Small White Onions	20
Thyme	1 tsp.
Oregano	1 tsp.
Bay Leaves	4
Ground Black Pepper	1 tsp.
Sweet Basil	1 tsp.
Garlic Cloves, mashed	4
Green Peppers, diced	6
Mushrooms, quartered	½ lb.
Olive Oil	3 cups
Chili Sauce	4 cups
Catsup	2 cups
Pimientos, canned	3 oz.
Ripe Olives	20
Green Olives	20
Dill Pickles, diced	3

Method

Put carrots, celery and small white onions in water with spices which have been put in bag. Boil until barely tender.

Saute garlic, green peppers and mushrooms for 5 min. in olive oil. Combine all ingredients and mix thoroughly. Store in jar; this relish can be kept for several weeks.

To Serve

Combine on antipasto tray with salami, ham, tuna, salmon, meat or poultry.

ITALIAN TOMATO SALAD

Yield 20

Ingredients

Tomatoes, sliced in very thin circles	20
Onion, sliced into thin rings	1 large
Green Peppers, sliced into thin rings	2
Dressing	
Italian Dressing	1½ cup

Method

Arrange sliced tomatoes in single layer on china or glass platter with onion slices and green pepper rings on top of tomatoes. Use machine for slicing, if available. Pour dressing over all ingredients.

VICTORIA SALAD

Yield 20

Ingredients

Belgian Endive, split crosswise and leaves separated	8
Green Beans, cut, frozen	1 lb.
Tomatoes, sliced	5
Dressing	
Olive Oil	2 pt.
Wine Vinegar	1 pt.
Salt	1 tsp.
Pepper	1 tsp.
Chives or Scallions	2 tbsp.

Method

Blend dressing ingredients and mix with endive and beans.

To Serve

Place salad mixture in center of bowl or platter and arrange thin tomato slices around it.

SALAD CHRISTOPHER

Yield 20

Ingredients

Green Beans, frozen, cut	5 lb.
Pimientos, canned, diced	7 oz.
Red Onion, diced	1
Dressing	
Italian Dressing (omit oregano)	1½ cup

Method

Blend ingredients with dressing. Garnish with red pimiento cuts or strips.

GUACAMOLE SALAD

Yield 20

Ingredients

Tomatoes, cut in wedges	5
Chili Peppers	5
Romaine or Head Lettuce	2 heads
Dressing	
Avocadoes, ripe, peeled, stone removed	8
Lemons	juice of 2
Onion, quartered	1
Garlic Cloves	2
Liquid Hot Pepper Sauce	1 tsp.
Salt	
Pepper	

Method

Mix all dressing ingredients in blender until smooth. Separate heads of lettuce or romaine into leaves.

To Serve

Place all blended ingredients on romaine or head lettuce leaves. Garnish with tomato wedges and chili peppers.

JELLIED SALMON, CELERY AND CUCUMBER SALAD

Yield: 24 4-oz. molds or 3 large fish molds.

Ingredients

Prepared Lemon Gelatin	3 oz.
Hot Water	1½ qt.
Plain Gelatin	2 tbsp.
Cold Water	1¼ qt.
Vinegar (or sweet pickle juice)	1 cup
Salt	3 tbsp.
Pepper	¼ tsp.
Onion Juice	1 tbsp.
Red Salmon, flaked	3 lb. cans
Cucumber, diced	3 cups
Celery, diced	3 cups

Method

Dissolve lemon gelatin in hot water. Add plain gelatin which has been soaked in 1 cup of the cold water.

When it is thoroughly dissolved, add the remaining qt. of cold water, the vinegar, salt, pepper and onion juice. Cool until mixture begins to congeal.

Mix the partly congealed gelatin with the flaked salmon, celery and cucumbers. Mold and chill until firm.

Serve this jellied salmon, celery and cucumber salad on lettuce with mayonnaise.

PLACKY (Russian Bean Salad)

Yield 20

Ingredients

Navy Beans, dry, large white	2 cups
Olive Oil	¾ cup
Carrots, diced	2
Celery Stalks, sliced	4
Fresh Dill, chopped or Dried Dill	2 tbsp.
Parsley, chopped	2 tbsp.
Garlic Cloves, minced	4
Ground Black Pepper	1 tbsp.
Lemons	3

Method

Boil beans in plenty of water (after soaking overnight).

Saute garlic, carrots and celery in olive oil. Add mixture to cooked beans, add rest of seasonings, let cool and garnish with lemon wedges.

FRIED RICE

Yield 20 portions

Ingredients

Peanut oil	¼ cup
Pork, Chicken, Ham or Shrimp, cooked and diced	3 cups
Salt	1½ tsp.
Pepper	¾ tsp.
Eggs	2
Cooked Rice	12 cups
Soya Sauce	5 tbsp.
Scallions, chopped	3 to 4

Method

Heat oil. Add diced pork, chicken, ham or shrimp and salt and pepper. Stir and cook until mixture is hot and slightly brown.

Stir raw eggs into mixture cooking till there are cooked shreds of eggs throughout the mixture. Add cooked rice; continue to cook, stirring constantly until rice is slightly browned. Add soya sauce, cook about 3 minutes more, stirring constantly.

To Serve

Sprinkle chopped green and white bits of scallion over rice.

DESSERTS

RICE PUDDING WITH SWEDISH BERRIES

Yield 20 to 25 servings

Ingredients

Milk	2 qt.
Rice	2 cups
Sugar	1 cup
Vanilla	2 tbsp.
Cinnamon Stick, broken	1
Egg Yolks	6
Light Cream	2 cups
Cinnamon-Sugar, blended	1 cup

Method

Bring milk to a boil, add rice slowly and cook slowly over low flame until rice is well done. Add sugar, vanilla and cinnamon stick. While rice is still hot, combine egg yolks and cream and blend in thoroughly.

Pour mixture into baking pan, top with cinnamon-sugar mixture. Serve with lingenberries.

MARRON GLACE

Yield 20 to 25 servings

Ingredients

Syrup with bits of Preserved Chestnuts	1 No. 2½ can
Vanilla Ice Cream	1 gal.
Cream, whipped	1 pt.

Method

Pour syrup with bits of preserved chestnut over vanilla ice cream. Top with whipped cream. Add maraschino cherries and sugar wafers.

COCONUT PUDDING—STEAMED

Yield 20 to 25 servings

Ingredients

Granulated Sugar	1 lb. 8 oz.
Salt	½ tsp.
Shredded Coconut	1 lb.
Baking Powder	¾ oz.
Butter	12 oz.
Egg Whites	20
Cake Flour	1 lb. 8 oz.

Method

Lightly cream sugar, butter and salt. Add egg whites slowly, then coconut and cake flour which has been sifted with baking powder. Mix until very smooth.

Fill steamed pudding pans ¾ full and cover. Steam for 1½ hours. Can be cooked in double boiler also. Serve with hot vanilla custard sauce.

HOT VANILLA CUSTARD SAUCE

Ingredients

Milk	1 pt.
Sugar	½ cup
Vanilla	1 tbsp.
Cornstarch, diluted in water	1 tbsp.
Egg Yolks	6

Method

Bring milk to boil. Add sugar, vanilla and cornstarch which has been diluted in a little water. Remove from fire and add the egg yolks one at a time. Serve with coconut pudding.

BANANA OR MANGO CUSTARD PUDDING—BRAZIL

Use custard formula for caramel pudding, page 221. Sliced bananas or mango fruits are added to the mold.

DESSERTS

BLACK FOREST CHERRY CAKE

Yield 18 to 20 portions

Ingredients

Black Bing Cherries	1 No. 2½ can
Powdered Sugar	1 cup
Butter	½ lb.
Light Cream	1 cup
Chocolate Layers	
Baking Powder	1 tbsp.
Kirschwasser	3 oz.
Cornstarch	2 tbsp.
Egg Yolks	6
Flour	1 cup
Melted Bittersweet Chocolate	½ cup
Butter Cream Frosting	
or	
Whipped Cream	2 cups

Method

Drain cherries, mix with kirschwasser and set aside. After 15 minutes heat cherry mixture. Blend cornstarch with 5 tbsp. drained cherry juice; add to cherries, bring to boil and cook until slightly thickened.

Chocolate Layers

Cream butter and sugar, add well beaten egg yolks, beating until batter is light and fluffy. Add melted bittersweet chocolate, flour and baking powder. Pour batter into 4 well buttered, 9 in. layer cake pans and bake in 350°F. oven for 20 minutes or until cake tester comes out clean. Place on wire rack to cool.

Pipe buttercream or whipped cream border around edge of each chocolate cake layer and also spread butter cream frosting in center of each layer. Pour cool thickened cherry mixture inside butter cream border of bottom layer. Add second layer and press down to make layers stick together. Cover top and sides of cake with remaining butter cream frosting. Sprinkle top and sides with finely shaved bittersweet chocolate. Repeat process for remaining two layers to make second cake.

ORANGE BAVARIAN CREAM

Yield 20

Ingredients

Almonds, sliced	2 cups
Milk	3 cups
Sugar	1 cup
Egg Yolks	12
Gelatin, unflavored	3 oz.
Vanilla	2 tbsp.
Mandarin or Orange Segments	1 qt. can
Heavy Cream, whipped	1 qt.

Method

Whip egg yolks, sugar and vanilla over double boiler till thick, then add milk and let thicken again.

Dilute granulated gelatin in ½ cup mandarin orange juice from can.

Combine diluted gelatin with egg mixture and cool on ice.

Fold in whipped cream, almonds and pour into oiled mold.

Chill over night, then unmold in hot water (2 seconds).

Decorate Bavarian cream mold with mandarin orange sections and whipped cream.

GATEAU DES POMMES

Yield 2 cakes serving 18 to 20

Ingredients

Tart Dough—For 2 9-inch tarts	
Flour	3 cups
Butter or Margarine	2 cups
Sugar	1 cup
Baking Powder	1 tsp.
Eggs	2
Grated Rind of Lemon	1
Milk or Water, if needed	few drops
French Apple Tart Filling	
Cooking Apples	14
Sugar	½ cup
Water	½ cup
Butter	6 tbsp.
Apricot Jam	1 cup
Cinnamon	½ tsp.

Method

Step 1. Tart—Sift flour into bowl. Make a well in center of flour and put eggs, sugar, butter and grated lemon rind in well. Mix ingredients in well to a smooth paste, working with one hand. With the other hand quickly work in the flour, adding a very little ice water or cold milk if necessary to moisten the dough so it can be made into a ball. Ball of dough should clean bowl. Wrap dough in wax paper and chill for at least an hour.

Step 2. Filling—Pare, core and cut 8 apples into medium sized pieces. Put apple pieces in saucepan with sugar, water, and butter. Cover pan tightly and cook apples over moderate heat until tender.

To Assemble Gateau

Step 3. Line 2 flan pans with tart dough. Fill pans half full with stewed apples. Peel, core and slice remaining 6 apples. Arrange raw slices over stewed apples, overlapping slices starting from the center and working out in a spiral. Sprinkle sugar over apple slices.

Step 4. Bake in a 400°F. oven for 20 to 25 minutes until apples are tender and crust is golden. Add enough hot water to apricot jam so it will spread easily, then spread on top of tart to glaze.

PINEAPPLE UPSIDE DOWN CAKE

Yield 18 to 20 portions

Ingredients

Pineapple Slices	12-15
Cake Batter	
Flour, sifted	2 cups
Sugar	4 tbsp.
Eggs, well beaten	6
Baking Powder	1 tsp.
Butter	5 tbsp.
Milk	½ cup

Method

Step 1. Butter 2 8-in. round spring form cake pans and arrange pineapple slices in layer over bottom of each pan.

Step 2. Batter—Mix flour, baking powder, salt and sugar together. Cream butter into mixture. Beat eggs into mixture and add 4 tbsp. of milk or just enough to keep batter stiff.

Step 3. With spoon, spread dough on top of pineapple. Bake in 400°F. oven for about 25 minutes.

CARAMEL CUSTARD PUDDING

Yield 20 caramel custard cups

Ingredients

Eggs	6
Egg Yolks	4
Sugar	2 cups
Cream	1 cup
Milk	1 qt.
Vanilla Bean or Flavoring	2 tbsp.
Water	½ cup

Method

Step 1. Beat eggs, egg yolks and 1 cup sugar until well blended. Scald cream and milk with vanilla bean or vanilla flavoring. Remove vanilla bean, if used, from hot milk and gradually add milk to egg mixture, stirring constantly.

Step 2. Stir 1 cup sugar into heavy skillet, stirring over low heat until sugar browns. Be careful not to let sugar burn. Add water and boil to a syrup.

Step 3. Pour caramel into a mold or custard cups, turning mold or custard cups around during pouring so that caramel completely coats the insides. Let coating set, then pour custard into the mold or custard cups and put in pan of hot water.

Step 4. Bake in 350°F. oven in pan of water for about 30 to 45 minutes or until knife inserted in center comes out clean. Cool, then unmold on serving dish.

FRANCHIPAN TARTLETTES (Swedish)

Yield 20

Ingredients

Butter	8 oz.
Sugar	8 oz.
Almond Paste	1 lb.
Eggs	4
Bread Flour	5 oz.

Method

Filling

Soften almond paste with two eggs. Cream butter and sugar, add rest of eggs. Mix everything together till smooth.

To Assemble

Line muffin tins or similar mold with thin pie crust.

Fill lined tins or molds with franchipan mixture.

Bake for 30 minutes in moderate oven. Serve with powdered sugar on top.

DROP CAKES WITH CARAWAY SEEDS

Yield 20 cakes

Ingredients

Lemon Rind, grated	2
Sugar	1 cup
Butter	2 cups
Flour	3 cups
Baking Powder	1 tsp.
Whole Eggs	3
Caraway Seeds	½ cup

Method

Cream softened butter with sugar; add egg yolks and lemon rind and a few drops of ice water. Quickly work in sifted flour and baking powder until well blended.

Hand roll dough into 40 uniform balls. Place on baking pan; brush with one beaten egg; sprinkle with caraway seeds and bake in 350°F. oven until golden brown, about 15 minutes.

ST. HONORE

Yield 2 9-in. pies for 20 portions

Ingredients

Pastry for 9-in. pie crusts, ⅛ in. thick	2
Cream Puff Paste	recipe below
Cream Filling	recipe below
Water	⅔ cup
Sugar	1 cup
Whipped Cream	1 pt.
Maraschino Cherries	12

Method

Place circle of pie crust dough on sheet pan and perforate to prevent blistering during baking. Egg wash edge of crusts. Using pastry bag with plain round tube, pipe cream puff paste around edge of pie crusts. Bake in 400°F. oven until light golden brown. Cool. While pie crust and cream puff border are baking, also bake 8 miniature cream puffs and cool.

When cream puff border around edge of crust has cooled, cut ½ in. slice from top of it. Fill this cream puff shell with cream filling, then put top slice back in place.

Fill 8 miniature cream puffs from the bottom with cream filling. Boil water and sugar at 325°F. until it caramelizes. Dip tiny filled cream puffs in this coating and arrange around border edge of pie crust with sticky side down to hold puffs on border. Fill center of shell with cream filling. Decorate with whipped cream and garnish with maraschino cherries. Chill in refrigerator until time to serve.

CREAM PUFF PASTE BATTER

Ingredients

Butter	2 oz.
Water or Milk	½ cup
Flour	1 cup
Eggs	8

Method

Heat butter with water, add flour, cool. Add eggs one at a time, beating after each addition.

CREAM FILLING

Ingredients

Milk	1 pt.
Sugar	½ cup
Vanilla	1 tbsp.
Egg Yolks	4
Cream	½ pt.
Cornstarch	2 tbsp.

Method

Bring milk to boil, add sugar, vanilla and cornstarch diluted with a little water. Slowly add egg yolks one at a time. Stir in cream.

RUM BALLS

Yield 20

Ingredients

Cake Crumbs	3 lbs.
Dark Rum	1 cup
Chocolate Fudge	½ cup
Walnuts or Almonds, chopped	1 cup

Method

Moisten cake crumbs with rum. Crumble chocolate fudge into crumb mixture. Add nuts. Mix thoroughly. Form into small balls and roll in chocolate shots.

Make a pyramid of the balls on a round platter. Circle with candied mint leaves.

DESSERTS

CHESTNUT RICE (Austrian Dessert)

Yield 20

Ingredients

Chestnuts, boiled and peeled	3 lb.
Sugar, confectioners	1½ cups
Water	½ cup
Butter, melted	3 tbsp.
Dark Rum	3 oz.
Cream, whipped	3 cups

Method

Boil sugar and water to light syrup stage.

Add peeled chestnuts, butter, rum and nutmeg, if desired; simmer till chestnuts are mushy.

Force mixture through potato ricer, or finest blade of meat grinder.

Shape chestnut mixture into nice mounds. Sprinkle with cocoa and decorate with plenty of whipped cream. Serve chilled.

CARAMEL PUDDING—BRAZIL

Yield 20

Ingredients

Sugar	3 cups
Whole Eggs	12
Milk	2 qt.
Vanilla	1 tbsp.
Salt	pinch

Method

Take half the sugar and carmelize in skillet till reddish brown.

Grease metal pudding molds, either 20 individual molds or 2 qt. metal mold, with butter.

Pour a quarter of an inch of caramel sugar in each mold, let sugar set.

Mix milk, eggs, rest of sugar, vanilla and salt, using wire whip.

Pour into pudding molds and poach in pan of hot water in oven for 35 minutes. Cover while poaching.

Remove from mold right after poaching; serve well chilled with whipped cream.

INDIANER KRAPFEN

Yield 20 servings

Ingredients

Whole Eggs	6
Sugar	1 cup
Flour	1½ cups
Salt	pinch
Vanilla	1 tsp.
Baking Powder	1 tsp.
Chocolate Icing	2 cups
Butter, melted	½ cup

Method

Beat 6 whole eggs until light and fluffy, gradually adding sugar. Sift flour, baking powder, salt and add with melted butter.

Place mixture in a pastry bag and with plain large tube make 40 half balls. Bake in 350°F. oven for 10 minutes. Cool.

Remove center from 20 halves and fill with whipped cream or french vanilla cream. Top filled half with unfilled half; place balls on wire rack and cover with warm chocolate icing.

YULE LOG MADE WITH JELLY ROLL

Yield 20 to 25 servings

Ingredients

Eggs	8
Sugar	1 lb.
Powdered Milk	1½ oz.
Water	12 oz.
Cake Flour	1 lb. 5 oz.
Egg Yolks	4
Salt	½ oz.
Vanilla or Lemon Flavoring	to taste
Honey	3 oz.
Baking Powder	½ oz.

Method

Step 1. Mix eggs, sugar, salt, powdered milk and flavoring at high speed on mixer for approximately 10 minutes. Mixture should be lemon colored. Heat water and honey and slowly add to above. Sift cake flour and baking powder and fold into mixture.

Step 2. Line two 18-by 24-in. sheet pans with paper. Pour batter into sheet pans and bake in 375°F. oven for 15 to 20 minutes. Loosen cake from pan, turn out and roll. Unroll and fill with jelly (apricot, currant, cherry or strawberry), lemon cream, mocha cream or marshmallow filling or with ice cream. Roll up over filling.

Step 3. Cover log with frosting or butter cream and decorate. Slice into desired portion size.

ZUPPA INGLESE (Italian)

Yield 20

Ingredients

Sponge Cake, cut horizontally	1 sheet pan
Creme de Cacao, white	3 oz.
Orange and Lemon Rind, grated	1 ea.
Vanilla	dash
Rum	⅓ cup

Custard Sauce

Milk	1 qt.
Granulated Sugar	1 cup
Egg Yolks	8
Cornstarch	½ cup
Salt	½ tsp.

Method

Bring 3 pints milk to boil, add mixture of eggs, 1 pt. milk, cornstarch, sugar and salt, simmer 10 minutes (double boiler) and cool.

Divide Into Two Parts

Add some cream de cacao to yellow portion of sauce.

Add grated lemon and orange rind, vanilla and rum and enough red food coloring to make orange colored sauce.

Assembling

On an attractive large platter arrange the Zuppa. Cover bottom layer with cream de cacao sauce; top layer with rum sauce.

Pipe whipped cream over top and sprinkle with candied fruits and almonds.

Note: Sponge cake can be soaked over night in both sauces if advance preparation is desired. Use a deep platter.

Ideas for preparation and presentation of fresh fruit and cheese, together and separately, appear in Chapter IX, pp. 115 to 120.

RUSSIAN CHEESE CAKE

Yield 20

Ingredients

Cottage Cheese, unsalted and strained through sieve	6 cups
Egg Yolks	6
Sugar, granulated	2 cups
Egg Whites, beaten with half the sugar until stiff	8
Corn Starch	6 tsp.
Flour	6 tsp.
Sour Cream	½ cup
Lemon Rind, grated	1
Vanilla	1 tbsp.
Raisins	½ cup

Method

Cream sugar, egg yolks and flavorings.

Add cottage cheese, sour cream and fold in beaten egg whites.

Fold in flour and cornstarch which has been blended.

Pour mixture into cake mold lined with thin pie crust.

Bake in moderate oven for about one hour. Sprinkle powdered sugar on top of finished cake.

Note: Larger quantities can be made in a sheet pan.

CARROT CAKE

Yield 20

Ingredients

Sugar	1½ cups
Salad Oil	3 cups
Carrots, raw, grated	6 cups
Walnuts or Almonds, ground	2 cups
Whole Eggs	8
Cake Flour	4 cups
Baking Powder	2 tsp.
Cinnamon	4 tsp.
Salt	2 tsp.

Method

Cream sugar and eggs. Add oil and beat well.

Mix baking powder with flour and fold in rest of ingredients. Pour mixture into well-greased mold, which has been sprinkled with bread crumbs. Bake in moderate oven for 1½ hours. Sprinkle powdered sugar over cake at serving time.

ST. PATRICK'S DAY CREAM PIE

Yield 2 pies or 18 to 20 portions

Ingredients

Unflavored Gelatin	¾ oz.
Cold Water	½ cup
Sugar	1½ cups
Heavy Cream	1 pt.
Egg Yolks	6
Lime Juice	1 cup
Salt	½ tbsp.
Pie Shells	2 9-in.

Method

Soften gelatin in cold water and set aside. Slightly beat egg yolks with 1½ cups sugar in top of double boiler. Cook over bubbling water until slightly thickened, then add lime juice and a few drops of green vegetable coloring. Remove from heat and stir in softened gelatin, dissolving thoroughly. Cool.

Whip cream with remaining sugar and when egg mixture has cooled, blend all ingredients. Pour mixture into pie shells and refrigerate. When pies are well chilled, remove and cover with green fondant frosting and marzipan shamrocks.

SACHER TORTE (Chocolate Cake)

Yield 20

Ingredients

Butter or Half Butter and Half Margarine	1 lb.
Granulated Sugar	1 lb.
Semi-Sweet Chocolate	1 lb.
Cake Flour, sifted	1 lb.
Egg Yolks	15
Egg Whites (whipped with half the sugar)	15
Grated Lemon Rind	to taste
Vanilla	to taste

Method

Cream butter, half sugar, melted chocolate, lemon rind, vanilla. Add egg yolks and whip until very fluffy. Whip egg whites with remaining sugar until stiff.

Fold in stiffly beaten egg whites; then fold in flour.

Bake in moderate oven for about one hour in round tart molds.

Slice cooled cake in half horizontally, cover with raspberry or red currant jelly; cover outside of cake with jelly also. Coat with chocolate icing, made by combining 3 pt. granulated sugar and 1 pt. water, and boiling till it forms thread between fingers, then mixing with softened chocolate bar. Mix icing until smooth, then pour lukewarm icing over cake. Always serve Sacher Torte with whipped cream.

VIENNESE APPLE TARTS

Yield 20

Ingredients

1 - 2 - 3 Sweet Dough

Sugar	1 lb.
Butter or Margarine	2 lb.
Cake Flour	3 lb.
Cocoa	½ cup
Egg Yolks	2

Method

Mix like a pie crust.

Apple Filling

Either use about two pounds of ready made apple pie filling or make your own from tart apples, sugar syrup, cinnamon and grated lemon rind.

To Assemble

Cover cookie sheet with half the sweet dough and prebake for 10 min.

Spread apple filling about ¾ in. thick over prebaked shell.

Roll out other half of dough on cookie sheet. Chill in refrigerator until firm, then transfer to top of apple filling. Perforate top layer with fork. Brush with egg wash. Bake about 35 minutes.

When cold, cut into squares. Sprinkle with powdered sugar.

DESSERTS

BACCLAVA (Greek)

Yield 20

Ingredients

Strudel Leaves	1 lb.
Walnuts, chopped	3 lb.
Sugar	2 lb.
Butter, melted	1½ lb.
Cinnamon	to taste
Lemon Rind, grated	to taste
Orange Rind, grated	to taste

Method

Butter a half size hotel pan well. Cut strudel dough leaves to size of pan. (Strudel leaves may be purchased ready to use.)

Alternate strudel dough leaves in layers with filling (walnuts mixed with sugar, butter, orange, lemon rind, cinnamon).

Brush plenty of melted butter on each strudel leaf before filling.

When hotel pan is filled, bake at moderate heat for approximately 1 hour.

To Serve

Serve with hot honey sauce (heated honey diluted with some light cream), pour over each portion of bacclava (cut diagonally).

KEY WEST LIME CHIFFON PIE

Yield Portions for 18 to 20

Ingredients

Unflavored Gelatin	¾ oz.
Sugar	1¾ cup
Egg Whites	10
Egg Yolks	6
Lime Juice	1 cup
Salt	pinch
Green Vegetable Coloring	few drops (if needed)
Pie Shells	2
Whipped Cream	1 pt.

Method

Sprinkle gelatin over half a cup of cold water. In upper half of double boiler, combine slightly beaten egg yolks with 1½ cups sugar. When slightly thickened, add lime juice and a few drops of green vegetable coloring. Remove from heat. Add softened gelatin and stir until it dissolves. Cool.

Whip the egg whites, add salt and ¼ cup sugar. Add egg white mixture to first mixture which has been thoroughly cooled and blend the two mixtures well. Fill pie shells and place in refrigerator to chill until time to serve. At serving time, a little whipped cream can be piped from a star tube for decoration.

INDEX

INDEX

INDEX

INDEX

INDEX

INDEX

NOTES

NOTES